SOCIAL INDICATOR MODELS

Social Indicator Models

Edited by
Kenneth C. Land
and
Seymour Spilerman

Russell Sage Foundation   New York

Russell Sage Foundation
230 Park Avenue, New York, New York 10017

© 1975 Russell Sage Foundation. All Rights Reserved.
Library of Congress Catalog Card Number: 74-79447
Standard Book Number: 87154-505-5
Printed in the United States of America

THE CONTRIBUTORS

James S. Coleman
Professor of Sociology
University of Chicago

James A. Davis
Professor of Sociology
Director, National
  Opinion Research Center
University of Chicago

Beverly Duncan
Professor of Sociology
University of Arizona

Otis Dudley Duncan
Professor of Sociology
University of Arizona

Mark Evers
Instructor
Department of Sociology
Duke University

David L. Featherman
Associate Professor of Rural
  Sociology
University of Wisconsin,
  Madison

Robert M. Hauser
Professor of Sociology
University of Wisconsin,
  Madison

Kenneth C. Land
Associate Professor of Sociology
University of Illinois, Urbana

Judah Matras
Professor of Sociology
Hebrew University, Jerusalem

David D. McFarland
Assistant Professor of Sociology
  and Research Associate
Population Research Center
University of Chicago

Aage B. Sørenson
Assistant Professor of Sociology
University of Wisconsin,
  Madison

Seymour Spilerman
Professor of Sociology
University of Wisconsin,
  Madison

Arthur L. Stinchcombe
Professor of Sociology
  and Research Associate
Survey Research Center
University of California,
  Berkeley

Richard Stone
Professor of Applied Economics
Cambridge University

Kermit Terrell
Research Assistant
Center for Policy Research and
  Graduate Student
Department of Sociology
Columbia University

Donald J. Treiman
Associate Director
Center for Policy Research

James C. Wendt
Research Assistant
Survey Research Center
University of California, Berkeley

H. H. Winsborough
Professor of Sociology
University of Wisconsin, Madison

CONTENTS

FOREWORD

For almost a decade now the term social indicators has been appearing in the literature of the social sciences, social commentary and criticism, as well as in the more popular press. Although the term itself has been invoked to cover a wide range of referents—from the hortatory to the construction of mathematical models—there is scarcely a doubt that at least the reference is to quantative descriptions and analyses of social conditions and trends, designed both to inform public decision-making and to advance our knowledge and understanding of society.[1]

Regardless of one's stance in viewing the approaches and purposes of this social indicator effort, a common long-term objective is a rigorous analysis (model) of the interrelationships among aspects of the society—or as Land and Spilerman phrase it here, "interrelationships among social indicators." This volume, *Social Indicator Models*, is the first systematic attempt to focus directly on that objective.

Kenneth C. Land introduces his overview of social indicator models by recounting the recent history of the "movement" and the variations in its underlying rationales. For readers of the extant literature in the field, these rationales and purposes as well as criticisms of them are well-known, for they set the terms of the debate that characterized the field during the past several years. Land, however, synthesizes the best of the debates and related materials and suggests a new paradigm for consideration. It is open to argumentation and revision, as he notes, but it is a possible vehicle for organizing some current and future work. It is fully informed, well-considered, and an innovative contribution to the field.

Early in the resurgence[2] of the social indicators movement, Otis Dudley Duncan noted that the measurement of social change is basic to social reporting. In this connection he proposed the examination of current data sources and the

---

[1] Otis Dudley Duncan, "Developing Social Indicators," Department of Sociology, University of Arizona, Tucson (no date), mimeo.

[2] The antecedents of social indicator interests date back to at least the 1920s with William F. Ogburn and the beginnings of the President's Research Committee on Social Trends. See *Recent Social Trends in the United States*, New York:McGraw-Hill, 1933.

collection of "replicated" data. Land and Spilerman, in organizing the conference from which this volume emerged, used this approach in classifying one dimension of social indicator models. Following the theoretical and methodological paper by Stinchcombe and Wendt, the contributions of Davis, Duncan, Duncan and Evers, Treiman and Terrell, Winsborough, Featherman and Hauser detail possible applications of replication models. Longitudinal and dynamic models, the other classifying dimension, are explicated in the remaining papers by Stone, Matras, Coleman, Sørenson, McFarland and Spilerman.

It is a powerful set of contributors and array of papers. Russell Sage Foundation as sponsor, Land and Spilerman as conference organizers, editors and contributors have placed before the interested social science and policy-making communities a landmark volume. It is timely and welcome.

Eleanor Bernert Sheldon

ACKNOWLEDGMENTS

In addition to the contributors, we are indebted to a number of individuals for making possible the preparation of this volume. Daisy Helenius typed portions of the manuscript and attended to other administrative details. Jean C. Yoder provided capable editorial assistance. For their encouragement and generosity in making the volume possible, we are also grateful to Orville G. Brim, Jr., Hugh F. Cline, Eleanor B. Sheldon, and the Trustees of Russell Sage Foundation.

1

INTRODUCTION
Kenneth C. Land and Seymour Spilerman

INTERRELATIONSHIPS AMONG SOCIAL INDICATORS

The label "social indicators" has been with us for nearly a decade. It is now generally applied to indices of various social conditions within particular communities or societies; that is, to measurements of the contexts of the social life of members of a society. Moreover, it is generally held that such indicators are essential prerequisites to improved reporting on social conditions and on changes therein over time. Although somewhat controversial, it is also commonly held that social indicators potentially can be used to inform, and perhaps to guide, social policy in some more or less explicit way. (More details on the definition of, and rationales for, social indicators are given by Land in the next chapter.)

An interest in social reporting sooner or later leads one to focus on interrelationships among social indicators. For example, one may observe that the percentage of all adult women in the labor force has changed from 30 percent in 1940 to over 50 percent in the 1970s. But that simple indicator says nothing about changes (or nonchanges) in the relation of women's skills and efforts to the kinds of occupations that they have been getting or the remunerative compensation therefrom relative to their male counterparts. More generally, it says nothing about the *effects* of the movement of large numbers of women into the labor force. To answer these and a host of related questions requires a rather sophisticated analysis of interrelationships among social indicators.

As a somewhat different example, suppose that national sample surveys of the adult population of the United States taken in 1954 and 1972 showed that in 1954 only 28 percent of the adults indicated that an "admitted communist" should be "allowed to make a speech" in their community whereas the corresponding figure in 1972 is 53 percent. Although the change is striking and probably merits being reported, it indicates nothing about whether this is entirely due to the replacement of older cohorts of adults by younger more educated adults and to the positive association of young age and higher education with "allow" or whether the change also taps some degree of "real" change in the level of tolerance for public speeches by "admitted communists." Again, it takes a deeper analysis to answer these and related questions.

If the analysis of interrelationships among social indicators is essential for social reporting, it is all the more imperative for the guidance of social policy. We take "the guidance of social policy" to refer minimally to efforts to deal with present tendencies in the best possible way. Sometimes the "policy maker" can also envisage a "goal" or "objective" to be attained, but this is not essential to the argument. The basic point is that in order to deal with present social conditions and their changes the policy maker must possess knowledge regarding the interrelationships among social indicators. Ideally, such information will allow him: (1) to assess the impact of policy-manipulable variables on the "goal indicator"; (2) to ascertain how much of the levels and changes in the goal indicator is due to the impact of nonmanipulable variables; and (3) to determine some of the possible side effects or second-order impacts of changes in these variables.

In brief, both for reporting changes in social conditions and for the guidance of social policy, there are great benefits to be derived from the analysis of interrelationships among social indicators. It is these considerations which led Land to define the concept of a "social indicator model." (In the next chapter, Land elaborates on this notion.)

THE CONTENT OF THE VOLUME

In order to explore the notion of a social indicator model in various substantive contexts and relative to several uses, we organized a Conference on Social Indicator Models held July 12–15, 1972, at the Russell Sage Foundation. The conference was attended by over 20 social scientists, and, for the most part, the chapters in this volume are the products of the scholars who attended (we subsequently acquired the chapters by Matras and Stone).

Although these chapters deal with a diverse array of topics in a variety of ways, there are several characteristics which each shares. First, none of these chapters gets mired in the quicksand of grandiose social system models, which, for practical purposes, are not applicable to real social indicator data. Although numerous such "models" exist in the literature, they do not seem to have contributed to the analysis of social indicators, and each of our authors has avoided the temptation of adding yet another such model. Second, it is a characteristic of the following chapters that each addresses a specific set of social indicator data and constructs a corresponding analytical model with which to assay the various components of changes in the indicators. A third, and related, characteristic of the chapters is a concern with the analysis of social change. In short, the chapters included in this volume are best seen as explorations in the construction of models for the analysis of changes in specific areas of social indicators.

The chapters are collected into two groups, labeled replication models and longitudinal and dynamic models. As this distinction is elaborated by Land in the next chapter, replication models are built on the basis of data from repeated cross-sectional sample surveys. Because of this, the same individuals are not measured at the various time points, so that the observations are "macro-level" or percentage distributions. Even so, the various chapters vary in terms of the number of cross-sectional samples included. The minimum number of observations needed is, of course, two cross-sections, and several of the chapters use only two time points (Stinchcombe and Wendt, Davis, Duncan, Duncan and Evers, Featherman and Hauser). By contrast, the chapters by Treiman and Terrell and by Winsborough deal with three or more replications.

In contrast to replication studies, longitudinal studies are based on repeated observations on the same individuals or structural units ("micro-data"). The chapters by Coleman and Sørensen use longitudinal data in the investigation of social mobility. These papers also utilize dynamic (i.e., time-dependent) models in a much more explicit way than those in the replication section, although it does not follow that dynamic models are restricted to longitudinal data. Rather, it is the case that the larger number of time points available in a longitudinal study makes the use of an explicitly dynamic formulation more revealing and the testing of a dynamic model possible. The contributions by Stone, McFarland, and Matras review other dynamic models, some of which may be used with replication studies. Spilerman's chapter focuses on several conceptual issues in model construction and forecasting of social indicators. In particular, he discusses some conditions under which the forecasting of social variables is exceedingly difficult.

As noted by Land in the next chapter, it is likely that social indicator models will assume either a replication or a longitudinal form depending upon the type of indicator data to be analyzed and the types of effects to be incorporated into the model. We thus offer this volume as illustrative of some of the possible ways in which such models may be constructed and analyzed in several substantive contexts.

SOCIAL INDICATOR MODELS: AN OVERVIEW

Kenneth C. Land

RATIONALES FOR SOCIAL INDICATORS

The past decade has witnessed a great surge of interest in social measurement in the form of proposals for the development of "social indicators." Each of these proposals has been accompanied by some more or less coherent rationale for social indicators in the form of a description of the potential contributions of indicators to social analysis and social policy. On close examination, it is clear that the content of these rationales varies in emphasis, and it is useful to consider the main dimensions of the variation.

A Social Policy Rationale

Proposals for social indicators began to be advanced in the mid-1960s. Although the arguments advanced for social indicators in these documents are not completely homogeneous, there is one rationale which is found in several of them. Specifically, it is often proposed that social indicators can be used to:

Evaluate particular public (government) programs

Establish a system of social accounts analogous to the national economic accounts

Establish social goals and set social policy

Indeed, these are rather large claims for social indicators. Moreover, they occurred in several essays on, and proposals for, social indicators by social scientists, legislators, and governmental administrators which appeared during the years 1966–1969 and which have in common an interest in the information base for, or the consequences of, social policy decisions. These include: (1) *Technology and the American Economy* (1966), Volume I of the Report of the National Commission on Technology, Automation, and Economic Progress; (2) *Social Indicators* (1966), a collection of essays edited by Raymond Bauer and initiated by the American Academy of Arts and Sciences to study the impact of the space program on American society; (3) Senate Bill S.843, the "Full Opportunity and Social Accounting Act" of 1967; (4) the May 1967 and September 1967 volumes of the *Annals of the American Academy of Political and Social Science* edited by Bertram Gross and devoted to the theme, "Social Goals and Indicators for American Society"; (5) "Social Indicators: Statistics for Public Policy" (1968), an essay by Wilbur J. Cohen (then secretary of the U. S. Department of Health, Education, and Welfare); and (6) *Toward a Social Report* (1969), a report to the President prepared by the U. S. Department of Health, Education, and Welfare. Each deserves separate comment.

The National Commission on Technology, Automation, and Economic Progress (1966:XIV) was established by Public Law 88-444 in 1964 to identify and assess the pace and impact of current and prospective technological change on production, employment, and community and human needs, and to recommend actions which could be taken by private and public agencies with respect to technological change and its consequences. Its report, issued in 1966, was entitled *Technology and the American Economy*. With respect to its first goal, the commission (1966:109–110) concluded that although the rate of technological change had increased in recent years, its effects on employment could be controlled by governmental manipulations of aggregate demand. Furthermore, the commission (1966:110–112) made a number of recommendations for public and private policy changes which would facilitate adjustment to technological change and help attain human and community needs.

In its efforts to explain the relative lack of success of the nation in meeting human and community needs, however, the commission (1966:95) noted that, while we have begun to perfect an economic reporting system and to establish economic indicators that measure national performance, we do not have a continuous charting of social changes, and we are ill-prepared to determine our needs, establish goals, and measure our performance. Therefore, the commission (1966:96–97) made the following major recommendation:

> In an effort to improve the means of public decision-making, we propose that the government explore the creation of a "system of social accounts" which would indicate the social benefits and social costs of investment and services and thus reflect the true costs of a product. . . .
>
> A system of social accounts, if it could be established, would give us a broader and more balanced reckoning of the meaning of social and economic progress and would move us toward measurement of the utilization of human resources in our society in four areas:

1. The measurement of social costs and net returns of economic innovations;
2. The measurement of social ills (e.g., crime, family disruption);
3. The creation of "performance budgets" in areas of defined social needs (e.g., housing, education);
4. Indicators of economic opportunity and mobility.

Eventually, this might provide a "balance sheet" which could be useful in clarifying policy choices.

It would allow us to record not only the gains of economic and social change but the costs as well, and to see how these costs are distributed and borne.

Thus, impressed with the contribution to economic understanding of our "national income accounts" system, the commission advocated the creation of a parallel "system of social accounts." This notion was apparently proposed by the sociologist, Daniel Bell, as a member of the commission (see Bell, 1969:78). Its importance derives from the fact that it was the first proposal for social indicators to be endorsed by an official government panel. Furthermore, the proposal exhibits three claims for social indicators which have characterized the advocacy of social indicators for social policy decisions to the present. That is, the commission argues for the use of a system of social accounts (1) to evaluate specific programs, and (2) to develop a "balance sheet" in order (3) to help set social policy.

Social Indicators, a volume of papers edited by Raymond Bauer, was a second major contribution to the social indicator literature in 1966 which was motivated by a concern for public policy decisions. As noted above, the original mandate of the volume from the American Academy of Arts and Sciences (Bauer, 1966:2) was to investigate the consequences, particularly the second-order (or unintended) consequences, of the space program on American society. However, as the editor and his colleagues explored this problem, they became convinced that "the problem of measuring the impact of a single program could not be dealt with except in the context of the entire set of social indicators used in our society" (Bauer, 1966:1). Hence, they attempted to assess the present state of the art of providing social indicators, and to explore what would be required in the form of an improved informational system (Bauer, 1966:21).

The Bauer volume consists of four substantive chapters, each of which can be given only brief comment here. The first essay, "Social Indicators and Goals," by Albert Biderman, looks at existing social indicators in terms of their relationship to those national goals which have been set forth. For example, he shows (1966a:86–89) that data of any kind could be found in the major Census Bureau publications of historical series (U. S. Department of Commerce, 1960, 1962) for only 48 (or 59 percent) of the 81 goals set forth by the President's Commission on National Goals in 1960. Biderman then goes on to consider the ways in which statistical series originate and the multiple uses to which they are put (1966a:95–105). Finally, he examines various characteristics of indexes in such areas as education, unemployment, and crime.

The second major essay of the Bauer volume is "The State of the Nation: Social Systems Accounting," by Bertram Gross, who deserves considerable credit for stimulating the initial public and professional interest in social indicators and social reporting. In this essay, Gross delineates in a broad scheme what an ideal system of social statistics would look like. Specifically, he takes national income accounting as his model, extending it to a system of social accounting (Gross, 1966:162–171). This extension, in turn, is based upon a conception of society which Gross (1966:179–185) terms a "structure-performance model":

The structure of any social system consists of (1) people and (2) nonhuman resources (3) grouped together into subsystems that (4) interrelate among themselves and (5) with the external environment, and are subject to (6) certain values and (7) a central guidance system that may help provide the capacity for future performance. . . .

The performance of any social system consists of activities (1) to satisfy the interests of various "interesteds" by (2) producing various kinds, qualities, and quantities of output, (3) investing in the system's capacity for future output, (4) using inputs efficiently, (5) acquiring inputs, and doing all the above in a manner that conforms with (6) various codes of behavior and (7) varying conceptions of technical and administrative (or guidance) rationality.

Two additional essays complete the Bauer volume on social indicators: "Anticipatory Studies and Stand-by Research Capabilities," by Albert Biderman, and "Problems of Organizational Feedback," by Robert Rosenthal and Robert Weiss. The former essay is devoted to the need for stand-by research facilities to collect data on events falling outside regular statistical series (Biderman, 1966b:272). On the other hand, the latter paper is concerned with what to do with new information if it becomes available. Specifically, these authors are concerned with the problems and consequences, both favorable and unfavorable, of reporting information on the full range of impact of the organizations' actions (Rosenthal and Weiss, 1966:302–304).

This brief review of the Bauer volume cannot do justice to the contents of its essays. However, that is not the goal of the present statement. Rather, we wish to emphasize the influence of the Bauer volume on the development and orientation of interest in social indicators. This perspective is perhaps best illustrated by the opening statement of the editor (Bauer, 1966:1):

This volume is devoted to the topic of social indicators—statistics, statistical series, and all other forms of evidence—that enable us to *assess where we stand and are going with respect to our values and goals, and to evaluate specific programs and determine their impact.* (Italics added)

Thus, Bauer and his collaborators are seen to claim, as did the National Commission on Technology, Automation, and Economic Progress, that social indicators can help (1) to evaluate specific social programs, (2) to develop a balance sheet (or "system of social accounts") to assess where we stand in order (3) to provide a key to social policy development.

In February 1967, Senator Walter C. Mondale (Minn.) and ten other senators gave major political support to the notion of social indicators by introducing Senate Bill S.843, The Full Opportunity and Social Accounting Act of 1967. The structure of the bill, paralleling in many ways the Employment Act of 1946, provides for: (1) an annual Social Report of the President to be transmitted by March 20 of each year; (2) a Council of Social Advisors to assist the President in preparing the Social Report and carrying out related research activities; and (3) a joint committee on the Social Report (composed of eight senators and eight representatives) to review the Social Report and give its findings and recommendations thereon to the Congress by June 1 of each year (Senate Bill S.843, 1967:974—976). Of particular relevance here is the policy for which the bill is introduced (Senate Bill S.843, 1967:974):

> to promote the general welfare . . . to encourage such conditions as will give every American the opportunity to live in decency and dignity, and to provide a clear and concise picture of whether such conditions are promoted and encouraged in such areas as health, education, and training, rehabilitation, housing, vocational opportunities, the arts and humanities, and special assistance for the mentally ill and retarded, the deprived, the abandoned, the criminal, and by measuring progress in meeting such needs.

The bill further specifies (Senate Bill S.843, 1967:974) that the Social Report is to set forth: (1) the overall progress and effectiveness of federal efforts designed to carry out these goals; (2) a review of state, local and private efforts designed to create the conditions of the goals; (3) current and foreseeable needs in the areas served by such efforts and the progress of development of plans to meet such needs; and (4) programs and policies for carrying out the goals, together with recommendations for legislation as deemed necessary or desirable. In brief, the Mondale Bill is seen to be concerned, as were the National Commission on Technology, Automation, and Economic Progress and the Bauer volume on social indicators, with (1) specific government program evaluation, (2) general social accounting, and (3) social policy formulation.

Another event of major importance to the concern for social indicators for social policy in 1967 was the publication in May and September of two volumes of *The Annals* edited by Bertram Gross and devoted to the theme "Social Goals and Indicators for American Society." These two volumes contain some 21 essays by prominent social scientists and social commentators on conceptual and measurement problems in nearly as many aspects of social life. It is impossible to review the contents of the papers here. The interested reader is encouraged to seek them out for himself. Here it will suffice to note that, in conformity with his earlier work, the editor of the volumes continued to propose a rather broad system of social indicators to parallel the existing system of national economic accounts.

In an address to the Annual Meeting of the American Statistical Association in 1968 entitled, "Social Indicators: Statistics for Public Policy," Secretary of Health, Education, and Welfare Wilbur J. Cohen stimulated social indicator interest by appealing to the association of professional statisticians for help in the development of social statistics. In doing so, he made a distinction with respect to social statistics which is relevant here (Cohen, 1968:14):

> There are at least two types of information that the statistician must supply to policy-making officials and to the citizenry if we are to have rational methods of dealing with complex social and economic problems. First, there is need for statistics which indicate clearly and precisely present conditions in our society, including, for example, the magnitude of existing social problems and their rate of change. Second, there is a need for statistics which, given a sense of the problems which exist, can suggest the cost and effectiveness of alternative means of resolving these problems. We need, in other words, statistics which help policymakers identify and measure problems, and statistics which help them decide how best to use the available resources to solve these problems.

The Secretary then proceeded to identify the first type of statistics as "social indicators" and the second as "social accounts."

In 1966, Secretary of Health, Education, and Welfare John Gardner appointed a panel on social indicators composed of 41 social scientists and chaired jointly by Daniel Bell and William Gorham, with the latter replaced by Alice Rivlin when Gorham left HEW. *Toward a Social Report*, released in January 1969, is an HEW document based partly on the working papers of the appointed panel members and prepared under the direction of the economist Mancur Olson serving as Deputy Assistant Secretary for Social Indicators. It was released by Secretary Cohen to promote the further participation of the federal government in social indicator research (U. S. Department of HEW, 1969:iv). The volume includes chapters on health and illness, social mobility, the physical environment, income and poverty, public order and safety, learning, science and art, and finally, participation and alienation.

For the present review it is sufficient to note the aims of the report. First of all, the Secretary states in the letter of transmittal to the President that we must continue the allocation of resources to prepare a comprehensive social report, to develop social indicators to measure social change, and to "be useful in establishing social goals" (U. S. Department of HEW, 1969:iii). Second, it is stated in the introduction that a social report and a set of social indicators can provide "insight into how different measures of national well-being are changing" (U. S. Department of HEW, 1969:xii). Finally, it is said that the latter "might ultimately make possible a better evaluation of what public programs are accomplishing" (U. S. Department of HEW, 1969:xii–xiii). It is clear that these are the same claims which were advanced in the Report of the National Commission on Technology, Automation, and Economic Progress published three years earlier.

In summary, we have seen that several of the early proposals for social indicators advanced the rationale that social indicators can help (1) to evaluate specific social programs, (2) to develop a balance sheet or systems of social accounts, and (3) to set national goals and priorities. It is not difficult to find fault with this rationale, and it has been criticized by Duncan (1969) and Sheldon and Freeman (1970), in particular.

First, with regard to the setting of goals and priorities, Sheldon and Freeman (1970:99) remark that, although it would be foolish to argue against the use of indicators in planning and development, or to expect them to disappear as a means of influencing politicians and their electorates, it is naive to claim that social indicators in themselves permit decisions on which programs to implement and especially that they allow the setting of priorities. Essentially, their point is that priorities and goals are more dependent on national objectives and values than on assembled data.

Second, on the evaluation of specific social programs, Sheldon and Freeman (1970:100) argue that the use of indicators would require one to be able to demonstrate statistically that programs rather than uncontrolled variables determine changes (in the indicators). According to these authors, this is impossible at the present time, because contaminating variables cannot be controlled with presently available indicators. While agreeing with this criticism, Duncan (1969:6) also observes that not all social indicators are necessarily subjects for government programs. In brief, as Sheldon and Land (1972:139) have noted, the emerging consensus seems to be that the evaluation of specific government programs is primarily the province of "evaluation research," a somewhat specialized discipline with different research designs and measurement problems from those of social indicators.

Third, Sheldon and Freeman (1970:102–103) argue that the claim that social indicators can be used to develop a system of social accounts is not reasonable, because there is no social theory capable of defining the variables of a social system and the interrelationships among them. Similarly, Duncan (1969:3) notes that Gross's (1966) attempt to sketch the framework for a system of social accounts remains an inapplicable and unconvincing classification. He also observes that the national income accounts evolved from long and patient efforts devoted to interpreting numerical information already generated by the economy or to estimate specific quantities implicitly defined by accounting equations. Thus, he concludes that the idea of a system of social accounts is either premature or a faulty analogy with the economic accounts.

A Social Change Rationale

In addition to the social policy rationale for social indicators, we can identify a rationale which we shall loosely call a "social change" rationale. Whereas the social policy rationale has derived from the need to assess and guide public programs, the social change rationale originates from the observation that modern societies are undergoing far-reaching social change and from attempts to ascertain the rate and direction of such change. As with the social policy rationale, the social change perspective has several related components which describe the potential of social indicators to contribute to:

The measurement of social conditions (social states)

The supplementing of economic indicators with information on the "quality of life" or the "conditions of human existence"

The measurement of social change (changes in social conditions)

Although we have contrasted this rationale to the social policy perspective, it should be emphasized that the division is less than completely exclusive. Indeed, some of the three components described above can be found in the same publications which advanced the social policy perspective.

For example, with respect to the measurement of social conditions, Biderman (1966a:69) describes his focus on "quantitative data that serve as indexes to socially important conditions of the society: 'social indicators.' " Similarly, in his letter of transmittance of *Toward a Social Report* (1969:iii), the Secretary of HEW notes that the report was compiled in response to the President's request "to develop the necessary social statistics and indicators to supplement those prepared by the Bureau of Labor Statistics and the Council of Economic Advisors. With these yardsticks, we can better measure the distance we have come and plan for the way ahead." The Secretary then describes those aspects of the "quality of American life" with which the report deals.

In brief, we see that these documents clearly exhibit a concern for the establishment of social indicators to "measure social conditions" and, in particular, to "supplement economic indicators with information on the quality of life." Indeed, the use of the term "quality of life" has since become virtually identified as *the* rationale for social indicators. Insofar as the term refers to "the measurement of the social conditions of human existence," there is little ambiguity and the terminology seems appropriate enough. However, it is clear that several other meanings have become attached to the phrase. For example, although the quotation above uses the phrase in the sense of "social as opposed to economic," the Report of the National Goals Research Staff (1970) seems to use "quality of life" to refer to "qualitative as opposed to quantitative." Recently, Campbell and Converse (1972:10) have attached a third meaning, "subjective feelings as opposed to objective conditions," to an already overburdened term. This excessive use of the term "quality of life" and the resulting confusion of meaning leads to the conclusion that it serves more as a political slogan for social indicator advocates than as a convincing rationale for their development. Thus, like other political slogans, the phrase benefits from a nebulous meaning, in that this facilitates the use of the slogan for many different purposes.

The third component of the social change rationale outlined above was given a particularly strong impetus in a 1965 paper by Wilbert E. Moore and Eleanor Bernert Sheldon entitled "Monitoring Social Change: A Conceptual and Programmatic Statement." By social change, the authors meant "large-scale social structural transformations" which they proposed (Moore and Sheldon, 1965:144) to "monitor":

> *Monitoring* social change we mean in the full ambiguous sense of the term. We are concerned with "tuning in," with recording and verifying the messages we may get or produce relating to structural alterations. But we are also concerned with the use of such information for entry into the system, to alter the magnitudes, speed or even direction of change in terms of explicit, normative criteria. Many people are attempting to manipulate the system, and we think we have some obligation to unite such sophisticated skills as science affords us with such practical policies as explicit value-orientations validate.

The authors went on to state that they were preparing to ask experts in several areas to evaluate what we know about past and present trends and to prescribe what additional trend data are needed, and why. Moore and Sheldon proposed five major rubrics for examining structural changes in American society: (1) the demographic basis, including population magnitudes and geographic distribution; (2) major structural components, including the production of goods and services, the labor force, knowledge and technology, the family and kinship, religion, and the polity; (3) distributive features, including consumption, health, education, recreation and leisure; (4) aggregative features, including social stratification and mobility, and cultural homogeneity and diversity; and (5) welfare and its measurement. The major product of this effort is the volume *Indicators of Social Change: Concepts and Measurements* (1968) edited by Sheldon and Moore on the basis of the design reviewed above. It has been described as "the most comprehensive volume since *Recent Social Trends* [the report of the President's Research Committee on Social Trends (1933) under the direction of William F. Ogburn] on the major dimensions of American society" (Bell, 1969:78).

The "measurement of changes in social conditions" also was proposed by Otis Dudley Duncan in *Toward Social Reporting: Next Steps*, a monograph published in 1969. After considering and eliminating several of the components of the social policy perspective on social indicators described above, Duncan (1969:7) observes that the problem of the measurement of social change is basic to the success of social reporting. But perhaps even more important than this is Duncan's advocacy (1969:13) of the use of existing sources of data with the collection of new data as a strategy for measuring social change, which he calls "replication of base-line studies." This suggestion is further elaborated by the citation of examples of replication and base-line studies, as well as by guidelines and procedural suggestions.

A third publication contributing to the measurement of social change as a rationale for social indicators is *The Human Meaning of Social Change* (1972), edited by Angus Campbell and Philip E. Converse. Conceived of as a companion piece to *Indicators of Social Change*, the editors (1972:5) note that

> its main focus is upon a special class of such indicators that were largely bypassed in the original volume. Whereas the parent volume was concerned with various kinds of hard data, typically sociostructural, this book is devoted chiefly to so-called softer data of a more social-psychological sort: the attitudes, expectations, aspirations, and values of the American population.

Thus, the volume includes chapters on changes in the use of time, community social indicators, leisure, the subjective aspects of major social institutions (family, economy and work, politics, criminal justice), the black population, aspiration, satisfaction and fulfillment, and alienation and freedom.

A Social Reporting Rationale

A third identifiable rationale for social indicators places most emphasis upon:

The improvement of social reporting

The prediction of future social events and social life

To some degree, this represents an extension of, rather than a break with, past practice, since this society has been engaged in certain kinds of demographic and economic reporting and prediction for some time. What is new is the emphasis on periodic assessments of aspects of social conditions which have heretofore received only sporadic and unsystematic reporting.

The importance of the social reporting rationale lies in its capacity to serve as common meeting ground for both the social policy and the social change rationales. For, as Duncan (1969:7) has observed, . . . "an improved capability and capacity to measure social change is fundamental to progress in the field of social reporting. . . . " Moreover, it is clear that an expanded social reporting system is one possible application of social indicators to the guidance of social policy. Thus, in his introduction to *Toward a Social Report*, Secretary Cohen spoke of the document as a "preliminary step toward the evolution of a regular system of social reporting." Although social reporting is not as ambitious a goal as some of the promises which have been made for social indicators, it nevertheless represents a substantial increment in the systematic and periodic use of social statistics. Even more important, perhaps, is the emerging consensus among social scientists that improved social reporting is a realistic use of social indicators which is within the reach of our present capabilities.

DEFINING CHARACTERISTICS OF SOCIAL INDICATORS

With this survey of rationales for social indicators in hand, we may go on to examine the defining characteristics of social indicators. Given the divergent claims advanced for social indicators as summarized above, one might anticipate some corresponding controversy regarding the attributes of social indicators, and, indeed, one would not be disappointed. Major controversy has centered around the following definition advanced in *Toward a Social Report* (U. S. Department of HEW, 1969:97):

> A social indicator, as the term is used here, may be defined to be a statistic of direct normative interest which facilitates concise, comprehensive and balanced judgments about the condition of major aspects of a society. It is in all cases a direct measure of welfare and is subject to the interpretation that, if it changes in the "right" direction, while other things remain equal, things have gotten better, or people are "better off." Thus statistics on the number of doctors or policemen could not be social indicators, whereas figures on health or crime rates could be.

Sheldon and Freeman (1970:98) and Duncan (1969:3–4) have noted several flaws in this definition of social indicators, three of which are particularly salient here. First, Sheldon and Freeman argue that the position that indicators must be of "normative interest" is too restrictive since what is relevant today may not be so next year and vice versa. Second, Sheldon and Freeman observe that the requirement that indicators need to be measures of welfare is too confining in that it rules out many variables that may be relevant to an understanding of the indicator. Consider the examples cited in the definition. Would not statistics on the number of doctors or policemen be significant for a comprehension of health and crime rates and changes therein over time? In short, the definition of social indicators given in *Toward a Social Report* is too restrictive in that it excludes many variables from consideration which are relevant to an evaluation of the "condition of major aspects of a society." Third, Duncan notes that this definition and the discussion accompanying it clearly emphasize the desirability of a high degree of "aggregativeness" in a social indicator, which he argues may be premature.

On the other hand, as Sheldon and Freeman (1970:97) have pointed out, there is little agreement on the defining attributes of social indicators beyond the notions that: (1) social indicators are time-series that allow comparison over an extended period; and (2) social indicators are statistics that can be disaggregated (or cross-classified) by other relevant characteristics. Yet, even as the definition cited above was too restrictive, these attributes are probably not restrictive enough in that they do not distinguish social indicators from other social statistics. That is, given only these two criteria, there is little possibility of distinguishing the subset of statistics called social indicators from the set of all social statistics which are available in disaggregated time-series form. But one would probably not want to argue that these two sets are equal inasmuch as there exist many "social statistics" which are collected for administrative purposes and have little relationship to an "indexing" of social life. The latter probably should not be labeled as social indicators. Thus, the major definitional problem is to give a definition of social indicators which is neither too exclusive nor too inclusive.

These definitional problems have not been entirely resolved in recent social indicators work. For example, Campbell and Converse (1972:2–3) see the following two distinctive emphases associated with the definition of social indicators:

> First, the term is intended to convey a stress on descriptive measurement which is much more "dynamic" than most social science research has been to date. . . .
>
> Second, and perhaps more notable, the call to arms represented by the social indicators movement lays a heavy stress on policy relevance. . . .

In brief, Campbell and Converse (1972:3) see the defining characteristics of social indicators as (1) capacity to assess "the evolving quality of American social life" and (2) amenability "to manipulation through policy change."

As a second example, in his description of the criteria used to select statistical series for inclusion in the new federal social indicators publication, Tunstall (1971:109–110) notes:

> The choice of statistics has been based on two criteria. First, they must measure individual well-being. For each series, national totals are given in terms of persons or families and then broken down to reveal the age, sex, race, and other characteristics of those involved. . . .
>
> But we are not simply selecting information on people; we are also collecting information that reflects outputs. . . .

In brief, this set of defining criteria has close affinity to the definition advanced in *Toward a Social Report* in its emphasis on measures of "individual or family well-being" (welfare) and on measures of "desirable output."

It seems clear that one of the basic issues in the definition of the characteristics of social indicators is the extent to which social indicators are related to "policy" or "goal" appraisal. The derivation of such a relation has been much more obvious from a social policy than from a social change perspective on social indicators. Thus, there has existed some controversy over the primacy of this relation, for it implies a heavy emphasis on "output" or "performance" measures. Moreover, social policy advocates have often been content with such output indicators, whereas the advocates of social change analysis have sought to go beyond this narrow conception of social indicators to more general social description and analysis. For example, with respect to the two criteria described in the preceding paragraph, it is clear that the second is an "output" indicator criterion, whereas the first gives a weak attempt at social analysis, which we shall call an "analytic" indicator criterion. On the other hand, the first criterion seems completely arbitrary in its emphasis on the "individual or family" level of measurement, at least from a social change perspective. That is, such a criterion would rule out, for example, any consideration of system changes, except insofar as these are captured in the individual level measurements.

Types of Indicators and Social Indicator Models

To solve this problem of definition, it is convenient to think of three types of social indicators measuring social conditions, but each designed for different uses:

(1a) *Output descriptive indicators*: These are measures of the end products of social processes and are most directly related to the appraisal of social problems and social policy.

(1b) *Other descriptive indicators*: These are more general measures of the social conditions of human existence and the changes taking place therein.

(2) *Analytic indicators*: These are components of explicit conceptual models of the social processes which result in the values of the output indicators.

These three types are modified from those that appear in Sheldon and Land (1972:139), wherein it is also specified that each shares the attributes of being capable of collection in time-series form and the possibility of aggregation or disaggregation to whatever level appropriate for a particular analysis. Moreover, both (1b) and (2) might be viewed as indirectly policy related, for in the long run it will be these measurements and models that will provide guidance for social intervention.

Although the descriptive and output categories have been identified in the social indicators literature from the outset, the analytic indicator category was only implicit until it was identified and emphasized by Land (1971a). In brief, Land proposed that, in addition to the disaggregation and time-series criteria, social indicators are identified as components in a social system model (possibly including sociopsychological, economic, demographic, and ecological aspects) or some particular segment or process thereof. Thus, *for any particular social condition, social indicators are specified when some conception of the relevant social process is stated*. This criterion is important for at least three reasons. First, for a particular social condition, it is useful in identifying which output, descriptive, and analytic indicators are involved. Second, it allows one to focus on the relationships between indicators as these are specified in the model. This facilitates a decomposition of changes in the output indicators into those changes due to changes in other indicators, those due to random disturbances, and those due to shifts in the relationships of the output indicators to other indicators. It may well be the case that changes or shifts in such indicator-relationships are as important as changes in the output indicators themselves. Moreover, since they have been to some extent purged of the purely random variation which occurs in direct observations on descriptive indicators, these analytic indicators are possibly more basic indices of the underlying social condition being measured. Third, the position of an indicator within a social system model may be of strategic importance in determining its construct validity. That is, even though an indicator may be defined in the most rational way possible, the analyst must still provide evidence that the indicator measures what it is intended to measure. One way of making such a construct validation of an indicator is to study its behavior in relationship to other variables within the context of a model. Although such an investigation will in no case provide incontrovertible evidence on construct validity, it can provide information on how an indicator behaves with respect to other indicators.

These three types of indicators and their interrelationships are illustrated in Figure 2.1, where we have made the usual distinction between exogenous variables (those determined outside the model) and endogenous variables (those determined within the model). Within the class of exogenous variables, we have distinguished between *policy instrument descriptive indicators* (those exogenous variables which are manipulable by social policy) and *nonmanipulable exogenous descriptive indicators* (those exogenous variables which are not manipulable by social policy). Similarly, within the class of endogenous variables, we have distinguished between *output or end-product descriptive indicators* (those endogenous variables which define the social condition being measured and are the consequences of the social processes embodied within the model) and *side-effect descriptive indicators* (those endogenous variables which influence or

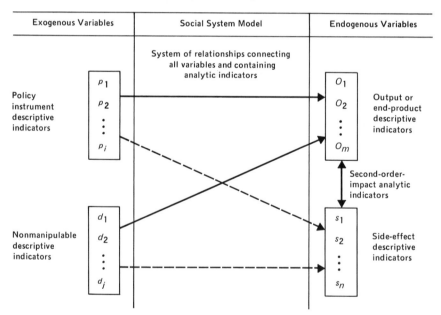

Figure 2.1. Relationships Among Output, Descriptive and Analytic Indicators

are influenced by, but do not define, the social conditions and social processes under consideration). Relating these four sets of indicators, we have a model or system of relationships which identify certain parameters or *analytic indicators* of the social processes specified in the model. We have indicated the main relationships determining the output indicators with solid arrows and those determining the side effects with broken arrows. A final arrow connects the set of output indicators with the set of side-effect indicators. We have labeled it as a *second-order impact analytic indicator*, because it seems to be the kind of relationship which Bauer and his colleagues were commissioned to study in their original social indicator effort. Furthermore, we have made this a two-headed arrow in explicit recognition of the fact that this relationship can be such that side-effect indicators both influence, and are influenced by, the social conditions measured by the output indicators. This is indeed another type of analytic indicator which could be added to the list given above.

It should be emphasized at the outset that the situation illustrated in Figure 2.1 is more of an *ideal* than an actual description of the current state of social indicators research. In fact, it is impossible to find any one social indicator study which has been successful in incorporating all of these types of indicators into an integrated model of a social process. As noted below, however, the configuration in Figure 2.1 is helpful in illuminating the measurement and analytical problems underlying social indicator efforts in several areas. Furthermore, the figure helps to illustrate the shortcomings of traditional social system models with respect to social indicators. That is, most sociological modeling efforts have concentrated on the analysis of the effect of nonmanipulable indicators on some output and side-effect indicators with only limited attention to policy instrument indicators and their relative impacts. On the other hand, most traditional operations research seems to emphasize the effects of policy instruments on output indicators without explicitly considering side-effect indicators or the influence of nonmanipulable indicators.

Suffice it to say at this point that Figure 2.1 incorporates most of the specifications for social indicators reviewed above. Moreover, by displaying the full arrangement of all components of a social indicator analysis of this pictorial form, we see that the various conceptions of social indicators which have been advanced in the literature are not necessarily contradictory; rather, their differences arise from an emphasis on different aspects of the analysis. Because the focus of Figure 2.1 is on social system models which specify social processes determining social conditions rather than more general social processes, we shall refer to a configuration such as that illustrated in the figure as a *social indicator model*. The remainder of this discussion essentially is an explication of the substantive contents and general analytical forms which social indicator models are likely to assume.

Before that, however, consider how the outline of Figure 2.1 could be applied to the problem investigated by Bauer and his collaborators—the assessment of the impact of the space program on American society. In this case, the basic end-product indicator was a successful moon flight, whereas the policy instruments pertained to the monetary, physical, and manpower resources allocated to the program. Nonmanipulable descriptive indicators included such constraints as the state of physical science and technology and the availability of trained manpower. Finally, side effects of the space program included indicators of the concentration of men and resources in particular occupations and geographical locales. Without elaborating further on the details, it seems clear that a social indicator model could be quite useful in organizing indicators pertaining to such a specific social program.

As a second example, consider a more generic social process such as education. For a social indicator model designed to represent the social processes which determine the education condition, one might specify output indicators relating to individual learning and attainment, policy instrument indicators relating to monetary, physical, and manpower resources committed to educational programs, nonmanipulable descriptive indicators pertaining to family environment and individual abilities, and side-effect descriptive indicators concerning individual occupational and income attainment, life style, cultural tastes, etc. Again, the perspective given in Figure 2.1 helps to organize indicators on education into a coherent example.

This last example helps to sharpen *a distinction between a social indicator model and a social policy model*. In brief, we have spoken in general of indicators as measuring social conditions, and, in particular, of measuring the social condition of education. But we have not imposed any additional structure on our model in the form of normative assumptions about preferred states of social conditions and objective functions to be optimized. For one thing, it should be clear that there is no necessary consensus on preferred social states. For example, some people may prefer a high divorce rate while others prefer a low rate, or some may prefer a high degree of political alienation while others prefer a low degree. Second, for purposes of research and development on social indicators and the associated models, it is not necessary to impose such normative considerations. They add nothing to the scientific development of social indicators and may even be a retarding force. Finally, such normative criteria serve to transform a social indicator model into a social policy model. In brief, given a policy maker can express his priority ordering and objective function for output indicators, a social indicator model can be analyzed to determine if the desired social state is feasible and, if so, what policy manipulations will be most likely to achieve the goal. But it must be emphasized that this presumes the existence of an adequate social indicator model on which to operate. The comments by Sheldon and Freeman reviewed on page 15 may be taken as a severe skepticism regarding the adequacy of currently available models in this respect. Moreover, these normative criteria constitute additional structure beyond that necessary to develop indicators and indicator models and derive from the values of policy makers or their constituencies, not from the indicators.

A PARADIGM FOR SOCIAL INDICATOR MODELS

The preceding discussion of rationales for, and defining characteristics of, social indicators and social indicator models has avoided several substantive theoretical foundational issues to which we now turn. The first issue has to do with *the proper scope and substantive contents of social reporting and social indicators*. This question is conveniently and quickly answered from a social policy perspective. For example, in the words of the Mondale Bill, the Council of Social Advisors would (among other things) "appraise programs and activities of the Government." In brief, the content of social indicators is to be determined by the specification of a close and direct relationship of social indicators to the evaluation of government programs. If, however, one accepts Duncan's (1969:6) position that "not all issues on which some report should be made are necessarily subjects for Federal programs," then one is faced with the necessity of spelling out some more or less explicit model of society from which the necessary social indicators are derivative, or, at least, derivable. Thus, the minimum contribution that we ask of a foundation for social indicator analysis is that it provide a theoretical context from which the contents of specific social indicators follow.

But beyond this lies the issue of *a guide to the analysis of social change*. Again, the social policy approach provides a marvelously simple solution to this issue. For as stated in *Toward a Social Report*, social indicators, by their very definition, facilitate normative judgments about social progress or decay. The image is that of the social engineer reading a set of "dials" which indicate the state of health of the society. There is no analogous component in the social change rationale for social indicators beyond the rather bland assumption that more information can help one to understand better the rate and direction of current "far-reaching social change." Thus, the second major foundational problem for social indicator analysis is that it give direction for the assessment of social change.

The Content of Social Indicators

Consider first the issue of social indicator content. It is well illustrated by the following list of content areas from Sheldon and Land (1972:146):

I. Socioeconomic Welfare
    1. Population (composition, growth, and distribution)
    2. Labor force and employment
    3. Income

4. Knowledge and technology
5. Education
6. Health
7. Leisure
8. Public safety and legal justice
9. Housing
10. Transportation
11. Physical environment
12. Social mobility and stratification
II. Social Participation and Alienation
1. Family
2. Religion
3. Politics
4. Voluntary associations
5. Alienation
III. Use of Time
IV. Consumption Behavior
V. Aspiration, Satisfaction, Acceptance, Morale, etc.

Sheldon and Land offer this as a tentative list of social indicator content areas, with due caution regarding "dangers of preemption in a premature selection of social indicators." The major problem with the list is that it was compiled in an almost totally eclectic fashion from the topics treated in such major social indicator publications as the following volumes: *Indicators of Social Change* (1968), *Toward a Social Report* (1969), and *The Human Meaning of Social Change* (1972). While there is nothing inherently wrong with such a procedure, especially at this stage in social indicators research, it fails to provide a rule for the systematic refinement and augmentation of the list, and it certainly provides little in the way of guidelines for the analysis of social change.

To some extent it seems clear, as Duncan (1969:5) has noted, that the contents of a periodic social report and (hence) of the associated social indicators will fluctuate and evolve over time. Moreover, it seems to be the case, on the basis of past unsuccessful efforts, that any useful paradigm for social indicator analysis will evolve from, or at least interact with, the development of empirical research. It is in this sense that the following effort should be taken. Thus, rather than beginning anew with some a priori theoretical scheme of society, we ask how the topics listed above can be utilized in the development of a theoretical framework.

One approach to a paradigm for organizing social indicator topics would be centered around a set of social "goals" or "concerns." This is the orientation of the new federal publication on social indicators (Tunstall, 1971).

The problem is that one is immediately confronted with the definitional referent of the "social" component of "social concerns." On the one hand, we can speak of "national" goals as these are specified by "national goals commissions." However, not only is there no necessary relation of the goals specified in this manner to the concerns of individuals, but this very easily can become a matter of partisan dispute. On the other hand, we can define "social concerns" in terms of the "needs" and "goals" of individuals. Apart from the obvious problems of defining individual needs or goals, this approach seems more defensible on other grounds. We shall reconsider a modified form of it below.

Another approach is to consider two related and complementary aspects of social activities: (1) their institutional organization, and (2) their distributive consequences. But which social activities? Certainly, some social activities should be indexed by social indicators, whereas others need not be. Thus, we need a decision rule to provide the basis for making such a distinction. One possibility is to list those activities which define a human society. For this purpose, consider the following tentative definition: A *society* is a politically organized, relatively self-sufficient population of human beings which maintains a culture and which is capable of existing longer than the life span of any individual member, the population being recruited at least in part of the sexual reproduction of its members (adapted from Parsons, 1966:2; Aberle, Cohen, Davis, Levy, and Sutton, 1950:110–111). There are several undefined terms in this definition which can be given their more or less standard social science meanings. Moreover, it is not necessary to get caught up in discussions of these activities as "functional prerequisites" for society and the associated problem of "whether societies can exist" without performing one or more of these activities; it is sufficient to observe that, for our purposes, these are the attributes which have been found to distinguish human societies from nonhuman societies. What is important here is that the definition provides a very specific set of activities around which to organize social indicators. In particular, the definition implies that a society carries out the following four classes of activities: (1) reproduction; (2) sustenance (deriving from the self-sufficiency condition); (3) maintenance of order and safety; and (4) socialization and cultural organization. To each of these types of activity, we can associate one or more standard social institution (not necessarily exclusively so) and several distributive consequences for the members of the society, as is illustrated in Table 2.1. That is, the second column of the table corresponds to the structural components by which a society reproduces itself, produces goods and services, maintains order and security, and organizes its knowledge and technology, whereas the third column lists the products of society—people, health, illness, jobs, goods, services, pollution, crime, justice, schooling, etc.—which are allocated among members.

This scheme is only illustrative of many possibilities. It will certainly undergo revision, if not total dismissal. However, let us briefly explore some of its attributes in light of previous comments. First of all, it clearly exhibits the basis for one of the fundamental criticisms made by social indicator analysts of our existing social statistical system (see, e.g., Tunstall, 1971:110): that it can provide many statistics on social institutions, but only inadequate measures of

Table 2.1. An Organization of Social Indicator Content Areas

Type of Activity	Institutional Organization	Distributive Consequences
Reproduction	Family Health care	Marriage Fertility Kinship Divorce Morbidity and health Mortality
Sustenance (production of goods and services)	Economy	Employment Income and poverty Consumption Leisure Housing Transportation Physical environment
Order and safety	Government Religion	Public safety and crime Legal justice Political and religious participation
Learning, science, and art	Knowledge and technology	Schooling Access to art

their distributive consequences (read: output or performance). Second, we observe that the scheme more or less adequately meets our first condition as stated above. That is, almost all of the social indicator content areas, as listed by Sheldon and Land (1972), are found in the third column of the table. Moreover, it is clear that new categories can be added if they fall under one of the four classes of activities, and the scheme can be further refined by respecifying some of the broad labels listed in the table.

On the other hand, this paradigm is little more than another institutional description of society (in particular, it is a modification of a scheme described by Sheldon and Moore, 1968:4). Moreover, like all such descriptions, the scheme must confront the fact that the institutions around which a society organizes its activities are mutually interdependent. Thus, we must solve *the problem of interchanges among the institutional components* if such a scheme is to be useful. This has been one of the most difficult questions for sociological theory. Parsons and many other functional theorists have approached the problem *at the institutional level* and have sought a solution in terms of the value-normative system of a society. Although some may disagree, it seems fair to say that such efforts have been less than completely successful, or at least that they have not resulted in empirically useful solutions. Another approach is to seek the solution to the problem of interrelationships, not at the institutional level, but *at the level of distributive consequences for individuals*. In particular, we propose that the interdependencies of the institutional components of society as measured by social indicators are best treated in terms of their distributive consequences as spaced over the life-cycles of individuals. As a specific example, consider health status. It is clear that conditions of health and illness of a society are affected not only by its health care activities but also by its other institutionalized activities. However, rather than attempt to specify interrelationships among the health care, family, economic, political, and cultural institutions, our suggestion is that such relationships be measured in terms of relationships among the distributed products of society, that is, in terms of interrelationships among the health, employment, income, schooling, and consumption properties of individuals.

A useful consequence of this proposal is that it allows us to relate our institutional analysis of society to one of the most powerful explanatory paradigms available in current social theory: the notion of *a life-cycle ordering of distributed social attributes* as it has been developed by Otis Dudley Duncan (Blau and Duncan, 1967; Duncan, 1967, 1968) and others over the past decade. Duncan has been particularly concerned with analyzing the process of social stratification and thus has developed a paradigm for the "socioeconomic life-cycle" (see, in particular, Duncan, 1967:87). Since we are here concerned with a broader set of variables, we give a schematic representation in Figure 2.2 of a *sociological life-cycle* (where we use sociological in its generic sense). The left side of the figure gives a rough ordering of socioeconomic status variables as these have been specified by Duncan and others, whereas the right side gives a list of the remaining categories from Table 2.1 together with some others. The diagram indicates with arrows the possibility of causal effects from the categories on the left to those on the right. Moreover, no causal ordering is postulated among the entries on the right, although specific models could be generated to exhibit such an ordering. Nor is the diagram intended to rule out the possibility of causal influence from the categories on the right to those on the left. For example, it may be that illness (on the right) should be given a nonzero effect on schooling, employment, income, and consumption, as well as on some of the categories on the right. Finally, it should be observed that, by selecting particular combinations of the variables in the figure, one could specify different (although not necessarily mutually exclusive) paradigms, that is, a *socioeconomic life-cycle* (relating socioeconomic status variables), a *socioreproductive life-cycle* (comprising family and health categories), a *sociopolitical life-cycle* (referring to a participation in political, religious, and voluntary organizations), and a *sociocultural life-cycle* (referring to schooling and other cultural categories).

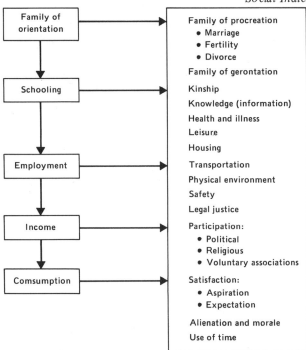

Figure 2.2. Schematic Representation of the Sociological Life-Cycle

The scheme in the figure is, of course, nothing more than a general paradigm out of which particular models can be specified. However, we shall not present such models here. Suffice it to say that tentative models have been applied in the literature and are undergoing continuous revision, estimation, and further elaboration. For our purposes, it is clear that, insofar as specific life-cycle models relate distributed social products (education, occupation, income, consumption, health, social participation, etc.) of individuals, the corresponding estimated parameters represent analytical indicators of the functioning of the various social institutions indexed by the variables of the model.

With respect to the criteria stated above for a framework for social indicator analysis, an examination of Figure 2.2 shows that our proposed paradigm is capable of accommodating all of the social indicator content areas listed by Sheldon and Land (1972) and then some. In particular, we see that the scheme now incorporates the social stratification and time-use categories, as well as the social psychological categories of satisfaction, alienation, and morale.

More generally, our proposal to focus on distributive consequences at the level of the individual provides a simple basis for further augmentation and refinement of social indicator content areas through the use of the notion of the life-space of an individual introduced by Sheldon and Land (1972:139–140).

For present purposes, it is convenient to think of the *life-space* of an individual as consisting of three measurement domains: (1) *objective conditions* (the external physical and social conditions of the individual's existence); (2) *subjective value-context* (the individual's beliefs, expectations, and aspirations); and (3) *subjective well-being* (the individual's feelings, satisfactions, and frustrations concerning components of the first two sets). These three domains of the life-space are arranged in Figure 2.3 according to the way in which they are ordinarily conceived in social theory. That is, it usually is assumed that objective conditions and subjective value-context mutually affect each other and that these two determine subjective well-being, although perhaps not in any simple linear, additive fashion. Of course, the precise specification of a specific identifiable causal ordering between the first two domains depends upon the variables and time span being considered. For example, for a set of cross-sectional observations, it may be sufficient to specify that both objective conditions and subjective value-context are exogenous and thus leave uninterpreted any observed correlations between the two sets of indicators.

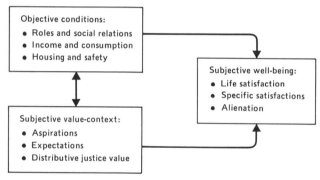

Figure 2.3. Domains of the Life-Space

Some illustrative component indicators are also shown in each of the boxes in Figure 2.3. The key to using the notion of a life-space to augment and refine social indicator content areas lies in the specification of each of these boxes as measurement domains. A measurement domain is usually conceived of as consisting of an infinite (or at least very large) set of specific measurement items possessing some particular empirical referent and some particular degree of covariation with the common core measured by all the items (see, e.g., Nunnally, 1967:175). Thus, with respect to Figure 2.3, we conceive of three measurement domains referring to the objective conditions, subjective value-context, and subjective well-being of an individual's life-space. Given this conception, we can refine these three measurement domains into more specific subdomains consisting of subsets of measurement items, where by more specific we mean a less general empirical referent. In Figure 2.3 we have refined each of these three domains into three subdomains. But there is nothing to stop the refinement process at this point. For example, the housing category could be partitioned into indicators of housing quality and housing privacy, each of which could be refined again and again. Moreover, the definition of a set of subdomains at any particular level of empirical referent is to some degree arbitrary. The only criteria which can be applied are the degree of specificity required in a particular investigation and the standard homogeneity requirements for well-defined measurement scales. But the main point is that the notion of a life-space can be used in this way to refine and augment a set of social indicators, which is one of the goals for a foundational paradigm stated above.

A Social Transformation Strategy for the Analysis of Social Change

Our second requirement for a suitable paradigm is that is must provide guidance for ordering social indicators in such a way as to facilitate the analysis of social change. Although the paradigm described above does not pretend to provide a grand analysis of social change, it can be useful in the dissection of social trends.

The basis of a strategy for the analysis of social trends lies in the realization that the notion of a life-cycle ordering of the distributed products of society leads naturally to the study of aggregates of individuals in terms of the concept of a *cohort* (Ryder, 1965). In particular, by suitably defining aggregates of individuals who experience the same event (e.g., birth) within the same time interval, we can study both *intracohort temporal development* by observing particular cohorts throughout their life cycle and *intercohort comparative careers* by comparing the temporal development of various cohorts (Ryder, 1965:861). Thus, given an observed *historical change* in the values of a social indicator during some time interval, our paradigm would suggest a decomposition of the change into at least the following (not necessarily mutually exclusive) five *components of social transformations*: (1) a *life-cycle change*, consisting of that portion of the total historical change associated with the aging of the cohorts that make up the population; (2) a *cohort change*, consisting of that portion of the total historical change accounted for by the replacement of older cohorts in the population by younger cohorts; (3) a *period change*, consisting of that portion of the total historical change associated with the unique historical characteristics of a given observation period; (4) a *social-structural change*, consisting of that portion of the total historical change accounted for by a change in the efficacy of various social institutions for particular distributional processes; and (5) a *residual change*, consisting of that portion of the total historical change unaccounted for by life-cycle, cohort, period, and structural changes. There are several analytic problems in executing such a decomposition which stem from the fact that the period of observation (P) is an exact sum of the cohort (*C*) and its age (*A*); that is, $P = C + A$ (see, e.g., Riley, 1973). Nevertheless, with suitable data and specific models, an adequate decomposition often can be made.

A somewhat similar approach to the analysis of social change has been developed by Richard Stone (1971; see also Chapter 10) under the name of demographic or social accounting. However, there are at least two major differences between the social transformation strategy to be outlined here and that presented by Stone. First, Stone has emphasized the use of a cohort model to describe the entire population of a society as individual cohorts age and progress through various stages of the life-cycle, whereas the present strategy is equally well applied to samples from populations as to entire populations. Second, Stone's strategy is more or less closely tied to a particular, albeit quite general, formal model (an input-output transition matrix representation of cohort flows), whereas the strategy stated here is more general in that it allows several formal representations (one of which is Stone's formalization). Nevertheless, for a broad variety of social conditions, it is clear that Stone's formalization is an appropriate model of the type described here.

Without going into an elaboration of specific social indicator models, it is impossible to explicate the meaning of each of these components in great detail. A couple of illustrative examples will have to suffice. First, in an analysis of the cumulative divorce records of marriage cohorts (defined as couples married within a given year), Land (1971b) found that the divorce trajectories of the cohort could be approximated by an exhaustible Poisson process model with two parameters: one for the transition rate of the process and a second for the total percentage of the initial cohort that will ultimately become divorced. In this case, the model provides for the computation of life-cycle changes of the divorce condition of a given cohort in terms of the estimated parameter values associated with that cohort. On the other hand, cohort changes may be computed by comparing the parameter estimates for different cohorts. Comparing the 1949 and the 1958 marriage cohorts, for example, we find that the estimated total percent divorced moved from 16.56 to 20.13 while the transition rate declined from 0.2529 to 0.1862. In brief, while the estimated ultimate divorce percentage of these cohorts has increased, the transition rate has decreased. Thus, more couples will ultimately become divorced in the 1958 cohort than in the 1949 cohort, but they are doing so at a somewhat slower initial velocity so that the density of divorces is spread out over more years of the cohort's marriage cycle rather than being bunched up in the initial years.

As a second example, consider Duncan's (1968) analysis of discrimination against blacks. Although his model and equations need not be reproduced here, it should be noted that he showed the differential efficacy of various socioeconomic characteristics of family of orientation for son's number of school years completed, occupational status, and income level for blacks and whites taken separately. Moreover, he used cohort comparisons to estimate changes in the associated parameters (a social structural change).

These examples illustrate two types of models which may be used in an analysis of social change. In brief, Land used a dynamic model to represent the time-dependent nature of marriage cohort divorce trajectories, whereas Duncan employed a static model to represent the relationships between socioeconomic characteristics of family of orientation and son's educational, occupational, and income attainments which presumably are not subject to life-cycle effects during middle adulthood. Thus, Land's model incorporates both life-cycle and cohort effects, whereas Duncan's model only allows for cohort effects. Logically, a third type of model would incorporate only life-cycle effects. Moreover, all of these types of models may or may not incorporate period effects. All of these effects measure the impacts of social transformations; they differ, however, in the way in which each makes use of the passage of time.

On the other hand, both of these examples are similar in another respect: neither employs time-ordered micro-data. By *micro-data*, we mean time-traces of observations on the states occupied by individuals in the cohorts. Rather than employing micro-data, both of the above models rest on *macro-data* which give the sample aggregate proportions relating to the number of individuals in each measured state for each time period. Table 2.2 gives a cross-classification of social indicator models by type of data and type of transformation effect.

In terms of this table, we see that Land's model is of Type 3, while Duncan's is of Type 7. But there are 14 other types of models in this classification, some of which incorporate nontrivial combinations of transformation effects and data types.

Consider now the relative merits of the types of models displayed in Table 2.2 with respect to the components of a social indicator model as illustrated in Figure 2.1. Clearly, the types of effects to be incorporated into the model will depend upon the types of changes in the output and side-effect indicators which the exogenous variables are assumed to produce and which are to be measured by the model. For example, to ascertain whether educational discrimination against blacks is having a lesser impact on successive birth cohorts, one might specify a model of Type 7 or Type 8. On the other hand, to distill out both cohort and life-cycle effects in party identification, one might specify a model of Type 3 or Type 4. As a somewhat different example, consider the problem of assessing the impact of an experimental education program, such as Head Start, for a sample in which there is no cohort replacement. In this case, one would probably specify a model of Type 9 or Type 10 which would facilitate the separation of effects due to maturation from those due to the impact of the program.

In each of these examples, we have offered two possible types of models, distinguished only by the type of data to be employed. This represents another

Table 2.2. A Cross-Classification of Social Indicator Models by Type of Social Transformation Effects and Type of Data

Type of Social Transformation Effects			*Type of Data*	
			Macro-Data	*Micro-Data*
Cohort	Life-cycle	Period	Type 1: cohort, life-cycle, period, macro model	Type 2: cohort, life-cycle, period, micro model
		No period	Type 3: cohort, life-cycle, macro model	Type 4: cohort, life-cycle, micro model
	No life-cycle	Period	Type 5: cohort, period macro model	Type 6: cohort, period, micro model
		No period	Type 7: cohort, macro model	Type 8: cohort, micro model
No cohort	Life-cycle	Period	Type 9: life-cycle, period, macro model	Type 10: life-cycle, period, macro model
		No period	Type 11: life-cycle, macro model	Type 12: life-cycle, micro model
	No life-cycle	Period	Type 13: period, macro model	Type 14: period, micro model
		No period	Type 15: no effects, macro model	Type 16: no effects, micro model

decision that must be made in the specification of a model suitable for the analysis of social change. The distinction is between a model based on micro-data (and thus utilizing information on the time-traces of observations on the states occupied by individuals) and a model based on macro-data (and thus utilizing only information on aggregate proportions of individuals in each measured state for each time period). This characterization suggests that the decision should be based on how essential it is to have information on which individuals have made transitions during a time interval as opposed to information only on the aggregate proportions in each state at the time points.

But the decision should also be tempered by a consideration of the methods (and hence the cost) by which each type of data may be collected. In brief, macro-data arise from repeated samples from a population wherein it is not essential to have the same individuals in the sequence of samples; that is, macro-data are produced by what Duncan (1969) has called *replication studies*. On the other hand, micro-data arise from repeated observations on the same individuals so that individual time-traces of state-occupancy are preserved; that is, micro-data are produced by *longitudinal studies* (e.g., panels, life histories, population registers). Although longitudinal studies preserve information on individuals, they are also substantially more expensive in terms of cost per unit observed than are replication studies. This cost consideration taken together with recent advances in methods of statistical inference for aggregate time-series data (see, e.g., Lee et al., 1970) seems to indicate that much social indicator model construction should rest on replication studies except when a clear and compelling argument can be made for a longitudinal study. On the other hand, it might at some point be sensible to consider extending Sheldon and Land's suggestion (1972:145) for a National Youth Panel ("covering the ages 10 to 29 to be surveyed periodically over these years with respect to their achievements and participation in the major institutions of the society with respondents dropped at age 30 and replenished with a new sample from the youngest cohort each survey period") to cover a full range of age intervals from birth to death, thus constituting a National Population Panel from which cohort, life-cycle, and period changes in various aspects of an individual's life-space could be studied.

CONCLUSION

In sum, we began by describing three rationales for social indicators: social policy, social change, and social reporting. We observed that each of these rationales, although differing in emphasis, shares various common characteristics. We concluded that advocates of both the social policy and social change rationales could agree on the centrality of improved social reporting. That is, an improved capacity to measure social change is necessary to improved social reporting and these two, taken together, seem to be preliminary, if not necessary, to the expanded use of social indicators in the guidance of social policy.

We next surveyed various definitions of social indicators, observing that major discussion has centered around whether or not social indicators need to have a normative direction and how much emphasis should be placed on output indicators. We circumvented this issue by recognizing the existence of two types of indicators: descriptive (including output indicators) and analytic. Analytic indicators arise within the context of a social system model relating various kinds of indicators, which we called a social indicator model. We then noted that a social indicator model could be transformed into a social policy model with the addition of a suitably specified objective function and an optimization criterion, but that these considerations are not necessary to the construction of the basic model.

A final section addressed two foundational problems for social indicator models: (1) the scope and substantive contents of social indicators; and (2) the provision of a guide to the analysis of social change. Regarding the first issue, we began with an institutional description of society and observed that certain problems of institutional analysis could be handled by focusing on the distributed products of society at the level of the individual. This led to the characterization of the sociological life-cycle of an individual and then to the definition of an individual's life-space as consisting of three measurement domains: (1) objective (social and physical) conditions; (2) subjective value context; and (3) subjective well-being. It was observed that this notion of a life-space provided a means for the successive refinement and augmentation of a list of social indicators. On the second foundational issue, we noted that the organization of individuals into cohorts permits an explicit recognition of four forms of social transformation effects: cohort, life-cycle, social-structural, and period. Together with a distinction between micro-data and macro-data, we then specified 16 possible types of social indicator models which may be employed in various situations. We finally observed that the decision to employ one type of model or another depends both upon the types of transformation effects to be specified and upon the type of data required.

REFERENCES

Aberle, D. F., Cohen, A. K., Davis, K. A., Levy, M. J., and Sutton, F. S.
  1950 "The functional prerequisites of society." Ethics 60 (January): 100–111.
Bauer, Raymond A.
  1966 "Detection and anticipation of impact: The nature of the task." Chap. 1 in Raymond A. Bauer (ed.), Social Indicators. Cambridge, Mass.: Massachusetts Institute of Technology Press.

Bell, Daniel.
  1969   "The idea of a social report." The Public Interest 15 (Spring):72–84.
Biderman, Albert D.
  1966a   "Social indicators and goals." Chap. 2 in Raymond A. Bauer (ed.), Social Indicators. Cambridge, Mass.: Massachusetts Institute of Technology Press.
  1966b   "Anticipatory studies and stand-by research capabilities," Chap. 4 in Raymond A. Bauer (ed.), Social Indicators. Cambridge, Mass.: Massachusetts Institute of Technology Press.
Blau, Peter M., and Otis Dudley Duncan.
  1967   The American Occupational Structure. New York: Wiley.
Campbell, Angus, and Philip E. Converse (eds.)
  1972   The Human Meaning of Social Change. New York: Russell Sage Foundation.
Cohen, Wilbur J.
  1968   "Social indicators: Statistics of public policy." The American Statistician 22 (October):14–16.
Duncan, Otis Dudley.
  1967   "Discrimination against Negroes." The Annals 371 (May):85–103.
  1968   "Social stratification and mobility: Problems in the measurement of trend." Chap. 13 in Eleanor Bernert Sheldon and Wilbert E. Moore (eds.), Indicators of Social Change: Concepts and Measurements. New York: Russell Sage Foundation.
  1969   Toward Social Reporting: Next Steps. (Social Science Frontiers, No. 2.) New York: Russell Sage Foundation.
Gross, Bertram M.
  1966   "The state of the nation: Social systems accounting." Chap. 3 in Raymond A. Bauer (ed.), Social Indicators. Cambridge, Mass.: Massachusetts Institute of Technology Press.
  1967a   (ed.) "Social goals and indicators for American society: I." The Annals of the American Academy of Political and Social Science 371 (May).
  1967b   (ed.) "Social goals and indicators for American society: II." Annals of the American Academy of Political and Social Science 373 (September).
Land, Kenneth C.
  1971a   "On the definition of social indicators." American Sociologist 6 (November):322–325.
  1971b   "Some exhaustible Poisson process models of divorce by marriage cohort." Journal of Mathematical Sociology 1 (July):213–232.
Lee, T. C., G. G. Judge, and A. Zellner.
  1970   Estimating the Parameters of the Markov Probability Model from Aggregate Time Series Data. Amsterdam: North-Holland.
Moore, Wilbert E., and Eleanor Bernert Sheldon.
  1965   "Monitoring social change: A conceptual and programmatic statement." Social Statistics Proceedings of the American Statistical

Association, pp. 144–149. Washington, D. C.: American Statistical Association.

National Commission on Technology, Automation, and Economic Progress.
1966   Technology and the American Economy. Washington, D. C.: U. S. Government Printing Office.

National Goals Research Staff.
1970   Toward Balanced Growth: Quantity with Quality. Washington, D. C.: U. S. Government Printing Office.

Nunnally, J. C.
1967   Psychometric Theory. New York: McGraw-Hill.

Parsons, Talcott.
1966   Societies: Evolutionary and Comparative Perspectives. Englewood Cliffs, N. J.: Prentice-Hall.

President's Research Committee on Social Trends.
1933   Recent Social Trends. New York: McGraw-Hill.

Riley, Matilda White.
1973   "Aging and cohort succession: Interpretations and misinterpretation." Public Opinion Quarterly (Spring).

Rosenthal, Robert A., and Robert S. Weiss.
1966   "Problems of organization feedback process." Chap. 5 in Raymond A. Bauer (ed.), Social Indicators. Cambridge, Mass.: Massachusetts Institute of Technology Press.

Ryder, Norman B.
1965   "The cohort as a concept in the study of social change." American Sociological Review 30 (December):843–861.

Senate Bill S.843
1967   "The full opportunity and social accounting act of 1967." American Psychologist 22 (November):974–976.

Sheldon, Eleanor Bernert, and Howard E. Freeman.
1970   "Notes on social indicators: Promises and potential." Policy Sciences 1 (April):97–111.

Sheldon, Eleanor Bernert, and Kenneth C. Land.
1972   "Social reporting for the 1970's: A review and programmatic statement." Policy Sciences 3 (Summer):137–151.

Sheldon, Eleanor Bernert, and Wilbert E. Moore (eds.)
1968   Indicators of Social Change: Concepts and Measurements. New York: Russell Sage Foundation.

Stone, Richard.
1971   Demographic Accounting and Model-Building. Paris: Organization for Economic Cooperation and Development.

Tunstall, Daniel B.
1971   "Developing a social statistics publication." Pp. 107–113 in Proceedings of the Social Statistics Section, 1970. Washington, D. C.: American Statistical Association.

U. S. Department of Commerce.
1960   Historical Statistics of the United States, Colonial Times to 1957. Washington, D. C.: U. S. Government Printing Office.

1962   Statistical Abstract of the United States, 1962. Washington, D. C.:
           U. S. Government Printing Office.

U. S. Department of Health, Education, and Welfare.

1969   Toward a Social Report. Washington, D. C.: U. S. Government
           Printing Office.

3

THEORETICAL DOMAINS AND MEASUREMENT IN SOCIAL INDICATOR ANALYSIS *

Arthur L. Stinchcombe and James C. Wendt

PART I: THE CONCEPT OF A THEORETICAL DOMAIN

The purpose of this chapter is to suggest a general approach to the theory of measurement which rests on the idea of a *theoretical domain*.[1] By a theoretical domain we mean a set of *possible* uses to which a concept, and correlatively the measures of a concept, might be put. It consists of the set of other concepts (with their correlative measures) which may enter into theories together with the concept to be measured. The definition of a concept must be formed in the light of the uses to which it is to be put. But the difficulty with this pragmatist axiom is that it seems to rest concept formation, and therefore measurement theory, on scientifically arbitrary explanatory motives of individual scientists. The idea of a theoretical domain of possible uses is directed at the problem of taking some of the arbitrariness out of the philosophical notion of explanatory purpose or use. This will allow us to define in a satisfactory way some traditional measurement concepts and to reconceive what the technical apparatus of statistical measure-

*The research for this chapter was done in connection with the Social Indicators project of the Survey Research Center at the University of California, Berkeley. The project is supported by a grant from the National Science Foundation. Part of this material has been published in *Acta Sociologica,* vol. 16, nos. 1 and 2 (1973), pp. 3-12 and 79-97, and is reprinted by permission of the Editor.

[1] The general problem of the project is to develop measures in the attitudinal areas of race prejudice, political alienation, and the status of women, which will remain valid over time. This chapter is an outgrowth of methodological discussions of validity of measures over time in the project.

ment theory is trying to do. The idea is that if we can show an irreducible core of meaning of a concept in *all* its possible uses in a given theory, this provides a firm basis for the analysis of the meaning of the statistical behavior of measures of a concept.

The plan of the chapter is as follows. In this first part, we will define and illustrate the idea of a theoretical domain, and define the crucial subsidiary concepts of the *span* of a theoretical domain and a set of spanning concepts, and a *causal locus* in such a domain. In Part II, we will turn to the conceptual and methodological status of *time* in such domains as a central feature of permissible relations between concepts. In particular we will treat ordinary concepts of causality (where time enters as an ordinal), concepts of an event (where time enters as a boundary which creates causal unities), concepts of rates of change (where time enters as a differential), concepts of cumulation and equilibrium (where time enters as the span of an integral), and concepts of a context or "spirit of the times" (where time enters as a summarizer of nondomain variables and concepts). The combination of this philosophical treatment here, and the analysis of the role of time, will then allow us to discuss in terms of these ideas some traditional measurement concepts, such as construct validity, predictive validity, reliability and the corresponding estimate of validity, unidimensionality, and communality from factor analysis. Finally, in Part III, we will apply this treatment of the notion of a theoretical domain and of the role of time to an analysis of the stability of the meaning of attitude scales over time.

Elements of a Theoretical Domain

The most fundamental choice of a theory is its choice of the *unit of analysis*. The fundamental requirement of a unit of analysis is that it be a boundary within which the concepts of a theory have an invariant causal relation to each other. In social science probably the three main choices of units of analysis are the act or decision (e.g., marginal economics, symbolic interaction in sociology, the early Parsons, and most experimental social psychology choose this unit), the individual (attitude studies, intelligence studies, and other predispositional studies choose this unit), and the group (e.g., Durkheim, cross-national statistical studies, choose this unit).

The postulate that the act or decision is a unit is seen for example in the theory of the firm, in the notion that as the relative costs of labor or capital change, a man or firm will substitute the cheaper factor for the dearer one; or in the symbolic interactionist postulate that individuals' definitions of the situation of an action may change so that the same "objective" events have different consequences at different times for the same person. In both cases the act is conceived of as a boundary within which variables have an invariant relation of cause and effect (relative costs to substitutions, definitions to responses), while individuals and groups do not (in that theoretical domain) have such invariances.

That is, there is no variable describing a firm or an entrepreneur which will predict whether it substitutes labor for capital in the marginal theory of firm behavior. Only by describing variables that characterize decisions or acts can the substitution be predicted.

Likewise when we describe an individual as having an authoritarian personality or high verbal ability, and so predict his ethnic attitudes or his school performance, we postulate the causal unity of the individual in these respects. We do not study in such a theory how some situations make us all submissive (e.g., concentration camps) or authoritarian (e.g., emergencies that are our responsibility). Nor do we notice that intelligent people talk more intelligently in a seminar than in a bedroom. The skin of a person is conceived to be a boundary within which authoritarianism bears an invariant relation to ethnic attitudes and intelligence to school performance.

We study nations as units in the theory of money, because we think national economies rather than individuals determine the value of a currency. Likewise nations have suicide rates, advanced economies, and other characteristics that bear invariant relations to still other characteristics of nations.

Such choices of units of analysis are of course theories. If it should turn out that there are characterologically labor-substituting entrepreneurs, who substitute labor, whatever its cost, marginal economics will not work. If it should turn out that people's intelligence varies erratically according to how they define the situation (e.g., as one appropriate for thought), then the unit of analysis in intelligence studies is wrong. If individuals exchange francs for dollars at a rate that strikes their fancy in a particular situation, depending on the age, sex, and social standing of the person who offers dollars, then nations are not the right units in theories of currencies.

The theories that form the basis for the choice of units of analysis are, however, psychologically intractable. If one tells a good psychometrician that a trial is a more intelligent social situation than reading a news story (in the sense of being cognitively adequate in analyzing the question of guilt or innocence), and that the same man as a juror is more intelligent than as a reader, he is likely to be either bewildered or irritated. Social situations are not the sorts of units to which the variable "intelligence" applies, and imagining invariances in the relations between social arrangements and cognitive effectiveness is just not his business. Units of analysis are deep parts of the paradigms within which routine science is done.

The psychological intractability for investigators of units of analysis is not as damaging as it might be, as long as the methods of analysis used do not find invariances that are not there. The unit of analysis merely constitutes a lower boundary on a theoretical domain, a black box whose causal unity is taken as unproblematic. A theoretical domain cannot include concepts and variables whose argument—the unit to which they apply and within which they have invariant relations to other variables—is not itself in the theoretical domain.

The unit of analysis is the set of X's in the "for all X" in the formal statement of a scientific law: "for all X, if X has value A_1 on variable A, then X has value B_1 on variable B." It is the set of entities to which variables A and B apply. Usually laws which are true for one set of units of analysis are not true for others. For instance, laws about the relation of age, genetic endowment, schooling, and so on, to intelligence of individuals have very little to do with the intelligence of a juror as compared to a reader of the crime news. When scientists read the epistemologist's restatement of their laws with the "for all X" phrase, their casual acceptance of the formulation is a measure of the psychological intractability of units of analysis. It is almost always easy to think of X's to which the variables apply in some sense, to which the law in one theoretical domain does not apply. Scientists assent to the "for all X" because they have a hard time thinking about any other kind of X's than the ones that define their theoretical domains.

A second kind of element of a theoretical domain is a *set of environments* within which the invariances hold. The complete statement of a scientific law would usually have the form: "There exist environments within which, for all X, if X is A_1 then X is B_1." The statement of this restriction is sometimes part of the meaning of the phrase *ceteris paribus* in economics.[2] Usually, however, this restriction of a theoretical domain to certain environments is hinted at by calling the theory a "model" rather than a "theory" (see Papandreou, 1958:101−120).[3] That is, a model is a "sometimes true theory." In the extreme, it might be true only in one environment. Thus a "model of the American economy" may fit American economic experience quite well by setting the over time coefficient relating consumption and national income at 0.7. It might be that no other country in the world has the same coefficient, and that the author of the model has no idea at all why it is 0.7 in America and nowhere else. This model is a "sometimes true theory" which is true in exactly one environment.

There are two things we mean when we say that a "model" becomes a "theory." One alternative is that the science specifies more and more exactly, in general terms, to which environments the model applies. This is done by describing idealized environments (sometimes called "closed systems") within which the model applies. For instance, Newtonian mechanics applies in a vacuum, at low speeds, without significant light pressure, etc. The second

---

[2] The more responsible meaning of *ceteris paribus* is: "this relation holds, other things being equal, and the rest of the theory tells what those other things are." It is only because the economist is willing to tell what other things have to be equal that he has a disprovable theory.

[3] What we have called "environments," Papandreou calls a "social space." Chapter 6, "Models versus Theories," is about the logical problem of specifying the "social space" within which economists' models holds.

alternative is to develop the theory by incorporating environmental variables. For example, a more complex version of Newtonian mechanics enters the viscosity of the medium into the system of equations, with a vacuum having a viscosity of zero, the effect of air at low speeds of the ball at Galileo's tower being near enough to zero, and the viscosity of the ground at the bottom of the tower where the balls hit being very large indeed; another level of complexity enters the specific gravity of the medium and buoyancy effects; and so on. Eventually by hooking enough auxiliary theories to the model it becomes applicable to more environments; in the limit to all environments.

Environments are nearly as psychologically intractable for the working scientist as units of analysis. We observe that intelligence tests predict cognitively effective behavior in classrooms but do not predict very well cognitively effective behavior in everyday life. Rather than reconceive intelligence so that it applies to everyday life, the usual solution is to shrug at the low correlation and go on about a psychometrician's business. (The source of the difficulty is fairly obvious, we think. Suppose that the role of engineer actually required people to solve problems like those they had in engineering classes, each by himself. Then about 30 percent of all components would fail, which means about 100 percent of all bridges would come crashing down. Only the most insane engineering firm would set up a social structure as likely to produce errors as a classroom examination structure. The intelligence test predicts success in a situation designed to maximize the probability of a wrong answer. As an exercise the reader should try to convince a psychometrician to measure the talent for getting the right answer on examinations when everybody in class is trying to help the student get it right, including the teacher. If he is an ordinary scientist, he will not understand the problem. Everyday life is built with a social system which would be plagiarism and cheating on an examination.)

The third main element of a theoretical domain is a *set of concepts*, a set of names of theoretical variables. The set of concepts specifies a substantive focus of a theoretical domain. It is the set of phenomena which the theory to be developed hopes to account for, together with the set of phenomena which will hopefully account for them. Thus the theory of stratification in sociology hopes to account for the patterns of inequality among men in social life and consequently for patterns of change and revolution in patterns of inequality. The legitimacy of stratification systems, the socially organized educational and career sequences, the impact of existing inequalities on what happens to a man in career sequences and consequently the patterns of cumulation of inequality (or its converse, social mobility), are the central phenomena to be explained. Causes in the history and economy of societies, causes in the characteristics of individuals, and causes in chance events or career contingencies, are therefore also constituents of the theoretical domain. Likewise effects of stratification positions and patterns, such as life styles, political and social participation, the segregation of social classes and ethnic groups in social life, in conviviality, in marriage, are included in the focus of substantive concern.

For the theory of intelligence the consistent efforts of psychometricians to eliminate items from the tests which are too contaminated by social experience, stratification position, or amount of education, indicate a boundary on the conceptual domain. If an intelligence test turned out to be a measure of the cultural richness of the home environment, a good scientist in the field would be unhappy. Of course an overall theory of cognitive effectiveness would have concepts in it of the cultural richness of the environment of individuals and of their schooling. The point is that the conceptual domain of the ordinary theory of intelligence is deliberately restricted to other connections than those between social and educational experience and cognitive effectiveness.

The importance of the conceptual domain for the theory of measurement derives from the purpose of defining a concept. The purpose of a concept is to identify phenomena that bear invariant relations to other phenomena, as cause, effect, manifestation, or whatnot. The definition of concepts that bear invariant relations to everything whatsoever is an inherently impossible task. Mass may bear an invariant relation to accelerating forces in Newtonian mechanics, but not to evolutionary advantage in biology, nor to chemical reactions, nor to the legal provisions about damages in automobile accidents. Mass is, of course, a relevant concept in those theoretical domains as well as in mechanics. But it has to be properly combined with metabolism rate to give food requirements, with molecular weight to give the number of reacting ions, or with the value of the thing crashed into to give damages. But the key invariances in the other conceptual domains are invariances about food requirements, numbers of ions, and value of damages, and mass plays a completely different theoretical role than in mechanics. The variations in mass above which an accident-causing car totally wrecks the car it hits is irrelevant to the insurance theory of accidents, while a Newtonian analysis will go on to analyze how small a package the acceleration made of the resulting wreckage.

Thus the central criterion for a concept in a theoretical domain is that, for the boundaries specified by the units of analysis and the environments in which the theory is to apply, the concept should be defined to occupy a stable place in the conceptual domain of a theoretical domain. That is, for all the arguments of the concepts, all the X's of the "for all X," the phenomena or aspects of events identified by the concept should bear invariant relations to the phenomena identified by the other concepts in the domain. It is no argument against the concept of mass in mechanics that it does not bear an invariant relation to the number of ions or to the food requirements of animals. The number of ions and food requirements have nothing to do with motions under accelerating forces.

By analogy to the statistical terminology, we can call such concepts as the number of ions or food requirements or accident damages *orthogonal* to the theoretical domain of mechanics. This does not mean of course that ions, food requirements, and damages are uncorrelated with mass. Instead it means that these correlations are irrelevant to the connection between mass and accelerating forces; that the relation between mass, acceleration, and force is invariant with respect to the number of ions, the food requirements, and the damage of a given mass. The assumption of orthogonality in this sense is the justification for the boundary around a conceptual domain.

A final element of a theoretical domain, which we will analyze extensively in the second part of this chapter, is a *set of functional forms* for the relations between concepts. When we say that a concept must bear "invariant relations" to other concepts in a domain, we have to specify the classes of relations permitted in order to investigate the invariance. If for example the force applied to a mass can cumulate over time, adding more and more acceleration to the mass, the force embodied in the moving mass does not bear an invariant relation to the instantaneous acceleration of the mass at a given moment, but to the temporal integral of that acceleration. Without specifying that temporal integrals are permitted functional forms, we cannot specify the relations between acceleration and force within which the two concepts have to have invariant relations.

Functional forms generally are divided into major classes according to the role of change in them (stochastic versus deterministic forms), and according to the role of time in them (for example, "instantaneous" forms in which the value of variable B is thought to depend on the value of A immediately, "differential" forms in which the rate of change of B is thought to depend on the value of A, "equilibrium" forms in which the cumulated changes on B are thought in the long run, as time goes to infinity, to depend on the value of A). The distinction between stochastic and deterministic functional forms is familiar from the social science literature, and will not be elaborated here. The role of time will be dealt with in the second part of this chapter.

The elements of a theoretical domain then are four: (1) a set of arguments of the concepts, the units of analysis, which are thought to be sufficiently causally unified so that some variables which characterize them are causes or effects of other variables which describe the same units; (2) environments within which the theories constructed in the domain are supposed to hold, varying from the "sometimes true" models that hold in a particular or idealized environment to the set of all possible environments; (3) a substantive focus defined by the set of concepts to whose mutual relations the theory to be developed will be responsible; and (4) a set of functional forms for the formulation of invariant relations between the concepts.

Spanning Sets of Concepts

A crucial subset of the conceptual domain is a set of concepts in terms of which all the invariant relations of the domain can be stated, with only definitional relations between this subset and the other concepts of the domain. This subset varies with the type of functional forms allowed in the domain. For example, if all the relations between variables are linear instantaneous stochastic relations with mutually orthogonal error variance or "specific variance," then the factors of ordinary factor analysis are a spanning set of concepts. That is, given the definition of all the variables in terms of the factors by their factor loadings and their means and variances, all the relations among that set of concepts (for those units of analysis in that environment) can be stated in terms of the (usually smaller) set of relations among the factors. The set of factors then is said to span the common variance of the variables. The language comes from linear algebra, in which a basis set of vectors is said to span a vector space if all other vectors can be described by linear combinations of the basis set.

The case of factor analysis shows that the spanning set of concepts of a theoretical domain is not unique. Any rotation of the factor space which does not reduce its dimension, or any set of the original variables whose vectors of correlations with the others are mutually linearly independent, also spans the theoretical domain (provided always that the functional forms are restricted to linear stochastic relations).

This nonuniqueness of the spanning set of concepts also applies to other theoretical domains. For example, the relation $f = ma$ that relates force to mass and acceleration in mechanics will permit all the equations to be stated in terms of any two of them. We can define acceleration as a function of force and mass, and state the equations of motion in terms of force and mass alone. Or we can define force in terms of mass and acceleration, and state all the equations in terms of those two concepts. Any pair of the concepts can serve to span that part of the theoretical domain spanned by the three concepts, as long as only the relations of classical mechanics are allowed between concepts.

There are two senses to the idea of spanning concepts, a theoretical one and an empirical one. If all variables or concepts in a theoretical domain are theoretically allowed to be related to all the others by all the permissible functional forms, then theoretically the spanning set of concepts will be the whole set of concepts. It sometimes happens, however, that on theoretical grounds one is willing to specify nonexistence of some relations. For example, in econometric practice one often specifies a set of zero coefficients in order to identify a system of structural equations. In psychometric theory one often uses the postulate that the correlations among a set of items are entirely due to their measuring a single concept, which also involves theoretically specifying a number of zero relations. The number of zero relations specified by the theory might be sufficient to reduce the necessary number of concepts in the theoretical domain below the complete list of variables; in the case of psychometric practice, that is the purpose of specifying theoretically the zero relations.

Further, sometimes, as in the example of the equation $f = ma$ in mechanics or

$Q = MV$ (relating the quantity of money spent in a given time period, Q, to the money stock, M, and the velocity of circulation, V, in the quantity theory of money), one of the concepts may be regarded as defined by the other two, and therefore theoretically dispensable.

Factor analysis on the other hand reduces the number of concepts that span a theoretical domain on empirical grounds. Once the forms of relations permitted are specified, the number of independent concepts required to completely describe the actual empirically present set of relations in a body of data can be derived from the analysis of the data (the rank of the correlation matrix with communalities in the diagonal). It is also possible to say of any given set of variables or concepts whether they constitute such a spanning set (if the rank of their correlation matrix is the same), and to derive from the data the definitions of the remaining concepts which will enable the complete set of relations to be described in terms of the spanning set. In this case the theoretical system does not specify the zero relations necessary to reduce the conceptual domain to a spanning set; instead the data specify which relations can be taken to be zero for any given spanning set of concepts.

The relationships of a system of equations or laws relating the concepts of a theoretical domain can be stated in terms of any spanning set of concepts. This of course includes the set of all the concepts of the domain, but also includes all the subsets of concepts which include a spanning set. Between any two sets of spanning concepts there will exist a transformation or "rotation" that allows any laws statable in one spanning conceptual scheme to be stated in terms of the other one. The transformation will neither add nor subtract information from the theory, though of course it may greatly increase the intuitive comprehensibility of the theory or the ease with which its results can be related to other theories in closely related theoretical domains. Any given formulation of the theory is therefore a member of the set of acceptable theories given by all the information-free transformations which allow it to be restated in terms of the other spanning sets of concepts. The theory, strictly speaking, is that part of any given statement of it which remains invariant under the permissible information-free transformations.

The Causal Locus of Concepts in a Domain

By the *causal locus* of a concept in a theoretical domain, we mean those aspects of its relations to other concepts which are invariant under the information-free transformations of the theoretical domain. For example, the angles of any given variable with every other variable in a factor space is invariant under all rotations of the factor space (which do not move the null vector). Thus one description of the causal locus of a variable or concept in a theoretical domain in which only linear stochastic functional forms are allowed is the complete set of angles of the variable with all other variables, combined with its communality, mean, and standard deviation. All the information about how it will enter into any rotation of the factor space, or any regression equation on the other variables in the matrix, is contained in this information. This information can be transformed in various ways without loss of information. For example, the set of angles of the variable with a spanning set of concepts (e.g., a set of factors), plus the definitions of other variables in terms of those factors, is also a complete description of the causal locus of the variable. Two variables then would have the same causal locus if they had the same set of angles with the factors, or with all the other variables in the space. This would mean that no statement exists in any of the permissible statements in all the permissible transformations of the theoretical domain which would distinguish between the two variables, which would make them have different causes or different effects.

By a causal locus then we mean a set of relations to other variables in a domain. If two variables or phenomena have the same causal locus, that means that they are caused by the same phenomena and cause the same phenomena, in the same proportions. For example, weight measured at the surface of the earth occupies the same causal locus as mass. As long as we restrict ourselves to a domain with constant gravitation, the same entities that are heavy also have large mass. Weight is a perfect measure of the amount of force needed to accelerate an object, and the amount of force a moving object will give off when it crashes into something. Within the domain of classical mechanics defined by constant gravitation, then, weight and mass are interchangeable concepts, with the same causes and the same effects. No way of stating the laws of mechanics can be found which will distinguish these two concepts if gravitation is not allowed to vary. Hence within that domain, they occupy the same causal locus. In domains of varying gravitation, such as the solar system, they are of course distinguishable concepts, and do not occupy the same causal locus. This shows the relativity of the idea of causal locus to the theoretical domain. It is because, within the domain of constant gravitation, mass and weight occupy the same causal locus that we can use weight as a measure of mass in that domain. It is because weight varies with both distance and mass in the solar system that we cannot use weight as a measure of mass in astronomy.

Thus the task of the theory of measurement is to specify the signs by which one recognizes whether two phenomena do, or do not, occupy an identical causal locus. A question of constructing intelligence tests, for example, is: Do vocabulary size and verbal reasoning performance have the same causes and the same effects, so that both phenomena may indifferently be taken as measures of verbal ability, or do they occupy distinct causal loci so that we have to theorize about the causes of vocabulary and its effects separately from the causes and effects of verbal reasoning ability? Or we ask whether distrust of people in general has the same causes and effects as hatred of ethnic minorities, so that we can talk of hostility as a syndrome in personality theory, or whether instead people learn the two kinds of hatred separately. The technology of statistical measurement theory is directed at classifying together, for a given theoretical domain, those phenomena occupying a single causal locus, which can therefore be taken as "measures" of a "concept" which occupies that locus in the theoretical system.

Conclusion

The point of this definitional work is to pose the problem of measurement in a philosophically adequate way. The problem of measurement is the accurate description of a causal locus in the sense just defined. That is, a measure is valid to the degree that it identifies a unique causal locus in a theoretical domain. Different measures of the same concept should identify the same locus, that is, undergo identical transformations when a theoretical domain is restated in a new set of spanning concepts, and enter in an identical way in all the statements of laws in each. The usefulness of a spanning set of concepts in a theoretical domain is that it simplifies the analysis of causal locus, since a complete description of the causal locus of a variable can be given in terms of any spanning set of concepts.

In the second part of this chapter, we will analyze the various functional terms used in social science theoretical domains. In particular, the role of time in the relations between variables needs analysis, in order to extend the theory of measurement to the analysis of social change. Then we will reanalyze some traditional concepts of measurement theory in the light of the philosophical position outlined here.

PART II: THE ROLE OF TIME IN A THEORETICAL DOMAIN

Time and Functional Forms

The practical usefulness of the ideas of spanning sets of concepts and of the causal locus of a set of measures or a concept depends on our capacity to manipulate the total set of interrelations among concepts in the domain. For example, the capacity of factor analysis to identify a set of spanning concepts for a conceptual domain depends on the simplicity of the linear nature of the permitted stochastic relations, as well as on some assumptions about the stochastic elements.

In most disciplines the kinds of relations among concepts permitted in a theoretical domain include some interaction of the causal variables with time in the determination of dependent variables. Time is centrally involved in all sorts of notions of causation, and people get terribly mixed up in reasoning about causation because they do not have a clear analysis of the relation of time to the functional forms permitted in the theory. And if a causal locus is to be defined as a set of variables having the same "causal relations" to other variables, "causal relations" has to be a strongly defined idea.

Take for example the problem of what it is about intelligence that is normally distributed. One classical way of formulating the problem is that *at a given age* the number of items answered correctly (or the score if computed otherwise) is normally distributed. A second way (the original way) of formulating the relation was that Mental Age divided by Chronological Age was normally distributed, with mental age being measured by the mean age of people who got the same number of items right as the subject. The difficulty with the first formulation is that it takes each age as a theoretically separate entity, and does not formulate the relations between the distributions at one age and another in any clear way. The difficulty with the second formulation is that it formulates the relation in an incorrect way, especially as people approach the age range of 15−17 when their scores stop improving much. That is, there is no age which has the same mean score as a 17-year-old who has had previously an IQ of 130.

Perhaps what is normally distributed is the differential of intelligence scores with respect to time, the rate of change of intelligence scores. We think that from the addition theorem for the normal distribution it follows that an integral over a given time period of a normally distributed time differential will be normally distributed.

The means and variances of the distributions of differentials depend on age, with the mean change per year approaching zero at around 15−17 years of age. The means and variances of the differentials also probably depend on the level of cultural richness of the society (e.g., perhaps primitive societies approach mean differentials of zero at younger ages than advanced societies), and on the heterogeneity of experiences at an age (e.g., the variance of the differentials probably decreases as a given age group approaches 100 percent in school, and probably increases as an age group goes from zero to 50 percent in school).

The point of such a reformulation is that it mirrors the observation of change over time much better than the first formulation (for example, it explains the increased variance of intelligence test performance distributions with age); it allows the formulation of propositions about both the mean and the variance as functions of social and educational experience; it does not create fictional mental ages over 17 as does the classical formulation; it predicts the temporal degradation of the correlations between intelligence scores (i.e., the fact that the more years intervene between one intelligence measure and the next, the less well the second can be predicted from the first).

But the central point for this chapter is that the lack of specific theory about time and functional forms in ordinary psychometric theory, specifically the lack of the concept of a distribution of the time differentials in test performance, makes a number of causal problems very hard to formulate.

A similar example from sociology is the confusion over the causal status of Protestantism and capitalism in Max Weber's theory. Weber talked about this relation as one of "elective affinity," i.e., some kind of mutual causation. With an ordinal conception of time, that is, with the common before-and-after treatment model borrowed from experimental psychology of what causation means, sociologists and historians have got into fruitless arguments about which came first, capitalism or Protestantism.

If we define C as the proportion of all economic social relations which have a bourgeois capitalist character, and P as the proportion Protestant in a social order, and denote by R_i the other causal variables facilitating capitalism and by X_j those encouraging Protestantism, and assume linear relations of the differential, the causal notion of "elective affinity" is easily formulated by a pair of differential equations in time and the causal variables:

$$\frac{dc}{dt} \quad = \quad a_c + b_{cp}P + \Sigma_i b_i R_i \qquad (3.1\text{a})$$

$$\frac{dp}{dt} \quad = \quad a_p + b_{pc}C + \Sigma_j b_{pj} X_j \qquad (3.1\text{b})$$

That is, the rate of growth of capitalist social relations depends on the level of Protestantism in a society and on various other variables (summed up in Weber's concept of "rationalization" of society). The rate of growth of Protestantism depends on the level of capitalism in a society and on various other causes of Protestantism. In such a system neither one of the variables precedes the other in time. They both grow together, each in a smooth curve whose slope depends on social conditions. The pulse conception of a "treatment" in ordinal time completely misses the causal character of "elective affinity."

Both of these examples have to do with the lack of time differentials among the functional forms of a theoretical domain. Similar difficulties are created when the theoretical domain lacks clear equilibrium concepts. An equilibrium relation is one in which the causal variables or concepts predict where a dependent variable will end up, no matter where it started. That is, it predicts the cumulative change that a variable will undergo as time approaches infinity (as the economists say, "in the long run"). This cumulative change depends on where the dependent variable starts and on the equilibrium value predicted by the causal variables.

Consider the following problem in the study of the social causes of attitudes by panel studies in which respondents are reinterviewed over time. We quite often find that the social variables that predict the cross-sectional correlation do not predict, or do not predict with the same coefficient, the changes over time. For example, workers are more likely to vote left at a given time, but are not in the aggregate usually more likely to change leftward between two elections. That is, between two elections it can happen that middle-class and working-class Republicans are equally likely to change to Democrats and not be replaced, even though the overall result of workers being more Democratic could not have come about by such a pattern of change. Consequently, studying changes of individuals in short periods in order to establish causation for the overall pattern of association between social variables and attitudes quite often does not work.

A very similar situation occurs in the stock market. The relative values of different stocks at a particular time depend on the relative profitability of different firms. But a bull market is not created generally by an increase in overall profits in the economy, and highly profitable firms move up in a bull market about equally with relatively unprofitable firms. Thus a "panel" study in which stocks are "reinterviewed" before and after a bull market will not identify the same causes of high stock prices as a cross-sectional study at any given time.

In both these examples, what may be going on is that the variability among individuals or stocks of party loyalty or stock price is the end result of an equilibrating type of causal system. Over the long run leftism or stock price is determined by the general characteristics of the unit of analysis, class position or profitability. At any given time most of the units of analysis are in equilibrium states, in which their relative degrees of leftism or their relative stock prices are in congruence with the values of the independent variables. Such a process might be for workers a social one, in which the historical experience of working-class leaders and organizations fills working-class social environments with leftist interpretations of politics, leftist general policy preferences, and so on. Then the relative leftism of a worker at a given time might be in congruence with the proportion of all political discussion in his lifetime social environment filled with these leftist elements of working-class culture.

We will not expect however that working-class culture will change much between elections, while candidates and economic conditions and losses or wins in warfare will change. Likewise the causes of a bull market are quite different from those that act over time to bring the value of a stock into a relatively stable price-earnings ratio. The price-earnings ratio increases for all stocks in a bull market.

That is, the causes that operate through equilibrium relations have played themselves out, have already had their effect for most of the units of analysis. There is no further causal force there. This will tend to happen when the causes operating through equilibrating functional forms are relatively permanent characteristics of the units of analysis, such as class position or basic relative profitability, for in that case the cause has a long time to reach its equilibrium effect.

When the time span of significant transients associated with permanent causes in equilibrating processes are large compared to the time between panels, but small compared to the lifetime of the values of those permanent causes for each unit, we will find very little of the equilibrating *process* between the panels, but much of the *cumulative results* of the process in the variability among individuals at a single point in time. Therefore the causes found in over-time studies are likely to be different than those in cross-sectional studies. That is, presumably, the reason why the "face sheet data" of surveys (biographical information such as race, education, occupation, age, parent's party affiliation, region where the respondent grew up, etc.) have generally powerful effects in differentiating individuals at a given point in time, and minor effects in panel studies of over-time changes.

There seem to be six main causal notions of the relations between variables which conceive the role of time differently. These we will call (1) ordinal time with the cause as an "event"; (2) instantaneous time, in which the values of the causal variable are thought to determine the values of the dependent variables without important temporal lags—a regression equation conception of time; (3) a permanent or predispositional conception of time, in which permanent qualities of the unit of analysis are thought of as causing events which are manifestations or indicators of the permanent quality—a conception of constants such as is often found in psychometric theory; (4) time as a differential, in which the rate of change of a variable is thought to be determined by its causes; (5) time as a transient in equilibrating processes, so that causes have their full effects of determining equlibriums only as time approaches infinity (or more practically after considerable time); and (6) time as a measure of variations in contextual variables such as the "spirit of the times."

Ordinal Time

Ordinal time dominates the behavioral science's and history's conceptions of causation, perhaps because the dominant paradigms of studying causation have been the psychological experiment and the narrative. The philosophical introduction to this conception of cause for a modern person is usually in Hume. A change in a causal variable is thought of as an "event," a bounded thing whose place in time can be described sufficiently well by a point. The time periods before and after the event are identifiable. Changes in the dependent variable that come after the event (e.g., after the treatment in a psychological experiment, after the fall of the Bastille) can be identified as effects.

The effort at "periodization" in history is a particularly amusing misapplication of conceptions of ordinal time to processes where they do not fit. Thinking of causation in terms of events, but recognizing nevertheless the relative slowness with which some variables rise or decline (e.g., the variable of romanticism in literature, or the introduction of the factory system into the economy of England, or the rising power of the bourgeoisie), there is a vain attempt to construct an event which started the romantic period, or which was the "takeoff to sustained growth," or the "bourgeois revolution." To be caused, a change in a variable has to come after an event, and if there is no such event people tend to invent one. For the analysis of socially important variables, ordinal time and the pulse conception of a cause as an event are hardly ever adequate, and before and after are not meaningful concepts. The conception mainly applies in the psychological laboratory.

Instantaneous Time

There are two conceptions of the role of time which justify the use of systems of linear (or polynomial) equations, without time as a variable, to represent the connections between cause and effect. The first is a conception of instantaneous effect. As soon as a cause changes, whether as an "event" or a smooth change, its effect changes, so there is always a one-to-one relation between the values of the causal variables and the values of the effect variables. This one-to-one relationship allows us to use time only in the definition of the unit of analysis. That is, since we conceive instants of time to be boundaries within which the relation between concepts is invariant, each observation taken at one time is independent of observations taken at other times and gives direct information about the connections of a system of equations in which time is not a variable. Time appears in such systems of equations only as a subscript on observations, since subscripts on observations perform the scientific function of identifying units of analysis.

With such a conception of the role of time in a theoretical system, "studying social change" is the same thing as studying causation. The reason a dependent or effect variable has changed is that its causes have changed, and so on back to the variables at the boundaries of the theoretical domain (the "exogenous" variables). Among sociologists the phrase, "social change is not a separate subject," is a moderately accurate predictor of an instantaneous conception of time and causation.

Of course none of us believes literally in instantaneous causation if we think about it. What we believe instead is that the time of significant transients is small relative to the times between observations, or that the transients will be randomly distributed because the changes in causal variables are randomly distributed in time.

Predispositional Causation

A third kind of causal conception or treatment of time in a theoretical domain also justifies linear (or polynomial) treatments of causal connections without time as a variable. This is the predisposition model. The basic idea is that causal variables do not change, or their change is so slow that it can be ignored. If we ask, for example, how fair the tracking of different races, social classes, or sexes in American high schools is, we may study how far we can predict that tracking by measures of verbal and quantitative ability taken in the ninth grade. The presumption here is that (1) there is a relative ability which has various manifestations (answering a bunch of items on an ability or achievement test) in the ninth grade, and (2) that quality has other manifestations at different times which result in teacher and counselor judgments which push people into various tracks. The mapping of items on the tests into scores on the permanent quality is presumed to be a one-to-one mapping in the ninth grade, justifying the linear treatment of measurement problems in psychometric theory. The quality being relatively permanent justifies test-retest estimates of the reliability of measurement. The slow change of the quality justifies linear regression of later high school experience on ninth-grade scores.

That is, the unit of analysis is thought to be an individual at any or all points in time, rather than an individual in his current state as in the instantaneous conception. Since either form of causal idea justifies causation being formulated in linear or other one-to-one functional forms without time as an explicit variable, social science practice mixes the instantaneous and predispositional causal notions indifferently, except when over-time data are available. Then social scientists get confused.

Time as a Differential and Rates of Change

Almost all sciences that regularly analyze change eventually go to a differential equation formulation of causal connections. Here time enters explicitly as a differential in the definition of the dependent variable. A particularly easy example is a simple growth process, in which the percent change in a given quantity is thought to be constant in time. That is, the growth of a quantity is thought to depend on the size the quantity has already reached. The romance of population and ecology with exponentials in time, and the doom of being three deep on the surface of the earth by the year 2200 at present rates of growth, are due to the power of the causal imagery of constant percentage growth.

The differential equation for a dependent variable having a constant percentage growth rate is:

$$\frac{dY}{dt} = bY \qquad (3.2a)$$

or

$$\frac{dy/dt}{Y} = b \qquad (3.2b)$$

where b is the percentage rate of growth. Integrating and setting Y at time 0 equal to Y_o, this gives rise to a temporal equation:

$$Y_t = Y_o e^{bt} \tag{3.2c}$$

The simplest of all functional forms of the differential equation type illustrates the central distinction between these and the ordinal, instantaneous, and predispositional conceptions of time and causation. There is no longer a one-to-one relation between the values of the causal variables (in this case, causal variables determining b) and of the effect variables. There is not even a one-to-one mapping between a variable and itself at different points in time. Instead the relation between one variable and another, or one variable and itself, is one-to-many. The different values of the many have time subscripts, and given the time interval there is a one-to-one mapping. But each time point has its own mapping of variables on each other.

The illustration given above of the causal conception of "elective affinity" in Weber's theory of Protestantism and capitalism also illustrates this point. The fundamental difficulty most social scientists have had with this conception is the restriction of their causal notions to one-to-one mappings without time as an interacting variable.

Time as the Limit of Equilibrating Processes

A theoretical system may have causal relations in which the influence of time disappears in the long run—that is, equilibrium relations. For example, in Fouraker and Siegel's *Bargaining Behavior* (1963) the payoff matrix to which the subjects are exposed predicts a certain equilibrium at which their bargains will end up. The subjects spend some time casting about to find this equilibrium bargain, and then tend to settle down at that bargain in repeated trials. The theory of what the equilibrium will be in the long run does not predict very well at all the transient curve which the subjects will go through to reach the equilibrium. Instead the causal process has the form that as long as the subjects are away from the equilibrium value, they will continue to change their behavior to bring themselves closer to it, but when they get to the equilibrium they stop changing.

Economics is full of such causal arguments. The long-run equilibrium for a railroad, after certain technical innovations, was to have all its traction by diesel engines. It is quite a separate study to explain the differentials in the rate of substitution of diesel traction for steam in different firms, than to predict where they will all end up (see Mansfield, 1963a, 1963b, 1963c). The theory of the rate of approach to equilibrium, or of the exceptional circumstances that may keep a firm or a bargaining pair away from it, is a theory of the conditions that predict rationality, or of more subtle aspects of rationality. The theory of the equilibrium is a theory of what rational men will do.

A similar causal conception occurs in James S. Coleman's (1964) treatment of the social causes of attitudes in *Introduction to Mathematical Sociology*. The idea is that the members of a group or social category are exposed to a random series of shocks that move them sometimes toward, sometimes away from, the attitude. The ratio between frequencies of these shocks toward and shocks away from the attitude determines the expected proportion of a group which will, in the long run, be favorable. If the mix of shocks changes in a given social group, there will be a transient response of the group proportion until it settles down at a point where an equal number of people in the group move toward and away from the attitude. The theory of the mix of shocks may take a simple linear form with no time variable in it, so that the prediction of the equilibrium proportion favorable in a social group is of a form as simple as the prediction of the long-run rate of dieselization. But the theory of the transient by which the group gets to a new equilibrium requires equations in which time enters as an explicit variable.

Perhaps the simplest form of equilibrating theory is one in which the causal force pushing a variable toward the equilibrium is proportional to the distance from the equilibrium. That is:

$$\frac{dx}{dt} = -b(x - x^*) \quad (b > 0) \tag{3.3}$$

where b is a measure of the strength of the equilibrating causal process, x^* is the equilibrium value of x, so $(x - x^*)$ is the distance of x from the equilibrium, and the minus sign on the positive coefficient indicates that if x is above the equilibrium it tends to go down, if below it tends to go up. Clearly x will keep changing until $(x - x^*) = 0$, or until x is equal to its equilibrium value. Furthermore over time x will approach the equilibrium, and the farther away it is, the faster it will approach.

Theories like Mansfield's (1963b) about the rate of dieselization or like Fouraker and Siegel's (1963) about conditions of rational bargaining are theories about the causes of variation in the size of b. The theories of the long-run equilibrium in both cases are theories about the size of x^*. The theory of the transient that x will follow in reaching the equilibrium must be more complex than the theory of the equilibrium value, if only because it involves estimating b and keeping track of the difference between x and x^* over time. Any sophisticated theory of what determines how far x gets out of equilibrium because of the temporal variation in conditions determining x^*, and of how big b is, will tend to make the theory unmanageable.

Note however that the size of b determines how well one can predict x from

x^* if he takes samples at a given point in time. Suppose, for example, we are trying to predict the response of public opinion to a change in the international power situation, say to the developing conflicts between China and the Soviet Union. The equilibrium favorableness toward China might be predicted from the degree of opposition between the United States and Russia, and the degree of opposition between China and Russia, on the basis of an equilibrating causal process that makes the enemy of my enemy into my friend. That is, if x is public opinion, and x^* is the opinion compatible with current power interests, Equation (3.3) predicts that public opinion will move toward x^*. But x^* will move away from x whenever the power situation changes, dragging x along with some lag. The larger b is, the less the lag. Henry Kissinger and other Metternich types of diplomats have a very high b, since the free movement of their favorableness is not restricted by ideological friction nor by ignorance and error. The educated but nonideological patriotic public concerned with foreign affairs learns fast, but not as fast as Kissinger. The more simple-minded anticommunist public learns to distinguish China from the Soviet Union much more slowly. The stratification of the public into layers that have not caught up with the new equilibrium will depend both on the distance the equilibrium opinion toward China has moved recently, and the different rates of response of different opinion strata.

The degree of nationalism of a public can be defined as the amount of public enthusiasm for policies which increase national power. Supposing (what is false) that the level of concern with foreign affairs in different countries and at different times within the same country is constant, this definition is equivalent to defining nationalism as a large b coefficient in a public. In a nationalistic public when war is declared, the enemy defined diplomatically becomes the enemy of the public, and new allies become "Uncle Joe" (a name for Stalin in the United States during World War II). When the war comes to an end, and the spoils are being divided among the victors, old allies quickly become new enemies and Alger Hisses who do not adapt fast enough become enemies of the public.

In a nationalistic public, then, the state of public opinion can be well predicted from the current diplomatic interests of the country. Because the b response coefficient is high, the transients of lag of the public behind the diplomatic and military apparatus are short, and one can predict directly from the x^* of current equilibrium power interests, the x of public opinion. The theory of public opinion is then simplified to the theory of the power interests of the country.

Generally speaking one would imagine that Metternichs will be able to operate effectively only when *either* the mobilization of a country does not depend on public opinion, *or* in highly nationalistic publics. When the response of the public to changes in the power situation is sluggish but when public opinion is influential, juggling alliances is likely to produce alienation. For example, one reason Frederick of Prussia in the eighteenth century could get away with rapid shifts in alliances without undermining the regime or the army's supplies was that he was not surrounded by an independent intelligentsia. Louis XV who tried to respond by allying with Austria, an ancient enemy of France, had a relatively powerful public opinion which responded slowly to the shift, still liking Frederick and hating Vienna. (Of course it was also relevant to the public response that France lost the war.) If we predict alienation from the regime by the distance between the policy followed and public opinion, high rates of change of x^* plus low response coefficients b will tend to increase alienation. Conversely, alienation from the regime will tend to lower the response coefficient, in the extreme making the enemies of one's government one's friends, with a positive coefficient in place of $-b$, and a nonequilibrating system.

We will therefore expect the set of spanning concepts of a theoretical system involving equilibrium causal connections to be larger if the response coefficient is small, requiring dynamic theories to take account of the transients. If the transients can be ignored, the concepts which span the theory of comparative statics, i.e., of the determinants of equilibrium states, will serve to span the theoretical domain.

Time as a Context

Finally we find interpretations, especially in history, in which time appears to be acting as itself a causal variable. If one says, for example, that the United States had an imperialistic policy due to nationalistic sentiments around 1900, but a policy of restriction of immigrants due to the same sentiments in the early 1920s, it looks as if time were interacting with sentiment, playing the role of a cause in the theory.

When we examine such theories more closely, what we usually find is that time is standing as a proxy for other causal variables, such as concern over southern and eastern European immigration of Catholics and Jews, war weariness, the fact that all the rich areas of the third world had been conquered by 1920, and so on. Such variables are thought to have an overall impact on elite and public opinion, which shapes the cognitive definition of the costs and benefits of policy options, shapes the saliency of various policy issues, and shapes the emotions which are called up by specific policies or social objects. That is, they affect the "spirit of the times."

It is important not to confuse such a use of time in a theory as a summary measure of causal variables, with the uses of time in the *form* of causal relations. Such contextual use of time is *not* a "form" into which one puts a causal variable. Time is a *measure of causal variables* in this case, not a conception of how causes work through time.

Measurement Concepts Redefined

Construct Validity. "Construct validity" usually is defined as the degree to which a measure of a concept actually reflects the concept. That is, it is an estimate of the closeness of what was actually measured to what the scientist wanted to measure. Thus it is the central heading in psychometric textbooks in which the will of the scientist comes into play. It therefore presents a crucial test of whether the philosophical orientation of this chapter resolves the problem of scientific subjectivity to which it is addressed. A concept in a theoretical domain is a *hypothesis* that there exist phenomena whose variation occupies a certain causal locus in a theoretical domain. Usually in fact one is not interested in a concept unless it brings economy into the description of the domain. This means more specifically that a concept is a hypothesis that some *set* of phenomena occupy an identical causal locus in the theoretical domain.

The causal locus that one is looking for may be more or less completely described by the theory. For example, the causal conception of the "need for achievement" (see McClelland, 1961) is that a set of phenomena, saliency of achievement aspects of situations, occupy an identical causal locus in a theoretical domain of concepts explaining motivational differences among individuals in meeting standards of excellence. This causal locus is supposed to be of a relatively permanent predispositional kind, so that the same people over time will be high in need for achievement. It is supposed to be motivationally significant, so it is supposed to explain differentials in performance, especially where motivation is a critical variable in that performance. It is supposed to be motivationally significant especially when the performance is perceived as relevant to socially reinforced standards of excellence, such as grades in school or money in economic life. It is supposed to have its roots in some experiences in early life which contribute to the attachment of cathexis to socially instituted standards of performance. The experiences which contribute to it are expected to lie in the family environment which varies among children within a society (rather than only to lie in, say, school experience, which is more uniform), and also to experiences with a general cultural atmosphere as reflected in variations in folktales or children's books in different societies.

Thus the hypothesis involved in the concept of achievement motivation is a relatively detailed description of the causal locus into which phenomena of saliency of achievement themes are supposed to fit. This richness of the description of the causal locus allows a rich development of alternative measures of the concept, and provides multiple checks of the equivalence of different measures.

The central point here is that a measurement hypothesis of this kind has multiple implications, and therefore multiple ways of being disproved. Consequently the question of whether some particular phenomenon measures the concept has multiple tests. The winnowing of measures to get conceptual purity can therefore go forward in many directions.

Of course one of the consequences of such a test of a measurement hypothesis can be that none of the phenomena tested occupy the causal locus in question. It may be, for example, that the saliency of achievement is situationally variable rather than characteristic of personalities, or that saliency of achievement increases anxiety rather than performance in achievement situations, or that schools homogenize populations by inducing a common level of achievement motivation, or that motivation accounts for very small variance in achievement while ability and opportunity explain nearly all of it.

It can also happen that the investigation might show that the concept can be reduced to some other concept(s). For example, the number of achievement themes in projective tests may measure the length of the response or verbal productivity, and verbal productivity may predict achievement and be located in distinctive family and school environments; cross-cultural variations in verbal productivity may account for the number of motives attached to characters in children's books and hence in particular the number of achievement motives; Protestant sectarians may be more verbally productive than Catholics because they may be more literate and more experienced at speaking in meetings on abstract questions, and so on (see Entwisle, 1972). Or people with high abilities may be more reinforced in achievement-oriented situations, and learn to have high achievement motives because they achieve.

That is, the investigation may show that the causal locus hypothesized bears such a relation to other causal loci so that the theory can be restated without that concept with no loss of information. Once one has shown that verbal productivity and saliency of achievement occupy the same causal locus in a specific theoretical domain, he can still choose to call it need for achievement if he likes, but this is not likely to suggest fruitful directions for further theoretical development.

Conversely, the result of the investigation may be that the set of phenomena thought to occupy a distinct causal locus actually occupies two or more, with different causes and different effects. For example, it may turn out that saliency of achievement in school situations is almost independently distributed of saliency of achievement in athletic situations, and that these two variables predict different achievements, have different locations in the class structure, vary across cultures in different ways, and relate to the economy of hunting and gathering tribes where athletic achievements are economically crucial differently than to the economy of scientific cultures. In sum, construct validity refers to a rich set of measurement criteria derived from a complex description of the causal locus that a measure is supposed to occupy. Measures have multiple chances of being rejected, and the statement that a phenomenon measures a concept carries more information than in other measurement strategies.

The point then is that when we elaborate for a particular concept what it is substantively supposed to mean, we do so by analyzing its relations to other concepts in the theoretical domain, to its causes and effects. These are analyzed (in this case) by predispositional forms of the relationships among variables, and with individuals as the units of analysis, because of the character of the units and forms extant in the theoretical domain. Thus McClelland's will actually has nothing to do with the construct validity of the measures of achievement motivation, but instead the criteria are the public property of all of us who work in that theoretical domain. Entwisle (1972) can give evidence about the construct validity of McClelland's (1961) measures as well as can McClelland.

Unidimensionality. Unidimensionality may be simply defined as a characteristic of a *set* of phenomena, that they all occupy a single causal locus in a theoretical domain. It can be shown that if only linear stochastic relations are allowed, this is equivalent to the criterion that variations in the phenomena have angles of zero in the factor space which spans the theoretical domain. Further, it is a consequence of unidimensionality in a domain with linear relations that phenomena occurring with different frequencies will form a Guttman scale structure if they are unidimensional with respect to each other, though the reverse does not apply. That is, one cannot prove that a scale is unidimensional in a domain by showing that it has a Guttman scale pattern, for one also has to show that none of the items have different causes or different effects than the scale. Likewise it follows that the correlations among phenomena or items occupying a single causal locus will be products of their validities, though one cannot estimate validities of items from interitem correlations directly unless they are unidimensional.

Reliability. When the central causal conceptions in a theoretical domain are predispositional, then remeasurement of the same predisposition at different times sorts out that part of the phenomena used for measurement which fit a causal locus of a predispositional kind and those which are variable in time. An estimate of how well the phenomena measure a permanent variable is called the reliability of the measure. Where the relations in a theoretical domain are limited to linear stochastic relations, the reliability is defined as the correlation between two measures of the permanent predisposition.

An alternative estimate can be derived from two or more measuring instruments (e.g., two or more items in a test, two or more judges) measuring the same predisposition at the same time, provided some estimate of their relative measuring power is available. These estimates depend on a prior determination that the phenomena which are observed by the two instruments occupy the same causal locus in the theoretical domain.

The assumption behind these procedures is that all of the aspects of the phenomena that are permanent predispositions are included in the theoretical domain. For example, if an intelligence test (in a linear domain) has a reliability of r_{ii}, then its correlation with the underlying predisposition should be $\sqrt{r_{ii}}$. From this fact, and the corresponding estimates of reliability for measures of achievement, we can figure out how much of the predisposition measured by the intelligence test predicts *any* of the measures of achievement, or is predicted by *any* of the measures of presumed causes of intelligence (genetic heritage, amount of education, social conditions). It usually turns out that some proportion of the predisposition's variation has neither causes nor effects in the theoretical domain. (See the section, "Communality and Orthogonality to the Domain," page 63.) It is as if one estimated the true masses of some bodies by several weighings, and then found that only part of the variation in mass among those bodies caused variable behavior in a mechanical system. One could be confident that there was a permanent characteristic of the body which was reflected in the measurement phenomena produced by weighings, but that characteristic includes some components which have no effects in the theoretical domain.

The central conclusion that psychometricians draw under these circumstances is that there are inadequacies in the theoretical domain, rather than in the concepts. For example, one thing that may account for a proportion of the reliable variance in intelligence not being causally effective in the system is that other variables also determine achievement (motivation, quality of teaching, culture exposure), and that these are not adequately conceptualized and measured. Thus it is possible that the predisposition "intelligence" adequately explains the residual variance in the predisposition of "capacity to solve algebra problems," once the motivational, teaching, and cultural exposure variables are taken into account.

A second thing that may be wrong with a theoretical domain is that the functional forms used do not adequately mirror the causal process. For example, it may be that intelligence does not "add" to exposure to good teaching, but rather "multiplies" the effect of good teaching. Thus in an environment filled with good teaching, intelligent people learn more; but in an environment of poor teaching, neither intelligent nor unintelligent people learn much. Such a nonlinear causal connection will not be adequately analyzed in a theoretical domain with only linear functional forms, and some variance in achievement will not appear to be related to the predispositions and variables in the domain.

The overall assumption then is that when the theoretical domain is properly specified, only the "measurement error" will turn out to be orthogonal to the domain. All of the variation in the true values of the predispositions will have effects in the domain, unless it is purely a dependent variable.

Predictive Validity. When the primary reason for being interested in a theoretical domain is a practical interest in controlling or responding to a variable included within it, one wants to view the whole domain from the perspective of the valued variable. For example, if one wants to control nervous breakdowns in combat (but not by controlling the amount of combat), one may want to respond to the probability of nervous breakdown by assigning healthy men to combat, and assigning others to quartermasters. The causal locus of interest then is viewed as an effect, and one wants all the predictors of that effect that lie within the theoretical domain which can be measured before the event.

There are two basic strategies for doing this in the psychometric literature. One is simply to start with a very long list of phenomena thought to reflect or measure any possible prior causal locus in the domain, and to select as predictors any phenomena that work as predictors. The second is to use some procedure to distinguish distinct causal loci among the predictors, construct independent measures of each by combining the phenomena which show the characteristics of .occupying the same causal locus, and then construct the prediction by specifying the relation of the effect variable to these distinct causal loci. The first of these is roughly the procedure followed in constructing the Minnesota Multiphasic Personality Inventory, the second in constructing the set of Graduate Record Examinations. The second procedure allows much more use of the intelligence of the investigator in further improvement of the prediction, in the elimination of redundancy from the measures, in the estimation of the theoretical adequacy of the prediction, and so on.

The central criterion of predictive validity of a phenomenon is that it measures some causal locus which stands prior causally to the effect of interest. The other causal loci in the theoretical domain, which do not have causal implications for the variable of interest, are ignored.

Communality. The term "communality" is used in factor analysis, but the concept involved is intimately related to the approach of this chapter. In some ways the purpose of this chapter can be conceived as the explication and extension of the idea of communality as the mother concept of measurement theory. Technically the concept of communality is that part of the variance of a phenomenon used as a measure of a concept which is related to a set of spanning concepts (the "factors" of factor analysis) by the functional forms allowed in the theoretical domain (in factor analysis, linear stochastic relations).

In practical factor analysis the set of spanning concepts are estimated, and consequently the communality is estimated. Further it is often the case that many of the concepts in a theoretical domain are left out of the original variables of a factor analysis, and only "nearby" causal loci are included. Consequently the spanning concepts located in factor analysis usually span only a subdomain of the theoretical domain. Consequently the communality commonly estimated is not a proper estimate of the communality in the theoretical domain. Finally, many factor analysis explications turn the fact, that distinct causal loci in a theoretical domain with linear forms can be described (in relation to other causal loci) as having a component orthogonal to other loci, into a fundamental theoretical fact. This orthogonal romance makes it difficult to translate the usual factor analysis language into the approach of this chapter. For all these reasons the explication of communality here will be much more contentious than would ordinarily be justified.

Communality and Orthogonality to a Domain. The presumption of factor analysis is that each variable has a "specific variance" or "unique variance" which is orthogonal to the space spanned by the factors. This is equal to $1 - h_i^2$, where h_i^2 is the communality of variable i. In the usual discussion this is broken down into "reliable" specific variance and "error" variance. That is, one part of the variance which is orthogonal to (uncorrelated with) the factor space spanned by the factors is *also* orthogonal to the communality of repeated measures of the same variable, i.e., to the reliability. This doubly orthogonal component is conceived of as error of measurement, or unreliability of the phenomenon as a measure of a predisposition. The remaining part of the unique variance which is not included in the communality, i.e., is orthogonal to the common factor space, is thought of as a measure of the inadequacy of the theoretical domain, as "reliable specific variance."

Thus one of the ways to explore how far the reliable variance of a predisposition (say intelligence) predicts the reliable variance of achievement is to compare the communalities of each in a factor analysis with their reliabilities. An overall assessment of the adequacy of a theoretical domain in this sense would be a comparison of the communalities of a factor analysis including *repeated measures of all the variables* with the communalities found in a single cross-sectional factor analysis of all the variables, for the reliable specific variance of each variable would form a separate factor involving the repetitions of measures.

Note, however, that all this reasoning depends on the applicability of the predispositional model of causation. If the underlying variables which the phenomena measure are changing, then the reliability will not accurately locate measurement error. If, furthermore, the predispositions measured at time 1 are causes of differential rates of change in the other predispositions, then the "reliable specific variance" of such a cause at time 1 will predict some of the other variables at time 2, even though it did not predict those other variables at time 1. Hence the difference in the communalities between a cross-sectional and over-time factor analysis will underestimate the reliable variance in the cross-section whenever a differential equation causal model is appropriate.

If over-time measures are included, some part of the "unreliable" variance of the phenomenon may have causes and effects at a given time so the communality in the extended domain including repeated measures may exceed the reliability of the measures. For example, suppose that there are in fact menstrual mood swings, and suppose that they affect many areas of life of which we have measures. Suppose that the test-retest time span was two weeks. Then mood measures will have very low reliability, but many effects at each time period. The communality of a mood measure in a cross-sectional factor analysis will be larger than its reliability in such a case.

The communality of a variable is then an estimate of the degree to which it occupies its particular causal locus in a theoretical domain. The components of that communality, i.e., the factor loadings of the variable, describe that causal locus in terms of a set of spanning concepts, the factors. The transformations of the factors ("rotations") leave the communality unchanged, as any measure of the character of a causal locus should be.

The communality will, however, generally be changed when the theoretical domain changes. The change in the communality of a variable when repeated measures are included in the domain is one type of such change, where the domain is extended by changing the functional forms permitted (linear relations over time as well as with other variables). This change in functional forms also changes the set of spanning concepts, since all the predispositional concepts associated with each variable (i.e., the "reliable specific variance") are added to the domain.

The set of spanning concepts can also be changed directly, by adding other phenomena to the factor analysis. A measure of accumulated experience with good teaching added to a domain having intelligence measures and achievement measures will increase the communality at least of achievement measures, since more of the variation in achievement is in the theoretical domain spanned by ability and teaching than in that spanned by ability alone.

In general the communality of a variable will be increased by increased dimension of a theoretical domain only if the immediate causal locus of a variable is affected. If we think in terms of causal arrows, only if arrows are added by adding concepts which enter or leave a given causal locus will the communality of a variable at that locus change. Otherwise put, if a variable still lies only in the subspace spanned by the original set of spanning concepts, or by a subset of them, we get no additional information about that causal locus by adjoining spaces which are orthogonal to that subspace, even if some of the other variables partly in that subspace have components which lie in the adjoined space and hence have their communality increased.

For example, if we suppose that good teaching does not affect intelligence, and that intelligence does not cause people to select good teaching (both unlikely hypotheses), then adjoining a space spanned by good teaching and intelligence-achievement to the intelligence-achievement space will not increase the communality of intelligence.

Validity and Communality. The set of angles with the factors, implied by the factor loadings of a given variable, describe the causal locus of that variable in the theoretical domain spanned by the variables included in the analysis, with linear stochastic functional forms. The communality of a variable describes the proportion of the variance of that variable which lies in that causal locus. Thus the square root of the communality of a variable is the correlation of the variable with the causal locus described by its factor loadings.

A comparison of this observation with the discussion of construct validity above shows that communality (or usually it is more convenient to use its square root) is the best measure of construct validity in a domain with linear functional forms. The adequacy of communality as a measure depends on the variables included in the factor analysis actually spanning the theoretical domain, or at least that subdomain that has any direct relation to the causal locus. Note that if causes or effects of the causal locus have been left out of the factor analysis, the communality will be an underestimate of the construct validity as defined above. Note also that if the concept of the causal locus includes "whatever is predispositional in the phenomenon," this requires the presence, in the set of variables factor analyzed, of repeated measures of the variable.

Review and Conclusions

The philosophical purpose of defining the concepts of theoretical domain, spanning concepts, and causal locus, is to be able to describe the set of scientific uses to which a particular concept is to be put. The uses of a concept are relative to the theoretical domain in which it lies, but are determinate once the domain is specified. The pragmatist criterion of concept formation, that a concept be defined by the uses to which one intends to put it, does not make the criteria of concept formation depend on the arbitrary will of the scientist.

A theoretical domain is bounded from below by a conception of the unit of analysis. The unit of analysis is any sort of observable boundary around events or phenomena, within which the causal connections between concepts in the domain are hypothesized to be invariant (deterministically or stochastically). It is bounded from above by the hypothesis describing the environments within which these invariances hold. It is bounded in the rear by the hypothesis that some of the variables in the domain (e.g., the masses of rigid bodies in mechanics) are not determined by the variables in the system, are "exogenous." It is bounded forward by the hypothesis that there are no further variables which are not orthogonal to the relationships or coefficients in the functional forms of the domain. The rear and forward boundaries determine the substantive content of the domain.

It is finally bounded in structure by the functional forms of causal connections allowed in the domain, especially by the role of time in them. Time may enter the causal scheme as ordinal, instantaneous, or predispositional, in which case the equations of the domain do not generally involve time as an explicit variable. Time may enter into the functional forms as a differential in a rate of change, in which case it enters directly into the equations. Time can enter as a variable in the transients of an equilibrating system, in which case the relations break apart into two classes: relations predicting equilibriums, not involving time ("comparative statics"); and relations predicting transients ("dynamic models"). The relations of comparative statics do not involve time in the equations—those of dynamic models do.

These boundaries on units, environments, substance, and functional forms determine spanning sets of concepts, sets which suffice to describe all the causal connections in the domain. Different spanning sets are related to each other by information-free transformations of the set of relations in the domain. The causal locus of a phenomenon in the domain is the set of characteristics of the relations of that phenomenon to others in the domain which are invariant under the permissible information-free transformations.

The idea of a causal locus in a theoretical domain can be used to define in a general way the traditional conceptions of psychometric measurement theory, including construct validity, unidimensionality, reliability, predictive validity, and communality, and to specify their interrelations. Thus it lays a philosophical groundwork under the technology of psychometric measurement.

PART III: MOVING TOWARD APPLICATION: THE STABILITY OF MEANING OF SCALES OVER TIME[4]

The case of weight as a measure of mass discussed above illustrates a general problem of measurement. As long as gravity remains constant, the force generated by gravity acting on a body (i.e., its weight) is directly proportional to its mass. When we move to a new situation in which gravity varies, weight is no longer proportional to mass, but proportional to gravity times mass. Thus a measurement analysis technique which was appropriate to show whether two concepts were indistinguishable on the surface of the earth would not show us what would happen if gravity varied.

Consider now two questions on civil liberties attitudes: Should communists be allowed to teach and should socialists be allowed to teach? They are asked first at the height of the Cold War, in 1954 (see Stouffer, 1955). At that time we can presume that the distance in "degree of obnoxiousness" between communists and socialists was roughly constant in the population. Then internal analysis might show answers to the questions to be highly correlated, and each to have about the same causes (e.g., education, cosmopolitan experience) and the same effects (e.g., recommendations of policies restricting academic freedom).

Now suppose NORC asks these questions again near the tail end of an unpopular war, at a time when China plays ping pong and Russia participates in

---

[4] The applications technology used here was developed by James C. Wendt.

SALT talks. The distance between communists and socialists in obnoxiousness may well be reduced substantially, and consequently the questions have changed their *meaning relative to each other*. We have then a causal system that can be represented as shown in Figure 3.1. The crucial observation here is that because $O(t)$, obnoxiousness of communists, is a function of time, the meaning of the questions that make up a "scale" of civil liberties attitudes changes over time. This is because these causes differently affect the answer to questions about communists than to questions about socialists.

Suppose that one found (we do not) that all the movement of the scale scores between 1954 and 1972 was due to the communist items. Then one would not want to say people had gotten more liberal, without investigating whether the meaning of communists had changed. If socialists, atheists, homosexuals, felons, prostitutes, etc., still elicited the same degree of repressive response, and only communists were treated better, one would be leery of too much enthusiasm about liberalization.

This would be true *even if* the new answers showed that by treating communists as equally obnoxious as socialists gave the investigator a good scale in 1972. We would infer that we were in a system of constant differences in relative degree of obnoxiousness in 1954, and in a different system of constant differences in 1972. In the same way, relative weights of people could have changed between those two dates because at the second date some of the men were weighed on the moon. We would be suspicious now that the weight of men might not bear such an invariant relation to mass as we had previously supposed.

The point here is that by changing the theoretical domain (in particular, the environments within which the theory is supposed to hold), we have changed the nature of the causal locus of attitude toward communists, or weight. Invariances that previously held about these causal loci no longer hold, so what it is that a given phenomenon measures also changes.

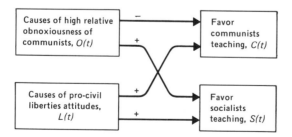

Figure 3.1. Causal Diagram for Changes in Civil Liberties Items

Practical Implications for Measurement Over Time

If we want to develop, say, attitude measures that remain valid over time, the above argument implies that we must specify a larger theoretical domain for such measures than we do for measures in a cross section. In the case of men on the moon, the larger domain includes gravitation as a variable rather than as a constant, and requires us to know something about how it varies before we can analyze what weight measures, at what causal locus the phenomenon of weight is located. With such a theory we can see, for example, that balances on the moon will measure mass, but spring scales will not, and neither will measure mass in a free-falling spaceship. We need a comparable extension of the theoretical domain for an attitude scale in order to use it in over time studies.

Let us suppose for example that the meaning of adjectives in a semantic differential analysis of the concepts "atheist," "socialist," and "communist" does not change over time. A better assumption would be that the rate of change of meaning of adjectives is very slow, so that we can practically ignore it. Then we extend the theoretical domain to include the variation of obnoxiousness of these three concepts—communists, socialists, and atheists—measured against the stable grid of adjective meanings. In this case then we could correct the attitude questions by rescaling the objects in them by their degree of obnoxiousness. The question of change in attitudes toward communists would then break down into two questions: "Has there been a change in liberalism toward objects of a given degree of obnoxiousness?" and "Has the degree of obnoxiousness of communists changed?"

But this is in a sense a fake solution to the problem, because it rests entirely on the movement of the concept relative to a grid which is *assumed* to be fixed. In the long run, we will not be satisfied with a procedure which rests so strongly on such weak theoretical foundations as linguistics can provide us. How do we know that an adjective such as "crazy" does not drastically change meaning over time? The question is whether we can, from the above considerations, derive some alternative (or supplementary) criteria for diagnosing or predicting how different elements in the new theoretical domain are likely to behave.

Consider again the causes $O(t)$, causes of change in obnoxiousness of communists, and $L(t)$, causes of changes in liberalism. Suppose that we have some measures which give us variations on O and L. Then consider comparing the anticommunist civil liberties scale with one such as an antiatheists scale, which is not affected by O. We will find that both scales will be related to L, but only the communist scale would be related to O.

If we could find such measures which do not respond to O, then as O becomes a function of time, $O(t)$, the meaning of the civil liberties attitude measures changes, but the meaning of the anchors we have cast to measure obnoxiousness ought not to change. Which is what we wanted to know about the grid for measuring obnoxiousness. Thus the key aspect of finding stable anchors against which to judge *which* causal locus a given change represents, is *to measure the causes of the different kinds of changes.*

Clearly the theoretically simplest way to do this is to let time pass, so that nature expands our theoretical domain for us. Then we study whether there is evidence that different measures of civil liberties move in the same direction at the same speed, or whether there are different pushes on different items. But this empiricist procedure is likely to be expensive, not only because we cannot decide what we have measured until we are old men, but also because we are likely to waste our resources by having to have a large number of measures, only a few of which work.

The alternative strategy is to find ways of expanding the theoretical domain by means of intelligence and analysis. *If* we can find *other* variance on L and O than that provided by history, *then* we can analyze the problem of the stability of measures with cross-sectional data. The importance of the philosophical approach for the problem of measurement over time, then, is to translate the problem of stability of meaning into a problem of the causal locus of an indicator in an expanded theoretical domain. Then other ways of expanding the domain become at least partial solutions to the problem of analyzing stability.

From "Application" to "What is Actually To Be Done"

What we usually in fact have in a cross-sectional study (which might be repeated over time) is a concretization of a group of sociologists' notions about the central elements in the theoretical domain, whose explanatory purpose is to explain differences among individuals. These elements come from the accumulated wisdom of the discipline (never leave out occupation, education, age, sex) or from known correlations in the literature that need elaboration (a domain with race prejudice would always include southern origin and religious affiliation, for example), or from theoretical developments for the study itself.

Some of these causal variables for cross-sectional differences may vary over time. Thus a better approximation to the theoretical domain within which items will have to occupy a stable place over time is the entire domain of the cross-sectional study. That is, instead of only asking whether an item bears such a relation to the universe of content (e.g., civil liberties) that it can be taken as a measure, we can easily extend the question to whether the various items occupy the same locus in the entire theoretical domain of the cross-sectional study. If the items do that, then it is at least somewhat less likely that there exists a cause bearing distinctively on one subset of items which is likely to push them in different directions over time. How adequate that "somewhat" is will depend, of course, on how far there is measured cross-sectional variation on variables like L and O in Figure 3.1. There are some contextual variables, such as the shifting national interest, which have little cross-sectional variation. Perhaps with delicate measures of exposure to the current international news, one could construct such a measure for a cross-sectional study. But it would be unlikely to cause great cross-sectional variation, and so to be omitted and not to tell us much if included.

The basic point then is this: The difficulty of the stability of measures over time is a particular case of the difficulty of whether measures which occupy a distinct causal locus in one theoretical domain occupy a distinct locus in an extended domain. A partial answer to that question is to examine their behavior in the most extended domain available. The most extended domain available in a cross-sectional study is the entire set of variables thought to be related to cross-sectional variation. Thus the analysis of measures needs to be extended to this domain of causes and effects, in addition to the regular internal consistency analysis.

A Rough Intuitive Application

In the set of items measuring political alienation in a cross-sectional study of the Bay area in the Berkeley Social Indicators Project, factor analytic studies indicated a dominant principal component and several dimensions of smaller importance. But this internal consistency analysis leaves the question of the interpretation of these dimensions open. The argument above suggests that we ought to look for dimensions that occupy distinct causal loci, in the sense of having distinct causes and effects.

In Table 3.1 a number of alienation items (or in one case a scale) are arranged into groups that apparently have different relations to education, age, and ideological self-description. (The correlation coefficients are from dirty data, because measurement analysis takes place early in survey analysis.) The items grouped under "Economic indignation" have generally small negative relations to education, small to medium negative relations to age, and small negative relations to ideological self-description. That is, the more alienated people on these items are slightly less educated than the average, slightly younger, and slightly more leftist.

The set of items grouped under "Left ideology" have generally small positive relations with education, middle- to large-size negative relations to age, and large negative relations to ideological self-description. That is, more alienated people on these items are somewhat better educated than average, younger than average, and substantially more left in self-description.

The set of items grouped under "Moralistic despair" are slightly negatively related to education, substantially positively related to age, and somewhat positively related to ideological self-description. That is, more alienated people on these items are somewhat less educated than average, substantially older than average, and somewhat more likely to describe themselves as conservative.

The argument above implies that these groups of items should be regarded as

Table 3.1. A Theoretical Domain Analysis of Alienation Items

	Education	Age	Ideological Self-Description	Item-to-Total Alienation
Economic indignation				
[16] Government not try to make streets safe	−0.08	−0.03	−0.11	0.42
[20] Dissat. with standard of living	−0.18	−0.11	−0.08	0.34
[22] Work dissatis.	−0.09	−0.26	−0.10	0.31
[23] Poor chance to get good work	−0.24	0.07	−0.06	0.33
Left ideology				
[3] Leaders dissatis.	0.13	−0.18	−0.40	0.66
[5] Need change in system	0.07	−0.19	−0.23	0.47
[6] Breaking law necessary	0.23	−0.36	−0.40	0.40
[8] Can't trust government	0.05	−0.16	−0.29	0.65
[9] No leaders share my beliefs	0.00	−0.17	−0.25	0.57
[10] No leaders tell truth	−0.04	−0.15	−0.26	0.62
[11] Country run by power elite	0.09	−0.19	−0.23	0.55
[56] Adjective check list	0.14	−0.28	−0.36	0.87
Moralistic despair				
[17] Courts too easy	−0.10	0.24	0.25	0.04
[19] Moral standards worse	−0.17	0.38	0.26	−0.01
[21] Standard of living getting worse	−0.03	0.38	0.01	0.13
[35] Doing badly moral standards	−0.02	0.18	0.11	0.29

occupying distinct causal loci in the cross section, because they evidently have different causes and different effects. But inspection of the last column of item-to-total correlations (the total was of some 64 alienation items, including the ones in the table) shows that on grounds of internal consistency, only three of the "Moralistic despair" items would have been eliminated from the scale on grounds of too little correlation with the principal component as measured by the total score.

The relations to age are particularly interesting from the point of view of the study of change. Age is not, of course, an ordinary kind of cause, but literally a measure of the passage of time. One should not make too much of this, since age measures causes such as life-cycle stage or farm origin or educational achievement as well as historical experience of the zeitgeist. Nevertheless we can ask the question: Supposing age measures the causal forces acting at the time people crystallized their attitudes in early adulthood, what would have been the effect on measures of alienation?

Clearly the answer we infer from Table 3.1 is that it would depend on the mixture in our alienation index of the three components. The item-to-total correlations show that this study had a heavy weighting of left ideology in the overall measure of alienation. The overall result would have been that alienation *as measured by this mix of items* would have increased substantially. If the scale had been developed during the Depression and had more items with economic indignation components, alienation would have remained about the same. If the measure had been developed in the time of the prohibition movement, and had had more items of moralistic despair, alienation would have declined.

In spite of the hazards of such a reckless use of age data for inferring historical trends, these results give some plausibility to the idea that in the expanded theoretical domain appropriate to studies over time, these different alienation items occupy distinct causal loci. Although at any one point in time, they may together form a scale that accurately differentiates those with negative affect toward the society from those with positive affect, this scale has an uncertain meaning for over-time studies.

How does this relate to the suggestions above about the change in meaning of objects such as communists? One possible way to interpret the results of Table 3.1 is suggested in the choice of labels for the groups of items. As is usual in studies based on variants of factor analytic techniques, theoretical recklessness comes in the choice of labels. The items have in common that they measure negative affect toward social objects. They differ, perhaps, in the objects. The first group has primarily to do with economic objects (the exception, crime in the streets, may possibly have to do with slum living); the second group with government policies, leaders, and structures; the third with moral behavior of the general population (one exception).

It looks as if education and youth make immorality less salient, less an object around which negative affect is organized. But they make government policies and leaders more salient. As immorality becomes a less obnoxious object, and government becomes a more obnoxious object, we would expect items measuring negative affect toward society which make use of those objects to move in opposite directions. Thus their place in an overall scale of negative affect would tend to change. It would do this in two ways. First, questions involving less salient objects would tend to become worse measures of overall affect. Second, highly indignant young people would find it easy to say that on morality we are doing OK, while highly indignant old people would find it easy to say the government was OK. Thus the scale position of different objects would be likely to change.

A Formal Approach to the Analysis

If we assume that the relations between variables are linear stochastic relations, then the logic of factor analysis can be extended to the problem above.

For what we want to know about a set of measures is not only whether they are unidimensional in the space spanned by proposed measures of the causal locus of alienation, but whether they are also unidimensional in the expanded space which includes proposed causes and effects of the variables. If the variables in Table 3.1 were factor analyzed in a factor space including measures of education, age, and ideological self-description, they would have different projections on those causes or effects. Thus there would be some dimensions of the space on which they would have distinct factor loadings. Rather than inspecting the correlation matrix, as we did to find the pattern in Table 3.1, we could have inspected the rows of factor loadings in the factor space describing the same matrix. If the rows of factor loadings corresponding to two items are proportional (within some estimate of the sampling error of factor loadings, a knotty problem), then they occupy the same causal locus in the expanded theoretical domain of the cross-sectional study, specifying that linear stochastic relations only are allowed in the domain.

REFERENCES

Coleman, James S.
   1964   Introduction to Mathematical Sociology. New York: Free Press.
Entwisle, Doris R.
   1972   "To dispel fantasies about fantasy—based measures of achievement motivation." Psychological Bulletin 77, No. 6: 377–391.
Fouraker, Lawrence E., and Sidney Siegel.
   1963   Bargaining Behavior. New York: McGraw-Hill.
McClelland, David C.
   1961   The Achieving Society. New York: Van Nostrand Reinhold.
Mansfield, Edwin
   1963a   "The speed of response of firms to new techniques." Quarterly Journal of Economics 67 (May): 290–309.
   1963b   "Intrafirm rates of diffusion of innovation." Review of Economics and Statistics 45, No. 4 (November): 348–359.
   1963c   "Size of firm, market structure, and innovation." Journal of Political Economy 71 (December): 556–576.
Papandreou, Andreas.
   1958   Economics as a Science. Philadelphia: Lippincott.
Stouffer, Samuel A.
   1955   Communism, Conformity, and Civil Liberties. Reprint edition, 1966. New York: Wiley.

4

THE LOG LINEAR ANALYSIS OF SURVEY REPLICATIONS *

James A. Davis

INTRODUCTION

Thanks to a little pamphlet (Duncan, 1969) and a lot of money, social indicator research will probably take the, route of replication rather than invention. Instead of developing brand new measures of the "Gross National This and That," we are more likely to see the exact repetition of previous bench mark studies. A number of such projects are currently in process, for example:

1. Duncan has replicated attitude items from past years in the 1971 round of the Detroit Area study.

2. David L. Featherman and Robert M. Hauser have received funding for a replication of the Blau-Duncan mobility research.

3. The National Opinion Research Center (NORC) has completed the first survey in an annual series of national surveys containing bench mark items from a variety of sources. (Data from the NORC General Social Survey are currently available to anyone at cost—$50.00 for two decks of IBM cards—from the Roper Public Opinion Research Center, Williamstown, Mass.)

4. For all practical purposes, the publication of a detailed index to the

*The research reported herein was supported by a grant from Russell Sage Foundation, NSF Grant GS31082X, and the perpetual generosities of The National Opinion Research Center and the Kiewit Computation Center of Dartmouth College. I am grateful to Stephen E. Fienberg for comments and criticisms of the original draft.

University of Michigan Survey Research Center Election Series (ICPR, 1971) amounts to a large grant to all of us for replication research.

But how shall we go about analyzing the data in replication studies? To narrow the field a little, I assume the situation to be something like this:

1. We have two or more surveys, identical in sampling plan and questionnaire content.
2. The content is divided into "dependent" variables such as attitude and opinion items, and "independent" background items such as Occupation, Education, Region, City Size, etc.
3. We want to know two things: (a) How much change has there been in the dependent variables? and (b) What role do the background items play in the changes?

The central principle is obvious: *merge the two data files and treat time as a variable.* That is, treat all of the data as a single study in which one of the variables is the date of measurement. The principle implies that no new methods need be developed. We may thus be able to avoid the fate of the panel study fad, which exhausted itself in producing fancy methodology and never got around to analyzing and reporting much in the way of results.

All that is required is a little thought about how to interpret various statistics when one of the variables is time. For example, what would it mean to find a correlation between one variable and time that vanishes when another variable is controlled?

Let us begin with standard regression procedures. There are two basic strategies: path analysis and analysis of covariance. We begin with path analysis and the generic path diagram shown in Figure 4.1.

Making the usual crucial, queasy assumptions about causal direction, Figure 4.1 gives us an ideal typical model. It says that: (1) time affects the level of the independent variable (e.g., educational levels are increasing); (2) the independent variable affects the dependent variable when time is controlled (e.g., educated people always tend to be more "liberal"); and (3) time may or may not affect the dependent variable when the independent variable is controlled. If the $X_1 Y$ path turns out to be negligible and the other two nonnegligible, we would conclude that change in the independent variable explains change in the

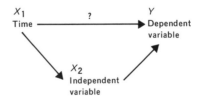

Figure 4.1. Generic Path Diagram for Replication Studies

dependent variable (i.e., the $X_1 Y$ zero order). If not, we can see how much of the change is "pure" and how much is due to the intervening variable.

The notion is more than statistical. It is one of our natural ways of thinking about social change. When we say that urbanization is destroying (or improving) family life, we are really saying that with appropriate data, we could substitute urbanization for X_2 and family life for Y, and obtain a model with nontrivial values for the two paths $X_1 X_2$ and $X_2 X_y$ only. As a more concrete example, Stouffer's classic 1954 study of tolerance argued that because educational attainment is increasing and education is correlated with tolerance, in the future we would see increasing tolerance in America (Stouffer, 1955:107–108). Stinchcombe (1968:60–79) discusses a variety of such theories, calling them "demographic explanations." Note that Stinchcombe divides demographic explanations into two components akin to $X_1 X_2$ and $X_2 Y$ (1968:73–79).

Path analysis is not the only method. One can also take an approach roughly like analysis of covariance and examine the regression of Y on time separately for various levels and combinations of independent variables. We have an excellent example of this in a monograph by Schwartz (1967). Schwartz examined poll data on racial prejudice in surveys from 1944 to 1965, regressing opinions on time within educational and regional subgroups. Generally speaking, she found the correlations to be linear and the slopes parallel, as shown in Figure 4.2.

The linearity of the relationships is of interest, since it suggests that racial attitudes are not much influenced by short-run episodes such as the 1954 Supreme Court decision or the 1957 Little Rock, Arkansas, confrontation.

The similarity in slopes is equally interesting since it suggests similar rates of

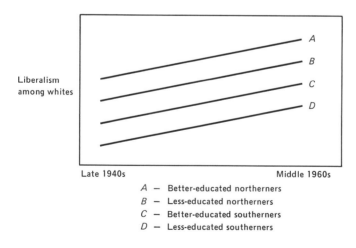

Late 1940s   Middle 1960s

A — Better-educated northerners
B — Less-educated northerners
C — Better-educated southerners
D — Less-educated southerners

Figure 4.2. Schematic View of Schwartz Data

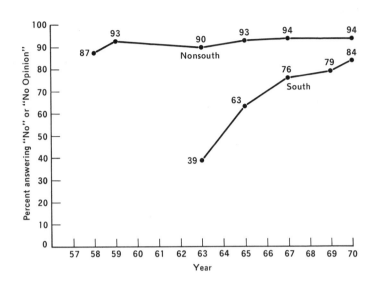

Figure 4.3. Time Trends on School Integration Item by Region[a]
[a] Number above the point is the percentage.

change in these subgroups. It is quite possible, however, for a different pattern
to emerge.

By piecing together data from various Gallup publications through the
1960s, we can trace answers to the question "Would you, yourself, have any
objection to sending your children to a school where a few of the children are
colored?" Figure 4.3 gives the percentages answering "No" or "No Opinion"
(versus "Yes") among white parents by region (N's not reported in the original
sources).

The lines are not parallel. Among nonsoutherners, the figures show an
essentially horizontal pattern of very high endorsement. Among southerners,
there has been a sharp increase throughout the decade; the regional gap is almost
closed by 1970.

If we look at the variants—"where half are Negroes" and "where more than
half are Negroes"—we see different patterns, which are not quite as pleasing to
the integrationist. Figure 4.3 should not be considered a prototype for race
relations items in the 1960s, but it does serve the purpose for which we chose it
by showing how differences in slopes can be interpreted as subgroup differences
in social change.

Just as the path model has a solid substantive base in demographic theories
of social change, the analysis of covariance approach is relevant to the question
of "massification versus differentiation" (Glenn, 1967). Is America becoming
more homogeneous in attitudes or is it really in some process of polarization,

with group differences increasing? For example, does it suddenly have a "generation gap?" The matter usually is left to what Stinchcombe calls "fact free" research, although Glenn's paper and an ingenious analysis of historical voting data by Stokes (1967) are excellent exceptions. General application of the covariance strategy could be most interesting, in the light of three possibilities:

1. Data showing converging regression lines (e.g., Figure 4.3) suggest "massification."
2. Data showing diverging regression lines suggest "polarization."
3. Data like Schwartz's (Figure 4.2) suggest a general secular trend with constant group differences.

To summarize the argument so far:

1. In analyzing survey replications the various data sets should be merged and time treated as a variable.
2. Existing multivariate techniques are probably quite adequate for such analyses, although it may be necessary to review their interpretations in the light of the unconventional research problem.
3. There seem to be two theoretical approaches to social change, each with a natural multivariate interpretation.
   a. Demographic explanations can be tested by path models in which time is the antecedent (exogenous) variable and a demographic item intervenes between it and the dependent variable.
   b. The massification-differentiation hypotheses can be tested by procedures similar to analysis of covariance, i.e., examining the relationship between time and the dependent item within levels or categories of the demographic items.

The further argument advanced in this chapter is that a new set of techniques for statistical analysis of attribute data enables us to combine these two strategies of analysis into a single system that is useful for analyzing the results of survey replications.

Since this is the first of three chapters in this volume using these procedures, I will begin with a description of the techniques and then illustrate their application to survey replications with a concrete example, a 1972 replication of Stouffer's tolerance items.

LOG LINEAR AND HIERARCHICAL MODELS

In the last few years statisticians have developed a set of novel techniques for analyzing categorical data called log linear and hierarchical models. Sociologists recently have become aware of these developments through the writings of Leo Goodman, a major contributor to the approach (Goodman, 1965, 1970, 1971, 1972a, 1972b, 1972c). Since many readers of this volume are not familiar with these tools, I will explain them here. I will treat log linear models first and then hierarchical models. No advanced mathematics is involved, but the materials are complicated and subtle. Therefore, I make no promise to thoroughly cover the topic. I intend to explain just enough so that the reader can follow the reasoning in this section. For a more thorough and precise coverage, see the Goodman papers cited and their bibliographic references. For a more popularized and longer explanation, see Davis (1972, 1973).

Log Linear Models

We begin with the classical factorial design for an experiment, a methodology seemingly quite distant from the analysis of surveys. Consider, for example, a factorial design with three "treatments," *A, B*, and *C*, and two levels within each. Following Finney (1960), the design can be represented as shown in Table 4.1.

Table 4.1. Notation for a Three-Treatment, Two-Level Factorial Design

Treatment *A*	Treatment *C*			
	No		Yes	
	Treatment *B*		Treatment *B*	
	No	Yes	No	Yes
Yes	*a*	*ab*	*ac*	*abc*
No	1	*b*	*c*	*bc*

For the sake of concreteness, imagine Table 4.1 to be an agricultural experiment in which beans are planted in eight rectangular plots. Three fertilizers, *A, B*, and *C*, are applied alone and in combinations. The particular treatment given each plot is indicated by the appropriate lower-case letter(s). For example, the "*ab*" in the upper right-hand plot of the left-hand box means that these beans were given fertilizers *A* and *B* but not *C*. (The comparison also could be made between larger and smaller dosages, rather than presence and absence.) The plot designated with the number "1" received no fertilizer at all. At the end of the experiment we can count or weigh the beans to establish the *mean yield* in each plot. These eight means are the basic information for analyzing the experiment.

By definition, *the main effect of A is the mean difference in yield between all plots containing "a" and all without "a."* For fertilizer *A*, we would estimate this number by (1) adding the four means in plots *a, ab, ac*, and *abc*; (2) subtracting the sum of the means in "1," *b, c*, and *bc*; and (3) dividing by four.

Factorial experiments can also have interaction effects, loosely defined as excesses or deficits in yield, associated with particular combinations of treatments. The *AB* interaction effect, for example, is half the difference between the mean effect of *A* at the upper level of *B* and that at the lower level of *B*. Because of space limitations I have no choice but to assume that the reader is familiar with the concept of interaction effects. It is explained in most elementary statistics texts in connection with analysis of variance.

With many variables and higher-order interactions, verbal definitions of effects become cumbersome. Finney (1960) has devised a routine for defining all possible effects in a two-level factorial experiment:

(1) For an experiment with *n* treatments *A . . . . N*, write out expressions of the following general form:

$$(a \pm 1) \quad (b \pm 1) \quad (c \pm 1) \ldots (n \pm 1)$$

(2) Define effects in terms of the capital letters of the treatment(s), e.g., "*ADF.*"

(3) To decide whether a particular term should have a plus or minus sign, use this rule: If the letter appears in the treatment, use a minus sign, otherwise use a plus sign.

(4) When signs have been given, multiply out the expression following the usual algebraic rules.

(5) The results of step (4):
  (a) will be a list of design cells with plus or minus signs;
  (b) when summed will be the treatment effect times 2^{n-1}

Let us follow these rules to obtain the *A* effect in our hypothetical example. After step (3) we obtain:

$$(a - 1) \quad (b + 1) \quad (c + 1)$$

which multiplies out to:

$$ab + a + ac + abc - 1 - b - c - bc$$

and since *n* = 3 (we have three treatments), $2^{n-1} = 2^2 = 4$, so we divide by 4.

In a two-level factorial experiment there are exactly as many orthogonal (mathematically independent) effects as there are combinations of capital letters. Table 4.2 gives the formulas for all the effects in Table 4.1.

The definitions and formulas can be extended to an indefinite number of treatments and to treatments with more than two levels, though we will stick with the two-level case here.

Table 4.2. Formulas for All Possible Effects in a Three-Treatment Factorial Design

4A	=	$(a - 1)(b + 1)(c + 1)$
	=	$abc + ab + ac + a - bc - b - c - 1$
	=	$(a - 1) + (ab - b) + (ac - c) + (abc - bc)$
4B	=	$(a + 1)(b - 1)(c + 1)$
	=	$abc + bc + ab + b - ac - a - c - 1$
	=	$(b - 1) + (ab - a) + (abc - ac) + (bc - c)$
4C	=	$(a + 1)(b + 1)(c - 1)$
	=	$abc + ac + bc + c - ab - a - b - 1$
	=	$(abc - ab) + (bc - b) + (ac - a) + (c - 1)$
4AB	=	$(a - 1)(b - 1)(c + 1)$
	=	$abc + ab + c + 1 - ac - bc - b - a$
	=	$[(abc + c) - (bc + ac)] + [(ab + 1) - (a + b)]$
4AC	=	$(a - 1)(b + 1)(c - 1)$
	=	$abc + ac + b + 1 - bc - ab - a - c$
	=	$[(abc + b) - (ab + bc)] + [(ac + 1) - (a + c)]$
4BC	=	$(a + 1)(b - 1)(c - 1)$
	=	$abc + bc + a + 1 - ac - ab - b - c$
	=	$[(abc + a) - (ac + ab)] + [(bc + 1) - (b + c)]$
4ABC	=	$(a - 1)(b - 1)(c - 1)$
	=	$abc + a + b + c - ab - ac - bc - 1$

Now, the log linear model:

1. Assume that Table 4.1 is no longer an experiment but is a table for the complete cross-tabulation of three dichotomous variables in a survey. The numbers associated with the eight cells (plots) are now case frequencies, not mean yields.
2. Assume that we take the natural logarithms of the eight frequencies and use them for analysis rather than the frequency counts. (We will see why in a moment.)
3. Assume that we calculate all the "effects" defined in Table 4.2. Let us interpret the meaning of main effects, two-variable interactions, and three-variable interactions under these assumptions.

The main effects, *A*, *B*, and *C*, can be interpreted as "partial skews." This is—as far as I can tell—a concept unique to the log linear model and not one of compelling interest to most investigators. But we need it to see the logic of the complete system. Consider the third line of the formula for 4*A* in Table 4.2:

$$(a - 1) + (ab - b) + (ac - c) + (abc - bc)$$

Inspection of Table 4.1 shows that within each parenthesis we compared a Yes cell on *A* and a No cell on *A* while the other two variables were held constant. Remembering that we are working with logs rather than frequencies and that subtracting logs is the same as taking a ratio, we see that the *A* effect will vary with the ratio of Yes *A* to No *A* within conditions. When the Yes *A* cell frequencies generally outnumber the No *A* cell frequencies, the *A* effect will be positive; when the highs and lows are equal, the effect will tend toward zero; when the lows outnumber the highs, the effect will be negative.

(Since the results are divided by four, and since division of a sum of logs is equivalent to taking roots, the main effects will be logs of geometric means of the Yes-No ratios and the other effects will be roots of various geometric means. In this condensed explanation we will omit this part of the analysis.)

A main effect of zero then is equivalent to saying that the Yes-No ratios for a particular variable average 1.00; i.e., the cells tend to show 50-50 splits. Positive and negative main effects may be interpreted as indices of skew in the item distributions—i.e., departures from 50-50 splits. They can be called "partial skew" effects because, unlike the traditional marginal distribution, they are assessed with the other variables held constant.

In most survey analyses, single-variable distributions are not of much analytical interest since item splits are greatly affected by small changes in wording and arbitrary collapsing. The analyst, therefore, will seldom focus on main effects. However, one technical point is worth consideration: since the experimental effects are orthogonal, the definition of skews implies that the other effects are independent of item splits. Thus, the analyst may use log linear techniques even when his items are badly skewed.

Before interpreting higher-order effects, we must review the concept, "odds ratio." Consider Table 4.3, a hypothetical table of raw frequencies. The odds that a Yes on *A* is Yes on *B* are 104 to 35, while the odds that a No on *A* is Yes on *B* are 12 to 216. If we take the *ratio of these two odds*, we get the odds ratio:

$$\frac{104/35}{12/216} = \frac{(104)\,(216)}{(35)\,(12)} = 53.486$$

Table 4.3. Hypothetical Fourfold Table of Cell Frequencies

Variable *A*	Variable B	
	No	*Yes*
Yes	35 ⌐a	104 ⌐ab
No	216 ⌐1	12 ⌐b

A well-known principle in contingency table statistics states that in a fourfold table the odds ratio will equal 1.000 when the variables are independent and depart from 1.000 when the two items are correlated.

Applying the factorial design notation to the hypothetical frequency table, Table 4.3, we obtain a general formula for the odds ratio:

$$\frac{(ab)\ (\text{``1''})}{(a)\ \ (b)}$$

Referring back to Table 4.2, let us look at the formula for the *AB* effect:

$$[(abc + c) - (bc + ac)] + [(ab + 1) - (a + b)]$$

If we remember that we use logs when calculating effects, and that the addition and subtraction of logs is equivalent to multiplication and division of the antilogarithms (antilogs), we can see that the term in the right-hand bracket is the log of the odds ratio for variables *A* and *B* when *C* is No. Inspection of Figure 4.1 shows us that the term in the other bracket is, of course, the log of the odds ratio for *A* and *B* when *C* is Yes. The results are similar for *BC* and *AC*.

Skipping the division by four and the powers and roots it involves, we see that two-factor effects are functions of the conditional odds ratios for two variables within levels of the third. In other words, *AB, AC,* and *BC* are a form of partial association for variable pairs.

The point is worth repeating: Two-variable effects in the log linear model are to be interpreted as partial associations among pairs of variables.

The interpretation of two-variable effects justifies the use of logs rather than frequencies. If we calculated experimental effects on the raw frequencies we would lose the crucial correspondence between independence and effects of zero. (Doubters should try the fourfold table where $a = 4$, $ab = 1$, $b = 4$, and "1" $= 7$, calculating both the odds ratio and the *AB* effect using raw frequencies.)

Finally, let us interpret the three-variable effect, *ABC*. To do so we (a) assume that Table 4.1 is a table of raw frequencies, (b) calculate the two conditional odds ratios for the relationship between *A* and *B*, and (c) find the ratio of these two ratios. The result:

$$\frac{[(abc)\ (c)]\ /\ [(ac)\ (bc)]}{[(ab)\ (1)]\ /\ [(a)\ (b)]} = \frac{(abc)\ (c)\ (a)\ (b)}{(ac)\ (bc)\ (ab)\ (1)} \tag{4.1}$$

Looking at the bottom line of Table 4.2, we see that those cells with positive signs appear in the numerator of Equation (4.1), while those cells with negative signs appear in the denominator. Remembering again that adding and subtracting logs is equivalent to multiplying and dividing frequencies, we see that the *ABC* effect will vary with the ratio of the two conditional odds ratios for the *AB* association.

So? If we consider the odds ratio as a measure of degree of association, and we certainly should, a little elementary algebra will demonstrate that:

1. When the two conditional odds ratios are identical, the *ABC* effect will be zero and there is no difference in magnitude for the two conditional associations.
2. When the *C* Yes association is more positive than the *C* No, the *ABC* effect will be positive.
3. When the *C* Yes association is less positive than the *C* No, the *ABC* effect will be negative.

The *ABC* effect is a measure of "specification," that is, the degree to which the magnitude of the partial association varies according to the level of the control variable.

We have developed the interpretation in terms of the relationship between *A* and *B* specified by the level of variable *C*. However, it is easy to show that identical results hold for the other two pairs. *When the ABC effect is nonzero, any one of the three variables specifies the association between the other two.*

It is possible to go on to four, five, or any number of variables and show that their higher-order interaction effects can all be interpreted as specifications of lower-level ones. Thus, an "*ABCD*" effect would tell us that we will get different values for the three-variable effects, *ABC, ABD, ACD,* and *BCD,* depending on the category of the fourth.

To summarize: When data are analyzed using the log linear model we can calculate a set of statistically independent effects that can be interpreted as: (a) partial skews, (b) partial associations, and (c) specifications and higher-order effects that are conditional effects on specifications.

Hierarchical Models

The new statistical procedures include two distinct systems of analysis, the log linear approach just explained and the hierarchical model approach. My own discussion uses only log linear effects, but other chapters use hierarchical models. It may be helpful to sketch them here.

The ground rules for this new approach are:

1. We work with contingency tables of frequencies, not logs.
2. There is no advantage in sticking to dichotomies.
3. The data properties at issue are partial skews, partial associations, specifications, and higher-order effects of the kind discussed above.

Hierarchical modeling concentrates on testing null hypotheses about the presence or absence of effects, rather than estimating coefficients that describe the magnitude of effects. Modeling may also be used to improve estimates of cell *frequencies* but this aspect is not important for replication studies. (For an extensive discussion of applications to cell frequency estimation, see Bunker, et al., 1969:237–286.) The logic of the procedure follows.

First, we consider all possible effects that could occur in the data, using capital letter notation as in Table 4.2. For three dichotomies there are seven possibilities.

Second, on the basis of theory, hunch, or trial and error, we decide to test the hypothesis that one or more of the effects are absent. Thus, for three variables, we might hypothesize skew effects and one or more partial associations, but no *ABC* effect.

Third, we proceed to physically construct a new set of modeled data in which (a) the effects hypothesized to be absent are set to zero, and (b) everything is unchanged. The procedure uses an iteration routine that cannot be explained here. (See Goodman, 1972b:1080–1085; or Davis, 1973:56–60.) It is easily programmed for a computer and is not impossible for hand calculations.

Fourth, we compare the frequencies in the original data with the frequencies in the modeled data. If our model fits—that is, if there is no significant difference between the modeled data and the raw figures in the sample—we accept the null hypothesis that the effects hypothesized to be absent are indeed absent. If our model does not fit—that is, if there is a significant difference between the modeled data and the raw figures—we reject the null hypothesis. For details on the actual significance testing procedures, see Goodman (1970).

The classic chi square test for significant association in a two-variable table is a special case for such modeling. We hypothesize that the *AB* effect is absent, use the expected frequencies to build a modeled set of data, and compare the actual and modeled data to test the null hypothesis. Thus hierarchical modeling is a generalization of classic procedures, not an alternative.

According to the logic of this procedure, if the model fits the raw data it does not mean that the effects *in* the model are significant. It means that the effects *excluded* from the model are *not* significant. Therefore, the research worker using hierarchical models generally proceeds by testing a series of models to find out what effects can be safely left out and what effects produce a bad fit when excluded. To show failure of fit when a particular effect is set to zero is equivalent to showing that the effect in question is statistically significant.

The goal is to construct a final model which contains the minimal number of effects sufficient and necessary to fit the data. There often is, but need not be, a unique final model.

So far it would seem that the two systems differ only in the apparatus for making the calculations. Nevertheless, the notion of "hierarchy" constitutes an important logical difference between the two systems. To develop the notion of "hierarchy," we proceed as follows:

1. To define the model being tested we describe it by a set of capital letters and parentheses, designating the effects that are *not* set to zero. As an example, consider the model:

$$(ABC)\,(DE)\,(F)$$

It says that we can have a three-variable interaction for A, B, and C, a partial association for D and E, and a skew for F.

2. Any letter or combination of letters that does *not* appear within the same parentheses is set to zero in the model. In our example, Variable G does not appear. The model says that, in effect, G is not skewed and is totally independent of all the other variables. The letters C and D do appear, but they do not appear together in the same parentheses, so our model will set CD to zero.

3. Any subset of the letters within a pair of parentheses cannot be set to zero. In our example, the presence of (ABC) means that not only will we permit that three-variable interaction, but also that we cannot hypothesize zero values for AB, AC, BC, A, B, and C.

Point 3 is the hierarchy property. It means that we cannot use any old combination of effects for our model. We must use systems where the allowed effects form logically consistent Chinese boxes.

One might think that the hierarchy property means that this approach is less useful than the log linear model system. Things are not that clear-cut. In defense of the hierarchical model we must note that:

1. The log linear model is very cumbersome and difficult to interpret where the data are not all dichotomies. The hierarchical model system has no such limitation.

2. While there are significance tests for log linear models (Goodman, 1970:229, Equation 2.9, and 233, Equation 3.4), they have different powers for different levels of effect. The matter cannot be explained here, but it amounts to saying that higher-level effects have to be much stronger to achieve statistical significance. This is not true in hierarchical models.

3. There is a rule of thumb in many areas of science that higher-order effects are weaker than lower-order ones. Thus, hierarchical models may be particularly appropriate.

4. In practice, a major use of hierarchical models is to demonstrate that there are few or no higher-order effects. Once this is done, the analyst can then proceed to examine his associations using other techniques, including log linear effects.

To summarize: Log linear models and hierarchical models have two common assets. They both allow one to study higher-order effects in contingency tables in a straightforward fashion. They both allow the analyst to describe his findings in a concise fashion—a list of effect parameters or a concise alphabetical model.

Log linear models have the advantage of describing the magnitude of the effects and allowing one to examine any possible combination of effects.

Hierarchical models have the advantage of simple extension beyond dichotomies and have similar power against null hypotheses of different levels.

We can now turn to the main topic: how to apply log linear techniques to replication studies. The procedure is actually rather simple. Just as log linear models turn out to be a reinterpretation of experimental effects when the cell data are logs of frequencies, their use in replications requires only that we interpret the various coefficients when one of the variables is time. The main conclusions are these:

1. A Time × Dependent effect is a measure of change.
2. Differences between the zero-order Time × Dependent effect and its value when a background item has been controlled provide the grist for the path strategy.
3. Time × Dependent × Background effects can be interpreted in terms of the analysis of covariance or massification-differentiation strategy.
4. Since 2 and 3 are orthogonal, both research strategies are incorporated in the same analysis.

That is all there is to it, but it may be useful to work through a concrete example to see how the technique actually works. We will illustrate with a replication of the Stouffer tolerance items.

THE STOUFFER REPLICATION

The 1972 NORC General Social Survey is a 1,613-case personal interview sample of the continental United States noninstitutionalized population 18 years of age and older. It is a multistage probability sample down to the block level, with quotas applied at the final stage. Interviewing took place in February and March of 1972. In this study, nine questions were taken verbatim from Stouffer's 1954 study of tolerance of communists and other deviants. His cross-section sample has a total of 4,933 cases. The replicated items are presented in Table 4.4.

With the exception of Stouffer's study, we know little about trends in these items. Hyman and Sheatsley (1953) assembled a set of similar questions from Gallup and NORC polls, and concluded that restrictiveness toward communists increased during the period from the middle 1940s to the early 1950s. For example, on the item, "Communist Party members should *not* be allowed to speak on the radio," they report 40 percent agreement in 1943, 39 percent in 1945, and 57 percent in 1948 (Hyman and Sheatsley, 1953:8). For the item, "In peacetime, Socialists should not be allowed to publish newspapers," they report agreement percentages of 25 percent in 1943, 29 percent in 1945, and 39 percent in 1953 (Hyman and Sheatsley, 1953:16).

Table 4.4. Replication Items

35. There are always some people whose ideas are considered bad or dangerous by other people. For instance, somebody who is against all churches and religion. . .
    A. If such a person wanted to make a speech in your city (town, community) against churches and religion, should he be allowed to speak, or not?

    Yes, allowed to speak .... ·1
    Not allowed 2
    Don't know 8

    B. Should such a person be allowed to teach in a college or university, or not?

    Yes, allowed to teach 4
    Not allowed 5
    Don't know 8

    C. If some people in your community suggested that a book he wrote against churches and religion should be taken out of your public library, would you favor removing this book, or not?

    Favor 1
    Not favor 2
    Don't know 8

36. Or consider a person who favored government ownership of all the railroads and all big industries.
    A. If such a person wanted to make a speech in your community favoring government ownership of all the railroads and big industries, should he be allowed to speak, or not?

    Yes, allowed to speak 1
    Not allowed 2
    Don't know 8

    B. Should such a person be allowed to teach in a college or university, or not?

    Yes, allowed to teach 4
    Not allowed 5
    Don't know 8

    C. If some people in your community suggested a book he wrote favoring government ownership should be taken out of your public library, would you favor removing this book, or not?

    Favor 1
    Not favor 2
    Don't know 8

37. Now, I should like to ask you some questions about a man who admits he is a Communist.
    A. Suppose this admitted Communist wanted to make a speech in your community. Should he be allowed to speak, or not?

    Yes, allowed to speak 1
    Not allowed 2
    Don't know 8

    B. Suppose he is teaching in a college. Should he be fired, or not?

    Yes, fired 4
    Not fired 5
    Don't know 8

    C. Suppose he wrote a book which is in your public library. Somebody in your community suggests that the book should be removed from the library. Would you favor removing it, or not?

    Favor 1
    Not favor 2
    Don't know 8

I am not aware of any replications of the Stouffer items on a national sample since 1954. Now, 18 years after Stouffer's research, the republic is again extricating itself from a stalemate in Asia, and high public officials are again asking whether all our citizens are equally dedicated to anticommunism. It is thus of some interest to compare the 1972 NORC results with Stouffer's 1954 data.

Change in the Dependent Variables

In examining the Stouffer and NORC data, we begin with the correlation between time and tolerance. If time is a variable, the correlation between time and the dependent variable should be the central focus when the log linear model is used to analyze a replication. Table 4.5 gives the data for the item "Communist Speech" in the Stouffer and NORC studies (Question 37A in Table 4.4).

The Stouffer figures are taken from the ICPR code book. For the 1972 data, 68 cases—respondents 18 to 21 years of age—have been excluded to make the samples comparable (thus, the total equals 1,545 rather than 1,613).

Obviously, there has been some change. We find 53 percent saying "Allow" in 1972, compared with 28 percent in 1954.

Let us calculate the various effects for Table 4.5. We can extract: (a) the grand mean or average of all the cell logs, a result with no importance here, (b) the *A* effect, (c) the *B* effect, and (d) the *AB* effect.

We will report not effect parameters per se, but "normed effect parameters" (Davis; 1972). The actual effect parameter is a log of some root of a geometric mean of odds ratios, with the root depending on the number of variables in the effect. To make results comparable for effects with differing numbers of variables, and to make the results vary between +1.00 and −1.00, we (a) multiply

Table 4.5. Time (*B*) By Communist Speech (*A*)

		(*B*)	
		1954	*1972*
(*A*)	Allow to speak	1,328	827
	Not allow	3,373	706
	N	4,701	1,533
	Don't know and no answer	232	12
	Total	4,933	1,545

by the root in question, (b) shift from logs to antilogs, and (c) apply the formula:

$$\frac{[\text{result in } (b)] - 1}{[\text{result in } (b)] + 1}$$

The result of this process is that for dichotomous variables, the normed AB effect parameter in a zero-order table is Yule's Q. Thus, each effect can be compared in strength to the familiar coefficient Q in the zero-order tables. Table 4.6 presents the results.

Table 4.6 may be read this way:

1. The row variable, Item A, "Allow To Speak," is scored positive. If the ratio of "Allow" to "Not Allow" averaged 50-50 over the two studies, the coefficient would be 0.00. (Strictly speaking, the value would be 0.00 if the geometric mean of the Allow/Not Allow ratios were 1.00. We will use "average" for simplicity.) The negative value of -0.19 means that, controlling for time, "Allow" is less popular than "Not Allow."

2. A similar interpretation of the B variable, time, tells us that our sample is much smaller than Stouffer's since the coefficient is -0.46.

3. The row-column interaction effect, AB, has a value of $+0.49$. As scored, it means that the categories "Allow-1972" and "Not Allow-1954" have larger values than one would anticipate on the basis of the A and B effects taken separately. (Of necessity, the other two cells have deficits.) In other words, there is a correlation between time and tolerance of communist speeches.

Simple significance tests may be made for each effect (Goodman, 1970:229, Equations 2.8 and 2.9), but we shall save them for the climactic multivariate finale.

Table 4.6 is not in itself a strong argument for the log linear model since the most interesting result, the AB correlation, is identical to what we would get if we ran Yule's Q for Table 4.5. The A effect is not particularly interesting since the marginal distributions of attitude items are so heavily influenced by question wording. The B effect is a mechanical artifact of sample sizes and would seldom be of interest when comparing sampled replications.

Table 4.6. Normed Effects in Table 4.5

Effect	Positive Categories	Magnitude
Row (A)	Allow	-0.19
Column (B)	1972	-0.46
Row-column interaction (AB)	Allow-1972	$+0.49$

Things become a little more interesting if we add a second item, giving a three-variable, *A* by *B* by *C*, design with time and two dependent variables. Let us add "Communist Book" (Item 37C in Table 4.4). Table 4.7 gives the frequencies.

After the cell frequencies are transformed into natural logs, seven effects and a grand mean can be calculated. The grand mean and the single-variable effects, *A, B,* and *C*, are not of much interest, but the two-.and three-variable results are worth examination, and are presented in Table 4.8.

Table 4.8 can be interpreted as follows:

1. The Book × Speech coefficient is the partial correlation between the two items, controlling for time. We may think of it as the average consistency of the two items. Its value, +0.86, indicates a high level of consistency in both studies.

2. The Book × Time coefficient is a partial correlation between book and time, controlling for speech. It may be thought of as the increase (or decrease) in tolerance of communist library books, comparing groups similar in tolerance of communist speeches. The positive value of +0.37 reveals an increase in tolerance.

3. The Speech × Time coefficient may be interpreted in the same way as point 2 above. Tolerance of communist speeches shows an increase of +0.32, about the same in size as that found for communist library books. When communist book is controlled, the coefficient is reduced 14 points from the zero order in Table 4.6. Some, but not much, of the increased tolerance of communist speeches is accounted for by changes in attitudes toward communist books.

4. The last coefficient, Book × Speech × Time, is a three-variable interaction effect or specification. Here it is best interpreted as a change in the correlation between book and speech. If it were positive, we would infer that the correlation between the two items is increasing; if negative, we would infer the opposite. Since the value is zero, we infer that—while tolerance of communist speeches and tolerance of communist books have both increased—the consis-

Table 4.7. Communist Speech (*A*) By Communist Book (*B*) by Time (*C*)

(*A*) Communist Speech	(*C*) 1954 (*B*) Communist Book		(*C*) 1972 (*B*) Communist Book	
	−	+[a]	−	+
+[a]	424	835	148	666
−	2,790	437	527	174
N		4,486		1,515
Don't know and no answer		447		30
Total		4,933		1,545

[a]For both *A* and *B*, + is the more tolerant response; − is the less tolerant response.

Table 4.8. Two- and Three-Variable Effects in Table 4.7

Effect	Positive Categories	Magnitude
Book × speech	+ +	+0.86
Book × time	+ 1972·	+0.37
Speech × time	+ 1972	+0.32
Book × speech × time	+ + 1972	0.00

tency in responses to the items has remained the same. Such effects can be of considerable interest when one is working with replications of attitude scales.

The design of Table 4.7 can be extended to any number of dependent variables, but it may not be desirable. When working with scale items, such a design tends to control out the underlying common dimension. That is, the design tells us about change and consistency in the items after partialing out what the items are supposed to measure.

There is an alternate strategy that can be used with multiple items that I find more informative. It turns on the fact that the log linear model works just as well when the cell value is the log of some odds ratio as when the cell value is the log of a frequency. This means there is nothing to stop us from treating the set of items as a row or column variable and their change (+ vs. – by time) as the dependent variable.

The possibility is particularly interesting for the Stouffer items since they may be viewed as a two-variable design in which the rows are types of deviants (atheists, socialists, communists) and the columns are manifestations that the citizenry will or will not tolerate (teaching in a college, giving a speech, have one's book in the library). Table 4.9 gives the raw materials for the analysis. Because of the author's laziness, 18- to 20-year-olds were not removed from the NORC data, but it can be seen from Table 4.6 that, at least in the case of communist speech, it makes little difference.

Each of the nine cells in Table 4.9 presents: (a) the fourfold frequency table for tolerance by time, (b) the odds ratio or ratio of the two diagonal products (e.g., for the upper left-hand corner, $518 \times 4402 / 299 \times 979 = 7.790$), and (c) Yule's Q for the fourfold table. Each of the nine Q's is positive, with a range from +0.27 to +0.77.

Just as experimental designs can be extended beyond two levels, log linear effects can be calculated when the variables are not dichotomies. The result is a set of coefficients associated with each category of each variable and each combination of categories from different variables. For details on the calculations, see Davis (1972) or the discussion of row and column effects in any text on experimental design or analysis of variance.

(If extension beyond dichotomies is so natural, why did we limit our introduction to the all-dichotomy case? The first reason is sheer simplicity of

Table 4.9. Replication Data for the Nine Stouffer Items Rearranged as a Row and Column Design[a]

| | Teach | | Speech | | Book | |
	1954	1972	1954	1972	1954	1972
Communist:						
+[b]	299	518	1,328	835	1,318	851
−	4,402	979	3,373	721	3,248	681
Odds ratio	7.790		2.942		3.080	
Q	+0.77		+0.49		+0.51	
Atheist:						
+	587	644	1,833	1,049	1,739	975
−	4,153	894	2,967	527	2,925	577
Odds ratio	5.097		3.222		2.842	
Q	+0.67		+0.53		+0.48	
Socialist:						
+	1,626	899	2,889	1,241	2,597	1,086
−	2,646	595	1,512	293	1,704	409
Odds ratio	2.459		2.217		1.742	
Q	+0.42		+0.38		+0.27	

[a]Differences between column sums and totals (1954 = 4,933; 1972 = 1,613) are due to "don't know" and "no answer" responses.

[b]+ = the more tolerant response; − = less tolerant response.

exposition. The second is that the survey analyst usually is interested in finding a single number to summarize the degree of relationship between two variables, e.g., the *AB* effect. In the case of two dichotomies, one such number emerges. In larger designs, there are many such numbers and no obvious way to combine them into a single coefficient.)

If we transform the nine odds ratios to their logs and calculate the various row, column, and interaction effects, we can see whether there is a pattern in these associations. Table 4.10 gives the normed effect parameters.

The cells are not independent samples in this design since the same respondents (all the cases in both studies) appear in each of the nine cells (Table 4.9). Thus, the assumptions for significance testing are not met. This probably should make the test more conservative since cell differences are not affected by respondent sampling error.

Although significance tests were not run, looking at the data, I would interpret in the following way:

1. There has been a general increase in tolerance across the nine items, the

Table 4.10. Normed Effect Parameters for Odds Ratios in Table 4.9.

Normed parameter	Value
Grand mean	+0.52
Row categories:	
Communist	+0.20
Atheist	+0.10
Socialist	−0.29
Column categories:	
College teacher	+0.28
Speech	−0.10
Library book	−0.18
Row-column interactions:	
Communist teacher	+0.28
Socialist speech	+0.25
Socialist book	+0.05
Atheist speech	0.00
Atheist book	0.00
Communist book	−0.05
Atheist teacher	−0.05
Communist speech	−0.23
Socialist teacher	−0.25

geometric mean of the cell odds ratios being +0.52 (normed). (In this design, unlike Tables 4.5 and 4.7, the grand mean has substantive interest.)

2. While all items showed an increase in favorability, there are relative differences:

   a. Considering type of deviant, communists showed a relatively greater increase in tolerability; socialists showed a relatively lesser increase, though all three socialist Q's are positive.

   b. Considering type of manifestation, deviant incumbency in college teaching showed a relatively greater increase in tolerability; the presence of intolerable library books showed a relatively lesser rate of increase, though all three library Q's are positive.

   c. In terms of specific combinations, communist teachers and socialist speakers showed an increase even higher than that associated with their row and column categories; communist speakers and socialist teachers showed a relatively lesser rate of increase in tolerability, though their Q's are positive.

I'm not sure that the results yield incisive interpretations, even ex post facto. My intuition tells me that (outside of California) individual college teachers are less in the public eye this round than they were in the early 1950s, which might have something to do with the row effects. One might think that the lesser progress in tolerating socialists could be a ceiling effect, but the 1972 data show 60 percent tolerant for socialist teachers, 73 percent for socialist books, and 81 percent for socialist speakers—so there is still some room for progress in civil liberties here in the Land of the Free. The interaction effects have no plausible pattern that I can discern, if indeed they are statistically significant.

Thus, we see that when examining dependent variables, the log linear model can be used to assess:

1. Change in a particular dependent variable
2. Change in consistency for pairs of independent variables
3. Relative rates of change in a set of dependent variables or vectors of dependent variables

Independent and Dependent Variables

The same techniques discussed above can be extended to analyses with both independent and dependent variables. We will examine the case of one independent and one dependent item, then of one independent and two dependent items, and finally, of three independent variables and a single dependent item.

Since education played such a large part in Stouffer's own analysis (1955:chap. 4), it is a good example of an independent variable, especially since changes in the level of educational attainment are one of the strongest trends in modern America. (For an interesting discussion of some political consequences of this, see Converse, 1972:322–337.) Table 4.11 gives the raw frequencies for

Table 4.11. Education (*A*), Communist Speech (*B*), and Time (*C*)

(B) Communist Speech	*(A)* Less than High School		*(A)* High School Graduate	
	(C) 1954	*1972*	*(C) 1954*	*1972*
+	582	200	738	622
−	2,119	400	1,238	312

1954 *N*	4,677	
Don't know and no answer	256	
Total	4,933	

1972 *N*	1,534	
Don't know and no answer	79	
Total	1,613	

education (dichotomized as high school graduate and higher versus less than high school graduate), communist speech, and time.

We can pluck out the same number of effects here as we did in Table 4.7, but it seems counterintuitive to look at education by time, controlling for communist speech, the dependent variable. For that relationship, we examine the zero order from a collapsed version of Table 4.11, following the spirit of path analysis. Table 4.12 reports the effects.

The first three rows in Table 4.12 correspond to the three arrows in Figure 4.1, and give us information in terms of the path approach. There is indeed a positive correlation between education and time (Q = +0.35) and an effect for education and tolerance of communist speakers, controlling for time (+0.49). This supports Stouffer's use of the demographic explanation model. However, the effect for speaker by time, controlling for education, is a healthy +0.42. This is less than the zero order (+0.49 in Table 4.3) but not much less. Increasing educational attainment appears to play a part in explaining the increased tolerance of communist speeches, but it is far from accounting for the change between 1954 and 1972.

The bottom row of Table 4.12 bears on the covariance strategy. The normed coefficient of +0.30 says that there is an interaction effect or specification. Mathematically, it makes no difference which of the three items we choose as the specifier, but two of the three possibilities seem interesting:

1. The correlation between education and tolerance of communist speeches is higher in 1972 than in 1954.
2. The increase in tolerance of communist speeches between 1954 and 1972 is stronger among the better educated.

The result is formally akin to diverging lines in Figure 4.2 and thus consistent with the "polarization" rather than the "massification" hypothesis.

Table 4.12 provides simultaneous findings on both theories of social change. Which theory emerges as best is hard to say, though one might argue that the "differentiation" effect of 0.30 is larger than the reduction (0.49 − 0.42 = −0.07) in the demographic partial. Without taking sides on the matter, I fear that the demographic explanation will have tough sledding in replication studies like these. While the multivariate principles of log linear models are not fully worked

Table 4.12. Normed Effects for Data in Table 4.11

Effect	*Positive Categories*	*Normed Coefficient*
Education × time (zero order)	High school graduate, 1972	+0.35
Education × speaker	High school graduate, +	+0.49
Speaker × time	+, 1972	+0.42
Speaker × education × time	+, High school graduate, 1972	+0.30

out, I suspect that the folk wisdom, "small correlations never explain larger ones," will apply. Even such a massive social trend as our increase in educational attainment will—I predict—produce effect parameters smaller than the attitude and opinion changes to be explained. The hypothesis is almost pure conjecture, although informal inspection of the Schwartz data on racial attitudes for a similar span (1940s to early 1960s) seems to give change parameters roughly equivalent to the Stouffer items.

The problem is not a trivial one and presents a considerable challenge to investigators. How can we account for social change in attitudes and opinions when they are changing faster than the variables we introduce to explain them? The invocation of "secular trends," "zeitgeists," and similar specters will not fill the gap for long.

Turning next to cases with more than one dependent item, we can treat each as a variable, as in Tables 4.7 and 4.8, or we can combine them into a single variable, as in Tables 4.9 and 4.10. We will illustrate the second approach, using the items communist book and communist speaker. Since we are not interested in the effect, education by time, controlling for tolerance, we need only analyze the data in Table 4.13.

The normed effects are presented in Table 4.14.

Just as in Table 4.10, the grand mean can be interpreted. Here it is a sort of partial correlation between time and tolerance, controlling for education and specific item content. For comparison, we can use the grand mean we obtain if we analyze only communist speech and communist book in Table 4.9 rather than all nine items. Comparing this "zero order" of 0.512 with the partial of 0.436, we can say that education accounts for only a small amount of the general increase in tolerance for the two items.

The education effect of +0.167 says that increases in tolerance on the two items have been greater among the better educated.

Table 4.13. Correlations Between Tolerance Items and Time

	Item	
Education	*Communist Book*	*Communist Speaker*
High school graduate	2.840[a]	3.344[a]
	+0.479[b]	+0.540[b]
Less than high school graduate	2.434[a]	1.820[a]
	+0.418[b]	+0.291[b]

[a]Odds ratio for the fourfold table, tolerance by time.

[b]Yule's Q for the same fourfold table.

Table 4.14. Normed Effect Parameters for Table 4.13

Effect	*Positive Categories*	*Normed Value*
Grand mean	–	+0.436
Education	High school graduate	+0.167
Tolerance	Communist speaker	–0.000
Education × communist speech	High school graduate, communist speaker	+0.221

The 0.000 value for communist speaker says that the rate of change for the two items has been identical.

The interaction effect of +0.221 says that communist book had a faster rate of increase among the less educated, and communist speaker had a relatively more rapid rate of change among the better educated.

The design could be extended to all nine items in Table 4.1 with no difficulty.

As a final case, the design may be expanded to include any number of independent variables. We shall treat education, age, and region as an illustration, since these were important variables in Stouffer's original analysis. As in Tables 4.11 and 4.12, it seems best to begin with the independent variables to see whether they have any time effects that might help to explain trends in the dependent items.

The data for region (south versus other) by age (40 and older versus 21 to 39) by education by time were run on the Dartmouth Time-Sharing Interactive Log Linear Program written by Stephen Haines, Dartmouth 1971. We chose the two-tailed 0.05 level for significance. Because both samples are clustered, we multiplied the 1.96 normal curve value for 0.05 by the cabalistic number 1.67 that many people believe to be a reasonable compensation for clustering. Thus, we recognize as significant at the 0.05 level all effects where the parameter was 1.96 × 1.67 = 3.27 times its estimated standard deviation.

Table 4.15 reports the four two-variable-and-higher effects that are significant.

Table 4.15. Significant Effects for Region by Education by Age by Time

Effect	*Positive Categories*	*Effect Divided by Standard Deviation*	*Normed Effect*
Region × education	South, high school graduate	8.58	–0.31
Education × age	High school graduate, 40+	16.14	–0.54
Education × time	High school graduate, 1972	12.22	+0.41
Age × time	40+, 1972	5.23	+0.20

Of the 11 possible effects (excluding single-variable, i.e., partial skew effects), 4 are significant at the 0.05 level:

1. There is a negative partial correlation between region and education in both studies. Southerners are less likely to have high school degrees.
2. There is a negative partial correlation between education and age in both studies. Older respondents are less likely to have high school degrees.
3. There is a positive partial correlation between education and time. The 1972 respondents are more likely to have high school degrees.
4. There is a positive partial correlation between age and time. The 1972 respondents are more likely to be over 40 years of age.

None of the interaction effects were statistically significant. It appears that the increase in educational attainment was essentially similar in all age and regional combinations, and that the increase in age was essentially similar in all educational and regional combinations.

Table 4.15 suggests two hypotheses in the path tradition. The increase in education might produce an increase in tolerance, while the slight aging of the population might have the opposite effect if Stouffer's 1954 age-tolerance relationships hold in 1972.

Now we are ready to add the dependent variable. A five-variable analysis was run using communist speaker as dependent, and a parallel run was made with atheist speaker (Item 35A in Table 4.1) as dependent. Table 4.16 gives the statistically significant results involving the dependent variables.

The first three rows of Table 4.16 are a successful replication of Stouffer's major findings. We have significant partial associations across the two studies for age (older people are less tolerant, controlling for region, education, and time), region (southerners are less tolerant, controlling for age, education, and time), and education (high school graduates are more tolerant, controlling for age, region, and time).

Row four gives us the partial relationship between time and tolerance. It is positive for each item, and when we compare the magnitudes with the zero-order

Table 4.16. Statistically Significant Associations with Tolerance Items

Tolerance by	Communist Speaker Effect Divided by Standard Deviation	Normed Effect	Atheist Speaker Effect Divided by Standard Deviation	Normed Effect
Age	5.71	−0.22	9.89	−0.22
Region	6.59	−0.25	8.56	−0.33
Education	11.39	0.41	14.59	0.52
Time	11.9	0.43	14.12	0.51
Time X education	3.28	0.24	−	−

Q's in Table 4.7 (+0.53 for atheist speech and +0.49 for communist speech), we see that demographic trends do not account for the changes seen.

Only one interaction effect was significant in either analysis. The rate of change for communist speaker was higher among the better educated, but it was not for atheist speaker. This is consistent with the results in Tables 4.13 and 4.14.

DISCUSSION AND CONCLUSIONS

Our analysis of the Stouffer items has been fragmentary because our purpose is methodological. But the topic is so interesting that some inferences should be stated, if only as tips to others who will be working with these materials.

First, there clearly has been a general increase in tolerance in the 18 years since the Stouffer research. A nontrivial positive correlation between the items and time turns up for each of the nine questions and in every population subgroup we have seen.

Second, the trends cannot be accounted for by the demographic explanation approach. The appropriate demographic correlations do turn up in the data, and education does appear to reduce the correlations slightly, but the increase in tolerance seems to be far beyond anything that could be accounted for by demographic shifts in the last two decades. This approach seems rather like using glacial trends to predict changes in the weather over a period of a few days.

Third—and here I feel on the most shaky ground—, of the three covariance "models," the Schwartz parallel trend version looks best so far. There certainly is little evidence for massification, and the education polarization effect does not seem to be general across the items.

In sum, what seems to be going on is a remarkable continuity in the system of correlations involving tolerance and its predictors, but striking changes in the marginal frequencies for the dependent and some independent variables. To the extent that this pattern turns out to be characteristic in replication studies, our theoretical tools are sharply challenged since, of all the possibilities, the Schwartz pattern is least interpretable by conventional theoretical wisdom.

Turning to methodology, I conclude on the basis of this trial run that the log linear model can be of considerable use in the analysis of replications. Not only does it pull out effects cleanly and clearly, but the effects turn out to be of some theoretical relevance.

Of course, the technique has a number of limitations and problems.

First, when the time span between different studies is as long as this one, cohort change should be taken into consideration. (See Glenn and Zody, 1970; Klecka, 1971; and the later chapters in this volume.) Almost all of the 21- to 39-year-olds in Stouffer's data have moved on to the 40 plus group by 1972.

Without introducing detailed cohort controls, we have no way to distinguish between attitude change and the replacement of a cohort by persons with different attitudes. (See Converse, 1972, for an interesting discussion of this matter.)

Second, as it stands, the technique cannot be used to compare replications unless the time difference is identical. Our time span is 18 years, but using the General Social Survey we will be able to compare the 1972 and 1973 Stouffer results. Obviously, lower time coefficients should be expected. Need we do more than divide each time coefficient by its span to obtain comparability?

Third, the log linear significance test has decreasing power against more complex effects. Higher-order effects must be much stronger than lower-order ones to reach statistical significance. This means that we must be very careful when screening effects on the basis of significance alone because it is a procedure that loads the dice against finding interactions.

Fourth, log linear effects are especially sensitive to small cell frequencies. Each is a function of the geometric mean (cube root) of some odds ratios, and geometric means are especially sensitive to small values. For example, consider the three values 2, 4, and 8. Their product is 64 and the geometric mean is 4.000. If we raise the smallest number by 1 we get $3 \times 4 \times 8 = 96$ and a geometric mean of 4.578, while raising the largest number by 1 gives $2 \times 4 \times 9 = 72$ and a geometric mean of 4.160. Partial Q's (Davis, 1971:86) do not have this property since each conditional Q is weighted by the frequency of differing pairs involved. When specifications (interaction effects) are negligible, it may be preferable to use partial Q's and test for significance by summing chi squares over the conditional association tables.

The log linear approach certainly has limitations, but our analysis of the Stouffer replication data leads me to the opinion that it may be rather useful for such studies since it provides more information than classic contingency table analysis, and its parameters give direct interpretation to important sociological models for analyzing social change.

REFERENCES

Bunker, John P., William H. Forrest, Jr., Frederick Mosteller, and Leroy D. Vandam.
    1969   The National Halothane Study. Bethesda, Md.: National Institute of General Medical Sciences.
Converse, Philip E.
    1972   "Change in the American electorate." Pp. 263–337 in Angus Campbell and Philip E. Converse (eds.), The Human Meaning of Social Change. New York: Russell Sage Foundation.
Davis, James A.
    1971   Elementary Survey Analysis. Englewood Cliffs, N. J.: Prentice-Hall.

1973   "The Goodman system for significance tests in multivariate contingency tables." Chicago: National Opinion Research Center. In Herbert L. Costner (ed.), Sociological Methodology. San Francisco: Jossey-Bass.

1972   "The Goodman log linear system for assessing effects in multivariate contingency tables." Chicago: National Opinion Research Center. (Lithographed.)

Duncan, Otis Dudley.

1969   Toward Social Reporting: Next Steps. (Social Science Frontiers, No. 2.) New York: Russell Sage Foundation.

Finney, D. J.

1960   An Introduction to the Theory of Experimental Design. Chicago: University of Chicago Press.

Glenn, Norval D.

1967   "Massification versus differentiation: Some trend data from national surveys." Social Forces 46 (December): 172–180.

Glenn, Norval D., and Richard E. Zody.

1970   "Cohort analysis with national survey data." The Gerontologist 10 (Autumn):233–240.

Goodman, Leo A.

1965   "On the multivariate analysis of three dichotomous variables." American Journal of Sociology 71 (November):290–301.

1970   "The multivariate analysis of qualitative data: Interactions among multiple classifications." Journal of the American Statistical Association 65 (March):226–256.

1971   "The analysis of multidimensional contingency tables: Stepwise procedures and direct estimation methods for building models for multiple classifications." Technometrics 13 (February):33–61.

1972a   "A modified multiple regression approach to the analysis of dichotomous variables." American Sociological Review 37 (February): 28–46.

1972b   "A general model for the analysis of surveys." American Journal of Sociology 77 (May):1035–1086.

1972c   "Causal analysis of panel study data and other kinds of survey data." (Memorandum.)

Hyman, Herbert, and Paul B. Sheatsley.

1953   "Trends in public opinion on civil liberties." Journal of Social Issues 9 (Number 3):6–16.

Inter-University Consortium for Political Research Survey Research Archive (ICPR).

1971   Continuity Guide to Questions Asked in the CPS/SRC American Election Studies Series, 1952–1970. Ann Arbor, Mich.: Inter-University Consortium for Political Research.

Klecka, William R.

1971   "Applying political generations to the study of political behavior: A cohort analysis." Public Opinion Quarterly (Fall):358–373.

Schwartz, Mildred A.
   1967   Trends in White Attitudes toward Negroes. (Report No. 119.) Chicago: National Opinion Research Center.
Stinchcombe, Arthur L.
   1968   Constructing Social Theories. New York: Harcourt, Brace & World.
Stokes, Donald E.
   1967   "Parties and the nationalization of electoral forces." Pp. 182–202 in W. N. Chambers and W. D. Burnham (eds.), The American Party Systems. New York: Oxford University Press.
Stouffer, Samuel A.
   1955   Communism, Conformity, and Civil Liberties. Reprint edition, 1966. New York: Wiley.

5

MEASURING SOCIAL CHANGE VIA REPLICATION OF SURVEYS *

Otis Dudley Duncan

In *Toward Social Reporting: Next Steps* (1969) I argued that a promising strategy for enhancing our capability to produce useful indicators of social change is to carry out replications of studies conducted a number of years ago. If the replications are done carefully, differences between the original and the new findings should represent reliable estimates of the direction and degree of social change over the intervening period. The final recommendation in that memorandum was to "Sponsor a pilot project on replication studies: one sufficiently small in scale to be manageable but sufficiently ambitious to yield substantively interesting results." It was noted that the files of the Detroit Area Study (DAS) exemplify the situation in which several base-line studies are available and certain aspects of each of them could simultaneously be replicated in a single omnibus study.

So persuasive was the argument supporting this recommendation that I resolved to act on it myself, and the Russell Sage Foundation agreed to support the effort by way of a generous grant. In consequence, the 1971 DAS was

*This research is supported by Russell Sage Foundation, whose grant supplemented the regular budget of the 1971 Detroit Area Study (DAS). The research has been made possible by the extraordinary cooperation and high competence of the Director of DAS, Howard Schuman. I should like to make special note of the dedicated efforts of Elizabeth Fischer, Teaching Fellow in DAS, and the important contributions of the other teaching fellows and students in the course. Getting the process of data analysis under way was possible only because Beverly Duncan lent a capable hand at the critical time. I wish to thank J. M. Coble, R. W. Nylund, and James Carr for assistance in programming and computing. For patient counsel on statistical problems, I am indebted to Leo A. Goodman, although he bears no responsibility for any misuse of the methods he has exposited.

designed as an omnibus replication of several earlier surveys. This chapter is a progress report. It summarizes the background and rationale of the study, describes its design, and presents some illustrative preliminary findings. It is complemented by a separate summary report on substantive results (Duncan, Schuman, and Duncan, 1973) which will be followed by more intensive analyses of particular aspects of the data obtained.

ANTECEDENTS

The Detroit Area Study was established at The University of Michigan in 1951. It was supported initially by a grant from the Ford Foundation, but since 1958 The University of Michigan has taken financial responsibility for DAS. The main objectives of DAS are to provide practical research training for graduate students, to serve as a resource for basic research, and to provide reliable data on the Greater Detroit community. Surveys have been conducted annually since 1951–1952 on a variety of subjects of both topical and basic theoretical interest. Probability sampling has been used in all surveys, which typically have covered a cross section of the adult residents of metropolitan Detroit with a sample of about 700. The population has sometimes been more narrowly defined, however, in the interest of a more sharply focused research design. The position of Faculty Participant in DAS is filled each year by a different member of one of the several cooperating departments of the university. As of mid-1969, some seven books had been published on the basis of DAS materials, as well as some fourscore articles and chapters in books. More than two dozen Ph.D. dissertations have been drawn from the same source. There is also an extensive file of technical memoranda and occasional reports.

There are suggestive precedents for the current interest in replication studies in DAS. It is significant that one of the earliest DAS inquiries was conceived as an exploration of *changes* in child-rearing practices. The authors (Miller and Swanson, 1958:216) noted, however, that it was difficult to establish base-line observations from available historical records. They went on:

> What we can do is to make a first investment in providing the materials for later and longitudinal research on changes in child care. We can present the findings from our study in such a way that they may provide bench marks against which future investigators can match their own results.

Another early DAS investigation was conceived as an explicit replication. Janowitz and Wright (1956) were interested in assessing the trend of prestige of public employment. Accordingly they took care to duplicate some of the key questions used by L. D. White in a study of this topic in Chicago in 1929. Comparison with White's results—despite some uncertainty due to the change in study locale and sampling plan—indicated a marked upward shift in the prestige of public employment between 1929 and 1954.

Apart from one-time replications, DAS in its first decade of operation was exploited to some degree as a source of annual time-series observations. Recurrent reports were issued on annual changes in family income (DAS, 1956; 1960) and ownership of television sets (DAS, 1959), for example. While similar data are available nationally, very few localities possess an annual measurement of income changes, and the record of the rapid diffusion of television in the community during the 1950s is likewise nearly unique.

More recently, replication of selected earlier DAS inquiries has been of interest to the permanent director of DAS, Howard Schuman. In the 1965–1966 study he conducted a small-scale replication of that part of the 1957–1958 study which dealt with the relationship of religious affiliation to the "Protestant Ethic." In this case, however, the main import of the replication was to suggest a reassessment of the original results, rather than to provide a measurement of change (Schuman, 1971).

Similarly, in the 1968–1969 study of white attitudes on urban problems Schuman repeated a question asked in 1956:

One day a six year old asks her mother if she can bring another girl home to play. The mother knows that the other girl is a Negro, and that her own daughter has only played with white children before. What should the mother do? Here are three possible responses.
1. She should tell her daughter that she must never play with Negroes; or
2. The daughter should be told that she may play with Negro children in school, but not at home; or
3. The Negro child should be permitted to come to the home.

The following is the percentage distribution of responses (omitting NA's) of household heads and wives, ages 21–64:

Alternative	1956	1969
1. (Never)	12	2
2. (In school)	47	22
3. (At home)	41	76
Total	100	100
(Number)	(529)	(563)

The very substantial change shown here is consistent with other evidence, compiled by Schwartz (1967), of rapid changes in white attitudes toward Negroes. (Incidentally, I wish to note a major oversight in failing to cite the Schwartz study as an important prototype in *Toward Social Reporting: Next Steps*.)

Experience with these two small-scale replications was encouraging in contemplating a more ambitious effort along the same lines. It was of special interest, moreover, to replicate the "Protestant Ethic" and "playmate" items again in 1971, since this opens up the possibility of detecting both short- and long-run changes.

An important step that facilitated the present venture in replication and will encourage future efforts of the same kind was taken about eight years ago when the basic DAS punched-card files were reproduced on magnetic tape. Data going back two decades are now relatively easily accessible.

PRELIMINARY STEPS

The decision to devote the 1971 DAS to the attempt to measure change was reached in the fall of 1969, and initial work began shortly thereafter. We first had to decide which studies were most promising as sources of base-line measurements. Two considerations dominated this decision. First, we wanted the time span to be as great as possible, on the theory that the measurement of *trend*, if only two observations are available, is more reliable if those observations are widely spaced than if they are close together. (In one important domain, that of racial attitudes, we decided at a rather late stage of the preliminary work to make an exception, because of the importance of the topic, the likelihood that changes have been occurring rapidly, and the lack of earlier base-line measurements.) The second major criterion was that the base-line study pertain to a cross-section population, or some appreciable segment thereof. These two criteria quickly led us to focus on the studies conducted during the 1950s, with the aforementioned exception. Difficulties with the documentation of the 1952 survey led us finally to limit our field to the seven surveys conducted in 1953–1959 and the 1968 survey of racial attitudes.

Despite the work on the DAS archive that had been done earlier, there was much more that needed to be done to make the base-line studies fully accessible for our purposes. Their tape files were checked for consistency with extant tabulations. New tapes were created to secure a format compatible with currently available programs. The sample design of each study was reviewed and, in some instances, reconstructed from files of memoranda. The index to questions used in DAS surveys and the bibliography of publications and documents were reworked for our purposes.

Involvement of student participants in the project began in the fall term of 1970, at which time they were in a one-hour course, the DAS proseminar. The general purpose of the proseminar is to provide a period of relatively leisurely consideration of the scientific objectives and implications of the forthcoming survey prior to the somewhat hectic period of questionnaire design, pretesting, and field work. In the present case, there were presentations to the students concerning the general rationale of social indicators, the specific role of replication studies in developing indicators, and the particular resources of the base-line studies represented in DAS files. Students then nominated particular questions for inclusion in the omnibus replication and justified such nominations on the basis of their study of DAS documents and publications, other pertinent literature, and, where necessary, new tabulations from the DAS data file. Each student was asked to prepare a research memorandum of about ten pages, which would:

a. Summarize his investigation of items on a given topic as candidates for replication
b. State and justify his recommendations for choices of items for replication
c. Review literature that may be relevant to this decision, previous results with the items, and available data collected with these items
d. Suggest hypotheses about what changes may be detected in replicating these items
e. Indicate any additional questions or procedures needed to probe the meaning of the items recommended
f. Enumerate what other items will be needed to provide statistical controls and interpretations
g. Describe any new items that might be useful in extending our knowledge of the topic

The product of this effort was a set of some 13 memoranda delineating topics for study and listing appropriate items for inclusion in the 1971 survey. At about the same time, the study directors, working with the DAS teaching assistants, reviewed the entire set of prospective base-line studies to make sure that no promising item had been overlooked. It may be worthwhile to indicate the criteria for selection that were suggested to the students and followed by the principal investigators in making tentative selections. (General guidelines for replication studies are suggested in *Toward Social Reporting: Next Steps*.)

First, we wished to concentrate on topics for which DAS seems rather uniquely valuable. If indicators of a given type were already available in other sources and were of a quality that DAS could not easily improve upon, we did not wish to emphasize them as items for replication studies. Thus, while DAS might be used for studies of trends in political party identification, materials for this kind of research that are, on the whole, better suited to the purpose are available elsewhere. (This did not entirely rule out the possibility of carrying questions on party identification in the 1971 survey, if these were thought to be needed for the interpretation of other items.)

Second, items selected for replication should hold some promise for development into standard social indicators of the kind that would warrant periodic repetition for the foreseeable future. This tended to rule out not only items concerning particular public personalities or sporadic events (such as reactions to the 1955–1956 Detroit newspaper strike) but also items of mainly local significance.

Third, the replicated items should, at any rate ideally, be those for which we have some favorable evidence concerning their "validity." This criterion is somewhat difficult to state and even more difficult to implement in a clear way.

Still, the principle is obvious: a questionnaire item to be useful as an indicator needs to stand for something more than itself and to do so in a dependable manner. For some kinds of items, validity can be presumed because numerous replications have provided evidence of their predictable behavior. For others, where no such extensive body of experience exists, we must rely on evidence of meaningful covariation of item responses with other items. For exploratory purposes almost any item can be justified for inclusion in a questionnaire; for serious efforts at measuring social change, one wants to depend on the kind of item for which we can claim we know something about "how it works."

The difficulty in implementing the third criterion suggests the value of the intensive review provided in the students' memoranda. The aggregate amount of intellectual input to the project provided by their efforts considerably exceeded the amount that could otherwise have been devoted to the task in the period of time available.

A final step in the compilation of a set of eligible questions involved a relaxation of the criterion that our work would be focused on relatively long-run changes. At the suggestion of an interested student, we included several questions from the 1968 survey, "Negro Attitudes in Detroit," which involved a sample limited to black respondents. Although the three years elapsing between the base-line study and the replication was a rather short period, it was thought to be one during which exceptionally rapid changes, with respect to this subject matter, might have occurred. In light of the results obtained, it appears that this element of flexibility in our study design was most fortunate.

By the beginning of the winter term, then, we had constructed a tentative list of questions for inclusion in the 1971 survey. The number of attractive questions was larger by a considerable factor than the number that could be included in a single interview. Hence, we engaged in a systematic appraisal of all the prospective items. Students were assigned subsets of questions and asked to rate them in terms of relevance to the survey objectives and suitability as questionnaire items in general. Some questions were eliminated on the grounds that in the base-line study the frequency of "no answer" was excessively high or because there appeared to be difficulties in administering or coding them. Others were sacrificed when it became apparent that useful information could be obtained only with an excessive expenditure of time. All these decisions were argued out in conferences involving the principal investigators, teaching assistants, and interested students.

The surviving items were included in a tentative questionnaire used in the first pretest. Each student conducted two interviews in Jackson, Michigan. All the interviews were done in a day's time, so that certain aspects of the usual sampling and field procedures were not closely simulated. However, the student interviewers were encouraged to give primary attention to problems arising in the conduct of the interview itself due to ambiguities of wording, lack of clarity in instructions, resistance of the respondent, and the like. Analysis of the marginal distributions and interviewer comments led to the deletion of a number of questions—a contingency that had been anticipated by the inclusion of a somewhat larger number than it seemed feasible to carry in the final questionnaire.

The second pretest, conducted some six weeks later, was directed more to the training of interviewers than to the selection of questionnaire items. But experience in that pretest was useful in resolving some issues about the order of questions and clarity of instructions.

DESIGN OF THE 1971 SURVEY

Perhaps the quickest way to convey a sense of the scope of our study is to list the topics on which we have one or more measures of change. In the following list, not all topic headings are self-explanatory; but these are intended only to suggest the diversity of subject matter covered in the survey.
1. Marriage, Family, Age and Sex Roles
    a. Life-cycle and fertility: sex and age; household composition and relationships; marital history; children ever born
    b. Ideal family size
    c. Division of labor
    d. Decision making
    e. Values in marriage
    f. Satisfaction with marriage
    g. Child rearing
    h. Meaning of work for women
2. Civics and Public Affairs
    a. Political information
    b. Prestige of public employment
    c. Political particiation
    d. Political ideology
    e. Confidence in institutions
    f. Confidence in political process
3. Participation and Alienation
    a. Informal activities
    b. Associations
    c. Morale
4. Religion
    a. Preference, affiliation
    b. Belief
    c. Interest, practice
    d. Communal sentiment
    e. Ethics and values

5. Class and Race
   a. Schooling
   b. Job
   c. Income
   d. Standard of living
   e. Subjective class identification
   f. Socioeconomic background
   g. Race, nativity, nationality
   h. Black racial experiences and attitudes
   i. White racial attitudes

The more standard or "census"-like items in the list (1a, 4a, 5a–g) are available in several or all of the base-line surveys. But these are, of course, matters on which there are many other sources of information: the decennial census, the Current Population Survey, and national polls and surveys. Hence, we shall be using these items primarily as statistical controls in the analysis of change rather than as ways of describing change in themselves. Items under 5h derive from the 1968 survey. Most of the remaining items come from one or another survey done during 1953–1959, sometimes from more than one such survey.

We strongly, and for the most part successfully, resisted the temptation to invent "new" questions or to borrow questions from studies other than those serving as our base-line measures in Detroit. There are, however, four new questions that are specifically designed to aid in the analysis and interpretation of data on social change. For example, following the question on the hypothetical child's playmate mentioned earlier, we added the question, "How do you think you would have answered this question about 15 years ago?" By matching birth cohorts of respondents in the 1956 and 1971 studies, we can actually ascertain whether the aggregate retrospective data are veridical. Thus, we may learn whether respondents are fully conscious of the extent to which attitudes on this topic actually are changing. Finally, we can investigate correlates of the respondent's perception of change or stability in his own attitude.

Three of four other questions were added in the form of additional probes to replicated questions. Although the probes are not available from the base-line studies, we may hope that they will nevertheless help in the interpretation of any changes we may detect in the main questions.

The questionnaire includes some 200-odd questions asked of respondents. But no individual was asked all these questions. Certain questions were asked only of specified categories of respondents: married persons, married women, mothers of children under 19 years old, blacks, whites, Catholics, Protestants, Jews. The restriction in each case is, of course, implied by the subject matter of the question. Certain of these restrictions apply to the entirety of some of the base-line studies: the 1953 survey was limited to mothers, the 1955 survey to wives, and the 1968 survey to blacks. A different kind of restriction applies to the 1957 survey; it was limited to residents of Wayne County, the central county of the Detroit metropolitan area. And the 1968 survey was confined to the city of Detroit. The unusually large size of the 1971 sample, compared with previous DAS samples, was dictated by the decision to replicate not only the earlier general cross-section surveys but also these surveys restricted to subpopulations.

Primarily to keep the interview to a manageable length, we also resorted to the device of constructing two forms of the questionnaire, each including certain questions not contained in the other. Each form was administered to a random half of the sample. The two forms differ, as well, in respect to the order of certain questions and, in a few instances, the wording of some questions. There were two reasons for these variations. First, we suspected that responses to some kinds of questions are affected by the context. If a respondent is asked whether he is working class or middle class, the answer may differ according to whether this question precedes or follows one asking for his occupation. Second, some questions appeared in more than one base-line study in slightly variant wordings or formats. We hoped that use of both forms of a question would shed light on the sensitivity of response to such variations and possibly provide splicing measurements that would be useful in the future.

Except for the 1957 and 1968 surveys, all our base-line studies were carried out as samples of the population residing in an area defined as that part of the Detroit Standard Metropolitan Statistical Area (SMSA) which was tracted as of 1950, but excluding the city of Pontiac. In 1950 this area contained about 88 percent of the population of the three-county SMSA but less than half its land area. Cursory study of the 1960 census data on journey to work suggests that the study area at that time closely approximated the zone of heavy commuting into Detroit. However, a few suburban areas with moderately high commutation rates were not included. These same areas were found to have grown rapidly following 1950. We resolved to seek comparability in terms of the concept of a metropolitan population unit—rather than in terms of a fixed geographic area—and therefore decided to enlarge the study area slightly to take account of the spatial expansion of that unit. With the additions made for the 1971 survey, we estimate that the DAS study area contained about 85 percent of the 1970 Detroit SMSA population.

Like most of the base-line surveys, the 1971 survey was a multistage area probability sample of households in the study area. (The 1958 and 1959 samples were drawn from city directories.) Details of the sample design are provided in a memorandum by Elizabeth Fischer (1971), who also reviewed the sampling procedures for the several base-line studies. Apart from the definitions of the target populations, variations in which were noted earlier, there do not seem to be major differences among the samples that will require special procedures in effecting analytical comparisons and estimates of change.

Response rates varied among the base-line surveys between 82 percent

(1958) and 87 percent (1956 and 1957). In 1971 we went to 2,344 sample addresses and secured interviews at 1,881 of them, for a response rate of 80.2 percent. The median length of the interview was 60 minutes, so that something more than minimal respondent cooperation was needed to complete an interview. We have no evidence, however, that the length of interview significantly affected the response rate; only 14 interviews were broken off after getting underway.

The base-line studies of the 1950s were all done in the winter months, January—March. In 1971, to conform with more recent practice, we conducted the interviewing in the late spring and summer. Interviewing was begun by student participants in DAS in late April. As their work was completed, the interviewing was taken over by the professional field staff of the Survey Research Center, who remained in the field through the first part of September. Altogether, 19 percent of the interviews were secured by students and 81 percent by professional interviewers.

Both cadres included black and white interviewers. We took advantage of this circumstance in replicating the 1968 experiment of assigning black and white interviewers to black respondents at random. Schuman and Converse (1971) noted that a number of questions asked of black respondents produced rather different marginal distributions, according to the race of interviewer. The race-of-interviewer effect, however, was not observed in all questions having explicit racial content, nor was it confined to such questions. Clearly, in the absence of control for the effect, comparisons between surveys intended to provide estimates of change may be confounded with this source of bias. We shall be interested to learn, not only whether the previously observed interviewer effects were recapitulated in 1971, but also how such effects may interact with other factors producing change in the attitudes of black respondents.

STRATEGIES OF ANALYSIS

Some references to analytical problems have already been made. These tend to suggest that our problem will not always be as simple as computing the percentage answering "yes" to a question and comparing it with the corresponding percentage in, say, 1955. Such changes in "marginals" are, of course, of interest. But we must be sure, first of all, that they are not spurious. The inference that a change has really occurred, given a difference between the two percentages, is always subject to the uncertainty created by sampling error. We propose to cope with this problem by computing routinely the likelihood-ratio chi-square statistic (Wilks, 1935) for the $2 \times k$ contingency table giving the k-category response distributions for the respondents interviewed in 1971 and in the base-line survey. A significant value of this statistic will tend to assure us that we are detecting real change. A nonsignificant value will suggest that the change, if any, was too slight to be detected with samples of the size we are using. At least for the time being, we shall interpret these chi-square statistics as though the data arose from a process of simple random sampling, even though the actual samples were not of that design. For many items pertaining to attitudes and personal behavior, it appears that the effect of areal clustering on standard errors of proportions is not great.

One advantage of the likelihood-ratio statistic is that it is well suited to the analysis of contingency tables which are to be partitioned into subtables (Goodman, 1968:1102–1103, 1117, 1122–1123). The utility of this kind of analysis is suggested by the example in Table 5.1. We see from the percentage distributions that there was a shift between 1956 and 1971 in the proportions in each of the four categories produced by this question. The value of χ^2, the likelihood-ratio chi-square statistic, for the 4 × 2 table is 38.61; with 3 degrees of freedom, the probability of a value this large, if there were no real change in the distribution, is less than 0.001. If we look at just the first three rows of the table, regarded as a 3 × 2 contingency table, we find $\chi^2 = 0.12, d.f. = 2, P > 0.9$. Aggregating these three rows so as to compare the aggregate with the fourth row in a 2 × 2 table, we obtain $\chi^2 = 38.49, d.f. = 1, P < 0.001$. The χ^2 values for the two subtables sum to the overall χ^2 value: $38.49 + 0.12 = 38.61$. Thus, the entirety of the relationship between year and response is due to the elevated

Table 5.1. Distribution of Responses to a Question with Four Alternatives, 1956 and 1971

*People feel differently about making changes in the way our country is run. [In order to keep America great.] * Which of these four statements do you think is best?*	Number		Percent	
	1956	*1971[a]*	*1956*	*1971[a]*
1. We should rarely, if ever, make changes in the way our country is run.	16	15	2.1	1.6
2. We should be very cautious of making changes in the way our country is run.	370	393	48.9	42.5
3. We should feel free to make changes in the way our country is run.	277	293	36.6	31.7
4. We must constantly make changes in the way our country is run.	94	223	12.4	24.1
	757[b]	924[c]	100.0	99.9

*Wording included only in 1956 survey.

[a]Question asked only on Form A.

[b]Excludes 40 respondents who did not choose one of the four alternatives.

[c]Excludes 12 respondents who did not choose one of the four alternatives.

frequency of the fourth category in 1971 as compared with 1956. We can merely report that the proportion responding, "We must constantly make changes . . . ," went from 12 percent in 1956 to 24 percent in 1971, without discarding any information about the pattern of change. A considerable amount of experience with this kind of analysis suggests that the eyeballing of percentage distributions is a poor way to pick out relationships which warrant reporting and discussion. Several mistakes are possible and all are likely to occur: the analyst will focus on change in the percentage in the modal category, even though this may not be where the significant shift occurs (see Table 5.1 for such an example); the analyst may ignore small categories, even though these are the ones where significant shifts do occur; the analyst may make several ostensibly distinct statements about the pattern of change, even though only one such statement (as in this example) suffices to cover the matter, additional statements being redundant if not misleading. The reporting of tabular data, even with the aid of this statistical method, remains an art rather than a procedure that can be made completely explicit and mechanical. (Among other things, there is more than one way to partition a table with several degrees of freedom, and the choice needs to be made in such a way that the result is illuminating.) Nevertheless, the statistical technique tends to impose a certain discipline upon the process of reporting that often has been lacking in survey research.

Another consideration in the reporting of changes is the comparability of study design. If the base-line study only provides information on the responses of housewives, we must take care to extract a comparable set of replies from the 1971 replication. Adjustments will need to be made with regard to the factors of age, family status, race, and geographic location, since the several base-line studies did not secure the same coverage in these regards. Apart from differences in the populations covered in two surveys, we must take into account changes in composition of the covered population. As compared with the 1950s, the 1971 Detroit area population included a larger proportion of black persons, more home owners, more persons with college training, and so on. The statistical procedures to be illustrated later are well designed to effect adjustments for such changes in composition as may prove relevant in interpreting shifts in the distributions of responses to survey questions.

In the analysis of change, however, we shall seldom be content with measuring shifts in marginal distributions of individual questions, even if these can be shown to be substantial and reliable. Instead, we shall be involved in multivariate analysis in three respects. First, we shall frequently want to look at sets of items within a particular indicator domain. Where two or more items share a common content, analyzing their joint changes should be more informative than studying them one at a time.

Second, we shall often be concerned with indicators defined by the pattern or degree of association between items. For example, an intensification of class consciousness might be inferred from a shift toward stronger association between "objective" status position and "subjective" class identification, rather than from a change in the marginal distribution of either of these.

Third, we shall, of course, be concerned to localize any observed changes as to the sectors of the population in which they are most pronounced. To the extent that this can be done, we will have clues as to the causal interpretation of changes. Specifically, we intend to make thorough application of the strategy of cohort analysis. The 1971 respondents have been coded by individual birth years, so that we can match almost exactly any birth cohort that can be defined by age at any of the base-line dates. Both the base-line and the replication studies will provide intercohort, time-constant comparisons. Comparisons between the base-line and the replication samples will provide age-constant intercohort comparisons as well as intracohort comparisons. The ascertainment of the cohort pattern of change is a logical component of the interpretation of change in terms of any fixed or nearly fixed characteristic, such as ethnic origin, religious preference, or educational attainment. To the extent possible, moreover, we shall want to distinguish between changes attributable to maturation or aging as such and those attributable to factors in the social milieu that change over time. While such distinctions can seldom be made with certainty, cohort analysis is an indispensable aid.

The cohort approach is compromised to some degree by the fact that the metropolitan community is by no means a closed population. Several of the base-line studies, however, include questions on length of residence in the community, and we also included such an inquiry in the replication. Judicious cross-classification by duration of residence may help us to infer whether turnover in the composition of birth cohorts due to migration is a factor in producing observed changes. Other census-type variables (occupation and income, for example) may be used as control factors to a similar purpose.

It appears, therefore, that we shall be carrying out intensive manipulations of the data records from as many as nine different surveys, since the tabulations already made from the base-line studies will seldom be appropriate for the new use that we are making of those studies. Both the volume and complexity of the data-processing operations present challenges an order of magnitude greater than those faced by the typical one-time survey project. The problem of reconciling alternative patterns of population coverage as between surveys has been mentioned, as well as the problem of achieving nearly exact cohort matches— each of which requires a fresh set of operations for each comparison between the omnibus replication and the particular base-line study under examination. In addition, codes for dependent, independent, and control variables differ from one survey to another. Our general strategy has been to incorporate maximum detail in the code for the 1971 data so that with alternative patterns of aggregation we can achieve the best possible matches with the several base-line studies. But such a strategy is, of course, expensive in terms of programming and data-processing operations.

GENERATION GAP AND COHORT CHASM

In the remainder of this chapter I want to report some results of analyses made thus far of the responses elicited by two questions:

A18, B19. Here are two statements. Will you tell me which one you agree with *more*.

1. First, the younger generation should be taught by their elders to do what is right.
2. Second, the younger generation should be taught to think for themselves even though they may do something their elders disapprove of.

B20. How do you think your (father/mother) (PARENT OF SAME SEX AS R) would have answered this question when you were growing up? Which one would (he/she) have agreed with more? (REREAD ALTERNATIVES)

All respondents were asked the YG (younger generation) question. Only a random half (Form B) were asked the Parent question, since it was not a replication of any previous survey item and was included for experimental purposes. The YG question was originally asked in 1956. My purpose in presenting our first results with these questions is to exemplify the methods which we expect to be using, since some features of them are rather novel. In selecting an example for such presentation, I have been influenced by the substantive interest of these results; but further work with the data may lead to changes in interpretation.

We discover, to begin with, that 53.7 percent of the 756 respondents answering the YG question in 1956 preferred the "do right" alternative, as compared with 50.1 percent of the 1,814 respondents in 1971. This would not appear to be a promising beginning for a report on social change, inasmuch as χ^2 = 2.76, *d.f.* = 1, $0.25 < P < 0.50$; so that we could not state with assurance that any real change has occurred.

We find, moreover, that this question is strongly related to the respondent's education, so much so that one is almost tempted to regard the YG question as a rough-and-ready measure of "enlightenment," if not, indeed, of "intelligence." Knowing that the distribution of educational attainment has shifted upward, we must consider the possibility that the change from 53.7 to 50.1 percent favoring "do right," even if it were real, might merely reflect the changing level of schooling in the Detroit population. What we must study, therefore, is a three-variable problem: response to the YG question by year by education. The form of the problem is familiar enough; it is paradigmatic in the survey analysis tradition. Yet it is only quite recently that we have really learned how to carry out an efficient analysis. A common procedure in that tradition, for example, is to collapse the education distribution into two or three categories, so as to examine, say, the six percentages of respondents saying "do right" for the cells of the year-by-education table. In peering at these percentages the analyst attempts to answer several questions: does education affect response to the YG question? If so, is the overall change in YG response due solely to the shift in education? Do all education groups change to the same degree, or do the changes differ by education?

A systematic attack on the whole package of relevant questions is afforded by the procedures of multiway contingency table analysis proposed by Goodman (1969, 1970, 1971, 1972a, 1972b). (See also Fienberg, 1970, 1972, and other references given by both authors.) This work has at last supplied us with the tools required to carry out the tasks we have been attempting to do with our bare hands these past several decades. As one gains facility with these tools and comes to appreciate something of their rationale in statistical theory, it becomes apparent that many of the procedures followed on the "bare hands" approach were ill-advised or, at any rate, not optimal. With samples of the size we are using here, for example, there is no real reason to initiate the analysis by collapsing education into only three categories. Indeed, although I do not propose to go into the matter here, the statistical methods themselves can shed light on the issue of whether such aggregation is advisable and, if so, how it should be done.

A salient feature of these methods is that they take a consistent approach to the question of what is meant by "association" and "interaction" of qualitative variables. The common, and less disciplined practice of survey analysts, by contrast, is to shift back and forth among percentages, ratios, differences between percentages, ratios of such differences, or various ad hoc "indexes," as inspiration dictates. The methods in question also provide a clear and rational separation of distinct but related hypotheses that the analyst may wish to examine. It usually turns out that there are more "angles" to a subject than one is likely to attend to in the absence of formal guidelines. Hence, there is a strong liability to quixotic choices in deciding what to look at or what to discuss. As a final remark, I note that these methods promise to restore to the survey craft the disciplined use of tests of statistical significance. There really can be no "issue" here, "methodologists" of various persuasions to the contrary notwithstanding. From samples we can only make fallible inferences, and to appreciate their fallibility we require the formal apparatus of probability. The literature has been polluted by announcements of "effects" that are nothing other than the normal fluctuations of random sampling. Perhaps as deplorable is the fact that we have habitually overlooked effects of genuine interest by failure to carry out appropriate tests. Please note that I referred above to the *disciplined* use of significance tests, not to their mechanical use. With the results of appropriate tests in hand, the imaginative analyst will see additional leads to pursue and further questions to raise, just as he always has. Fortunately, the nature of the new methods is such that there is relatively little hazard of confusing the test of significance with a measure of association or importance of variables, to mention only two vulgar errors that seemingly discredited statistical tests in the past.

To return to the subject: after this hortatory digression, we want, at this stage of the analysis, to look at the three-way table classifying respondents simultaneously by response to the YG question by year by education. A stepwise examination of hypotheses pertinent to such a table yields, in summary, the following results.[1] The hypothesis of mutual independence of the three variables is rejected: $\chi^2 = 318.2$, $d.f. = 28$ (with ten education classes, two years, and two response categories), $P < 0.001$. On the other hand, a model that uses all three sets of two-way marginals fits the data quite well: $\chi^2 = 6.49$, $d.f. = 9$, $P = 0.69$. We find, however, that it is not really necessary to use the YG response-by-year marginals to secure a good fit; using only the response-by-education and education-by-year marginals we find that $\chi^2 = 7.42$, $d.f. = 10$, $P = 0.69$. Moreover, the difference between the two fits given by $\chi^2 = 7.42 - 6.49 = 0.92$, with 1 degree of freedom, is not significant. There is, therefore, no need for a year effect in the model, in agreement with our original result that the difference between years is not significant. Here, however, we test a different hypothesis, inasmuch as education has been held constant. Although the model does not include a year effect, a difference between years is implicit in the fitted counts, owing to the facts that the education distribution does change and the YG response is related to education. In fact, if we aggregate these counts over education categories, they imply that 55.2 percent of the 1956 respondents favored "do right," as compared with 49.5 percent of the 1971 respondents. Thus, in bringing education into the picture, we have more than accounted for

---

[1] For the benefit of the reader who wishes to check the steps in the analysis, the following makes the procedure more explicit: Let the YG question be designated as variable A with I $(= 2)$ categories; let year be variable B, with J $(= 2)$ categories; and let education be variable C, with K $(= 10)$ categories. Following Goodman (1970: Table 3), we represent the hypotheses to be tested (or models to be considered) by the sets of marginals to be fitted. The hypothesis of mutual independence involves fitting the three one-way marginals, $[A]$, $[B]$, $[C]$, this is hypothesis no. 5 in Goodman's table, with degrees of freedom $= IJK - I - J - K + 2$. The next hypothesis considers the fit of a model using all the two-way marginals, $[AB]$, $[AC]$, $[BC]$, which is Goodman's hypothesis no. 1, with degrees of freedom $= (I - 1)$ $(J - 1)(K - 1)$. We next fit only two of these two-way marginals, $[AC]$ and $[BC]$, which is Goodman's hypothesis no. 2 (with appropriate labeling of variables), so that we have degrees of freedom $= (I - 1)(J - 1)K$. The fourth and last hypothesis in this paragraph of the text involves comparing the fits of the two preceding models. Since these are hierarchical hypotheses, in Goodman's meaning of the term, we may test the difference in goodness of fit in the following way. Let χ^2_1 be the likelihood-ratio chi-square statistic for a model taking the form of hypothesis no. 1 (as labeled in Goodman, 1970; Table 3) and d_1 be the degrees of freedom for testing that model. Let χ^2_2 and d_2 be similarly defined for a model taking the form of hypothesis no. 2. Then, to test whether the inclusion of $[AB]$ in no. 1 improves the fit by comparison with no. 2, we use $\chi^2 = \chi^2_1 - \chi^2_2$ with degrees of freedom $d_1 - d_2 = (I - 1)(J - 1)(K - 1) - (I - 1)(J - 1)K = (I - 1)(J - 1)$.

the aggregate shift from 53.7 to 50.1 percent reported earlier. The actual shift is not quite so large as that "expected" on the basis of educational change.

Implicit in the results already summarized is the finding that the three-way interaction, response-by-education-by-year, is not significant. That is, these data do not suggest that the association of response with education changed its nature or intensity between 1956 and 1971. In that event, and in the absence of any difference between years other than that implicit in the changing distribution of schooling, we are justified in estimating a single set of education effects for the two years from the fitted frequencies. Although these effects are handled within the model as odds ratios, they may be transformed, for ease of presentation, into percentages of respondents endorsing the "do right" alternative, by educational level: less than 1 year of schooling, 100.0 percent; 1 to 4 years, 82.2; 5 or 6 years, 78.0; 7 years, 58.1; 8 years, 70.2; 9–11 years, 54.7; 12 years, 47.5; 13–15 years, 39.3; 16 years 35.5; 17 or more years, 23.7. Our work thus far, therefore, has yielded a beautiful regression of YG response on education, but nothing to report about social change, except that responses are changing no faster than one would expect on the basis of educational change.

It is useful at this point to remind ourselves of the demography of educational change. Exceptions granted (in view of the prolongation of schooling and the popularity of adult education), one may to a first approximation think of educational attainment as a fixed characteristic as far as adults are concerned. In that event, the adult population will change its educational distribution over time in one of three ways: selective migration, differential mortality, and the attrition of older (less well-educated) cohorts by mortality *pari passu* with the introduction into the adult population of more recent (more highly educated) cohorts. The pace of educational change in recent decades has been such that the third source is especially important. Thus, we find that the proportion of high school graduates in the 1956 DAS sample was 44 percent, as compared with the 63 percent observed in 1971. But if we eliminate from the 1971 sample those too young to have been included in the 1956 study, the figure is only 53 percent. If we confine our attention to this portion of the 1971 sample in making comparisons with 1956, educational change will be less of a factor with which to reckon. At the same time, we will be looking at change in a constant set of cohorts, albeit cohorts that are closed to neither mortality nor migration.

For this constant set of cohorts, the picture of aggregate change in response to the YG question is quite different from that cited earlier. For 1956, the proportion saying "do right" was 53.7 percent (as before), but in 1971 it rose to 58.7 percent. Thus, the direction of intracohort change was opposite to that noted for the total adult population, which was a mixture of intracohort and intercohort changes. Evidently, the YG question is one on which the younger and the older cohorts take rather different views. Moreover, the aggregated

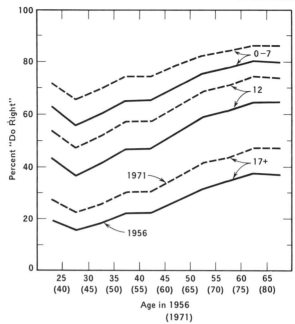

Figure 5.1. **Fitted Percentages of Respondents at Selected Educational Levels in the Seven Oldest Cohorts Endorsing the "Do Right" Alternative to the Younger Generation Question: 1956 and 1971.**

intracohort changes are in the direction opposite to what we would expect from the slight rise in (reported) educational levels of these cohorts over the 15-year period.

The salient results are illustrated in Figure 5.1, which depicts the proportion endorsing the "do right" alternative as a function of birth cohort, education, and year. These percentages are based on the fitted counts from a four-variable problem in which it was found that the data can be adequately reproduced by taking account of all six sets of two-way marginals but disregarding any higher-order interactions:[2] χ^2 = 170.44, *d.f.* = 177, P = 0.62. Each set of two-way marginals, moreover, contributes significantly to the fit. This means, in particular, that there are distinct effects due to education, cohort, and year, on the response to the YG question. The graph shows only selected education groups, but these adequately reflect the monotonic pattern of decreasing percentages saying "do right" with increasing education. The cohort pattern,

---

[2] This is hypothesis no. 23 in Table 4 of Goodman (1970). Its fit is compared with that of each of the six models of the form of no. 24 in his table obtained by omitting one set of two-way marginals from the six sets fitted in no. 23. The nature of tests of this kind was illustrated in footnote 1.

too, is nearly monotonic: the earlier the year of birth, the higher the proportion saying "do right." The pattern of roughly parallel lines is, of course, a property of the particular model adopted here in view of the finding of a nonsignificant three-way interaction of cohort by education by YG response. (The lines are not actually parallel on the percentage scale, but on the log-odds scale in terms of which the underlying model is stated.) Results with the same model also imply that at each educational level within each cohort there was a substantial increase in proportion of "do right" responses between 1956 and 1971. (As we shall see, this increase actually is noteworthy only for the seven oldest cohorts.)

Let us now consider the "new" cohorts—persons under the age of 36 in 1971. They may appropriately be compared with persons of the same age (actually, 21–34) in 1956 to secure a measure of intercohort change with age held constant. In 1956, 46.7 percent of these young adults said "do right"; in 1971, only 34.2 percent of their successors gave this answer. It is pertinent again to consider what differences in educational attainment between the two sets of cohorts may have had to do with this change. If we fit the three-way table, YG response by education by year,[3] using only the two sets of two-way marginals—YG by education and education by year—we find that the fitted counts imply 41.2 percent endorsement of "do right" by the young cohorts in 1956 and 36.7 percent by their successors in 1971. Educational change may well be a factor in the intercohort change, but clearly falls short of accounting for the full extent of the latter. We are not surprised, therefore, that this model does not provide a very close fit to the data: $\chi^2 = 11.92, d.f. = 7, P = 0.10$. A much better fit is obtained using all three sets of two-way marginals: $\chi^2 = 6.01, d.f. = 6, P = 0.42$. Moreover, the improvement in the fit secured by allowing the year effect as well as the education effect is highly significant: $\chi^2 = 11.92 - 6.01 = 5.91$, $d.f. = 1, P = 0.015$.

The upshot of our analysis, therefore, is that, while education is a powerful source of differentiation of the population with respect to the issue tapped by the YG question, it is not a major explanatory factor with respect to the pattern of change in responses to the question. Some part of the differences among cohorts (and, thus, some part of the change effected by the succession of cohorts) is no doubt due to their differences in education. But there are also strong intercohort differences not attributable to education; and the intracohort changes cannot be explained by education at all.

We will do well, therefore, to extract from the data as much information as we can concerning the pattern of cohort differentiation and change. Figure 5.2 displays this information in terms of both the observed percentages saying "do right" and the percentages computed from the fitted counts. The results of the

---

[3] The models considered in this paragraph are the same in form as those discussed in footnote 1.

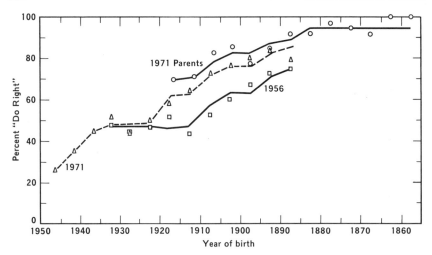

Figure 5.2. Observed and Fitted Percentages of Respondents Endorsing the "Do Right" Alternative to the Younger Generation Question or Reporting that Their Parents Would Have Done So, by Year of Birth or Approximate Year of Birth of Parents: 1956 and 1971.

investigations leading to these particular fits may be summarized briefly:[4] The three youngest cohorts in 1971 differ reliably among themselves and from the three youngest cohorts in 1956. For the latter, there was no significant intracohort change between 1956 and 1971, nor do the three cohorts differ significantly among themselves. For the older cohorts (35 and over in 1956, 50 and over in 1971), there are significant intercohort differences and there is a significant intracohort change but no significant three-way interaction of YG response by cohort by year. Hence, the model assumes the same change for each of these cohorts; this is represented by the quasi-parallel lines for the seven oldest cohorts in the figure.

What happened between 1956 and 1971, therefore, was a polarization of age groups, or the creation of a "cohort chasm" (this concept is to be distinguished from that of "generation gap," to which we come presently). The same set of facts could, of course, be summarized by stating that the relationship between "age" and YG response became more pronounced between 1956 and 1971. The choice between the two formulations is somewhat analogous to the choice between two rotations in factor analysis. My contention is that here, and perhaps in other problems, one gets closer to "simple structure" with the description rendered in terms of cohort differences and cohort changes than in terms of age differences and changes in their pattern. What is perhaps most

---

[4] The models and tests used here are of kinds mentioned in the preceding footnotes.

provocative is that only the seven older cohorts participated in the 1956–1971 rise in proportion favoring "do right." If this change were to be interpreted as a reaction or countertrend to the movement for autonomy of youth, then it is perhaps significant that adults under 35 in 1956 sat at the fulcrum of the seesaw.

Figure 5.2 includes, in addition to the material already discussed, the data on how respondents reported the views of their parents. Whereas 51.8 percent of the 1971 respondents to Form B themselves favored "do right," no less than 83.2 percent of them averred that this alternative would have been preferred by their parents. This, then, is the "generation gap," properly understood. The gap occurs for respondents of all ages, so that today's young adults are by no means unique in perceiving the older (i.e., parental) generation as more authoritarian than themselves. The presentation of the data on the Parent question in Figure 5.2 makes use of a somewhat questionable device: the alignment of the parents of a given cohort with the respondents of the cohort 30 years older. (See Duncan, 1966, for an exposition of the conceptual difficulties intrinsic to such juxtapositions of intercohort and intergenerational comparisons.) Despite the fact that this produces only the roughest approximation to a classification of parents by their own birth cohorts, it does make quite plausible the possibility that part of the generation gap is a matter of biased perception on the part of the offspring. If the comparison of parents with older respondents is in any measure trustworthy, it appears that respondents have rather considerably overestimated the frequency of their parents' endorsement of "do right." Even in 1971, the difference between older respondents and parents is appreciable. But the report on the parent nominally refers to the time at which the respondent was "growing up." Hence, the 1956 data should provide a better estimate of what the parents actually thought than the 1971 data. If so, then a very major part of the generation gap is a function of biased perception.

Despite the substantially fictitious assumption that is involved in doing so, we fit the differences among parental cohorts with the same set of cohort effects used for the seven older cohorts of 1956 and 1971 respondents. This involves the three-way problem, YG response (or, in the case of the parents, their attributed response) by cohort by the three-category classification: 1956 respondents, 1971 respondents, and parents of 1971 respondents. A model using all sets of two-way marginals fits the data quite well:[5] $\chi^2 = 8.93, d.f. = 12, P = 0.71$. Hence, in terms of the statistical criterion, we are justified in making the three curves quasi-parallel. We also find that differences among parents and the two groups of respondents contribute significantly to the fit of the model.

For the six oldest cohorts of "parents," we have no respondents old enough to provide a cohort match. It would appear that these cohorts approach the asymptote of 100 percent endorsement of the "do right" alternative (if the

---

[5] See footnote 1 for a formal representation of a model of this kind.

respondents' reports of parents views were taken as veridical). Actually, the 2 × 6 table, Parent question by parental cohort, produces a nonsignificant chi-square test: $\chi^2 = 5.05, d.f. = 5, P > 0.25$. Hence we have shown all "cohorts" of parents born before 1935 as endorsing the "do right" alternative to the extent of 94.4 percent.

Figure 5.2 provides us with a record, albeit a distorted record, of nearly a century of social change. (The distortions are not without analogy to the rock strata that geologists interpret as reflections of geological processes.) The record suggests a nearly 180° turn from a position of heavy endorsement of the view that parents should first of all teach their children the right thing to do, to the view that their obligation is to teach children to think for themselves. For the reason already indicated, the actual change is probably less than the intergenerational comparisons suggest. Moreover, the record of a single age cross-section, like that produced by the 1956 survey, is seen to be a very fallible basis for inferences about change.

Now that we know just a little bit more about how the change did occur, we have a broader field for speculation about the dynamics of our society than we had before. The value of improved measures of social change, which replication studies aim to supply, is not that they necessarily resolve theoretical issues concerning social dynamics or settle pragmatic issues of social policy, but that they may permit those issues to be argued more productively.

REFERENCES

Detroit Area Study.
   1956   "Family income in the Detroit metropolitan area: 1949–1955."
           (Mimeographed.)
   1959   "Television set ownership in Greater Detroit: 1950–1959." (Mimeo-
           graphed.)
   1960   "Family income in Greater Detroit: 1951–1959." (Mimeographed.)
Duncan, Otis Dudley.
   1966   "Methodological issues in the analysis of social mobility," in N. J.
           Smelser and S. M. Lipset (eds.), Social Structure and Mobility in
           Economic Development. Chicago: Aldine.
   1969   Toward Social Reporting: Next Steps. (Social Science Frontiers, No.
           2.) New York: Russell Sage Foundation.
Duncan, Otis Dudley, Howard Schuman, and Beverly Duncan.
   1973   Social Change in a Metropolitan Community. New York: Russell Sage
           Foundation.
Fienberg, Stephen E.
   1970   "The analysis of multidimensional contingency tables." Ecology
           51 (Number 3):419–433.
   1972   "The analysis of incomplete multi-way contingency tables." Bio-
           metrics 28 (March):177–202.

Fischer, Elizabeth.
  1971   "Sampling memorandum for the 1970–1971 Detroit Area Study."
          Preliminary draft (ditto).
Goodman, Leo A.
  1968   "The analysis of cross-classified data: Independence, quasi-indepen-
          dence, and interactions in contingency tables with or without missing
          entries." Journal of the American Statistical Association 63 (Decem-
          ber):1091–1131.
  1969   "On partitioning χ^2 and detecting partial association in three-way
          contingency tables." Journal of the Royal Statistical Society, Series B,
          31:486–498.
  1970   "The multivariate analysis of qualitative data: Interactions among
          multiple classifications." Journal of the American Statistical Associa-
          tion 65 (March):226–256.
  1971   "The analysis of multidimensional contingency tables: Stepwise
          procedures and direct estimation methods for building models for
          multiple classifications." Technometrics 13 (February):33–61.
  1972a   A modified multiple regression approach to the analysis of dichoto-
          mous variables." American Sociological Review 37 (February):28–46.
  1972b   "A general model for the analysis of surveys." American Journal of
          Sociology 77 (May):1025–1086.
Janowitz, Morris, and Deil Wright.
  1956   "The prestige of public employment: 1929 and 1954." Public
          Administration Review 16 (Winter):15–21.
Miller, Daniel R., and Guy E. Swanson.
  1958   The Changing American Parent. New York: Wiley.
Schuman, Howard.
  1971   "The religious factor in Detroit: Review, replication, and reanalysis."
          American Sociological Review 36:30–48.
Schuman, Howard, and Jean M. Converse.
  1971   "The effects of black and white interviewers on black responses in
          1968." Public Opinion Quarterly 35 (Spring):44–68.
Schwartz, Mildred A.
  1967   Trends in White Attitudes toward Negroes. (Report No. 119.)
          Chicago: National Opinion Research Center, University of Chicago.
Wilks, S. S.
  1935   "The likelihood test of independence in contingency tables." Annals
          of Mathematical Statistics 6:190–196.

6

MEASURING CHANGE IN ATTITUDES TOWARD WOMEN'S WORK*

Beverly Duncan and Mark Evers

An imaginative social analyst might see in a set of measures on attitudes toward women's work made some 15 years ago the roots of the current controversy surrounding sex discrimination in the job market. That women should have any kind of work was distinctly a minority sentiment among the survey respondents. Most often endorsing the sentiment, however, were the young females, those under the age of 35 at the time of the 1956 survey. Least often endorsing the sentiment were young males.

The analyst might adduce both the passage of time and the timing of events in explaining why the issue now is newsworthy. The young adults of 1956 had not yet left their teens at the onset of American involvement in World War II, when a war-induced labor shortage brought unprecedented numbers of women into the work force to fill a variety of traditionally male jobs. They witnessed soaring female labor-force participation rates, especially on the part of mothers, coincident with a pool of unemployed among males of prime working age. They now have reached the ages when they occupy key decision-making roles in lobbies and legislative bodies, in courts and corporations.

---

*The work was carried out as part of the project, Indicators of Social Change from Replication Studies, directed by Otis Dudley Duncan and Howard Schuman and supported by Russell Sage Foundation. The second-named author held a fellowship from the National Science Foundation during the period the study was carried out. We acknowledge with gratitude the assistance of our co-workers, including: Linda Romagnoli, who participated with us in the coding exercises; J. Michael Coble, who provided programming support; Julie Umberger, Chih-Chien Lin, and R. W. Nylund, who helped process the survey data; and Viola Stafford and James Carr, who worked with us on the analyses.

The account of attitudes toward women's work that we present here is essentially a series of qualifications on the foregoing line of argument. We first describe a 1956 survey which serves as the base line from which to measure change and a 1971 survey in which the questions pertaining to women's work were replicated. We detect a change in the proportion of adults favoring restrictions on women's work and try to identify differentials by sex, age, and cohort. We then consider some problems in measuring and interpreting change in responses to open-ended questions about the kinds of work thought to be unsuitable for women. By way of summary, we take another look at the current controversy in the light of attitudes expressed by the respondents in 1956 and 1971.

Our analytical approach is similar to that of Davis (Chapter 4) and of Duncan (Chapter 5). Our data sets derive from surveys described by Duncan. We share with these authors an interest in exploring the possibilities of measuring change through replication. The distinctive feature of our report is the introduction of coding as an issue, one which we feel cannot be overlooked if open-ended questions are to be included among the items repeated in surveys.

THE SURVEYS

The Base Line: 1956

The base line survey was carried out by the Detroit Area Study (DAS), a continuing research and training program associated with the Department of Sociology at the University of Michigan. A description of the 1956 survey procedures, along with selected findings, was issued in 1957 under the title *A Social Profile of Detroit/1956*. Roughly speaking, the 797 respondents selected by an area-probability sample design represent the adult noninstitutional population in the Detroit urbanized area.

Four questions pertaining to the respondent's attitudes toward women's work followed inquiries on the current or usual occupation of the respondent, the determinants of occupational choice, and any occupational training received or wanted by the respondent. The questions read:

1. Now, about working women, why do you think most women work?
2. In what ways do you think women's reasons for working may be different from men's?
3. Do you feel that women have special problems in working? [if yes, ask 3a]
   3a. What would these be? [if occupational problems not mentioned, ask 3b]
   3b. What about in her occupation?
4. Are there some kinds of work that you feel women should not have? [if yes, ask 4a and 4b]
   4a. What are they? 4b. Why do you feel this way?

It is only responses to the fourth question that we examine here.

Responses elicited by the query about what kinds of work women should not have were assigned to one of nine substantive code categories or a residual category—reasons other than above, don't know, or not ascertained. Provision was made for coding the first reason mentioned and the second reason, if any. Seven substantive code categories were provided for classifying the respondent's basis for feeling that the work was unsuitable for women. The substantive code categories are defined by descriptive phrases, such as "factory jobs," "where they take the job away from men," "degrading, coarsening, cheapening, loss of dignity."

Insofar as we know, these data on attitudes toward women's work were not examined in detail by analysts associated with the 1956 DAS. Three paragraphs appear in the *Social Profile* cited earlier.

The attitudes which Detroit residents have toward women working outside the home often are associated with labor force status and sex. For example, while a comparatively small proportion of the total metropolitan population would place no restrictions on the work women can do, the view that any kind of work is all right for women is expressed less often by men than by women (Table 9). In addition, there is a tendency for women in the labor force, those who do take on the male occupational role, to resemble men in this respect more than do nonworking women.

Although the differences are not large, women not in the labor force show the least objection to females working at hard, dirty jobs (Table 9). Men, on the other hand, seem to be relatively concerned that women avoid these occupations. Only 15 percent of the housewives specifically identify physically demanding or dirty jobs as work that women should not do; men are relatively twice as likely as are housewives to prohibit women from holding these jobs. Being both female and exposed to the realities of job problems, employed women have attitudes toward women's work that are intermediate between those of men and those of housewives.

From 31 to 35 percent of both sexes believe that women should not be engaged in blue collar factory jobs. Although factory jobs are pointedly identified by a large number of Detroit area residents as occupations women should not have, about one out of every five women in the greater Detroit labor force is now employed as a semiskilled machine operator in a factory. (*Social Profile*, 1957:45–46)

The accompanying tabular presentation (Table 9) is reproduced in Table 6.1.

Given the differentials by labor-force status and sex shown in Table 6.1, we might expect the attitudes held by males and females, respectively, to become more congruent over time, as an increasing share of the females are "exposed to the realities of job problems." Examination of age-sex differentials offers an alternative basis for evaluating the probable course of change. The pattern of response which might most easily be interpreted as indicative of future convergence would be an increase in the sex difference with age. Assuming that there exist no aging effects as such, a lesser sex difference among the young might be taken to mean that males and females will come to hold similar

Table 6.1. Attitudes Toward Working Women Held by Men and Women in the Labor Force and by Women Not in the Labor Force (Percent Distribution)

| | Labor Force Members | | Nonworking Women |
Kinds of Jobs Women Should Not Have	Men	Women	
No restrictions	14	21	27
Jobs women should not have: all	86	79	73
Hard, dirty work	29	21	15
Factory work	31	31	35
Other kinds of work	26	27	23
Total	100	100	100
Number of cases	336	149	274

Source: From Table 9 in *A Social Profile of Detroit/1956.*

attitudes as older cohorts die out and are replaced by new cohorts reaching adulthood. We find the pattern of an increasing sex difference with age absent in the responses.

On the critical question of whether there should be restrictions on women's work, it is among the young respondents that the sex difference is most pronounced. At each age, females are more likely than males to favor no restrictions on the kinds of work done by women; but the percentage-point difference falls from 16 at ages 21–34 to 5 at ages 35–49 and 4 at ages 50 and over. The relevant data are shown in Table 6.2.

A closing of the "sex gap" in attitudes becomes less plausible when the differentials by age and sex, as well as the differentials by work status and sex, are examined. Only a second reading on the attitudes toward women's work held by males and by females can resolve the issue.

Table 6.2. Attitudes Toward Working Women Held by Men and Women of the Specified Ages: Respondents in 1956 Detroit Area Study (Percent Distribution)

| | | Men | | | Women | | |
Jobs Women Should Not Have	Total	21–34	35–49	50+	21–34	35–49	50+
No restrictions	20	12	18	15	28	23	19
Should not have:							
Hard, dirty work	23	26	31	32	17	17	20
Factory work	32	35	21	33	29	36	36
Other kinds of work	25	27	30	20	26	24	25
Total	100	100	100	100	100	100	100
Number of cases	787	139	121	110	162	141	114

The Replication: 1971

The survey carried out by the DAS in 1971 is described in Chapter 5 in this volume. Among the items from earlier surveys included in the 1971 survey was the four-question sequence relating to attitudes toward women's work. The 1,881 survey respondents again are a sample drawn from the adult noninstitutional population in the Detroit urbanized area.

Although the study design does not permit us to measure the influence of the prior question sequence on responses to the women's work questions, we cannot rule out an intersurvey difference in frame of reference. Respondents in the 1956 base-line survey had been lead to think about jobs and the meaning of work, occupational choices, and training.. Those in the 1971 survey had been formulating their opinions about presumably controversial topics of current concern—the adequacy with which various groups were performing, the costs and benefits of government, the range over which the right of free speech extends. The four-question sequence relating to women's work was common to the 1956 base line survey had been lead to think about jobs and the meaning of nature and basis, that is our focus. In both surveys that question was posed after respondents had considered why women work and whether they have special problems.

The view that women should have any kind of work remains a minority sentiment among Detroit residents although the proportion concurring has risen from a fifth to a third over the past 15 years. Females again are found to favor no restrictions more often than do males, and the sex differential remains as large as in 1956. It is no longer only among the young respondents that the sex differential is pronounced; females in each age group now are appreciably more likely to favor no restrictions than are their male age-mates.

As a loose statement of major changes, the foregoing paragraph may suffice. It is necessarily vague with respect to the magnitude of the sex differential and change therein, for commonly used measures of such a differential may be interpreted to support divergence or an absence of change, or even convergence. (We leave aside for the moment problems of significance in the statistical sense.)

The proponent of convergence might select as a measure the ratio of the female to the male percentage favoring no restrictions; the ratio decreases from 1.60 in 1956 (24/15) to 1.46 in 1971 (38/26). The critic of the convergence hypothesis need only note, however, that each respondent must answer "no" or "yes." Although the ratio of the female to the male percentage answering "no" converges toward unity, the ratio of the female to the male percentage answering "yes" is 0.89 in 1956 (76/85) as compared with 0.84 in 1971 (62/74), which might be taken to signify divergence.

Two sounder measures of the differential are presented in Table 6.3. The percentages of males and females, respectively, answering "no" to the question "Are there some kinds of work that you feel women should not have?" are

Table 6.3. Age-Sex Differentials in a "No" Response to Q4: Are There Some Kinds of Work that You Feel Women Should Not Have?

	Percent Answer "No"			Odds−Answer "No": 100[a]		
Year and Age	Male	Female	Diff. M − F	Male	Female	Ratio M/F
1956						
21 and over	15	24	−9	18	32	0.57
21 to 34	12	28	−16	14	38	0.36
35 to 49	18	23	−5	22	31	0.73
50 and over	15	19	−4	18	24	0.76
1971						
21 and over	26	38	−12	35	62	0.57
21 to 34	30	43	−13	42	75	0.56
35 to 49	27	39	−12	37	63	0.59
50 and over	21	33	−12	27	49	0.54
50 to 64	22	31	−9	28	46	0.62
65 and over	19	37	−18	23	58	0.40

[a]Number of respondents answering "no" per 100 respondents answering "yes."

shown in the first two columns. The percentage-point difference appears in the third column: the sex differential is found to increase from 9 to 12 points between 1956 and 1971. Shown in the fourth and fifth columns are the odds that males and females, respectively, answer "no." The ratio of the male to the female odds appears in the sixth column: the sex differential stands at 0.57 in both 1956 and 1971.

How do we choose between the percentage-point difference, which is consistent with an argument for divergence, and the odds ratio, which is consistent with an argument for stability? We are reasonably sure that in a community as large as Detroit the sex ratio is not subject to large fluctuations or rapid change. We cannot, however, discount the possibility of large fluctuations or rapid change in the attitudes held by Detroit residents toward women's work. The odds ratio can remain invariant given a constant sex ratio and a shift in the proportion of respondents who answer "no." It will remain invariant if the relative number of "no" responses increases at the same rate, or by the same factor, for males as for females. Identity between males and females with respect to this rate squares with our notion of a constant sex differential. Analytically, therefore, we prefer to work with the odds ratio; and we conclude that no change in the sex differential has occurred.

IDENTIFYING PATTERNS OF CHANGE

We have found an absence of change in the sex differential associated with an upward shift in the proportion of adults favoring no restrictions on women's work. The finding cannot be taken to mean that the men and women who had reached adulthood by 1956 were changing their attitudes from a restrictive to a nonrestrictive position at the same rate over the 1956–1971 period. About a third of the 1971 respondents had reached their majority since 1956. Death had reduced the ranks of the older groups. A variety of patterns of change within and between cohorts could give rise to the finding.

The 1956 Cross Section

In the initial year, it is only among the youngest age group of respondents that the sex differential is sufficiently large to be significant in the statistical sense. Consider the 12-cell table, the columns of which are a "no" and a "yes" response, respectively, and the rows of which are sex (male, female) within age group (21–34, 35–49, 50 or more). The chi-square value is found to be 14.30, which with 5 degrees of freedom is associated with a probability of occurrence of about 0.02. The partitioning summarized below shows that the differentiation among the 12 cells traces mainly to the sex differential among young respondents.

Groups compared	Chi-square	df	P
M 21–34, F 21–34	11.46	1	0.001
M 35–49, F 35–49	1.08	1	0.3
M 50+, F 50+ ..	0.58	1	0.4
35–49, 50+ ...	1.00	1	0.3
21–34, 35+ ...	0.18	1	0.7

Nonetheless, the sex-response relation among young respondents cannot be shown to differ significantly from the relation among older respondents. We reach this conclusion by comparing the observed frequencies in the 12 cells of the age-by-sex-by-response table with expected frequencies calculated on alternative assumptions about the relations among age, sex, and response. We first consider models that assume (a) mutual independence among age, sex, and response and (b) three-way interaction, respectively. The model assuming mutual independence does not provide a satisfactory fit to the observed frequencies; the model assuming three-way interaction does provide an adequate fit. We then ask, however, whether models which assume (c) a constant sex-by-response relation within age groups also can provide an adequate fit to the observed frequencies; the answer is yes.

The model assuming (a) mutual independence takes as given only the numbers of respondents in each age group, of each sex, and in each response category; it assumes that the distribution of respondents by one characteristic— say, response—is identical within each subpopulation defined by a combination of the other characteristics—say, each age-sex group. In contrast, the model assuming (b) three-way interaction takes as given the numbers of respondents in each age-sex group, in each age-response group, and in each sex-response group;

it permits the distribution of respondents by response to vary among age-sex groups. Still another model (c) takes as given the numbers of respondents in each age group and in each sex-response group; it assumes that response is related to sex, but that the relation is constant over age groups. We have calculated expected frequencies in the 12 cells of the age-by-sex-by-response table for models (a), (b), and (c), respectively, and compared them with the observed frequencies.

Model	Chi-square	df	P
(a) Mutual independence	14.85	7	0.04
(b) Three-way interaction	3.49	2	0.17
(c) Sex-response and age	5.06	6	0.5

The model assuming three-way interaction does not provide a significantly better fit to the observed data than does the model which takes as given only the sex-response relation and the age distribution (chi-square value 1.57, df 4, P 0.8). Indeed, the expected frequencies calculated on either set of assumptions imply a constant odds ratio of 0.57 for each age group.

It is tempting to think that had the number of respondents in 1956 been larger, a stronger sex differential among the young might be documented; but only a weak case can be made for such age patterning with the data at hand. The results of our statistical tests are ambiguous. We can reject with considerable confidence the notion that males and females were equally likely to favor no restrictions on women's work in 1956. We can show that such differentiation by age and by sex as was present in 1956 traces primarily to the different attitudes held by young males and young females, respectively. We cannot, nevertheless, reject the possibility that the sex differential was constant over age groups in 1956.

1971 Contrasted with 1956

The results of statistical tests again are ambiguous when we examine intracohort changes between 1956 and 1971 and the differentiation by age and sex in 1971. Recall that in the 1956 data set the odds ratio is significant only for the youngest cohort, but that the odds ratio for the youngest cohort cannot be shown to differ significantly from that for the older cohorts. We now find that the odds ratio is significant for each cohort in the 1971 data set although for no cohort can the 1956 odds ratio be shown to differ significantly from the 1971 odds ratio.

Differentiation within the 12-cell table, the columns of which are response and the rows of which are sex within cohort, could be attributed mainly to the sex differential within the youngest cohort for the 1956 data set. Differentiation within the corresponding 12-cell table based on 1971 data cannot be attributed in such large measure to a single source. A partitioning of the table based on

1971 data, similar to the partitioning reported earlier for the table based on 1956 data, is summarized below.

Groups compared	Chi-square	df	P
M 35–49, F 35–49	8.48	1	0.004
M 50–64, F 50–64	4.81	1	0.03
M 65+, F 65+ ..	7.57	1	0.01
50–64, 65+ ...	0.09	1	0.8
35–49, 50+ ...	5.32	1	0.02

The chi-square value for the 12-cell table is 26.27, which with five degrees of freedom is associated with a probability of occurrence of 0.001.

The observed frequencies of the year-by-sex-by-response table for the cohort aged 50–64 in 1971 (35–49 in 1956) are fit satisfactorily by a model which takes as given the numbers of respondents in the respective years and in each sex-response group (chi-square value 3.64, *df* 3, *P* 0.3). Observed frequencies of the tables for the younger and older cohorts are fit adequately by models which take as given the numbers of respondents in each sex-response group and each year-response group (chi-square values of 2.04 and 1.74 for the respective cohorts, both *df* 2, *P* 0.4). In each case, a constant between-years odds ratio is implicit in the model which provides an adequate fit.

By way of summarizing the intercohort differences and intracohort changes, we compare observed frequencies with expected frequencies calculated on alternative models for the 24-cell table of response by sex by cohort by year. The model assuming mutual independence among the four items—response, sex, cohort, and year—does not provide an adequate fit (chi-square value 117.22, *df* 18, *P* < 0.001). The observed frequencies are fit adequately by a model which takes as given (a) each of the six two-way classifications among the four items, that is, the numbers of respondents in each response-sex group, in each response-cohort group, and so on or (b) each of the four three-way classifications among the four items, that is, the numbers of respondents in each response-sex-cohort group, in each response-cohort-year group, and so on. The observed frequencies also can be fit adequately by a model which takes as given (c) only the numbers of respondents in each sex-response group, in each year-response group, and in each year-cohort group.

Model	Chi-square	df	P
(a) 6 2-way classifications	6.70	9	0.7
(b) 4 3-way classifications	3.72	2	0.15
(c) Sex-response, year-response, and year-cohort	12.75	14	0.5

Neither the model incorporating (a) all two-way classifications nor the model incorporating (b) all three-way classifications provides a significantly better fit to the observed frequencies than does the model which takes as given (c) only the sex-response, year-response, and year-cohort classifications (chi-square value 6.05, *df* 5, *P* 0.3 and chi-square value 9.03, *df* 12, *P* 0.7, respectively).

In substantive terms, then, the main features of the data set are the sex differential in response, the year effect on response, and the fact of differential mortality by age. Our analyses are fully consistent with respect to two points: women more often oppose restrictions on women's work than do men; and relatively more adults oppose restrictions now than did so 15 years ago. We are reluctant to reject the possibility that the intensity of the sex-response relation differs among cohorts or over time because of the ambiguity in our analytical results, but such variation cannot be documented firmly with this data set.

One hunch remains to be examined: that the group reaching adulthood since 1956, those aged 21 to 34 in 1971, are as sharply differentiated by sex on the issue of restrictions on women's work as were young adults in 1956. It is the case that the 1971 odds ratio for the group aged 21–34 in 1971 cannot be shown to differ significantly from the 1956 odds ratio for the group aged 21–34 in 1956. A model which takes as given the year (group) by response and the sex by response distributions for the pooled years (groups) provides a satisfactory fit to the observed frequencies (chi-square value 1.65, *df* 2, *P* 0.4).

A sound, though perhaps sociologically unexciting conclusion to be drawn from the analyses is that an odds ratio of 0.57 cannot be rejected as a reasonable estimate for any cohort in either year. Our model of change would posit that male and female adults were changing their attitude from a restrictive to a nonrestrictive position at the same rate and that the intensity of the sex differential among those reaching adulthood was the same as among their elders.

Reasons for Restriction

It is possible, however, that significant convergence or divergence in the attitudes held by males and females, respectively, will appear when the bases of their support for restrictions on women's work are examined. Two types of work frequently mentioned as unsuitable for women in the base-line survey received comment from the 1956 DAS analysts: factory jobs and hard or dirty jobs. These items differ with respect to change in frequency of mention between base line survey and replication; and models which adequately describe the data sets typically must incorporate a year-response relation. It is tempting to interpret the year effects on response as meaningful substantively, but the year effect is confounded with the coder effect. What we are measuring is change in the frequency with which coders chose a given category to characterize an often vague response.

To reinforce the point that responses are not easily characterized, we record answers to the questions "What are they [kinds of work women should not have]?" and "Why do you feel this way?" given by five respondents who favor restrictions on women's work.

Respondent 1. What kinds: Uh, a woman is not qualified as a foreman. Why: because women are more emotional.

Respondent 2. What kinds: Political office, shop work. [Interviewer probe: anything else?] Being president of a company. Why: I just don't think women have the aggressive power to get things done.

Respondent 3. What kinds: Machinery and things like this. Why: They're just not the type of job women can handle.

Respondent 4. What kinds: Digging ditches, manual labor, working in sewers, collecting garbage. Why: It's the way I relate to a woman—they should be feminine—I can't think of any job that a woman couldn't do if trained but I wouldn't want to see her doing the ones I mentioned.

Respondent 5. What kinds: Factory work. Why: Man's job woman should be more like secretary, doctor, or something besides factory work.

We turn now to a consideration of the problem coding presents in replication studies.

CODING AND REPLICATION

In assessing change in the proportion of respondents favoring no restrictions on women's work, we did not consider the possibility that coding generated the differences between base line and current readings. Implicitly, we accepted as reliable the respondent's own coding of his full response to the question "Are there some kinds of work that you feel women should not have?" by a yes or a no. In fact, a respondent who endorsed the prohibition of legal restrictions relating to the employment of women, but was sympathetic to the use of informal sanctions to channel women away from unsuitable kinds of work might code his response as either yes or no; the proportion of such respondents selecting the no code may differ by year. We also accepted as comparable between surveys the essentially mechanical phases of the coding operation—the faithful transfer of the respondent's self-selected code to the tabulation.

An understanding of changes in attitudes toward women's work would seem to require the analysis of responses to such questions as what kinds of work they should not have and why some kinds of work are thought unsuitable. When attention turns from the respondent-coded questions to the open-ended questions, comparability in coding between surveys or the consistency with which responses can be categorized becomes a major issue. Responses obtained in a replication must be assigned to one of several predesignated code categories, the categories used in the base-line survey. For few open-ended questions has a standard set of coding procedures been developed, a counterpart to, say, the Alphabetical Index of Occupations and Industries.

No document detailing coding procedures followed in the 1956 base-line survey was available at the time the 1971 replication was undertaken. There remained only the listing of code categories, each identified by a descriptive phrase. During the summer of 1971, we carried out some coding exercises to determine how consistently responses could be assigned to the predesignated code categories used in the 1956 survey.

The Coding Exercises

Two sets of schedules were selected. The first included 93 schedules from the 1971 pretest; the second was a systematic sample of 76 schedules from the 1956 survey. Each response from the 1971 pretest was coded independently by three persons, two of whom then coded each 1956 response. Since the code assigned each 1956 response in the 1956 coding operation is known, we have three independently assigned codes for each response.

For the respondent-coded responses to the question of whether women should not have some kinds of work (Q4), discrepant code assignments must reflect either errors in the transfer of code from schedule to tabulation or differences in the disposition of schedules where neither yes nor no has been checked. The percentage agreement for coding pairs was high (98–99 percent), and discrepancies could be traced to differences in the disposition of unmarked or inconsistently marked schedules.

Roughly a quarter of the responses to the open-ended questions of what kinds of work are unsuitable (Q4a) and why (Q4b) were coded inconsistently. These inconsistencies, we think, trace mainly to a lack of fit between the response and any predesignated code category. No code can be said to be correct; two or more codes can be said to be plausible. The percentage agreement varies by question, by coding pair, and by survey year (66–86 percent over eight observations). Agreement between 1971 coders is not always greater for 1971 responses than for 1956 responses, however; nor is the agreement between two 1971 coders always greater than between a 1971 coder and a 1956 coder. (The percentage agreement was similar for Q4ab and Q1, but only two-thirds for Q2 and just over half for Q3ab.)

From the standpoint of replication, the relative number of responses coded consistently is no more important, and probably less so, than similarity in the relative frequency with which given codes are assigned. Although fully consistent coding guarantees similarity, inconsistent coding does not preclude similarity. In the course of the coding exercises, it began to appear that inconsistencies would not be patterned symmetrically although we did not have dual coding on a sufficient number of responses to identify noncompensating "exchange cycles" conclusively.

We did examine the predesignated coding scheme with a view toward reorganization for analytical use. (a) We felt that the distinction between first and second mention lacked merit since it depended so closely on phrasing—"like working real hard like assembly work" versus "ought to stay clear of factories, too hard for them"—and how many distinct mentions were perceived by the coder. (b) We combined codes with a common substantive theme if the distinctions between them, though conceptually real, could not be discerned reliably from the responses. Indeed, the 1956 DAS analysts had combined "Heavy work, hard work" with "Where working conditions bad, dirty, dangerous." (c) Finally, we thought there was justification for grouping responses similar in theme whether they were elicited by the question about kinds of work women should not have (Q4a) or the question of why (Q4b). Themes of hard work and of displacing men from jobs, for example, were present among the predesignated codes for the respective questions.

The results of these exercises were not encouraging from the standpoint of measuring change.

Recoding of 1956 Responses

Inasmuch as the full set of 1956 schedules remained on file, it was possible to have the same persons code all 1971 and 1956 responses. Four members of the coding staff of Michigan's Institute for Social Research were assigned to the project. Three were female; all would be members of our youngest cohort of respondents.

The coding of 1971 and 1956 responses was carried out in a prescribed sequence. Each of two coders was instructed to first code 100 of the 1956 responses, then to code 100 of the 1971 responses, and to code the remaining 100 of the 1956 responses assigned to her before completing the coding of 1971 responses. The other two coders alternated the 1956–1971 sequence, beginning with 100 of the 1971 responses. Each coder's assignment represented a systematic sample of 1956 responses, with the first coder assigned schedules bearing interview numbers 1–9, 40–49, 80–89, and so on.

We have, then, the code assigned by the 1971 coder for comparison with the code assigned by the 1956 coder to the answers given by the 797 respondents surveyed in 1956. We do not know the number of persons who participated in the 1956 coding operation, nor the sequence in which schedules were coded. In view of the complexity of the 1971 assignment procedure, however, it seems safe to assume that we do not have a 1971 coder paired with a single 1956 coder.

Our written instructions to coders were few. We designated the "other" code low priority, to be used only if no part of the response could be assigned a predesignated substantive code; no priorities were specified among the substantive codes. For training purposes, 15 responses to each question were selected from the schedules used in the coding exercises. (Included were the five responses reproduced earlier in this chapter.) The four persons assigned to the coding project and their supervisor coded these responses without prior

Table 6.4. Percentage of Responses Coded Consistently by 1956 and 1971
Coders, by 1971 Coder, for Selected Questions on Attitudes Toward
Women's Work

Item	All	1971 Project Coder				Coding Exercise
		1	*2*	*3*	*4*	
Q4a. Kind of work unsuitable	75	75	77	75	73	75
Q4b. Why work unsuitable	70	67	76	67	70	71
Number of responses	634	154	157	162	161	63

discussion. We then read to them the codes which we had selected as most appropriate, asking at the outset for reaction to our selections. Suggestions of alternative codings came almost wholly from the supervisor. We do not know whether the lack of comments on the part of the coders reflected disinterest, timidity, or agreement with our selections. From that point through the transfer of the codes to punch cards, the coding operation was out of our hands.

The percentage of responses which were assigned the same code by 1956 and 1971 coders appears in Table 6.4 for two open-ended questions. The percentage also is shown separately for each 1971 project coder. The similarity in results among coders and between project and exercise coding suggests that we have a fairly sound estimate of the inherent codability of these responses into the predesignated categories. Working independently, coders will select the same code from the 12 possible codes for kinds of work first mentioned as unsuitable for women about 75 percent of the time. They will select the same code from among the 10 possible codes for why the work is unsuitable about 70 percent of the time.

When we compare 1956 and 1971 code assignments within the framework of the grouped codes developed for analytical purposes in the course of the coding exercises, we find that code reorganization occasionally results in substantially improved comparability. The effect of reorganization is variable among items, however; and we do not think that these item-specific effects could have been forecast accurately on the basis of the coding exercises. By way of illustration, we describe the effects of code reorganization for three items.

We look first at the effect of a simple grouping of predesignated code categories, namely, the combination of the codes "Heavy work, hard work" and "Where working conditions bad, dirty, dangerous" which first was employed by the 1956 DAS analysts. Neither the percentage agreement between coders nor their similarity with respect to frequency of code assignment is improved by the combination. In only three cases (the cells identified as 1–2 and 2–1 in Table 6.5) did coders disagree as to which of the two codes best categorized the first mention in the response. In 79 cases (the cells identified as 3–4 and 4–3 in

Table 6.5. First Mentions of Hard, Dirty Work in Response to Q4a–What Kinds of Work Are Unsuitable for Women?–by Codes Assigned by 1956 and 1971 Coders, Respectively

Code Assigned by 1956 Coder	Code Assigned by 1971 Coder				Total
	(1)	*(2)*	*(3)*	*(4)*	
1–Heavy work, hard work	114	1	46	...	161
2–Where working conditions bad, dirty, dangerous	2	3	16	...	21
3–Code other than 1–2 above	14	3	598	17	615
4–Hard, dirty work, codes 1–2 above	...	...	62	120	182
Total	130	7	660	137	797

Table 6.5) the coders disagreed as to whether the first mention in the response was best categorized by either hard or dirty work. Moreover, frequencies in the off-diagonal cells which represent coding inconsistency do not compensate: hard, dirty work is perceived as the first mention in 182 of the 797 responses by the 1956 coder; it is so perceived in only 137 responses by the 1971 coder.

Our second example concerns the elimination of the distinction between first and second mention. The item is "Factory jobs" as a kind of work women should not have. In 19 cases the coders disagree as to whether factory jobs are mentioned first or second in the response; in 45 cases they disagree as to whether a mention of factory jobs is present in the response. As can be seen in Table 6.6, however, frequencies in the off-diagonal cells compensate in such a way that mentions of factory work are perceived as often by one coder as by the other irrespective of whether only first mentions or all mentions are considered.

Table 6.6. Mentions of Factory Jobs in Response to Q4a–What Kinds of Work Are Unsuitable for Women?–by Codes Assigned by 1956 and 1971 Coders, Respectively

Code Assigned by 1956 Coder	Code Assigned by 1971 Coder				Total
	(1)	*(2)*	*(3)*	*(4)*	
1–Factory jobs, first mention	222	7	19	...	248
2–Factory jobs, second mention	12	13	8	...	33
3–Code other than 1–2 above	14	4	498	18	516
4–Factory jobs, codes 1–2 above	...	...	27	254	281
Total	248	24	525	272	797

Table 6.7. Mentions of Hard Work in Response to Q4ab—What Kinds of Work Are Unsuitable for Women and Why?—by Codes Assigned by 1956 and 1971 Coders, Respectively

Code Assigned by 1956 Coder	Code Assigned by 1971 Coder				
	(1)	*(2)*	*(3)*	*(4)*	*Total*
1–Kind: "heavy work, hard work," or "where working conditions bad, dirty, dangerous"	146	42	21	...	209
2–Why: "too hard, too heavy, too dangerous"	9	78	17	...	104
3–Code other than 1–2 above	12	15	457	27	484
4–Hard work, codes 1–2 above	...	...	38	275	313
Total	167	135	495	302	797

The final example concerns pooling mentions of hard, dirty work elicited in response to the question of kinds of unsuitable work with those elicited as a response to the question of why the work is unsuitable. In 51 cases the coders disagree as to the query which elicited a mention of hard, dirty work; in 65 cases they disagree as to whether there is any mention of hard, dirty work. Only after pooling do the off-diagonal cells compensate. See Table 6.7.

Several pronounced exchange cycles, or patterned code interchanges, appear which we did not anticipate on the basis of the coding exercises. In each case, a relatively large number of the inconsistently coded responses are accounted for by the cycle; and the patterned interchanges result in a statistically significant difference in the relative frequency with which one or more codes were assigned. Even had we anticipated the cycles, code reorganization could not have resolved the problem, for grouping would yield a substantively uninterpretable category.

Retrospectively, we think that some exchange cycles were induced, or at least intensified, by our selection of examples for the coders' training session. Our suspicions about the influence of the training examples could be verified, of course, only by undertaking still another coding operation with new coders and a different training format.

We report here on only three patterns of code interchange. We can recall no action on our part that would have generated the first cycle; the third cycle is the one that we are most certain we induced.

Our first exchange cycle involves code assignments for the response to the question of why a given kind of work is unsuitable for women. The 1971 coders had a propensity to assign the code "not women's work" to responses which had been assigned either the code "takes men's jobs" or the code "degrading" by the

Table 6.8. Distribution of Selected Responses to Q4b—Why the Work Is Unsuitable for Women—by Codes Assigned by 1956 and 1971 Coders, Respectively

Code Assigned by 1956 Coder	Code Assigned by 1971 Coder				
	(1)	(2)	(3)	(4)	Total
1—Takes men's jobs	86	11	0	2	99
2—Not women's work; woman's place is in the home	3	56	5	23	87
3—Degrading, coarsening, cheapening; loss of dignity	0	13	73	15	101
4—Code other than 1—3 above	4	24	9	473	510
Total	93	104	87	513	797

1956 coder. The code "takes men's jobs" did not appear in our training examples, but the "degrading" code was used three times, for the responses: "It's the way I relate to a woman—they should be feminine . . . ," "because those jobs are not feminine," and "tends to deteriorate women, make more manly." The code favored by the 1971 coders was used twice in the examples, for the responses "man's job—woman should be more like secretary, doctor, or something besides factory work" and "She should be staying home with the kids." The patterns of interchange are shown in Table 6.8. Confusion of the "takes men's jobs" and "degrading" codes does not occur, but the net shift from these codes to the "not women's work" code is pronounced.

The second exchange cycle again involves code assignments for the reason the work is thought unsuitable. The 1971 coders had a propensity to assign the "too hard" code to responses which had been coded either "injurious" or "not capable" in 1956. In the training examples, the "injurious" code was used for the response "body not suited." The "not capable" code was used four times, for the responses "because women are more emotional," "I just don't think women have the aggressive power to get things done," "They're just not the type of job women can handle," and "The ones I've known haven't the capabilities to manage other people." The "too hard" code was used for the responses "Primarily I would say that they are strenuous types, and women are not suited for that" and "The work is too hard and really dangerous for most women," as well as for the response "They're just not capable, not strong enough." In assigning the "too hard" code to this last response, on grounds that capability here referred to physical strength, we may have induced the net shift from the "not capable" to the "too hard" code. The net shift from the "injurious" to the

Table 6.9. Distribution of Selected Responses to Q4b—Why the Work Is Unsuitable for Women—by Codes Assigned by 1956 and 1971 Coders, Respectively

Code Assigned by 1956 Coder	Code Assigned by 1971 Coder				Total
	(1)	*(2)*	*(3)*	*(4)*	
1–Injurious to health	28	19	0	6	53
2–Too hard, too heavy, too dangerous	2	149	5	20	176
3–Women not as capable, not as skilled; not as stable	0	26	31	13	70
4–Code other than 1–3 above	3	21	14	460	498
Total	33	215	50	499	797

"too hard" code is equally prominent, however, in the data displayed in Table 6.9.

The third exchange cycle involves code assignments for the kind of work thought to be unsuitable for women. We had noted in the course of the coding exercises a type of response framed in occupational or industrial terms, e.g., plumbing or construction, which was not readily accommodated in the predesignated coding scheme. Only three predesignated codes were described in these terms, namely, factory work, high administrative jobs, and the professions. For want of a better alternative, we selected the men's-work code for other

Table 6.10. Distribution of First Mentions in Response to Q4a—What Kinds of Work Are Unsuitable for Women?—by Codes Assigned by 1956 and 1971 Coders, Respectively

Code Assigned by 1956 Coder	Code Assigned by 1971 Coder				Total
	(1)	*(2)*	*(3)*	*(4)*	
1–Heavy work, hard work	114	33	11	5	163
2–Work usually done by men; truck, cab, bus drivers; job traditionally male	2	52	9	6	69
3–Factory jobs	8	13	222	5	248
4–Code other than 1–3 above	9	24	6	278	317
Total	133	122	248	294	797

occupationally or industrially defined kinds of work. We foresaw the risk of generating a net shift from factory work to men's work; we did not foresee that a net shift from hard work to men's work would be induced. The latter shift is the more prominent, however, in the data displayed in Table 6.10.

Since we have a specific notion about what produced the shift to men's work, we examine this exchange cycle in more detail. In Table 6.11 we reproduce the responses in which the first mention was thought to be hard work by the 1956 coder but men's work by the 1971 coder and in which the 1971 coder perceived no second mention of hard work. There are 25 such responses, 9 by females and 16 by males. Assignment of the hard-work code to the responses of three females (F7, F8, F9) and two males (M15, M16) seems more nearly correct than assignment of the men's-work code. In the other responses, however, work is described in the occupational or industrial terms which we had suggested were appropriately coded as men's work.

One other feature of this interchange merits comment: namely, the

Table 6.11. Responses Coded Hard Work in 1956 and Men's Work in 1971

F1. Being a mechanic, hotel porter
F2. Washing cars
F3. Not like Russia where they clean streets, work in mines, factory work
F4. Bending bows on top of cars
F5. Boilermaker—around a furnace or engineer on a train
F6. Wouldn't expect a woman to be a member of a road gang
F7. Hard labor they shouldn't have
F8. Painting—hard jobs
F9. Such terrible obvious things like coal mining which requires endurance and strength and I think a woman can't hold a very high executive office
M1. Don't work on the street or in blacksmith shop
M2. Hot steel molding, foundry, nothing to do with making a car
M3. Anything really manual like truck driving or driving a taxicab
M4. Construction work and stuff like that, any labor work
M5. Construction, manual labor, railroad work, fireman, switchman
M6. Manual labor—even secretarial positions in an office that is predominantly male
M7. Welding or wood work
M8. Digging ditches
M9. Plumbing and electrical, you can go down the whole building trade
M10. Digging ditches or any outside job—street cleaning or garbage collecting
M11. Bearings jobs [R works in auto plant]
M12. Try to put a woman on the press [R is press operator in auto plant]
M13. Women couldn't do my work—construction—and railroad [R is a plaster-tender on construction]
M14. Not like my kind [R is a charger in a foundry]
M15. Hard labor
M16. Some jobs they can't do—take a lot of strength and need a man, for example, construction, coal mining, and things like that; they do all right in offices, hospitals, small firms, white-collar jobs

selectivity by sex. If only the 374 responses given by males are examined, the difference between 1956 and 1971 coders with respect to the frequency of code assignment is clearly significant. The difference is only marginally significant for the 423 responses given by females. The number of times the respective codes were assigned is shown below.

	Males		*Females*	
	1956	*1971*	*1956*	*1971*
Hard work	99	79	64	54
Men's work	36	74	33	48

The largest single component of the difference is the net shift from hard work to men's work, a shift of 20 for the male responses and 11 for the female responses. The sex selectivity seems to trace to the propensity of males to describe kinds of work in occupational or industrial terms, in some cases by reference to their own jobs (e.g., M11–M14).

That the 1971 recoding of 1956 responses failed to reproduce the 1956 code assignments is clear. Moreover, when analyses of the type reported here are carried out separately for each of the four 1971 project coders, it becomes apparent that the differences between 1956 and 1971 code assignments do not trace to the idiosyncratic behavior of any one 1971 coder.

Coder versus Year Effects

We now can distinguish a coder effect from a year effect and need no longer try to estimate change from a measure in which year and coder effects are confounded. Specifically, we calculate the percentage of 1956 responses in which a given type of mention was thought to be present by the 1956 coder and 1971 coder, respectively, and the percentage of 1971 responses in which that type of mention was thought to be present by the 1971 coder. We then identify three effects: coder only (1956 responses, difference between 1956 and 1971 coders); coder and year; and year only (1971 coders, difference between 1956 and 1971 responses).

In the upper panel of Table 6.12, we show the percentage of respondents whose first mention in response to the query about kinds of work women should not have was factory work or hard, dirty work. The coder effect on mentions of factory work is negligible although the year effect, or change, is substantial. The coder effect on mentions of hard, dirty work is nearly as large as the year effect, however; and the effects combine in such a way that change, or the year effect, is underestimated by a measure in which coder and year effects are confounded.

The percentage of respondents mentioning factory work or hard, dirty work after the coding scheme has been reorganized to eliminate distinctions between first and second mentions and between responses to the "kinds of work" and

Table 6.12. Percentage of Respondents Mentioning Factory Work or Hard, Dirty Work in 1956 and 1971, Respectively, and Coder and Year Effects on Frequency of Mention

Type of Mention and Sex of Respondent	1956 Response 1956 Coder (1)	1971 Coder (2)	1971 Response and Coder (3)	Coder Only (2)-(1)	Effect Coder and Year (3)-(1)	Year Only (3)-(2)
First mention (Q4a)						
All respondents						
Factory work	32	32	12	0	-20	-20
Hard, dirty work	23	18	25	-5	2	7
Males						
Factory work	29	29	13	0	-16	-16
Hard, dirty work	29	22	31	-7	2	9
Females						
Factory work	33	34	12	1	-21	-22
Hard, dirty work	18	14	20	-4	2	6
Any mention (Q4ab)						
All respondents						
Factory only	21	21	6	0	-15	-15
Hard, dirty only	25	25	36	0	11	11
Factory; hard, dirty	15	13	8	-2	- 7	- 5
Males						
Factory only	19	19	6	0	-13	-13
Hard, dirty only	32	32	44	0	12	12
Factory; hard, dirty	16	13	9	-3	- 7	- 4
Females						
Factory only	22	23	6	1	- 6	- 7
Hard, dirty only	18	18	30	0	12	12
Factory; hard, dirty	15	14	8	-1	- 7	- 6

"why" queries appears in the lower panel of Table 6.12. The coder effect on mentions of factory work only or hard work only is negligible; the year effect is substantial—a decrease of 15 percentage points in mentions of factory work only, an increase of 11 percentage points in mentions of hard, dirty work only. Change in the percentage of respondents mentioning both factory and hard, dirty work is overestimated by a measure in which coder and year effects are confounded; the coder effect results in a 2 percentage-point drop in frequency of mention, the year effect in a 5 percentage-point drop.

We would be willing to generalize our experience only to the observation that how coding inconsistency will manifest itself is unpredictable. Precisely for this reason, the issue of coding takes on special importance in replication studies.

WORK WOMEN SHOULD NOT HAVE

Three-fifths of the 1956 respondents and half of the 1971 respondents mentioned either factory work or hard, dirty work as unsuitable for women. Objections to work in factories were voiced less often in 1971 than in 1956; in contrast, hard or dirty jobs were mentioned less often in 1956. That the year effect on each type of mention is similar for males and females is suggested by the data summarized in the lower panel of Table 6.12. The same data set reveals the strong relation between sex of respondent and the propensity to mention hard, dirty jobs, as well as the absence of a sex differential with respect to mentions of factory work. (Here and throughout the remainder of this chapter, our data set is 1956 and 1971 responses as categorized by 1971 project coders.)

The relation of each type of mention to year and sex, and also to cohort, can be described more systematically from the analytical results summarized in Table 6.13. To lend concreteness to these results, we show below the odds that a respondent of a given sex and cohort will mention factory or hard, dirty work, respectively, in each year. The odds are expressed as mentions per 100 nonmentions. The first line in each panel displays the odds implied by a relatively simple multiplicative model which provides a satisfactory fit to the observed data. Year and cohort effects are taken account of in model (q) for factory jobs; year, sex, and cohort effects are taken account of in model (k) for hard, dirty jobs. (Models are identified by line letter in Table 6.13.)

	1956			1971		
	21–34	*35–49*	*50+*	*35–49*	*50–49*	*65+*
	M F	M F	M F	M F	M F	M F
Factory						
Model (q)	47 47	46 46	·66 66	19 19	18 18	26 26
Observed	54 51	30 57	58 67	17 17	21 18	27 30
Hard, dirty						
Model (k)	75 41	96 53	84 46	105 58	134 74	117 65
Observed	59 50	88 47	107 43	108 58	137 81	127 46

The main features of the data set for factory work revealed by the implied odds are: the odds of a mention by a member of the oldest cohort are 1.4 times the odds of a mention by a younger respondent; the ratio of 1971 to 1956 odds is 0.4; and the odds of a mention are the same for males and females. For hard, dirty work, the odds of a mention by a member of the oldest cohort are 0.9 times the odds for a member of the middle cohort and 1.1 times the odds for a member of the youngest cohort; the ratio of 1971 to 1956 odds is 1.4; and the ratio of male to female odds is 1.8.

How do the response patterns of those who have reached adulthood since 1956 compare with those of young adults in 1956? Considering only the responses of persons aged 21–34 in 1956 and persons of the same age in 1971, we find that a model which takes as given the distributions of mention by year

Table 6.13. Analyses of Sex, Cohort, and Year Effects on Mentions of Factory Jobs and Hard, Dirty Jobs, Respectively, as Unsuitable for Women

Summary Measure and Data Set	Factory Chi-square	df	P.	Hard, Dirty Chi-square	df	P
Partition of sex-cohort differentiation, 1956						
Total	9.70	5	0.09	19.81	5	0.001
M 21–34 v. F 21–34	0.04	1	0.8	.48	1	0.5
M 35–49 v. F 35–49	5.51	1	0.019	6.08	1	0.014
M 50+ v. F 50+	0.31	1	0.6	11.44	1	0.001
35–49 v. 50+	3.83	1	0.05	0.18	1	0.7
21–34 v. 35+	0.02	1	0.9	1.62	1	0.2
Model with assumptions, 1956 data set						
a) Mutual independence	10.22	7	0.18	20.33	7	0.005
b) 3-way interaction	3.63	2	0.16	4.43	2	0.11
c) Diff. (a) – (b)	6.60	5	0.2	15.90	5	0.009
d) Sex-mention; cohort	–	–	–	6.63	6	0.4
e) Diff. (d) – (b)	–	–	–	2.20	4	0.7
f) Mention; cohort	13.24	8	0.10	–	–	–
g) Diff. (f) – (a)	3.02	1	0.08	–	–	–
Partition of sex-cohort differentiation, 1971						
Total	6.82	5	0.2	39.58	5	0.001
M 35–49 v. F 35–49	0.002	1	1	13.42	1	0.001
M 50–64 v. F 50–64	0.18	1	0.7	7.57	1	0.006
M 65+ v. F 65+	0.08	1	0.8	12.28	1	0.001
50–64 v. 65+	3.40	1	0.06	3.36	1	0.06
35–49 v. 50+	3.15	1	0.07	2.95	1	0.08
Model with assumptions, 1956 and 1971 data sets						
h) 6 2-way classifications	8.05	9	0.5	9.47	9	0.4
i) 4 3-way classifications	2.76	2	0.2	1.68	2	0.4
j) Diff. (h) – (i)	5.29	7	0.6	7.80	7	0.4
k) Sex-mention; cohort-mention; year-mention; cohort-year	–	–	–	14.04	12	0.3
l) Diff. (k) – (h)	–	–	–	4.57	3	0.2
m) Sex-mention; year-mention; cohort-year	–	–	–	19.72	14	0.14
n) Diff. (m) – (k)	–	–	–	5.68	2	0.06
o) Diff. (m) – (h)	–	–	–	10.25	5	0.15
p) Cohort-mention; year-mention; cohort-year; sex	12.13	13	0.5	–	–	–
q) Diff. (p) – (h)	4.08	4	0.4	–	–	–

and of sex provides an adequate fit for factory mentions (chi-square value 1.72, *df* 3, *P* 0.6). The implied odds of a factory mention are 53 for young adults in

1956 and 12 for young adults in 1971. A model which takes as given the distributions of mention by year and of mention by sex provides an adequate fit for mentions of hard, dirty work (chi-square value 1.87, *df* 3, *P* 0.4). The implied odds are 67 for young males and 45 for young females in 1956, 91 for young males and 62 for young females in 1971. Although we cannot make strict comparisons between the cohort analyses reported earlier and these analyses, the young adults of 1971 seem to resemble their elders with respect to the magnitude of the sex differentials. They voice objections to these kinds of work only slightly, if any, less often than do adults now in their late 30s and 40s.

An appreciable number of the respondents who mentioned either factory or hard, dirty jobs as work unsuitable for women mentioned both (lower panel, Table 6.12). Here we analyze mentions of factory work and mentions of hard, dirty work simultaneously to determine whether their relation differs by year, sex, and cohort. Our summary measure of the intensity of the relation between mentions is the odds ratio calculated from the fourfold table defined by mention of factory work (present, absent) and mention of hard, dirty work (present, absent).

Consider a 160-cell table displaying the relations among mentions of hard, dirty work (present, absent), factory-work mentions (present, absent), sex (male, female), cohort (ten identified by age in 1956 as 21–24, 25–29, . . . , 65 and over), and year of survey (1956, 1971). A model which takes as given the ten two-way classifications among the five items provides a more or less acceptable fit to the observed entries of the 160-cell table (chi-square value 122.10, *df* 104, *P* 0.11). An alternative model which takes as given the ten three-way classifications among these items provides an adequate fit (chi-square value 51.45, *df* 46, *P* 0.3), but the fit is not significantly better than that provided by the first model (chi-square value 70.66, *df* 58, *P* 0.12).

The foregoing results could be taken to mean that the relation between mentions of factory and hard, dirty work, respectively, is invariant by sex, cohort, and survey year. We cannot help but wonder, however, whether the model incorporating three-way classifications fails to provide a significantly better fit because negligible improvements in the estimation of demographic constraints, or relations among sex, cohort, and survey year, are associated with substantial losses in degrees of freedom. We, therefore, consider another model in which three-way classifications among the two types of mention and sex, cohort, and survey year, respectively, and two-way classifications among sex, cohort, and survey year are incorporated. This model provides an adequate fit to the data (chi-square value 100.27, *df* 93, *P* 0.3), and the fit is significantly better than that provided by the model incorporating only the ten two-way classifications (chi-square value 21.83, *df* 11, *P* 0.025).

The association between mentions of factory work and mentions of hard, dirty work (as measured by the odds ratio) is tighter for females than for males and became more intense between 1956 and 1971. Inspection of the odds suggests that the sex and year effects are to be explained on different grounds.

	Odds ratio	Odds (:100) of hard, dirty mention if factory mention	
		Present	Absent
Male 1956	0.77	68	88
Female 1956	1.44	59	41
Male 1971	1.22	144	118
Female 1971	2.30	125	55

Males and females who mention factory jobs differ little in their propensity to mention hard work; if no mention of factory jobs is made, however, males are much more likely to mention hard work than are females. In contrast, mentions of hard work on the part of respondents who mentioned factory work were much more common in 1971 than in 1956; no correspondingly large increase in mentions of hard work occurred on the part of respondents who did not mention factory work.

One might speculate that more limited acquaintance with the world of work leads females to equate a factory setting and physically demanding work. Objections to factory work for women based on physical demands of the job are more enduring than objections based on the possible displacement of men or coarsening of women (we have evidence that this is the case) because the former are less easily tested against reality. If this hunch is correct, the relation between mentions of factory and hard, dirty work should be loosest on the part of factory workers, most intense among those who have never been gainful workers.

As a check on our hunch, we array our data in a 96-cell table: four combinations of mentions (both factory and hard, factory only, hard only, neither) within each of four categories of sex and work status (male in manufacturing, other male, working female, nonworking female) within each of five categories defined by year and age (1956, aged 21–44; 1956, 45 and over; 1971, 21–35; 1971, 36–59; and 1971, aged 60 and over). A model which takes as given the three two-way classifications among the three items provides a more or less adequate fit (chi-square value 46.97, df 36, P 0.10). Calculations based on the model permit us to state: (a) respondents are differentiated by the fourfold classification of sex and work status to a significant degree; (b) the order of groups from loose to close association between factory mentions and mentions of hard, dirty work is males in manufacturing, other males, working females, and nonworking females; (c) the odds of a mention of hard, dirty work in the absence of a factory mention are highest for males in manufacturing, lowest for nonworking females. The findings are consistent with our speculation that the equation of factory with hard, dirty work is most pronounced on the part of persons least informed about the factory setting and physically demanding jobs.

One could argue that the hard-work response is a socially acceptable rationalization for the restriction of women's job opportunities and that manufacturing serves as a proxy for lesser education, fewer generations as an American urbanite, or any of a host of other characteristics posited to influence the male's view of the female role. We do not attempt to evaluate these alternative lines of argument here. Neither have we attempted to interpret intercohort differences in response pattern. We have at best illustrated that even when coding comparability in the narrow sense has been accomplished, the interpretation of response patterns to open-ended questions is fraught with difficulty.

THE SHIFT FROM A RESTRICTIVE POSITION

We now take a final look at responses to the question of whether there are kinds of work that women should not have (Q4). We noted earlier that the 1956 DAS analysts singled out for attention the differentials in attitude among males, working females, and nonworking females. Our analyses have focused on differentials by sex and age or cohort. We now combine these approaches, examining variation in response by sex and work status, by cohort, and by year.

We array our data in a 160-cell table: response to the question (no, yes) within four categories of sex and work status (male in manufacturing, other male, working female, nonworking female), within ten cohorts (defined by age in 1956 as $21-24, \ldots, 65$ and over), within survey year (1956, 1971). We find that the cell entries are not adequately estimated by a model which takes as given the six two-way classifications (chi-square value $126.94, df\,93, P\,0.01$), but that a model which takes as given the four three-way classifications does provide a satisfactory fit (chi-square value $30.26, df\,27, P\,0.3$). It is possible, however, to obtain a satisfactory fit also with a model which takes as given the two-way classifications of response by sex and work status, response by cohort, and response by year, and a single three-way classification describing the demographic constraints (chi-square value $76.31, df\,66, P\,0.18$); indeed, the model incorporating all three-way classifications does not provide a significantly better fit (chi-square value $46.05, df\,39, P\,0.3$).

We must accept as adequate a model based on the assumption that the relation between response and the respondent's sex and work status is invariant among cohorts and between years. The ordering of groups from greater to lesser propensity to oppose restrictions on women's work implied by the model is: working females, nonworking females, males outside the manufacturing sector, and males in manufacturing. Yet it was the finding that working females resembled males more closely in attitude than did nonworking females that received comment in the original analysis of the 1956 data set.

The presence of a differential between working and nonworking women in their attitude toward restrictions is, we believe, open to question in the 1956 data set (chi-square value 2.03, *df* 1, *P* 0.15). The presence of a differential in the 1971 data set is no more certain (chi-square value 1.84, *df* 1, *P* 0.18). Among 1971 respondents aged 36 or more (the cohorts surveyed in 1956), working women oppose restrictions more often than do nonworking women (chi-square value 5.17, *df* 1, *P* 0.02); no differential appears among the younger 1971 respondents, however (chi-square value 0.72, *df* 1, *P* 0.4).

The most striking feature of the data sets with which we have been working is the persistent sex differential in attitudes toward women's work. Our alternative models are consistent: the odds that a male opposes restrictions on women's work stand in a ratio of about 0.6 to the odds that a female opposes such restrictions. The ratio is invariant by cohort and year. It does not differ detectably between respondents who reached their majority after the date of the base-line survey and their elders.

A shift toward a less restrictive position occurred among members of each cohort, both males and females, between 1956 and 1971. The change did not occur differentially; instead the odds that a 1971 respondent opposes restrictions are about 1.6 times the odds for a 1956 respondent of the same sex and cohort.

Support for a nonrestrictive position is more widespread among the cohorts whose members were in their 40s in 1971, the teen-agers of World War II, than for any other cohort included in the base-line survey. From the standpoint of prospective change, the sentiments of those who have recently reached their majority are of special interest. The odds that a respondent who became 21 after 1956 favored no restrictions in 1971 were only 1.1 times the odds that a 40-year-old did so.

We incline to the view that it is the sex gap that merits attention in assessing the course of change in attitudes toward women's work. Given that males and females are represented in roughly equal numbers in the population, that a substantial sex differential in attitude persists at all ages, that a pervasive shift from a restrictive position is underway although restriction remains the majority sentiment, we conjecture that women's work will be among the controversial topics surveyed in future replications.

7

WOMEN, WORK, AND WAGES— TRENDS IN THE FEMALE OCCUPATION STRUCTURE*

Donald J. Treiman and Kermit Terrell

The period since 1940 has witnessed dramatic changes in the role of women. In 1940 about 30 percent of all adult women were in the labor force, while by 1970 fully half worked (U. S. Bureau of Labor Statistics, 1971:A–10). Little is known, however, about how the increase in the proportion of women working is related to changes in the occupational opportunities and experiences of women. What kinds of jobs have women been entering? Have new opporunities opened up or are women simply moving in increasing numbers into the jobs they have traditionally done? Indeed, what kinds of work have women done traditionally? What are the characteristics of jobs that are done mainly by women? And when women are employed, how are they treated? Are they overeducated relative to men doing the same work? Are they underpaid relative to their male co-workers once account is taken of their qualifications and amount of time spent working, or can the known income differences between male and female workers be attributed to the fact that men and women largely do different work? Finally, what are the effects of the movement of large numbers of women into the labor force? Is the position of women improving or declining relative to that of men?

Surprisingly little is known about these questions. We do know that some jobs are done almost exclusively by women and others almost exclusively by men, and that the sex composition of particular jobs tends to be highly constant over time (Hooks, 1947:67–69). In consequence, the labor force is and has been

*Preparation of this paper was supported by an NICHD grant to the Center for Policy Research to study "Female Occupational Structure–Determinants and Trends." We are indebted to Jonathan Kelley and Judith Herschman for their very helpful comments.

very strongly segregated by sex (Oppenheimer, 1970:Chap. 3; Gross, 1968; Hill, 1929:46–51). Moreover, in contrast to men, women are concentrated in a very small number of occupations. In 1970, about half of all working women were in only 20 occupations and no less than 30 percent were either elementary school teachers, retail sales clerks, bookkeepers, waitresses, or "stenographers, typists and secretaries"[1] (computed from Economic Report of the President, 1973: Table 33).

There is little definitive evidence as to why female workers are concentrated in particular jobs. Speculations include the demand for relatively skilled but poorly paid labor (Oppenheimer, 1968:224–226), the greater availability of part-time work in some jobs than in others (Ginsberg, 1968:197), ease of occupational entry or reentry, implicit norms prohibiting the supervision of men by women, and "tradition" (see Oppenheimer, 1968, for a review of these ideas). A major difficulty is that these explanations are basically ad hoc and lack rigorous empirical support. Changes in the sex composition of occupations are not well understood either. Oppenheimer (1973) has suggested that rising wage rates are one motivation for women to enter the labor force while Hodge and Hodge (1965) have argued that the entry of women workers tends to drive down wage rates. Similarly, it has been asserted both that the increasing availability of part-time work has pulled women into the labor force (Ginsberg, 1968), and, conversely, that the presence of larger numbers of working women led to the creation of more part-time jobs (National Manpower Council, 1957). In short, there is an abundance of questions and a paucity of answers regarding determinants and trends in the occupational status of women.

In general, previous attempts to analyze these various questions have tended to rely on fragmentary data for particular occupations. The only data available for any comprehensive set of occupations are those from the decennial population censuses, and they are somewhat limited in scope. In addition, the occupational classification used by the Bureau of the Census has changed with each new census, a disadvantage which enormously complicates longitudinal analysis. Nonetheless, these are the best data now available. In this chapter we propose to analyze data from the 1940, 1950, and 1960 censuses (the 1970 data are not available as this is written). Since the sexual composition of occupations cannot be understood independently of other aspects of the organization of work (e.g., differences in wage rates and hours worked by men and women), we

---

[1] This assertion points up the inherent difficulty in defining a "job." Obviously, the finer the definition of occupational categories, the less concentration is possible. Thus, for example, if stenographers, typists, and secretaries were treated as separate categories (as they were in the 1960 and 1970 censuses) women would appear to be less highly concentrated in a few occupations. We shall return to this issue in a more detailed way in the Appendix. The data referred to in the text were drawn from a tabulation of 197 specific occupational titles, grouped to allow a comparison of 1950, 1960, and 1970 census data.

Table 7.1. Percentage Distribution of Employed Civilian Labor Force Over
Major Occupation Groups, 1940—1970

Major Occupation Group	1940	1950	1960	1970
Professional and technical workers	7.5	8.1	11.0	14.4
Managers, officials, and proprietors	8.4	8.9	8.8	10.5
Clerical workers	10.4	13.2	15.9	17.6
Sales workers	6.5	7.1	7.6	6.0
Craftsmen and foremen	11.4	13.7	13.9	12.8
Operatives	18.5	20.4	19.7	17.6
Nonfarm laborers	6.9	6.1	5.0	4.6
Private household workers	4.7	2.6	2.8	2.0
Other service workers	7.3	7.8	8.9	10.4
Farmers and farm managers	11.6	7.8	4.1	2.3
Farm laborers and foremen	6.8	4.4	2.3	1.7
Total	100.0	100.1[a]	100.0	99.9[a]
N (thousands)	44,635	55,053	61,465	78,408

Sources: Subject reports on occupational characteristics from U. S. Bureau of the Census,
1942, 1943, 1953, 1963; Employment and Earnings, 1971.
Notes: Data from 1940—1960 classified according to the 1940 census detailed
occupational classification; 1970 data classified according to the 1960 census detailed
occupational classification. "Occupation not reported" is excluded from the totals in all
years.
[a]Differences from 100.0 percent due to rounding error.

propose to study trends and changes in a variety of occupational characteristics.
To provide a context for this analysis we begin, however, with a review of trends
in the distribution of the labor force over major occupation groups by sex and
race.

TRENDS IN THE COMPOSITION OF MAJOR OCCUPATION GROUPS

There has been striking change in some sectors of the labor force combined
with remarkable stability in other sectors. Table 7.1 shows the percent of the
total employed labor force[2] in each major occupation group for each decade
since 1940. Both the professional and clerical groups have grown markedly since
1940, while the farm categories have declined sharply. Aside from this, the only
notable shift has been a decrease in private household workers and an increase in

[2] In order to improve comparability over time, data are presented for the employed labor
force (which were the only data available for 1970) rather than the experienced civilian
labor force. However, a comparison of the employed and total ECLF distributions for 1940
through 1960 (not shown here) indicates that this decision has virtually no effect on the
results.

Table 7.2. Percentage Distribution of Employed Civilian Labor Force over Major Occupation Groups, by Race and Sex, 1940–1970

Major Occupation Group	White Male				White Female			
	1940	1950	1960	1970	1940	1950	1960	1970
Professional and technical workers	6.0	7.0	10.4	14.8	14.6	13.2	14.1	15.4
Managers, officials, and proprietors	10.7	11.5	12.0	15.2	4.4	4.8	4.3	4.8
Clerical workers	7.2	7.8	8.5	7.1	25.1	31.3	34.9	36.9
Sales workers	6.9	7.0	7.7	6.0	8.2	9.6	9.2	7.3
Craftsmen and foremen	15.8	19.5	20.8	20.6	1.2	1.6	1.3	1.0
Operatives	19.1	20.7	21.0	18.7	20.6	20.2	16.7	14.0
Nonfarm laborers	7.7	6.7	5.8	6.1	0.9	0.7	0.5	0.3
Private household workers	0.2	0.1	0.1	0.0	11.0	4.2	4.4	3.5
Other service workers	5.3	5.2	5.4	5.9	11.5	11.5	13.2	15.2
Farmers and farm managers	14.2	10.2	5.9	3.8	1.2	0.6	0.6	0.3
Farm laborers and foremen	6.9	4.3	2.4	1.7	1.2	2.3	1.0	1.4
Total	100.0	100.0	100.0	99.9	99.9	100.0	100.2	100.1
N (thousands)	30,509	35,973	37,834	43,937	9,517	13,550	17,549	26,076

Major Occupation Group	Nonwhite Male				Nonwhite Female			
	1940	1950	1960	1970	1940	1950	1960	1970
Professional and technical workers	1.9	2.2	4.1	7.9	4.3	5.5	8.1	11.5
Managers, officials, and proprietors	1.6	2.3	2.5	4.8	0.8	1.4	1.3	1.7
Clerical workers	1.2	3.2	5.8	7.5	1.0	4.5	9.5	19.7
Sales workers	1.0	1.3	1.7	1.7	0.6	1.4	1.9	2.7
Craftsmen and foremen	4.5	8.3	11.4	14.1	0.2	0.7	0.7	0.8
Operatives	12.3	20.5	25.3	28.1	6.7	14.9	14.0	17.0
Nonfarm laborers	20.7	23.0	21.0	17.4	1.0	1.5	1.1	0.8
Private household workers	3.0	1.1	0.8	0.2	58.7	41.4	36.9	18.0
Other service workers	12.3	13.6	15.0	12.8	10.6	19.0	22.7	26.9
Farmers and farm managers	21.5	13.6	4.8	1.5	3.2	1.8	0.7	0.1
Farm laborers and foremen	20.1	10.9	7.6	4.1	13.0	7.9	3.2	0.8
Total	100.1	100.0	100.0	100.1	100.1	100.0	100.1	100.0
N (thousands)	3,054	3,625	3,673	4,749	1,555	1,904	2,409	3,646

Sources: See Tabel 7.1.

other service workers. The service category as a whole has, however, continued to employ about the same proportion of the labor force throughout this 30-year period.[3]

How have these trends affected the occupational position of women and blacks?[4] Table 7.2 presents trends separately for white and nonwhite males and females. It is evident that the most dramatic shift has been the sharp increase in the status of black women workers. In 1940 about 60 percent of employed black women worked as domestic servants, whereas by 1970 less than 20 percent did so. This trend more than offset the increase in the proportion of black women doing other service work, so that the total percentage in service work of any kind dropped sharply. Furthermore, while black women were virtually excluded from clerical jobs in 1940, about 20 percent were in them by 1970. There was also a sharp increase in the proportion of professional workers, a similar increase in the proportion of operatives (which assuredly reflects the consequences of wartime demand), and a sharp reduction in the proportion of farm laborers. These trends indicate a marked upgrading of the occupational status of nonwhite women since 1940. Although nonwhite women still are disproportionately found in low status jobs, there is no denying that their position has improved substantially since 1940.

There has been a similar, although more modest, improvement in black males' occupational status. They made small but noticeable gains in all white-collar categories as well as in craft and operative jobs while the proportion who were farmers and farm laborers declined sharply. To some extent this reflects the general upgrading of the labor force but, as we shall see below, there was also an improvement relative to whites.

The distribution of white workers has been remarkably stable over this 30-year period. Male workers have shown small increases in the proportion of professional, managerial, and craft workers, and sharp reductions in the proportion in farming occupations, but these shifts corresponded to shifts in the total labor force. What is more interesting is that the occupational composition of white women has remained so stable in the face of the substantial increases in their labor force participation. There was a noticeable increase in the proportion of clerical workers although this was modest compared to that for black women, a small reduction in the proportion who work as operatives, and some reduction

---

[3] Obviously this shift does not necessarily imply that jobs once done in the household are now done outside the home, any more than the offsetting shifts in the proportions of white-collar workers and farm workers implies that farm workers are all becoming white-collar workers. Still, the shift in the relative size of the two service categories probably does reflect changes in the social organization of such services as cleaning, laundering, and meal preparation.

[4] Blacks constitute more than 90 percent of the nonwhite category and hence the two terms will be used interchangeably.

in the proportion of private household workers (which was partially offset by the increase in other service workers). But the basic stability is remarkable. The occupational position of white women will clearly need to be examined in more detail.

Table 7.3 allows us to look at the same data from a different perspective, focusing on the race and sex composition of workers in each occupational category. The left panel simply gives percentages. It allows us to ask what proportion of professional workers are white males, what proportion are white females, and so on. The "race-sex composition ratios" in the right-hand panel allow us to ask whether particular groups are disproportionately concentrated in particular occupations. Are white males, for example, overrepresented among managers, relative to their proportion of the labor force? To what extent are black females overrepresented among household service workers? What are the trends, if any, in these patterns? These ratios express the degree of overrepresentation or underrepresentation of particular race-sex categories in each major occupation group.[5] For example, the ratio of 0.8 for white males in professional occupations in 1940 indicates that only four-fifths as many white males were in these jobs as would be expected if all four race-sex categories had the same proportion of professional workers. In this sense, white males were underrepresented among professional workers in 1940. The use of such ratios is especially helpful given the changing sex composition of the labor force; they make it possible to assess trends in the relative concentration of women in particular occupational categories, controlling simultaneously for shifts in the distribution of the total labor force over major occupational groups and shifts in the proportion of women in the total labor force.

First, consider trends in the composition of the labor force. As we already know, women constitute a far larger proportion of the labor force than formerly. In 1940 less than a quarter of the labor force consisted of female workers, whereas by 1970 about 40 percent of all workers were women (details are in the top left panel). The trend toward increased labor force participation holds about equally for white and nonwhite women, and has had no effect on the racial composition of the labor force: blacks constituted about 10 percent of all workers throughout this period.

It is evident that major occupation groups differ substantially in their sex (and race) composition, and that the basic patterns have held constant since 1940 despite some minor trends. Managers, craftsmen, laborers, farmers, and

---

[5] Precisely, they give the ratio of the proportion of a given race-sex category, say white males, in a major occupation group to the proportion of the total labor force in that same major occupation group. An alternative definition, which yields an identical numerical value, is the ratio of the proportion of a particular major occupation group, e.g., professionals, that is in a particular race-sex category, e.g., white males, to the proportion of the total labor force that is in the same race-sex category.

Table 7.3. Composition of Major Occupation Groups by Sex and Race, 1940–1970

Major Occupation Group	Percentage Distributions				Race-Sex Composition Ratios[a]			
	1940	1950	1960	1970	1940	1950	1960	1970
Total employed civilian labor force								
White male	68.4	65.3	61.6	56.0				
Nonwhite male	6.8	6.6	6.0	6.1				
White female	21.3	24.6	28.6	33.3				
Nonwhite female	3.5	3.5	3.9	4.7				
No. in category (000's)	(44,635)	(55,053)	(61,465)	(78,408)				
Professional and technical workers								
White male	54.7	56.0	58.2	57.6	0.80	0.86	0.94	1.03
Nonwhite male	1.7	1.8	2.2	3.3	0.25	0.27	0.37	0.54
White female	41.5	39.8	36.7	35.6	1.95	1.62	1.28	1.07
Nonwhite female	2.0	2.3	2.9	3.7	0.57	0.66	0.74	0.79
No. in category (000's)	(3,353)	(4,481)	(6,754)	(11,291)				
Managers, officials, and proprietors								
White male	87.3	84.5	83.9	81.1	1.28	1.29	1.36	1.45
Nonwhite male	1.3	1.7	1.7	2.8	0.19	0.26	0.28	0.46
White female	11.1	13.2	13.9	15.2	0.52	0.54	0.49	0.46
Nonwhite female	0.3	0.6	0.6	0.8	0.09	0.17	0.15	0.17
No. in category (000's)	(3,754)	(4,894)	(5,408)	(8,233)				
Clerical workers								
White male	47.5	38.6	32.8	22.6	0.69	0.59	0.53	0.40
Nonwhite male	0.8	1.6	2.2	2.6	0.12	0.24	0.37	0.43
White female	51.4	58.6	62.7	69.7	2.41	2.38	2.19	2.09
Nonwhite female	0.3	1.2	2.3	5.2	0.09	0.34	0.59	1.11
No. in category (000's)	(4,653)	(7,241)	(9,773)	(13,800)				

Table 7.3. Composition of Major Occupation Groups by Sex and Race, 1940–1970 (cont.)

Major Occupation Group	Percentage Distributions				Race-Sex Composition Ratios[a]			
	1940	1950	1960	1970	1940	1950	1960	1970
Sales workers								
White male	71.9	64.8	62.9	56.0	1.05	0.99	1.02	1.00
Nonwhite male	1.0	1.2	1.3	1.7	0.15	0.18	0.22	0.28
White female	26.8	33.3	34.8	40.5	1.26	1.35	1.22	1.22
Nonwhite female	0.3	0.7	1.0	2.1	0.09	0.20	0.26	0.45
No. in category (000's)	(2,909)	(3,893)	(4,644)	(4,704)				
Craftsmen and foremen								
White male	95.0	92.9	92.2	90.2	1.39	1.42	1.50	1.61
Nonwhite male	2.7	4.0	4.9	6.7	0.40	0.61	0.82	1.10
White female	2.3	2.9	2.7	2.6	0.11	0.12	0.09	0.08
Nonwhite female	0.1	0.2	0.2	0.3	0.03	0.06	0.05	0.06
No. in category (000's)	(5,076)	(7,557)	(8,547)	(10,036)				
Operatives								
White male	70.4	66.4	65.4	59.5	1.03	1.02	1.06	1.06
Nonwhite male	4.5	6.6	7.7	9.7	0.66	1.00	1.28	1.59
White female	23.8	24.4	24.1	26.5	1.12	0.99	0.84	0.80
Nonwhite female	1.3	2.5	2.8	4.5	0.37	0.71	0.72	0.96
No. in category (000's)	(8,264)	(11,210)	(12,127)	(13,800)				
Nonfarm laborers								
White male	76.1	71.6	71.5	74.3	1.11	1.10	1.16	1.33
Nonwhite male	20.5	24.7	25.0	22.9	3.01	3.74	4.17	3.75
White female	2.9	2.8	2.7	2.2	0.14	0.11	0.09	0.07
Nonwhite female	0.5	0.8	0.8	0.8	0.14	0.23	0.21	0.17
No. in category (000's)	(3,074)	(3,372)	(3,093)	(3,607)				

Table 7.3. Composition of Major Occupation Groups by Sex and Race, 1940–1970 (cont.)

Major Occupation Group	Percentage Distributions				Race-Sex Composition Ratios[a]			
	1940	1950	1960	1970	1940	1950	1960	1970
Private household workers								
White male	2.6	2.3	1.8	0.0	0.04	0.04	0.03	0.00
Nonwhite male	4.3	2.8	1.7	0.6	0.63	0.42	0.28	0.10
White female	49.8	39.9	44.7	58.2	2.34	1.62	1.56	1.75
Nonwhite female	43.3	55.1	51.8	41.9	12.37	15.74	13.28	8.91
No. in category (000's)	(2,107)	(1,432)	(1,716)	(1,568)				
Other service workers								
White male	49.5	43.6	37.6	31.8	0.72	0.67	0.61	0.57
Nonwhite male	11.6	11.5	10.1	7.5	1.71	1.74	1.68	1.23
White female	33.8	36.2	42.3	48.6	1.59	1.47	1.48	1.46
Nonwhite female	5.1	8.5	10.0	12.0	1.46	2.43	2.56	2.55
No. in category (000's)	(3,240)	(4,271)	(5,456)	(8,154)				
Farmers and farm managers								
White male	84.1	85.7	88.3	92.6	1.23	1.31	1.43	1.65
Nonwhite male	12.7	11.5	7.0	4.0	1.87	1.74	1.17	0.66
White female	2.2	2.0	4.0	4.3	0.10	0.08	0.14	0.13
Nonwhite female	1.0	0.8	0.7	0.2	0.29	0.23	0.18	0.04
No. in category (000's)	(5,161)	(4,284)	(2,508)	(1,803)				
Farm laborers and foremen								
White male	69.4	64.5	63.5	56.0	1.01	0.99	1.03	1.00
Nonwhite male	20.1	16.4	19.5	14.6	2.96	2.48	3.25	2.39
White female	3.9	12.9	11.7	27.4	0.18	0.52	0.41	0.82
Nonwhite female	6.6	6.2	5.3	2.2	1.89	1.77	1.36	0.47
No. in category (000's)	(3,054)	(2,416)	(1,440)	(1,333)				

Sources: Computed from Tables 7.1 and 7.2.
[a] Ratio of proportion of workers in major occupation group who are of particular race and sex to proportion of all employed workers who are of the same race and sex.

farm laborers are overwhelmingly male; professional, clerical, sales, operative, and other service workers tend to have sizable proportions of both sexes, and private household workers are almost exclusively female. Blacks are only represented in substantial proportions in service, laboring, and agricultural jobs. The pattern of sexual segregation is, if anything, even more pronounced among blacks than among whites. Around half of all private household workers are black women and, increasingly, black women are to be found in other service work. Black men, by contrast, make up substantial proportions of both farm and nonfarm laborers and smaller but still substantial proportions of farmers and other service workers (although they are increasingly being replaced in these jobs by white and black women, respectively).

There are two notable trends in these data: first, a modest tendency for blacks (especially women) to improve their position over time; and second, the increasing domination of clerical, sales, and service work by women. However, the "composition-ratios" in the right-hand half of the table make it clear that the latter trend largely reflects the increased proportion of women in the labor force. The overconcentration of white female workers in clerical, sales, and service jobs has remained relatively unchanged since 1940 while the concentration of black women in these jobs has increased sharply (with the partial exception of private household work). This indicates that white females moved into these jobs just about as rapidly as they moved into the labor force. But black women moved into these particular jobs more rapidly than they moved into the labor force as a whole. By contrast, black women were moving rapidly out of farm laboring jobs where, however, they continued to remain overrepresented until 1970.

Of special interest from the standpoint of trends in female employment are the highest status occupations, those in the professional and managerial sectors. Ironically, equality of occupational opportunity by sex and race has substantially increased in the professional and technical category, but at a clear cost to white women. In 1940 white females were strongly overrepresented in these jobs, and black workers of both sexes sharply underrepresented, but by 1970 the ratios were all much closer to unity. In the managerial category, by contrast, the overconcentration of white males *increased* over time, albeit only slightly, while white females remained underrepresented by essentially the same amount. As with the other white-collar categories, blacks of both sexes increased their representation.

All in all, there has been a rather complicated interaction between shifts in the distribution of the labor force, increases in the proportion of working women, and (presumably) changes in norms regarding occupational discrimination by race and sex. The result has been a noticeable convergence in the occupational distributions of whites and blacks, particularly among females. Black women in ever larger numbers have broken out of the prison of domestic

Table 7.4. Indexes of Dissimilarity[a] in Distribution of Employed Civilian Labor Force over Major Occupation Groups by Race and Sex, 1940—1970

Comparison	1940	1950	1960	1970
Males vs. females				
White	0.46	0.43	0.44	0.44
Nonwhite	0.58	0.50	0.52	0.49
Whites vs. nonwhites				
Males	0.43	0.36	0.35	0.30
Females	0.62	0.52	0.45	0.30

Source: Computed from Table 7.2.

[a]The index of dissimilarity (Duncan and Duncan, 1955) is computed by summing one-half of the absolute value of the differences between the proportions of each category. The index is interpretable as the minimum proportion of either population being compared which would have to be shifted in order to make the two distributions equal.

service or unskilled farm labor to which they were largely confined in 1940 and have, for better or worse, come to largely share the occupational fates of white women. Trends in the occupational distribution of white women are not so obvious or so simple. Certainly, the major increase in white female employment since 1940 has been in clerical jobs, but the general pattern is one of no reduction in occupational segregation by sex among whites. These trends (and nontrends) are summarized in Table 7.4, which gives indexes of dissimilarity over major occupation groups between the two races.

What are the processes that create these gross trends? Precisely which jobs have women moved into as they have increasingly entered the labor force, and why have they gone into these jobs and not others? What special characteristics distinguish jobs which employ high proportions of women from those in which few women work? Finally, how similar are women workers to men doing the same work, and to what extent does this similarity depend upon the proportion of women workers? For example, do women have to be better qualified than men to break into jobs which are dominated by male workers, and do men have to be especially well paid to keep them in jobs in which most of their co-workers are women? Understanding of the sexual division of labor requires a detailed analysis of the structure of occupational opportunities and rewards for men and for women—an investigation of patterns of covariation among characteristics of specific occupations. It is to such an analysis that we now turn.

DATA AND PROCEDURES

In the remainder of the chapter we explore the interrelations among various characteristics of the detailed occupational categories of the U. S. census for the years 1940, 1950, and 1960, and also interrelations among changes in these characteristics over this 20-year period (recall that the 1970 data were not yet available when this chapter was prepared). Summary data on number of employees, levels of education, income, age, hours worked per week and weeks worked per year, class of worker (percent self-employed and percent in public employment), and urban concentration in each of the three census years are tabulated for each of 67 occupational categories, separately for males and females (and for some purposes for white males). In addition, the percent female is tabulated for each occupation.

There are several limitations to these data. First, in order to achieve comparability over time, we had to recode all the data into a single classification scheme. Unfortunately the 1940 data for females are available only in a highly truncated form, so the 1950 and 1960 data had to be substantially aggregated in order to match the 1940 classification. To explore the consequences of this loss of detail, we carried out extensive comparisons of the 1950 and 1960 data under two alternative classification schemes. These comparisons, reported in the Appendix, yield results which are qualititatively similar and yet sufficiently different to caution us about the severity of measurement problems in the study of social change. A second limitation is that these data do not permit a comparison between whites and nonwhites. Even with samples as large as these (the 1940 and 1960 occupational data are based on a 5 percent sample of the population and the 1950 data on a $3\frac{1}{3}$ percent sample), many occupational categories do not have enough nonwhite employees to give reliable estimates, especially when distinctions are made by sex. Using 100 sample cases as a minimum for inclusion, about a third of the 67 occupational categories would have had to be omitted for nonwhite males and nearly half for nonwhite females. Accordingly, we chose simply to drop the race distinction for the remainder of the analysis.

The rest of this chapter will consist of an analysis of the characteristics of *occupational categories*, not of individuals. But occupations differ substantially in number of employees—particularly when sex distinctions are taken into account. So we had to decide whether to treat each occupational category as a unit without regard to its size or to weight it proportionally to the number of incumbents. An interest in the occupational structure would appear to dictate an unweighted analysis—to determine, for example, what distinguishes occupations with high proportions of female workers from those with mostly male incumbents. But such an analysis does not tell us about the occupational experience of the average person, or the average woman. For that, we should weight our observations according to the total number of employees (or the number of female employees) in each occupation. Fortunately, weighting the observations has very little effect on the results, as is documented in the Appendix. Because of the greater conceptual clarity, the main analysis will treat each occupational category as a single observation, without regard to the number of workers.

DETERMINANTS OF OCCUPATIONAL COMPOSITION: CROSS-SECTIONAL ANALYSIS

We begin by asking what distinguishes "man's work" from "woman's work," i.e., what characteristics of occupations are associated with higher or lower proportions of female employees? We will study this question separately for 1940, 1950, and 1960, to determine whether the relations change over time.

There are theoretical reasons to expect a number of factors to be related to the proportion of women workers: (1) If Oppenheimer (1968) is correct in asserting that women workers are utilized by employers who need skilled labor but are unwilling to pay enough for it to attract males, we would expect to find disproportionately more women in occupations which pay poorly relative to the incumbent's education. (2) To the extent that women find part-time work more attractive, occupations in which the average hours worked per year is relatively low should have high proportions of women workers. (3) Because women ordinarily must combine outside employment with family responsibilities they are likely to prefer jobs in urban areas, because in such places services which relieve household chores—e.g., prepared food shops, laundries, etc.—are more readily available. Urban jobs should therefore have higher percentages of female workers. (4) We know that women are less likely to be self-employed than are men (U. S. Bureau of the Census, 1963:Table 21). This is presumably because they face discrimination when it comes to raising capital and organizing a business and in part because their greater home responsibilities (Hedges and Barnett, 1972) make it more difficult to devote as much attention to a business as men can. Hence women should be less likely to enter jobs which are largely done on a self-employed basis. (5) Insofar as public agencies are less discriminatory than are private businesses, jobs which are concentrated in the public sector should have higher proportions of women than other jobs. (6) Finally, we entertain two contradictory hypotheses about the relation between age and the distribution of women. Since women have much weaker labor force attachments than men, moving in and out of the labor force much more frequently (Saben, 1967), we would expect them to be underrepresented in those jobs which require substantial seniority for entry. Insofar as seniority can be measured by the average age of employees, we would expect fewer women in occupations where the average age is high. However, it may well be that age is not a good indicator of seniority, but rather that those jobs with many older workers are in fact declining occupations which are avoided by young workers. In this case, such jobs may be especially open to women, and would lead to a prediction of a positive effect of age on percent female.

Our strategy, then, is to regress the proportion of females in each occupational category on the set of occupational characteristics just discussed. Wherever possible, we characterize occupations by the attributes of their white male incumbents in order to avoid confounding the dependent and independent

Table 7.5. Correlations, Means, and Standard Deviations for Selected Occupational Characteristics

	E	I	A	H	SE	GE	U	Mean	S.D.
				1940					
F: % female	-0.02	-0.14	-0.08	-0.04	-0.16	0.15	0.30	34.4	30.3
E: Mean yrs. of school (WM)[a]		0.62	0.12	0.28	0.22	0.47	0.24	10.3	2.3
I: Mean annual income (TM)[b]			0.11	0.17	-0.23	0.39	0.36	1,132	578
A: Mean age (WM)				0.63	0.62	-0.03	0.20	39.7	5.1
H: Mean hrs. worked/yr. (TM)					0.52	0.10	0.18	2,022	439
SE: % self-employed (WM)						-0.24	0.05	17.6	27.4
GE: % govt. employed (WM)							-0.10	10.2	17.5
U: % urban (WM)								74.9	18.2
				1950					
F: % female	-0.05	-0.32	-0.02	-0.28	-0.23	0.14	0.23	37.5	29.3
E: Mean yrs. of school (WM)		0.81	0.08	0.30	0.26	0.47	0.35	10.6	2.4
I: Mean annual income (WM)			0.32	0.52	0.47	0.11	0.41	3,247	1,334
A: Mean age (WM)				0.45	0.52	-0.01	0.29	41.3	4.8
H: Mean hrs. worked/yr. (TM)					0.73	-0.05	-0.02	1,959	307
SE: % self-employed (WM)						-0.23	-0.10	15.6	24.6
GE: % govt. employed (WM)							0.14	10.9	17.0
U: % urban (WM)								76.6	19.7
				1960					
F: % female	-0.12	-0.40	-0.04	-0.32	-0.17	0.16	0.20	38.9	30.1
E: Mean yrs. of school (WM)		0.81	0.05	0.35	0.27	0.45	0.39	10.9	2.5
I: Mean annual income (WM)			0.32	0.63	0.43	0.07	0.43	5,389	2,379
A: Mean age (WM)				0.52	0.60	-0.07	0.29	41.6	4.9
H: Mean hrs. worked/yr. (TM)					0.63	-0.09	0.06	1,926	323
SE: % self-employed (WM)						-0.23	0.05	15.6	23.5
GE: % govt. employed (WM)							0.20	12.5	18.5
U: % urban (WM)								76.2	17.2

[a] White males.
[b] Total males; for these variables tabulations by race were not available.

variables. For example, mean incomes may be low in occupations which employ high proportions of women simply because women in general earn less than men. But this cannot account for any correlation between the mean income of white male incumbents and the percentage of female workers. In relating the percent female to the characteristics of white male incumbents, we assume that the attributes of these workers (who constitute the bulk of the labor force) set definitions of jobs for other workers as well (see Siegel, 1970). Means, standard deviations, and intercorrelations among the variables included in the analysis are presented in Table 7.5 separately for each of the three census years, and regression estimates are reported in Table 7.6 in both unstandardized and standardized form.

Income dominates the equations in all three years. Occupations in which white males are poorly paid, net of education, hours worked, and the other variables in the equation, have higher proportions of female workers than do other occupations. In 1950 and 1960 (but not in 1940) women were in occupations with high educational levels, net of other variables in the equation. Taken together, these results indicate that Oppenheimer's (1968) claim is correct: "women's work" is that in which men are underpaid relative to their education or overeducated relative to their earning power. However, the causal connection is unclear—to what extent are women limited to such jobs and to what extent does their presence force down wage rates for male workers? We will attempt a partial answer to this question later in the chapter, in our analysis of changes in occupational composition. Aside from the socioeconomic status of occupations, the other determinant of their sex-ratio is the extent to which white male incumbents are urban. As predicted, women are to be found in higher proportions in more urbanized occupations.

It is of particular interest to note what factors are *unrelated* to the sex composition of occupations. Contrary to expectations, women are *not* dispro-portionately concentrated in occupations which are characterized by short work years, high rates of public employment, or low rates of self-employment among white male workers, net of other factors. Nor is the proportion of women related to the mean age of white male workers. Although the zero order correlations are all in the direction hypothesized in our theoretical discussion, these correlations are apparently accounted for by the pattern of interconnec-tions among the various independent variables. Thus, we are left with the single strong finding: women work at jobs in which men are paid badly relative to their qualifications, their effort, and their other characteristics. Moreover, the strength of this pattern has been increasing over time, as indicated both by the steadily increasing size of the standardized coefficients for income and education and the increase in the explained variance; by 1960 about half of the variance among occupations in percent female can be attributed to variations in education, income, and urbanism.

Table 7.6. Regression of Percent Female in Occupations on Selected Characteristics of White Male Incumbents

Independent Variable	Metric Coefficients			Standardized Coefficients		
	1940	1950	1960	1940	1950	1960
Mean years of school	2.60	12.0[a]	11.5[a]	0.200	0.961	0.969
Mean annual income (000's)	-29.4[a]	-29.1[a]	-18.9[a]	-0.560	-1.32	-1.49
Mean age	0.303	1.12	1.21	0.051	0.184	0.196
Mean hrs. worked/yr. (00's)	0.267	0.298	1.33	0.039	0.031	0.142
% self-employed	-0.338	0.008	-0.039	-0.306	0.007	-0.030
% govt. employed	0.307	-0.386	-0.397	0.177	-0.224	-0.244
% urban	0.666[a]	0.664[a]	0.775[a]	0.400	0.406	0.443
Constant	-23.6	-93.3	-114			
R²	0.268	0.429	0.478			

[a]Significant at 0.01 level.

Table 7.7. **Intersex Correlations of Selected Occupational Characteristics**

Variable	1940	1950	1960
Number of workers	0.07	0.11	0.14
Mean years of school completed	0.97	0.97	0.98
Mean annual income	0.92	0.95	0.92
Mean residual income[a]	0.85	0.86	0.82
Mean age	0.80	0.67	0.65
Mean annual hours worked	0.91	0.82	0.75
% self-employed	0.98	0.96	0.93
% government employed	0.95	0.95	0.92
% urban	0.93	0.93	0.94
% married, spouse present	0.23	0.06	0.14

[a]Actual mean income minus income predicted from mean years of school completed and mean hours worked.

In characterizing occupations by attributes of white male incumbents we appear to risk misrepresenting the situation of the female labor force. For example, although there proves to be no relationship between the proportion self-employed among white male workers and the sex-ratio of occupations, there could be such a relationship when the proportion self-employed among female workers is considered, precisely for the reasons outlined above: where work is done on a self-employed basis, it is more difficult for women to manage. As it happens, our concern proves groundless because of the extraordinary similarity of the *occupational structure*—the pattern of interrelationships among occupational characteristics—for the male and female labor force. For the most part, occupational characteristics computed separately for male and female workers are extremely highly correlated, as the coefficients in Table 7.7 indicate. In occupations where men are highly educated, women are also highly educated; where men are well paid, women are also well paid (although, as we shall see, not as well as men); and so on. The only exceptions are in number of workers, as we have already noted above; and marital status, which will concern us below. Moreover, with the exception of marital status, essentially the same patterns of relationships among occupational characteristics hold for male and female workers, as can be seen in Table 7.8. In fact, the consistency of the relationships is astonishingly high even when the means and standard deviations differ (men earn more and work longer hours in the average occupation than do women, and there is more variability among occupations in these traits than for women). With respect to marital status, however, the differences between the sexes are pronounced. In high status occupations men are more likely and women less likely to be married than in low status occupations, although in the average occupation men are substantially more likely to be married than women. Interestingly, both men and women are less likely to be married in occupations

Table 7.8. Correlations, Means, and Standard Deviations for Selected Occupational Characteristics, Separately for Male and Female Labor Force (males above the diagonal; females below)

	F	E	I	R	A	H	M	Mean	S.D.
					1940				
F: % female		0.01	-0.02	-0.04	-0.31	-0.12	-0.40	29.7	28.4
E: Mean yrs. of school	0.01		0.64	0.00[a]	0.16	0.29	0.27	10.2	2.4
I: Mean annual income	0.03	0.71		0.77	0.15	0.16	0.46	1,132	578
R: Mean residual income	0.03	0.00[a]	0.71		0.08	0.00[a]	0.39	0.0[a]	446
A: Mean age	-0.34	0.17	0.00	-0.16		0.64	0.66	39.6	5.0
H: Mean annual hours working	0.00	0.31	0.21	0.00[a]	0.54		0.56	2,022	439
M: % married, spouse present	-0.38	-0.45	-0.31	0.01	0.02	-0.18		63.9	15.0
Mean	29.7	10.5	681	0.0[a]	37.1	1,775	35.9		
Standard deviation	28.4	2.3	345	244	6.1	386	9.3		
					1950				
F: % female		-0.05	-0.32	-0.41	-0.04	-0.27	-0.47	37.5	29.3
E: Mean yrs. of school	-0.05		0.82	0.00[a]	0.11	0.30	0.36	10.5	2.4
I: Mean annual income	-0.34	0.80		0.50	0.35	0.51	0.65	3,210	1,354
R: Mean residual income	-0.51	0.00[a]	0.51		0.25	0.00[a]	0.46	0.0[a]	680
A: Mean age	-0.05	0.01	0.11	-0.04		0.49	0.50	41.1	4.6
H: Mean annual hours working	-0.11	0.21	0.47	0.00[a]	0.37		0.55	1,959	304
M: % married, spouse present	-0.28	-0.46	-0.21	0.24	-0.15	-0.01		70.4	14.1
Mean	37.5	10.7	1,948	0.0[a]	39.7	1,650	48.1		
Standard deviation	29.3	2.3	776	402	4.9	286	9.1		

Table 7.8. Correlations, Means, and Standard Deviations for Selected Occupational Characteristics, Separately for Male and Female Labor Force (males above the diagonal; females below) (cont.)

	F	E	I	R	A	H	M	Mean	S.D.
				1960					
F: % female		-0.11	-0.40	-0.45	-0.05	-0.31	-0.51	38.9	30.1
E: Mean yrs. of school	-0.12		0.82	0.00[a]	0.06	0.38	0.31	10.6	2.8
I: Mean annual income	-0.36	0.81		0.46	0.33	0.62	0.64	5,282	2,396
R: Mean residual income	-0.46	0.00[a]	0.52		0.20	0.00[a]	0.36	0.0[a]	1,095
A: Mean age	-0.02	0.02	0.08	-0.04		0.53	0.51	41.5	4.8
H: Mean annual hours working	-0.13	0.18	0.42	0.00[a]	0.31		0.70	1,927	317
M: % married, spouse present	-0.09	-0.36	-0.18	0.02	-0.02	0.28		72.6	15.3
Mean	38.9	10.7	2,973	0.0[a]	42.3	1,537	56.5		
Standard deviation	30.1	2.4	1,298	675	4.0	284	9.1		

[a]Zero by definition of residual income variable (see Table 7.7).

dominated by women, and this pattern has been increasing over time for men and decreasing for women. It is not unlikely that this pattern of change is related to the relative loss of status of occupations dominated by women, a topic which we take up explicitly below. First, however, we must lay the groundwork with an explicit comparison of the socioeconomic position of men and women who do the same work.

It has sometimes been argued that women are relegated to jobs for which they are overqualified and are denied opportunities to employ their full capabilities. Taking educational attainment as a good indicator of skill, this proposition would imply that, job for job, women are more highly educated than men. However, this proves not to be the case. In the average occupation, women are hardly any better educated than men, but there is slightly less variance across occupations in the educational level of women workers (see Table 7.8). Moreover, as we noted above, the correlation between the educational levels of male and female workers is close to unity: in jobs where women are well educated, men are also well educated. However, when the mean years of school completed by females is regressed on the same variable for males, the slopes are in all cases less than unity, which (given that the means are essentially equal) implies that in jobs requiring the most education women tend to be less qualified than men whereas in the low skill jobs women tend to be better educated. It would be unwise to make too much of these differences, however, since the slopes are all near unity (ranging from 0.93 in 1940 to 0.86 in 1960), which is still another indication of the essential similarity in the skill requirements for male and female workers.[6]

Of course, it is possible that those occupations that employ large numbers of women require more education on the part of women workers than on the part of male workers. This, indeed, would be the prediction of the theory (Oppenheimer, 1968) that women tend to be employed in occupations in which it is difficult to recruit male workers. To the extent that this is so, employers may be forced to hire relatively less qualified males. To test this hypothesis, we computed the mean of the difference in the years of school completed by male and female incumbents of each occupation, with each category weighted proportionally to the number of females. This tells us whether the average female worker is better (or more poorly) educated than the average male worker in the same occupation. The answer is that she is not: for no year does this coefficient depart from zero up to the third decimal place. The average woman worker is exactly as well educated as the average man doing the same job.

---

[6] Of course, here as in the other analysis reported in this chapter, we must be sensitive to differences within occupational categories. To the extent that women are concentrated in the lower status jobs within a category, it may indeed be true that they are overeducated relative to men. But this is a level of specificity that is beyond our ability to achieve with the data at hand.

Table 7.9. Regressions over Occupations of Mean Income on Mean Years of School and Mean Hours Worked per Year, Separately for Male and Female Workers

	Metric coefficients			Standardized coefficients		R^2
	Constant	Education	Hours	Education	Hours	
1940						
Male	−372	153	−0.03	0.642	−0.021	0.405
Female	−401	105	−0.01	0.710	−0.012	0.499
1950						
Male	−3,636	411	1.29	0.732	0.289	0.748
Female	−2,162	251	0.87	0.731	0.319	0.732
1960						
Male	−6,313	589	2.78	0.684	0.367	0.791
Female	−3,274	402	1.28	0.757	0.280	0.729

Note: All coefficients significant at the 0.05 level except the hours-worked coefficients for 1940.

Moreover, since the difference in educational levels of male and female workers is uncorrelated with the sex ratio of occupations (see Table 7.10, below), it cannot be the case that in occupations where there are small proportions of women they must be unusually well educated in order to overcome entry barriers. Nor can it be the case that where there are small proportions of male workers, employers must bribe men to accept jobs by lowering the educational requirements for them.

Although women are not overeducated relative to men, they are very much underpaid. Job for job, women simply earn less than men do (Table 7.8) and since (as we just saw) they are about as well educated, this implies that the return on education is very much less for women than for men. However, since women also tend to work less than men, job for job (compare the means in Table 7.8), this may in part account for the observed income difference. To estimate the magnitude of these effects, we regressed mean income on mean education and mean annual hours worked over occupational categories, separately for male and female workers. The results are reported in Table 7.9.

Inspecting these coefficients, the general pattern is clear: the payoff for each additional year of schooling in all three years is for women about two-thirds of what it is for men, controlling hours worked; and hourly earnings for women are substantially less than they are for men,[7] controlling level of education. A

---

[7] In 1940 hours worked has no effect on annual earnings, net of education, but this may reflect the nature of the data more than social reality. The income measure utilized is mean annual income in 1939 for those individuals in each occupational category in April 1940; the hours worked variable is constructed by taking the product of "hours worked the previous week" in April 1940 and weeks worked the previous year (1939), again aggregated

striking feature of these data, which are based on occupational averages, is their similarity to individual level data. Here we show that, job for job, women benefit less from their investment in education or from their level of effort than do men; but we do not take account of the fact that men and women by and large do different work. However, data reported by Fuchs (1971) and others for individual workers show that the average hourly earnings of women are 60 percent of those for men, and that this ratio rises to about two-thirds when a variety of controls are introduced.

Not only are women paid less for doing the same work, but in 1950 and 1960 (although not in 1940) both women and men were paid less for doing "woman's work," that is, jobs with high proportions of female employees. This is true both with respect to actual income and with respect to the difference between actual income and income expected on the basis of education and hours worked, which we call "residual income" (Table 7.8). Recall that we argued above that women tend to be relegated to jobs which pay poorly relative to their educational requirements and other characteristics. It is of course possible to view the causal sequence as going in the opposite direction—jobs may pay poorly because they are mostly done by women and hence employers need not bid as high to attract workers (see Hodge and Hodge, 1965). Some evidence supporting this causal ordering is to be found in the fact that the difference between male and female mean income (actual or "residual") is on the average greatest in those jobs which employ small proportions of women (Table 7.10); in short, while both men and women profit by working in occupations dominated by men, the payoff for men is greater than for women. This may come about because employers have less incentive to pay men well where there are many women competing with them for the same jobs, and because women have to accept inferior wages in order to break into male-dominated occupations. In any event, the tendency for income differences to be greater in occupations which employ relatively few women is increasing over time, as the coefficients in Table 7.10 indicate.

Before turning to a general analysis of changes over time, however, one final difference between the male and female occupational structures must be noted—the tendency for the average hours worked by men to vary more with the sex ratio of occupations than the average hours worked by women in the same jobs. As Tables 7.8 and 7.10 indicate, women on the average work less than do men, but women doing "women's work" work hardly any less than women doing "men's work." By contrast, men doing "women's work" work substan-

---

over all incumbents of each occupation as of April 1940. Ordinarily these definitions of variables would have little consequence for data aggregated into occupational categories because of the enormous stability of occupational characteristics over time. But the labor market was so unstable in 1939–1940 that substantial error may have been introduced in the construction of these variables.

Table 7.10. Correlations among Measures of Differences between Male and Female Workers in Each Occupation

		EΔ	IΔ	RΔ	HΔ	Mean	S.D.
				1940			
F:	Percent female	-0.01	-0.08	-0.09	-0.30	29.7	28.4
EΔ:	Education difference		0.10	-0.24	0.17	-0.29	0.60
IΔ:	Income difference			0.87	0.10	451	292
RΔ:	Residual income difference				0.07	0.0[a]	270
HΔ:	Hours worked difference					247	181
				1950			
F:	Percent female	-0.00	-0.27	-0.19	-0.29	37.5	29.3
EΔ:	Education difference		0.48	-0.13	0.18	-0.16	0.56
IΔ:	Income difference			0.50	0.25	1,262	657
RΔ:	Residual income difference				-0.25	0.0[a]	393
HΔ:	Hours worked difference					308	179
				1960			
F:	Percent female	-0.04	-0.37	-0.28	-0.29	38.9	30.1
EΔ:	Education difference		0.62	0.03	0.21	-0.04	0.62
IΔ:	Income difference			0.48	0.50	2,309	1,293
RΔ:	Residual income difference				-0.08	0.0[a]	667
HΔ:	Hours worked difference					390	214

[a] Zero by definition of residual income variable (see Table 7.7).

tially less than men doing "men's work." The consequence, of course, is that the difference between the hours worked by men and by women is negatively correlated with the percent female in occupations. Taken together, the patterns we have been reviewing suggest that the position of women in the occupational structure has, if anything, become relatively worse over time. Although the evidence is not completely conclusive, differences between the characteristics of male and female workers, notably income, appear to be increasing over time, and to be increasingly correlated with the proportion of women in occupations. The obvious question is, then, how did this come about, how do transformations of the position of particular occupations occur? It is to these issues that we now turn.

STABILITY AND CHANGE IN OCCUPATIONAL STRUCTURE: LONGITUDINAL ANALYSIS

Although we know that the proportion of women in the labor force has been increasing steadily since 1940 and that the distribution of female workers over major occupation groups has changed substantially during that period, it is not at all clear precisely into what jobs, or what sorts of jobs, women are moving. The remainder of this chapter will directly address this question.

First, we shall want to ask how much stability there is in the sex composition of occupational categories, and what is the process of change. To do this, we consider the regression of percent female in 1950 on percent female in 1940 and the regression of percent female in 1960 on percent female in 1950, and also the corresponding regressions involving the number rather than the percentage of female workers in each occupational category. Table 7.11 presents the results of these analyses. Inspecting the coefficients in the table, a very interesting pattern emerges. First, there is substantial stability in sex composi-

Table 7.11. Intercensal Regressions of Percent Female and Thousands of Female Workers

	Percent Female		Thousands of Female Workers	
	1940–50	1950–60	1940–50	1950–60
Time 1 mean	29.7	37.5	157	239
Time 2 mean	37.5	38.9	239	297
Time 1 standard deviation	28.4	29.3	317	366
Time 2 standard deviation	29.3	30.1	366	486
Intercept	9.75	0.730	64.5	−16.1
Slope	0.936	1.02	0.990	1.31
r^2	0.83	0.98	0.78	0.97

tion, whether the actual number of females or the percent female is considered; but the stability is much greater for the 1950–1960 period than for the earlier period. Second, during the 1940–1950 period there was an across-the-board increase in the number of females in each occupation, which is manifest in the slope coefficient of virtual unity together with a positive intercept. In short, each occupation gained about 64,000 female workers on the average. But the slope of less than unity (together with a positive intercept) for the corresponding regression of percent female indicates that those occupations which had smaller proportions of women in 1940 increased their percent female more than did those occupations with higher percentages of females in 1940. Thus, the 1940–1950 transition was one in which formerly male-dominated occupations gained substantial proportions of women while the proportions of women in initially female-dominated occupations were relatively unaffected. By contrast, the 1950–1960 period was one of stability in the *proportions* of women in each occupational category, but not of the numbers of women. During this period those occupations which had more women to start with gained most rapidly in numbers of women workers, and those occupations with very few women actually lost women workers (the crossover point is about half a standard deviation below the 1950 mean). This combination of stability in the proportion of women and change in the number of women employed in particular jobs implies that occupations which were disproportionately heavy employers of women were growing in general, relative to those occupations employing low percentages of women; that is, not only were such occupations gaining in the numbers of female employees but of male employees as well, because otherwise the sex ratios would have changed. This pattern thus serves to confirm at the level of individual occupations what has already been observed in our analysis of shifts in the distribution of the labor force over major occupation groups (see Table 7.2).

Not only is the sex composition of the labor force highly stable over time, but other characteristics of jobs are extremely stable as well, especially between 1950 and 1960. Table 7.12 presents intercensal correlations of selected occupational characteristics, separately for male and female workers; and Table 7.13 presents similar correlations for the measures of differences between male and female incumbents of the same occupations which were analyzed above. Inspecting the coefficients in these tables, the general pattern is one of enormous stability in the occupational structure. Concentrating on the coefficients for women reported in Table 7.12, we note that between 1940 and 1950 there was a modest change in the relative numbers of workers in specific jobs, in the income return to particular jobs (especially when residual income—that is, income net of education and hours worked—is considered), in average age and average hours worked, and in marital status. These changes can hardly be considered large, however, since by most standards these coefficients are extraordinarily high.

Table 7.12. Intercensal Correlations for Selected Occupational Characteristics, Separately for Male and Female Workers

	Male		Female	
Variable	*1940– 1950*	*1950– 1960*	*1940– 1950*	*1950– 1960*
Number of workers	0.97	0.97	0.88	0.99
Mean years of school	0.99	0.99	0.98	0.99
Mean annual income	0.62	0.99	0.73	0.98
Mean residual income	0.38	0.93	0.45	0.95
Mean age	0.94	0.96	0.92	0.92
Mean hours worked	0.77	0.93	0.75	0.87
% married, spouse present	0.98	0.97	0.81	0.87

Moreover, between 1950 and 1960 both the relative number of women employed in various occupations and relative levels of income in different occupations stabilized, although the other characteristics just mentioned continued to exhibit moderate instability. Finally, with minor exceptions the male pattern is very similar to that for females, the only real difference being the greater stability for males in occupational differences in marital status. In consequence, even the differences between men and women workers in the same occupations are highly stable over time, especially between 1950 and 1960, as the coefficients in Table 7.13 indicate.

While this pattern of overwhelming stability in the occupational structure makes it relatively unlikely that movement of women into or out of particular jobs will be explained easily by reference to other occupational characteristics, it is nonetheless worthwhile to investigate this possibility, if only to attempt explicit tests of some of the claims that have been made regarding transitions in the occupational situation of women.

For example, Oppenheimer (1973:957) argues that "shortages in a preferred type of labor induce rising wages, which are an additional incentive for women to enter the labor force." To the extent that this is so, we would expect a positive correlation between change in the mean income of women in an

Table 7.13. Intercensal Correlations for Measures of Differences between Male and Female Workers in Each Occupation

Variable	*1940–1950*	*1950–1960*
Education difference	0.74	0.82
Income difference	0.52	0.97
Residual income difference	0.47	0.83
Hours worked difference	0.80	0.74

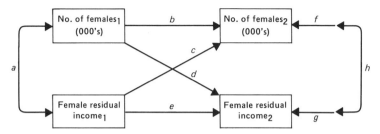

Figure 7.1. Number of Women and Female Residual Income

occupation and change in the number of female workers. Measuring change by simple difference scores,[8] this claim is not at all borne out: the correlation between change scores is −0.06 between 1940 and 1950 and −0.03 between 1950 and 1960.

However, it can be argued that the relevant variable is not income per se, but income returned to investment in éducation and working time. When one speaks of a high-paying job, one ordinarily means a job which pays well relative to time spent working and relative to other jobs requiring the same amount of training or skill. Accordingly, we utilize the residual income variable defined above (recall that this is the difference between actual income and income predicted from education and hours worked per year), and ask whether there is any correlation between change in the return on investment in education and effort and change in the number of women employed in particular jobs. The answer is no: the correlations are 0.10 for 1940–1950 and 0.11 for 1950–1960.

Clearly, if women are being drawn to particular jobs by rising wage rates (relative to investment), other factors are offsetting this tendency. One obvious possibility is that the availability of women workers drives relative wages down. To test this, we posit the model shown in Figure 7.1. In this model we posit stability over time in the relative numbers of women employed in particular jobs and in the income rewards to women for doing these jobs. However, we also allow the possibility that in occupations with large numbers of women at time 1, residual income drops relative to other occupations; presumably the mechanism for this is that in occupations with large numbers of women there are smaller

---

[8] Bohrnstedt (1969) argues that residual change scores based on the regression of the time 2 variable on the time 1 variable should be used in place of simple change scores ($c_x = x_2 - x_1$). Since simple change scores are likely to be correlated with the initial scores, the existence of a correlation between a second variable y_1 and the change score c_x may be due to the correlation of y_1 and x_1. This problem would not arise if residual change scores were used since they are not correlated with x_1 by definition. However, in a regression framework one can control for the correlation of two independent variables by including both in the regression equation and this seems to us a more straightforward procedure than the construction of residual change scores. Correlations merely tell us that two variables are related. If a correlation is interesting we can check for spuriousness by constructing the appropriate causal model.

inflationary pressures to raise wages than there are in other occupations (actually, in this case "number of female workers" serves as a surrogate for "proportion of females" because to use both variables in the model would unduly complicate it). And occupations which are economically rewarding at time 1 for women should, according to Oppenheimer (1973), attract additional women workers over time.[9]

The first panel of Table 7.14 presents the coefficients for this model, estimated both for the 1940–1950 period and for the 1950–1960 period. Inspecting the coefficients in the table, it is evident that the process differs rather substantially for the two periods. The return to investment in education and working time changes rather substantially from 1940 to 1950 (recall that the intercensal correlation is 0.45) and the pattern of change clearly was one in which occupations with large numbers of female employees in 1940 fared poorly in economic terms during the 1940–1950 period. Since this was a period of generally rising incomes, it is evident that women in occupations employing large numbers of women lagged behind the economic gains experienced by women in occupations where they were relatively scarce. During the subsequent 10 years, however, there was no tendency for occupations employing many women to lag in their economic returns to women; indeed, economic returns were highly stable between 1950 and 1960. There is no support whatsoever to be found for Oppenheimer's thesis that women move into jobs that pay them well. For neither period was there any tendency for initially high-paying occupations to attract disproportionate numbers of additional workers. And there is no substantial correlation between those determinants of time 2 income returns and time 2 numbers of women employees which are not accounted for by the time 1 characteristics; and, in fact, the correlation between the residuals (h) has the opposite sign in each of the two periods.

---

[9] We had initially thought of expressing this model, and some of the subsequent ones, in terms of the relationship between time 1 scores and change scores rather than in terms of the relationship between time 1 and time 2 scores. However, since the metric coefficients in one representation are straightforward linear transformations of the coefficients in the other, it seemed preferable to restrict ourselves to the simpler representation. But to illustrate the distinction, consider the structural equation for NF_2 (number of females at time 2) as a function of NF_1 and FR_1 (female rewards at time 1).

$$NF_2 = a + b(NF_1) + c(FR_1) + e$$

But, subtracting NF_1 from both sides, we have

$$(NF_2 - NF_1) = a + (b - 1)NF_1 + c(FR_1) + e$$

In short, the only difference between predicting time 2 scores and predicting change scores is that in the latter case 1 is subtracted from the coefficient for the time 1 variable. Similar isomorphisms can be shown for other models involving change scores as dependent and independent variables.

Table 7.14. Regression Coefficients for Path Models of Change in Occupational Structure

	1940–1950		1950–1960	
	Metric	*Standardized*	*Metric*	*Standardized*
Model 1–Number of women and female residual income (see Figure 7.1)				
a	–	−0.073	–	−0.345
b	1.02	0.884[c]	1.31	0.985[c]
c	−0.041	−0.027	−0.003	−0.003
d	−0.290	−0.228[c]	0.015	0.008
e	0.717	0.434[c]	1.60	0.950[c]
f[a]	78.7	0.464	−15.8	0.167
g[a]	37.5	0.863	7.25	0.321
h	–	−0.259	–	0.239
$r-\hat{r}$[b]	–	−0.104	–	0.013
Model 2–Number of women and hours worked by women (see Figure 7.2)				
a	–	0.013	–	−0.121
b	1.01	0.898[c]	1.31	0.986[c]
c	−6.56	−0.069	14.2	0.083[c]
d	10.3	0.080	−10.5	−0.061
e	−0.0017	−0.198[c]	0.000	0.031
f	0.559	0.754[c]	0.861	0.867[c]
g[a]	8.62	0.465	−89.1	0.161
h[a]	6.86	0.658	1.14	0.494
Model 3–Percent female and white male residual income (see Figure 7.3)				
a	–	−0.036	–	−0.402
b	0.929	0.903[c]	1.01	0.986[c]
c	−0.011	−0.167[c]	−0.000	−0.011
d	−7.39	−0.310[c]	−1.34	−0.036
e	0.560	0.376[c]	1.49	0.917[c]
f[a]	9.93	0.382	0.893	0.134
g[a]	210	0.868	69.4	0.363
h	–	−0.142	–	−0.122
$r-\hat{r}$[b]	–	−0.047	–	−0.006

[a]The appropriate constant terms are found in the metric column.

[b]For Models 1 and 3 (which are overidentified) $r-\hat{r}$ is a measure of how well the correlation between the two time 2 variables (r) is reproduced by the model ($\hat{r}$); obviously, the smaller the difference the better the fit.

[c]Significant at the 0.05 level (only coefficients b through e and, in Model 2 only, f, are tested for significance).

Although we can find no support for the proposition that women are seduced into the labor force by high-paying jobs, there is some reason to believe

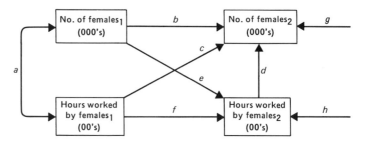

Figure 7.2. Number of Female Workers and Hours Worked by Women

that they are attracted to those jobs which can be done on a part-time basis (Ginsberg, 1968). Further, it may be that changes in the organization of work occur *in response* to the presence of large numbers of women workers (National Manpower Council, 1957), so that in such jobs more and more part-time positions become available. We do know that the number of part-time jobs has been increasing substantially during the same period that women have been moving into the labor force in large numbers (Ginsberg, 1968), but we do not yet know whether the particular jobs employing increasingly large numbers of women are those where part-time opportunities are increasing. To investigate these possibilities, we posit the model depicted in Figure 7.2, which relates the number of female employees at two points in time to the mean number of hours worked per year by women. In addition to the usual stability coefficients, the model allows the possibility that the number of female employees at one point in time affects the average number of hours worked ten years later; if the organization of work does change to accommodate the needs of women workers, this effect should be negative—in occupations with many women, women should work less at time 2 than would be predicted from hours worked at time 1. And if women are attracted to occupations where part-time opportunities are available, hours worked should have a negative effect on number of women employed at time 2, net of the number of women employed at time 1. To take account of the fact that part-time opportunities may have both an immediate impact (through' the ability of women in the labor market to find part-time work) and a delayed impact (because of the reputation occupations may acquire as being possible to do on a part-time basis), we posit paths to number of female employees at time 2 from hours worked at time 2 and hours worked at time 1.

Inspecting the coefficients for the model estimated for the same two periods as before in the second panel of Table 7.14, we note that once again the pattern changes over time. For the 1940—1950 period the number of women employed in an occupation at the beginning of the period does appear to have a negative effect on hours worked at the end of the period. However, hours worked in

1940 or 1950 had no effect on the movement of women into or out of particular occupations. The 1940–1950 period was thus one in which the organization of work was responsive to female employment but not conducive to it.

During the 1950–1960 period, by contrast, the number of women working initially had no impact on changes in hours worked, but hours worked did appear to affect the recruitment of women into particular jobs. Oddly, however, hours worked in 1950 had a positive effect on number of women employed in 1960, although hours worked in 1960 had a negative effect. It is difficult to understand this result, and further study will be required before any definitive claims can be made.

Thus far we have concentrated on changes in the characteristics of the female occupational structure but, recognizing that the occupational structure and occupational labor markets include both women and men, we now turn to investigation of the relationship between changes in the occupational position of women and of men. In particular, because women are apparently willing to work for lower wages than are males, the movement of women into particular occupations may drive down male incomes (see Hodge and Hodge, 1965; Taeuber et al., 1966). Conversely, it may be that those occupations in which male wage rates are falling for other reasons become available to women because men leave them for better paying jobs. To test these possibilities, we estimate the model presented in Figure 7.3 of the relationship between white male earnings and female occupational concentration. As before, we utilize the economic reward measure, income relative to income expected from education and hours worked. But in contrast to the above model involving female earnings, here we study the proportion of women in each occupation rather than the number. This reflects the theory that the sex-ratio of an occupation affects and is affected by the earnings of male workers. As before, we predict substantial stability in both the female concentration measure and the male earnings variable. But those occupations which have large proportions of women at time 1 should drop in male economic rewards relative to those occupations with smaller proportions of women, because in such occupations employers do not

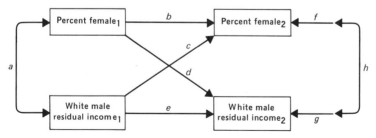

Figure 7.3. Percent Female and White Male Residual Income

find it so necessary to raise wage rates. And those occupations which pay men poorly relative to their education and working time should increase their proportions of female workers as males leave for better paying jobs and are replaced by women.

This is in fact what happens during the 1940–1950 period, but apparently not during the 1950–1960 period, as can be seen from inspection of the coefficients reported in the third panel of Table 7.14. The 1940–1950 period was one of substantial instability in wage rates (relative to education and hours worked) for white males, just as it was for females; and it was also a period in which there was some change in the sex composition of occupations, although this variable was much more stable. In any event, there was a strong propensity for those occupations with high proportions of females in 1940 to fare poorly with respect to changes in male economic returns during the 1940–1950 period. Obviously, men in those occupations with high proportions of women failed to experience the income gains that men with fewer women coworkers enjoyed, just as women in occupations employing many women fell behind other women in income gains. During the 1940–1950 period there was also a tendency, albeit a weaker one, for those occupations which paid men poorly at the beginning of the period to become more female dominated by 1950.

The 1950–1960 period, by contrast, was one of much greater stability both in the sex composition and in the economic status of occupations (as measured by white male economic rewards). Hence, there was little possibility that these variables could have much effect on each other; and indeed, although the paths are in the predicted direction, they are very small and are, with one exception, not statistically significant. It may be only when the occupational structure is fundamentally shaken, as by World War II, that much change of any kind at all occurs.

CONCLUSIONS

The most striking aspect of our analysis has been its overwhelming documentation of just how highly structured are occupations. Occupational characteristics computed from data for the male labor force are, with a few highly systematic exceptions, virtually identical to those computed from data for the female labor force. That is, jobs which employ well-educated men employ equally well-educated women; jobs which employ older men also employ older women; and so on. And even where there are average differences between male and female workers (e.g., women work shorter hours and earn less than do men), *interoccupational* differences for men are very highly correlated with those for women; that is, for example, occupations that pay men well also pay women well, although women systematically make less than men doing the same work.

Thus it is sensible to think of a single occupational structure, rather than of separate male and female occupational structures. However, despite the similarity in the pattern of interrelations among occupational characteristics for the male and female labor force, men and women are distributed very differently across jobs. Women tend disproportionately to be concentrated in occupations which require high skill but pay badly. Moreover, this tendency is increasing over time as are income differences between men and women doing the same work. The general pattern is one in which men who are employed in predominantly male occupations have benefited from the inflationary trend in wages since 1940 much more than have women in general, or men employed in predominantly female occupations.

This shift in the socioeconomic structure of occupations has been relatively independent of shifts in the sex composition of jobs since 1950, but was indeed related to changes in sex composition between 1940 and 1950. During the 1940–1950 period, which of course encompassed the period of great labor shortage during World War II, women moved into many jobs from which they previously had been largely excluded, as well as increasing their numbers in traditionally female jobs. However, the particular jobs which increased their proportion of female workers were precisely those in which men were paid poorly in 1940 relative to their education and hours spent working; and jobs which initially°had high proportions of female workers lagged behind in the income gains experienced by most jobs between 1940 and 1950. In short, the influx of women into the labor force between 1940 and 1950 was concentrated in jobs which were relatively undesirable from the standpoint of male workers. During the 1950–1960 period, by contrast, women simply moved increasingly into jobs in which they were already overrepresented; but since these were among the fastest growing jobs for both men and women, the sex composition of occupations was highly stable during this period. Indeed, the occupational structure as a whole was much more stable during the 1950s than during the previous decade.

What can we say about later years? The 1970 data will soon be available. Can we expect substantial change in the occupational position of women between 1960 and 1970? Probably not. Any effect of the Women's Liberation movement would not yet be evident and even if one sees the movement as a consequence rather than a cause of the changing position of women, the results of the present analysis strongly suggest that the occupational structure changes in a glacial way at best. Massive social changes, such as the labor demand occasioned by World War II, seem required to make any dent at all in the enormous stability of the occupational system. At best we can hope that the apparent trend toward *increasing* occupational disadvantages of women will be reversed; but genuine equality in occupational opportunities and rewards for men and women is still more a wishful hope that a realistic prospect.

REFERENCES

Bohrnstedt, George W.
   1969   "Observations on the measurement of change." Pp. 113–133 in Edgar
            F. Borgatta (ed.), Sociological Methodology 1969. San Francisco:
            Jossey-Bass.
Duncan, Otis Dudley, and Beverly Duncan.
   1955   "A methodological analysis of segregation indexes." American Socio-
            logical Review 20 (April):210–217.
Employment and Earnings.
   1971   17(May):Table A-19.
Fuchs, Victor R.
   1971   "Differences in hourly earnings between men and women." Monthly
            Labor Review 94 (May):9–15.
Ginsberg, Eli.
   1968   "Paycheck and apron-revolution in womanpower." Industrial Rela-
            tions 7 (May):193–203.
Gross, Edward.
   1968   "Plus ça change . . . ? The sexual structure of occupations over time."
            Social Problems 16 (Fall):198–208.
Hedges, Janice N., and Jeanne K. Barnett.
   1972   "Working women and the division of household tasks." Monthly
            Labor Review 95 (April):9–14.
Hill, Joseph A.
   1929   "Women in gainful occupations 1870 to 1920." Census Monographs
            IX. Washington, D. C.: U. S. Government Printing Office.
Hodge, Robert W., and Patricia Hodge.
   1965   "Occupational assimilation as a competitive process." American
            Journal of Sociology 61 (November):249–264.
Hooks, Janet M.
   1947   "Women's occupations through seven decades." Women's Bureau
            Bulletin No. 218. Washington, D. C.: U. S. Government Printing
            Office.
Kaplan, David L., and M. Claire Casey.
   1958   "Occupational trends in the United States 1900 to 1950." Bureau of
            the Census. Working Paper No. 5.
National Manpower Council.
   1957   Womanpower. New York: Columbia University Press.
Oppenheimer, Valerie Kincade.
   1968   "The sex-labeling of jobs." Industrial Relations 7 (May):219–224.
   1970   The Female Labor Force in the United States: Demographic and
            Economic Factors Governing Its Growth and Changing Composition.
            (Population Monograph Series No. 5.) Berkeley: University of
            California Press; Institute of International Studies.
   1973   "Demographic influence on female employment and the status of
            women." American Journal of Sociology 78(January):946–961.

Priebe, John A.
  1968   "Changes between the 1950 and 1960 occupation and industry classifications—with detailed adjustments of 1950 data to the 1960 classifications." Technical Paper No. 18. Washington, D. C.: U. S. Government Printing Office.
Priebe, John A., Joan Heinkel, and Stanley Greene.
  1972   "1970 occupation and industry classification systems in terms of their 1960 occupation and industry elements." Technical Paper No. 26. Washington, D. C.: U. S. Government Printing Office.
Saben, Samuel.
  1967   "Occupational mobility of employed workers." Monthly Labor Review 90 (June):31—38.
Siegel, Paul M.
  1970   "Occupational prestige in the Negro subculture." Sociological Inquiry 40(Spring):156—171. Reprinted in Edward O. Laumann (ed.), Social Stratification: Research and Theory for the 1970s. Indianapolis, Ind.: Bobbs-Merrill.
Taeuber, Alma F., Karl E. Taeuber, and Glen G. Cain.
  1966   "Occupational assimilation and the competitive process." American Journal of Sociology 72 (November):273—285.
U. S. Bureau of the Census.
  1942   U. S. Census of Population: 1940. The Labor Force. Washington, D. C.: U. S. Government Printing Office.
  1943   U. S. Census of Population: 1940. The Labor Force (Sample Statistics), "Occupational characteristics." Washington, D. C. : U. S. Government Printing Office.
  1953   U. S. Census of Population: 1950. Vol IV, Special Reports, Part 1, Chapter B, Occupational Characteristics. Washington, D. C.: U. S. Government Printing Office.
  1963   U. S. Census of Population: 1960. Subject Report PC(2)—7A, Occupational Characteristics. Washington, D. C.: U. S. Government Printing Office.
U. S. Bureau of Labor Statistics.
  1971   "Marital and family characteristics of workers, March 1970." Special Labor Force Reports, No. 130. Washington, D. C.: U. S. Government Printing Office.
U. S. Congress, Joint Economic Committee.
  1973   Economic Report of the President. Washington, D. C.: U. S. Government Printing Office.

APPENDIX: METHODOLOGICAL ISSUES IN THE TREND ANALYSIS
OF OCCUPATIONAL DATA

A generic problem in the analysis of social change is the necessity to rely
upon data initially collected for other purposes. This is particularly true in an
analysis of the American occupational structure, since the only data which
permit adequate assessment of changes in the characteristics of specific
occupations are those collected and published as part of the decennial census of
population. The difficulty, which tends to be shared by all statistical series
collected by public agencies, is that comparability in coding procedures is not
maintained across censuses. The dilemma is that any effort to improve data
collection procedures on the basis of experience inherently involves changing the
procedures from one census to the next, thus limiting comparability over time.

In particular, the occupational classification in use in 1940 by the Census
Bureau was substantially expanded in 1950 and was then changed again, albeit in
relatively minor ways, in 1960. Then in 1970 the classification underwent
another major revision. Although the Census Bureau has tried to minimize the
difficulties in comparing data over time by publishing conversion tables between
each pair of years (see Kaplan and Casey, 1958; Priebe, 1968; Priebe et al.,
1972) the conversions are of necessity only approximate. Comparability of the
1940 data with that for later years is limited further for our purposes because in
that year occupational characteristics of the female labor force were published in
a severely truncated occupational classification which aggregated occupations
with relatively few women in them more than occupations with substantial
proportions of female workers. The available data on the characteristics of
female workers in 1940 are not only much less detailed than the corresponding
data for males in 1940 and the data for both sexes in 1950 and 1960 but the
degree of aggregation is itself correlated with the major dependent variable of
interest, percent female in an occupation. Thus we were faced with a dilemma:
in order to analyze changes in the sexual composition of occupational categories
from 1940 to 1960, we were forced to recode our data for all three years into
the 1940 female classification; but by doing this we not only sacrificed the
wealth of detail available in the 1950 and 1960 classification schemes but also
ran the risk of distorting our results because of the special character of the 1940
aggregation.

The loss of detail in the 1940 classification is particularly troublesome
because of the possibility that it masks important sex differences within
occupational categories. For example, data from the 1960 census (U. S. Bureau
of the Census, 1963:2) show that 53 percent of secondary school teachers but
only 14 percent of primary school teachers were men, but the 1940
classification includes both of these titles (along with some others) in a single
category: "Teachers (n.e.c.) (including county agents)." Because examples of
this kind are manifold, it is possible that use of the 1940 classification

understates true differences in the occupational opportunities and rewards of men and women.

Since changes in classification schemes constitute an inherent problem in the analysis of social change, it occurred to us that it would be useful to conduct parallel analyses utilizing alternative classification schemes and to compare the results. Such a procedure should give us some indication of the robustness of our conclusions and, by extension, of the degree of caution that must be exercised in the analysis of social change. Accordingly, we present selected comparisons to the analysis reported in the main body of the paper for 1950 and 1960, based on the Census Bureau's 1950 occupational classification scheme which includes 430 lines. Further, for some comparisons we will restrict our analysis by omitting those occupations which employ very few women (see below for details).

Before proceeding to the analysis, it is instructive to compare the two classification schemes. As it turns out, it is not only in the 1940 female classification that we find a correlation between the level of aggregation and the sex composition of occupational categories. As the data in Table 7A.1 indicate, while the 1940 classification makes finer distinctions with respect to those occupations which are disproportionately female, the 1950 classification makes finer distinctions with respect to those occupations which have dispropor-

Table 7A.1. Comparison of Size of Occupational Categories under Two Classification Schemes (category sizes are in thousands of workers in Experienced Civilian Labor Force)

	1940 Classification		1950 Classification	
	Male Occs.[b]	Female Occs.[b]	Male Occs.[b]	Female Occs.[b]
1940 data (24.8% female)[a]				
Mean	631	482	–	–
Standard deviation	999	690	–	–
Number of occupations	33	34	–	–
1950 data (28.1% female)[a]				
Mean	1,105	651	109	209
Standard deviation	1,557	868	283	447
Number of occupations	30	37	326	104
1960 data (32.5% female)[a]				
Mean	1,055	812	117	285
Standard deviation	1,512	1,122	222	616
Number of occupations	35	32	355	75

[a]Percent female of total Experienced Civilian Labor Force.

[b]Male occupations are those for which the percent female is less than that for the total labor force; female occupations are those in which percent female is greater than or equal to that for total labor force.

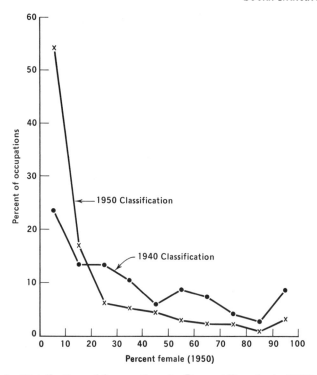

Figure 7A.1. Distribution of Occupations by Percent Female, in 1950

tionately *few* women. In the 1950 classification there are many more occupations in which women are underrepresented than in which women are overrepresented, and these categories are on the average less than half as large as those categories in which women are overrepresented. In consequence, there are many categories in the 1950 classification with too few female incumbents to allow reliable estimation of their characteristics. To overcome this difficulty, we restricted part of the analysis to the 225 occupational categories which had at least 3,000 female incumbents in 1950. This cutting point was established on the ground that the 1950 occupation data are based on a $3\frac{1}{3}$ percent sample of the population, so that a population estimate of 3,000 corresponds to a sample size of 100 cases, which we felt was the minimum base for making reasonably reliable estimates of occupational characteristics.

In consequence of the patterns of aggregation described above, together with the fact that females make up substantially less than half the labor force, the distribution of detailed occupational categories by percent female tends to be substantially more skewed to the right in the 1950 classification than in the 1940 classification (see Figure 7A.1). Fortunately, however, the other variables of interest do not seem to be severely affected by differences in the classification

Table 7A.2. Correlations, Means and Standard Deviation for Selected Variables, in 1950 Classification (1950 above the diagonal, 1960 below the diagonal)

		F	E	I	A	H	SE	GE	U	Mean	S.D.
F:	% female		0.05	-0.20	-0.03	-0.14	-0.06	0.05	0.11	19.4	25.0
E:	Mean yrs. of school (WM)[a]	0.01		0.71	0.13	0.42	0.22	0.30	0.36	10.2	2.0
I:	Mean annual income (WM)	-0.25	0.72		0.44	0.62	0.38	0.08	0.30	3,221	1,202
A:	Mean age (WM)	-0.06	0.09	0.45		0.58	0.35	0.14	0.06	40.1	6.1
H:	Mean hrs. worked/yr. (TM)[b]	-0.18	0.41	0.66	0.63		0.41	0.13	0.07	1,918	350
SE:	% self-employed (WM)	-0.05	0.21	0.38	0.38	0.37		-0.16	-0.03	11.8	25.5
GE:	% govt. employed (WM)	0.05	0.30	0.07	0.10	0.09	-0.15		-0.01	10.3	22.3
U:	% urban (WM)	0.11	0.42	0.31	0.07	0.07	-0.02	0.04		76.5	15.1
	Mean	19.4	10.2	5,311	40.7	1,908	12.3	10.5	75.0		
	S.D.	25.6	2.3	2,153	6.6	375	25.8	22.2	15.1		

[a]White males.

[b]Total males; tabulations were not available by race for hours worked.

schemes. Comparison of the means and standard deviations for selected variables in the 1950 classification scheme, shown in Tables 7A.2 and 7A.4, with the corresponding data in Tables 7.5 and 7.8 respectively, indicate that the distributions of these variables (as indicated by the first two moments) are nearly identical in the two classifications. Further, the distributions of white male occupational characteristics derived from the full 430 categories of the 1950 classification (Table 7A.2) are extremely similar to the distributions for the corresponding variables based on all males in each occupation derived from the truncated classification of 225 categories (not shown). Finally, the pattern of intercorrelations among occupational characteristics appears to be basically similar in the various classification schemes, with the exception, of course, of correlations involving percent female. In short, were we interested in characteristics of occupations other than the extent of female participation, we could expect our results to be relatively unaffected by the choice of classification. However, given that the sex ratio of occupations is the principal focus of our analysis, an explicit comparison of the results yielded by the alternative classifications clearly is required.

We start by analyzing the determinants of occupational sex ratios in a manner exactly parallel to that reported in Table 7.6 in the main body of the chapter—that is, we predict the percent female in jobs from the characteristics of their white male incumbents, utilizing the full 1950 classification of 430 categories. The regression estimates are reported in Table 7A.3. Comparing these coefficients with those reported in Table 7.6 based on the 1940 classification, it

Table 7A.3. Regression of Percent Female in Occupations on Selected Characteristics of White Male Incumbents, 1950 Classification

	Variable	Metric Coefficients		Standardized Coefficients	
		1950	*1960*	*1950*	*1960*
E:	Mean yrs. of school	5.44[b]	5.54[b]	0.422	0.498
I:	Mean annual income	−12.2[b]	−8.47[b]	−0.586	−0.712
A:	Mean age	0.889[b]	1.04[b]	0.218	0.268
H:	Mean hrs. worked/yr.[a]	−0.766	−0.686	−0.107	−0.101
SE:	% self-employed	0.029	0.042	0.029	0.043
GE:	% govt. employed	−0.047	−0.073	−0.042	−0.063
U:	% urban	0.207[c]	−0.207[c]	0.125	0.122
	Constant	−33.5	−37.0		
	R^2	0.155	0.193		

[a]Total males; tabulations were not available by race for hours worked.

[b]Significant at the 0.01 level.

[c]Significant at the 0.05 level.

is evident that in a gross sort of way the equations are similar, but only in a gross way. Both equations lead us to conclude that women are disproportionately concentrated in occupations which require high skill, pay badly, and are done by urban residents. Further, women appear to work at the same jobs as older white male workers, net of other factors, although the age coefficient is only significant in the 1950 classification. But despite the qualitative similarity of the equations in the two classifications, there are substantial differences in the size of various coefficients and a very large difference in their ability to explain variance in the dependent variable. In general, the coefficients are larger in the 1940 classification, which may reflect the higher level of aggregation. In any event, the results caution us not to make too much of the precise numerical values of the coefficients while at the same time providing some reassurance that our basic conclusions are sound.

We turn now to a second issue confronting the analysis of occupational data—whether or not to take account of differences in the number of workers in various occupations by weighting observations proportionally to their size. As indicated in the main body of this chapter, the argument against the use of weighted data is that our interest is in the characteristics of occupations, not in the occupational experience of individuals. In particular, we are interested in comparing the situation of men and women *doing the same work* and hence decided not to weight our observations to reflect the different occupational distributions of the male and female labor force. However, because female workers are heavily concentrated in a relatively few jobs, it is useful to explicitly compare the results that would be obtained through the use of weighted and unweighted data.

Table 7A.4 presents means, standard deviations, and correlations among education, hours worked, and income for the truncated 1950 classification. The top panel gives coefficients for the unweighted data while the bottom panel gives coefficients for males weighted proportionally to the number of males in each occupation and coefficients for females weighted proportionally to the number of females in each occupation. While some differences can be observed, the basic pattern is one of great similarity between the unweighted and weighted coefficients. Thus, on the basis of these data we need not be particularly concerned that our use of unweighted data for the bulk of the analysis unduly distorted the situation of the average woman worker.

This conclusion holds also when the regression of mean income on mean education and hours worked is computed both with unweighted and with weighted data. Table 7A.5 shows unweighted regressions in the top panel and weighted regressions in the bottom panel, separately for the male and female labor force. The basic picture yielded by the two sets of regressions is essentially the same: the returns to investment in education and effort are by and large much smaller for women than for men. However, the differences between the

Table 7A.4. Correlations, Means, and Standard Deviations for Selected Variables in the 1950 Truncated Classification, Separately for Males (above the diagonal) and females (below the diagonal)

	1950						1960					
	F	E	H	I	Mean	S.D.	F	E	H	I	Mean	S.D.
Unweighted data												
F: % female		0.01	-0.25	-0.28	32.0	27.6		-0.04	-0.27	-0.34	32.6	28.4
E: Education	-0.01		0.35	0.72	10.4	2.1	-0.05		0.35	0.71	10.4	2.4
H: Hrs. worked	-0.20	0.24		0.57	1,956	342	-0.20	0.17		0.56	1,930	379
I: Income	-0.35	0.65	0.61		3,190	1,255	-0.35	0.68	0.68		5,182	2,199
Mean	32.0	10.5	1,669	1,967			32.6	10.5	1,564	2,995		
S.D.	27.6	2.0	315	729			28.4	2.1	344	1,185		
Weighted data[a]												
E: Education			0.16	0.79	9.8	1.9			0.36	0.78	10.2	2.4
H: Hrs. worked		0.26		0.33	2,046	340		0.26		0.54	1,980	350
I: Income		0.77	0.55		2,891	1,215		0.82	0.58		5,090	2,206
Mean		10.6	1,598	1,662				10.9	1,477	2,595		
S.D.		2.1	256	592				2.2	256	981		

[a]Male data weighted proportionally to the number of male incumbents of each occupation; female data weighted proportionately to the number of female incumbents.

Table 7A.5. Regressions over Occupations of Mean Income on Mean Years of School and Mean Hours Worked per Year, Separately for Males and Females, 1950 Truncated Classification ($N = 225$)

	Metric Coefficients			Standardized Coefficients		R^2
	Constant	Education	Hours	Education	Hours	
			Unweighted data			
1950						
Male	−3,415	348	1.53	0.574	0.416	0.668
Female	−1,870	204	1.02	0.545	0.439	0.604
1960						
Male	−5,354	486	2.84	0.539	0.489	0.713
Female	−2,979	338	1.56	0.596	0.452	0.654
			Weighted data			
1950						
Male	−3,447	485	0.77	0.757	0.216	0.671
Female	−1,722	188	0.87	0.668	0.374	0.718
1960						
Male	−5,018	623	1.89	0.673	0.300	0.689
Female	−3,081	318	1.49	0.715	0.389	0.809

weighted and unweighted regressions that can be observed are of substantive interest—in the weighted regressions the difference in the return to investment in education for males and females is larger than in the unweighted regressions (in the weighted regressions the female coefficients are about 45 percent as large as the male coefficients, while in the unweighted regressions they are about 65 percent as large). This of course reflects the fact that part of the reason that women are paid more poorly than men on the average is that they are concentrated in low-paying jobs; but about two-thirds of the difference in the return to investment in education ($\cong 0.45/0.65$) can be attributed to the fact that, job for job, women are not as well paid as men even when differences in hours worked per year are taken into account.

8

AGE, PERIOD, COHORT, AND EDUCATION EFFECTS ON EARNINGS BY RACE
An Experiment with a Sequence of Cross-Sectional Surveys*

H. H. Winsborough

THE CURRENT POPULATION SURVEY AS A DATA SOURCE FOR MODELS OF SOCIAL CHANGE

A large fraction of the presently available indicators of the status of and change in American society are derived from the Current Population Survey (CPS) conducted monthly by the Bureau of the Census. Originally conceived of as a mechanism for collecting unemployment statistics, this large, highly

*The research reported here was supported by funds granted to the Institute for Research on Poverty at the University of Wisconsin by the Office of Economic Opportunity pursuant to the provisions of the Economic Opportunity Act of 1964. The conclusions are the sole responsibility of the author. Certain data used in this analysis were derived by the author from a computer tape file furnished under the joint project sponsored by the U. S. Bureau of the Census and the Population Council and containing selected 1960 census information for a 0.1 percent sample of the population of the United States. Neither the Census Bureau nor the Population Council assumes any responsibility for the validity of any of the figures or interpretations of the figures presented herein or based on this material. Data for the 1962 Occupational Change in a Generation Survey was kindly provided by David Featherman and Robert Hauser whose purchase of that data was supported by National Science Foundation Grant GI31604X. Current Population Survey person files for 1968 and 1970 were provided by Al Rosenthal of the Rand Corporation. Much of the computing for this paper was accomplished on the computing facility of the Center for Demography and Ecology, University of Wisconsin, Madison, which is supported by a "Centers Grant" from the National Institute of Child Health and Human Development, Grant Number 1-PO1-HD058F6-01A1. The assistance of Peter Dickinson in computational work is gratefully acknowledged. Criticism of a first draft of this chapter by I. Richard Savage, Stanley Masters, and Kenneth Land has been most helpful in preparing a final draft as have discussions with Otis Dudley Duncan, Karen Mason, and Charles Palit.

professional, and thoroughly routinized survey presently provides at least annual data on a whole host of social and economic variables.

It is my not-very-original contention that these surveys also provide a large and relatively untapped resource for the construction of models. Were basic CPS records for past and future data routinely made available to scholars, I believe a host of new and important social indicators would be forthcoming from the model building which would ensue. The argument of this chapter, then, is that the CPS archive represents an important resource for constructing interesting models of social change—models which can yield useful indicators as their by-product.

This argument will be made by example. I shall present a simple human capital model to explain individual earnings. Estimating the parameters of the model separately for blacks and whites should yield information on the changing sources of black-white income differences. This estimation requires tables of income by education, age, and race for several periods. Ideally, such tables should be constructed from a sequence of surveys conducted and processed in such a homogeneous way as to minimize "methods variance" between them. A sequence of annual CPS files from, say, 1960 to 1970 would be nearly ideal. Since these files are not presently in the public domain, I shall make do with surrogate sources which are generally available and rather widely used. On the one hand, I hope this strategy will provide a convincing argument for the potential utility of a model which requires repeated cross-sectional data. At the same time, the strategy will display the ambiguities of interpretation which arise from the compounding of "methods" and "real" effects.

The outline of the chapter is as follows: First, I shall discuss the model itself in order to make clear its data requirements. Second, I will discuss estimation of the model. Third, I will describe the data actually used to estimate parameters, and comment on some of the data's problems. Fourth, parameters will be estimated and the results discussed. Fifth, I shall discuss ways in which using CPS files would have made interpretation more secure. Finally, I shall consider some of the problems which my work suggests would be encountered in a facility designed to routinely estimate parameters of social change models from CPS files.

THE MODEL

The usual human capital model presumes children enter school with some level of human capital. This capital is a combination of innate ability and nonschool training. Although the value of this capital varies over individuals, its mean in the aggregate should vary only by birth cohorts as secular trends in ability and preschool training are captured and capitalized upon by each new school entrance cohort. Let us call this value A_c where the subscript specifies the relevant cohort.

Society requires that this preschool capital be invested in education for a period of time. Here I presume that investment increases capital at a rate r_i for the ith additional unit of schooling. Hence, the capital available on the termination of education after t years is $A_c \prod_{i=1}^{t}(1 + r_i)$.

On the termination of education, capital is invested in the labor market yielding income at some rate R during the first year. Ideally, the value of R is presumed constant over individuals but may vary by time period. Let us add a subscript p to R to indicate its variation by period. Thus, income in the first year of employment is given by:

$$I_{pct} = R_p \, A_c \, \prod_{i=1}^{t}(1 + r_i)$$

(Of course, the value of R_p for a period might be different between the races if only limited kinds of jobs were available to blacks and the supply or demands for those jobs were different from that of the labor force as a whole.)

Subsequent to the first year of employment, two things are presumed to happen. First, human capital is increased by virtue of the experience of working. Second, capital is depreciated by aging, and by obsolescence of both training and prior experience. One would like to measure experience and depreciation separately and directly but such measures are not routinely available. The best that can be done with available data is to presume individuals have been working since completing school and to use that elapsed time in years as a measure of experience (Thurow, 1968:235).

Formally, e, the index of experience, can be estimated by $y - (t + 6)$ where y is years of age, t is the termination level of schooling, and 6 is an estimate of age on entrance to school. Clearly, such a measure would also involve the best available index of depreciation, i.e., year of age. The balance of the two effects on the quantity of capital can be computed as $\prod_{j=1}^{e}(1 + \rho_j)$ where ρ_j is the rate of increase or decrease in capital during the jth year after leaving school and e indexes the number of years of experience.

Hence, our income model would become:

$$I_{pcte} = R_p \, A_c \, \prod_{i=1}^{t}(1 + r_i) \, \prod_{j=1}^{e}(1 + \rho_j)$$

In estimating parameters for models somewhat similar to this one, it is not uncommon to compute an experience index from the individual data. A simplification of the model makes this computation unnecessary and clarifies the interpretation. Suppose we think of computing the value of income from this equation for two individuals with different levels of education and, perhaps, ability, but of the same age in the same period. If the first individual has the minimum education for his group, his equation might be:

$$RA_1 \, (1 + r_1)(1 + r_2) \ldots (1 + r_t)(1 + \rho_1)(1 + \rho_2) \ldots (1 + \rho_{e-1})(1 + \rho_e)$$

where A_1 indicates his ability level. If the second individual has one unit more of education (and hence one unit less of experience) his equation would be:

$$RA_2 (1 + r_1) (1 + r_2) \ldots (1 + r_t) (1 + r_{t+1})(1 + \rho_1) (1 + \rho_2) \ldots (1 + \rho_{e-1})$$

where A_2 is his, perhaps greater, ability level. The ratio of the second income to the first is simply:

$$\frac{A_2 (1 + r_{t+1})}{A_1 (1 + \rho_e)}$$

the degree to which the investment of an additional year in education improves human capital over the improvement available by investing the year in work experience multiplied by an ability selection factor.

In general, then, if we define the rate of return to education, call it r'_i, as the excess over returns to capital via experience and recognize that it includes ability selection, our model simplifies to:

$$I_{pcyt} = R_p \, A_c \, \prod_{j=1}^{y} (1 + \rho_j) \prod_{i=1}^{t} (1 + r'_i) \tag{8.1}$$

where ρ_j is the return to the maximum level of experience of the year-of-age group y and A_c is the ability level of the earliest school terminators in cohort c.

ESTIMATION

The model of Equation (8.1) specifies the expected income of an individual of age y in the pth period (and consequently in cohort c) having units of education t. Writing Y_y for $\prod_{j=1}^{y} (1 + \rho_j)$ and T_t for $\prod_{i=1}^{t} (1 + r'_i)$, Equation (8.1) becomes:

$$I_{pcyt} = R_p \, A_c \, Y_y \, T_t$$

Multiplying and dividing by the mean income for the several ages, periods, and education groups and observing that $\bar{I} = \bar{A} \, \bar{R} \, \bar{Y} \, \bar{T}$, where means are geometric, yields:

$$I_{pcyt} = \bar{I} \, \frac{A_c}{A} \, \frac{R_p}{R} \, \frac{Y_y}{Y} \, \frac{T_t}{T} \tag{8.2}$$

Taking logs of both sides, using a caret to designate the log of the variable and adding a stochastic error term, Equation (8.2) becomes:

$$I'_{pcyt} = \bar{I'} + (A'_c - \bar{A'}) + (R'_p - \bar{R'}) + (Y' - \bar{Y'}) + (T' - \bar{T'}) + e \tag{8.3}$$

Given tables of means, variances, and numbers of observations for log income by age, period, and education, estimation of parameters in this model becomes a problem in the estimation of effect-parameters in a three-way analysis of variance design with unequal cell sizes. The model presumes there exist "main effects" for age, period, and education as well as "interaction effects" for cohorts. For a given educational level, these interaction effects for cohorts can be thought of as the series of diagonal interactions in the age, period table. As is common in analysis of variance problems, the parameters are not estimable without setting some side conditions. We first set the usual side condition that the weighted sum of effect parameters for each single effect (e.g., age or period) is equal to zero where the weights are the number of observations. This side condition is not by itself sufficient to make the parameters of Equation (8.3) estimable because of the linear constraints built into the design by the kind of interaction parameter specified. Perhaps the easiest way to appreciate these constraints is to observe that the birth date of a cohort is given identically by date of the present period minus the present age of the cohort. This constraint can be overcome by choosing not to estimate all of the cohort parameters. We accomplish this task by a side condition setting cohort effect parameters equal to zero for cohorts born from 1897 to 1904 and those born from 1934 to 1943.[1] With these side conditions estimation can proceed by least squares and the antilog of the parameters estimated for Equation (8.3) can be taken as estimates of the coefficient of Equation (8.2).

Note that this estimation technique does not permit estimation of preschool ability or the rate of return on human capital directly. It only permits an investigation of the proportionate deviation of these values from the mean taken over all of the data.

For education and age effects, however, it is possible to transform these "effect parameters" back into rates of return to capital for all but the first education or age category as follows: if γ_k is the estimate of T for the kth education category then:

$$\frac{\gamma_{k+1}}{\gamma_k} = \frac{\dfrac{T_{k+1}}{\overline{T}}}{\dfrac{T_k}{\overline{T}}} = \frac{T_{k+1}}{T_k} = \frac{\prod\limits_{i=1}^{k+1} (1 + r'_i)}{\prod\limits_{i+1}^{k} (1 + r'_i)} + (1 + r'_{k+1})$$

---

[1] For a concise discussion of estimable functions, see Scheffe (1959:13–19). For a more detailed discussion of the problem of estimability of cohort effects specifically, see Karen Mason et al., "Some Methodological Issues in Cohort Analysis of Archival Data," *American Sociological Review* 38(April): 242-258.

Thus, it is possible to find one's way back to the coefficients of Equation (8.1) for r' and ρ while for R and A one must make do with measures of proportionate change.

If one believes the model as presented, then the relative values for period parameters indicate the rise and fall over time in the rate of return on human capital. If the model is estimated separately for blacks and whites, a comparison of the range of these parameters for the two groups should answer the question: Is the rate of return to black human capital more sensitive to economic conditions than is white human capital?

An investigation of age effects should reveal the relative effect of experience versus depreciation of human capital. A comparison of the pattern of the parameters between the races should yield information on the relative experience-value of jobs available to blacks and whites.

An inspection of education effects is also of interest. Does the rate of return vary with level? Perhaps not. Thurow (1969) computed elasticity separately for elementary school, high school, and college training and found the elasticities increasing roughly proportionately to the added years of education. This finding would be consistent with a constant rate of return for an educational unit. If the rate of return is not constant, a comparison between the races should yield information on the differing pattern of rates of return to education. For example, is completing high school of less value to blacks than whites? If rates within races seem constant, then our model can be simplified to permit estimation of the two rates themselves and we can answer the question: Is there less payoff in education for blacks than for whites?

According to the model as described above, a comparison of cohort parameters should reveal any effects of the diffusion of preschool training via kindergarten, nursery school, etc., as well as any trends in innate ability accruing from improved nutrition, medical service, and the like. We shall find this an unsatisfactory explanation of the observed results.

Finally, we can investigate the adequacy of the model itself by comparing the variance between age-period-education groups in mean log income with the variance explained by our model.

If the model is not an adequate summary of the data, its only convenient elaboration consists in interacting education terms with age, period, and cohort terms. The latter interaction might be especially useful if there have been temporal trends in the quality of education. Age-education interactions might be useful if there is sufficient age segregation of jobs to create separate human capital markets by age. Beyond these elaborations, inadequacies in the model can only be explored by investigating residuals.

THE DATA USED IN THIS CHAPTER

Estimating the model just described requires construction of tables for males by age, education, income, and race for a series of cross-sections. Because the model investigates (among other things) cohort changes in income it requires that the surveys be evenly spaced in time, that a comparably fine age detail be available, and that there be sufficient surveys to yield a reasonable number of periods for most cohorts.

To satisfy these conditions within the collection of data available at the Wisconsin Center for Demography I chose to use the following files:

1. For 1960—The 1/1000 sample of the 1960 Census
2. For 1962—The Occupational Change in a Generation Survey (OCG)
3. For 1966—The 1966 Survey of Economic Opportunity (SEO)
4. For 1968—An extract for persons of the March CPS tape provided by the Bureau of the Census to the Bureau of Labor Statistics
5. For 1970—A similar extract for the March 1970 CPS

With the exception of the missing year 1964, this collection of surveys approximates a biennial sampling of the population. Each survey is large enough to support two-year age categories. Consequently, two-year birth cohorts can be followed with each being observed at five points in time. (I ordered tabulations from the March 1964 CPS from the Bureau of the Census but they did not arrive in time for inclusion in this analysis.)

On the surface, this set of surveys seems reasonably homogeneous. All sources derive from Bureau of the Census data collecting activities. The interviews were processed in somewhat similar ways. A fairly consistent set of coding procedures was used.

There are, however, some rather striking sources for "methods variance" among them. The method of enumeration varies. The sampling schemes are quite different. The same information is elicited by rather different questions. These differences are known to yield rather different distributions for basic variables.

At an even more operational level, consider the difficulties encountered with the variable income. The model requires a measure of earnings rather than total income. But the Occupational Change in a Generation Survey provides only total income, and that variable is coded in idiosyncratic categories ending in $15,000 and above. From the 1960 census sample, an earnings variable can be constructed by adding together wages and self-employment income but errors are introduced in that procedure by the unique coding scheme of that data set. There are $10 categories up to $10,000, where the category bounds shift to $1,000. CPS and SEO files, however, code earnings directly in single dollars with an open-ended upper category of $50,000.

Thus, despite the fact that each of the separate files is in its own right an important social science resource which has yielded—and will continue to yield—valuable returns to our knowledge of society, the files do *not* automatically aggregate to produce reliable indicators of social change. That sort of aggregation is possible only by giving detailed attention to replication, or by taking advantage of a facility such as the CPS whose basic design was created to produce social indicators (Duncan, 1969).

THE FINDINGS

Parameters of Equation (8.2) were estimated by the method discussed above for all nonfarm males between the ages of 25 and 64 in the periods 1960, 1962, 1966, 1968, and 1970. Sample weighting of cases was used as provided in each survey separately. Income was converted to 1960 dollars.

The correlation over individuals for our model is 0.336 for whites and 0.304 for blacks, while the value of the square root of the correlation ratio estimated from age, period, education cell means is 0.366 for whites and 0.399 for blacks.

Education

Table 8.1 presents parameter estimates for educational effects for whites and blacks. Columns 2 and 4 present parameters in the form of Equation (8.2). The numbers represent the proportionate deviation from the mean income attributable to being in the specific educational category. Columns 3 and 5 represent the numbers transformed into rates of return for the additional educational unit. Recall that these rates represent the return to human capital through investment in the additional unit of education compared to the return through the investment in work experience and that quantity multiplied by an ability selection factor.

Although effect parameters rise roughly linearly with increased education, there are notable rises and falls in the rate of return to an additional unit of education. In general, rates of return are highest for the completion of one of the traditional breaking points in the educational system, i.e., 8, 12, and 16 years. For both races the rates are also high for the 5–7 years level. Elsewhere I

Table 8.1. Parameters for Education by Race

Educational Level (1)	Whites		Blacks	
	Effect Parameters (2)	Rates of Return for Additional Unit (3)	Effect Parameters (4)	Rates of Return for Additional Unit (5)
0–4	0.2376	–	0.5422	–
5–7	0.5012	1.1094	0.8068	0.4880
8	0.7359	0.4683	0.9848	0.2206
9–11	0.9333	0.2682	1.0628	0.0792
12	1.1783	0.2625	1.4220	0.3380
13–15	1.2980	0.1016	1.5585	0.0960
16	1.7000	0.3097	2.0257	0.2998
17+	1.6251	−0.0441	3.0701	0.5156

have argued that it may be reasonable to regard accomplishing more than four years of schooling as an indicator of functional literacy. The high returns for the 5–7 level lend further credence to that notion (Winsborough and Dickinson, 1971).

In interpreting a finding of this kind—higher returns to the completion of a traditional break point—it is common to discuss the importance of a credential, such as a diploma, in our increasingly bureaucratized society. The details of our model suggest an additional plausible explanation. Recall that the relative rate of return in this model is multiplied by an ability selection factor. Perhaps these breaking points are important ability selection points. Some credibility can be accorded this argument by observing that most colleges and many high schools (and perhaps grammar schools in the past) have criteria for graduation which are more stringent than are those for continuance. Frequently a higher grade point average is required for graduation and certain kinds of courses must have been successfully completed by graduation time.

It could be argued that the foregoing overinterprets the rises and falls in the rates of return. A linear pattern appears to fit the effect parameters rather well. Perhaps the rates of return are simply deviations of the interpoint slopes from the total regression, i.e., from a constant rate of return. We find, however, that using a constant rate of return reduces the explained proportion of the variance between cell means by several points. This decrement is certainly statistically significant but more importantly, in my judgment, it is large enough to warrant substantive interpretation. If one wished to simplify the model, however, it seems clear that a constant, rather than a declining, rate of return is appropriate.

What are the differences between the races in these parameters? First, effect parameters show a greater range for blacks than for whites. Second, differences seem most dramatic where the fewest people are affected (and hence the parameters are the most unstable). The return for 5–7 years is greater for whites and the return for 17+ is greater for blacks. The exception to this rule is the markedly lower rate for blacks in the 9–11 category. Even though blacks show a somewhat higher return for the completion of high school, it is insufficient to compensate for the markedly lower parameter at the 9–11 level. The return for moving from grades 8 through 12 is for whites 0.60 while for blacks it is 0.44. Perhaps white employers have a tendency to take more seriously a white applicant's claim to "some high school" than they would a black applicant's claim.

Age

Table 8.2 presents parameters for age. Effect parameters have the expected general form. They rise to a peak around age 40 and then decline as the effects of "depreciation" overwhelm gains through experience. A plot of rates of return

Table 8.2. Parameters for Age by Race

	White		Black	
Age	Effect Parameters	Rates of Return	Effect Parameters	Rates of Return
26–25	0.6592	–	0.7454	–
27–28	0.8564	0.2992	1.0242	0.3740
29–30	0.9529	0.1127	0.9641	−0.0587
31–32	1.0635	0.1161	1.0846	0.1250
33–34	1.0895	0.0244	1.3450	0.2401
35–36	1.2126	0.1130	1.1202	−0.1671
37–38	1.2726	0.0495	1.3260	0.1837
39–40	1.3157	0.0339	1.6727	0.2615
41–42	1.2839	−0.0242	1.7000	0.0163
43–44	1.3050	0.0164	1.5289	−0.1006
45–46	1.2887	−0.0125	1.2449	−0.1858
47–48	1.2432	−0.0353	1.2100	−0.0280
49–50	1.2155	−0.0223	1.2100	0.000
51–52	1.1787	−0.0303	0.9648	−0.2026
53–54	1.0813	−0.0826	0.8021	−0.1686
55–56	0.9891	−0.0853	0.7493	−0.0658
57–58	0.7868	−0.2045	0.6072	−0.1896
59–60	0.7018	−0.1080	0.4547	−0.2512
61–62	0.4880	−0.3046	0.3416	−0.2487
63–64	0.2917	−0.4018	0.2478	−0.2746

by age suggest that a roughly linear decline is appropriate. It is interesting to note that the peak value for effect parameters occurs at roughly the same age for both races but the decline for blacks appears to begin about five years earlier than it does for whites. Again, we find a greater range of parameters for blacks than for whites.

Period

Table 8.3 presents effect parameters for periods. Recall that these parameters represent proportionate deviation in the rate of return to human capital and not the period-specific rates themselves. Thus, our model does *not* permit us to compare the rates themselves between the races but only permits us to investigate their comparative responsiveness to changing economic conditions.

In general, we observe the rising rates of return which would be expected over the period in question. The parameters for 1962 are the marked exception to the general pattern. Of course, a positive deviation from any trend would be expected for 1962 since the dependent variable in that period is total income rather than earnings. Because of this confounding of "methods" with "real"

Table 8.3. Parameters for Periods by Race

Period	White	Black
1960	0.8245	0.6404
1962	1.2143	1.2599
1966	0.9589	0.9898
1968	1.0512	1.1851
1970	1.0374	1.1130

effects it is difficult to say whether 1962 represents a real departure from the trend. Between the races we again find a greater responsiveness in parameters for blacks than for whites. This finding, of course, is consistent with the last hired, first fired effect.

Cohorts

Table 8.4 presents effect parameters for cohorts. In the presentation of our model we asserted that it was the preschool ability factor which should vary by cohorts. We expected changes in this parameter to reveal secular trends in kindergarten attendance, etc., as well as changes in ability due to improved level of living, improved medical services to children, better nutrition and the like. The pattern of these parameters, however, makes this kind of interpretation unreasonable. First, the parameters are higher for older black cohorts and perhaps for white cohorts also. They decline in the middle and finally rise to

Table 8.4. Parameters for Cohorts by Race

Birth Year	White	Black
1904–05	0.8615	1.3256
1906–07	0.9919	1.1775
1908–09	0.9398	0.9203
1910–11	0.9219	1.2326
1912–13	0.9255	0.9497
1914–15	0.9509	0.9624
1916–17	0.8852	0.9444
1918–19	0.9384	0.8285
1920–21	0.9461	0.7441
1922–23	0.9399	0.8429
1924–25	1.0475	0.7516
1926–27	0.9732	0.7834
1928–29	1.0009	0.9573
1930–31	1.0377	1.0310
1932–33	1.0929	1.0859

their highest levels for the youngest cohorts. But those cohorts are ones whose preschool experience was during the Great Depression, hardly a time of improved level of living.

What kind of alternative explanation can we produce for these results? Perhaps we have a cohort effect in the original meaning of that phrase. Perhaps variation in these parameters is negatively related to the relative size of the birth cohort. Keyfitz (1972) has recently presented cogent arguments to suggest that the economic advantage of being born into a small cohort and the disadvantage of being born into a relatively large one should be marked and persist throughout a lifetime.

The advantage of being in a small cohort is presumed to accrue to a person through his entering various levels of education at times when the schools are not crowded, entering the labor market with fewer competitors, and achieving promotions more rapidly because of a scarcity of appropriately aged alternatives. Probably the best index of this condition would be a sequence of variables for each cohort showing, at various ages, the proportion of the population which is older. Rather than construct such a series of variables I simply aggregated white births and white population to two-year groups from Coale and Zelnick (1963:21–23) and calculated the birth rate which "produced" each cohort. The correlation between the rates and the white cohort parameters is 0.78.

It is probably not worthwhile to perform the same computation for blacks since similarly reliable estimates for births and population are not available for many of the periods. An inspection of the available data, however, suggests a good correspondence.

A Summary of Black-White Differences

For every set of effect parameters we find a greater range of effects for blacks than for whites. For education and experience, perhaps there is a greater requirement for blacks than for whites to show some outward and visible sign of their human capital. For period and cohort effects, a last hired, first fired effect may be the most reasonable explanation wherein the behavioral motivation is simply racial prejudice.

An alternative explanation which has the virtue of explaining all four findings at once comes to mind. Perhaps primarily white employers have greater difficulty estimating the level of human capital for blacks than for whites. One might imagine the cultural and interpersonal separation of the races would make for great difficulty in assaying more subtle cues to ability level between races in the United States. Thus, one might expect that employers would lean more heavily on well-established criteria such as education and experience for blacks. At the same time, one response to economic recession or an oversupply of labor in a given cohort might be to reduce average uncertainty about the fit of ability to a given job. Such a response would account for the greater responsiveness of period and cohort for blacks since the employer's confidence interval about his estimate of a black's ability is presumed larger than it is for a white.

Investigation of Residuals

Overall the model predicts cell means rather well for whites and less well for blacks. Is there some pattern among the misestimations which would be helpful in revising the model? Several points of interest arise on the inspection of residuals.

First, there is a clear pattern of misestimation for 1962. For both races, income is underestimated at the older ages. Income is also overestimated for higher educational levels. It seems likely that this pattern is another effect of using total income rather than earnings for that period.

Second, for whites in 1960 there is exactly the reverse pattern of misestimation. The model overestimates at older ages and underestimates for higher educational levels. I think this pattern may derive from problems in measuring other nonwage and salary earnings in 1960. Particularly, I think the method of adding wage and salary income to self-employed income necessary with the 1960 1/1,000 tape may lead to discounting of the importance of the self-employed income component of earnings.

Third, there is a rather clear pattern of education-cohort interaction for both races. For more recent cohorts income is overestimated at the higher levels of education and underestimated at the lower levels. The pattern is such as to suggest a decline over cohorts in the average rate of return to a unit of schooling. One interpretation of this finding might be that the supply of well-educated people is rising faster than the demand for them. There is another interpretation which I think better fits history. The cohorts we are inspecting were educated during the drive for "universal" grade school and then high school completion. That process has surely resulted in a change in the ability selection factor which, in our model, modifies the rates of return to education itself. Thus, it seems to me that the cohort decline in returns to the completion of higher educational levels is likely to result from declining ability section over time.

Finally, there is no pattern of errors for blacks which is not extant for whites. Therefore, I find no simple explanation for the somewhat greater predictive power of the model for whites.

How CPS Files Would Have Been More Satisfactory

In several instances it has been necessary to explain findings by recourse to the peculiarities of one of the surveys. For 1962, period effects were overestimated and inspection of residuals revealed a pattern of deviation of

actual and predicted income by education and age. I explained these outcomes
as a result of the use of total income in that period. In 1960, I found a pattern
of education and age deviations which suggests that these data may have
discounted the nonwage and salary component of earnings in that period.
Perhaps that explanation would also account for the rather low period parameter
for 1960.

How have these obvious problems affected the estimation of other
parameters? It is difficult to say with a model as complex as this one, but there
has surely been an effect on the estimated age and education parameters as well
as on the period ones.

As one considers those methods effects which have *not* made themselves
obvious in the analysis, uncertainty increases even more rapidly. For example,
the surveys are likely to have rather different response rates for blacks, and the
pattern of selection bias in the returns among the surveys is probably not
negligible. Does this fact account for the less satisfactory fit of our model for
blacks? Perhaps so, but it would be a shame to allow the possibility of an
additional factor in the model for blacks to go unexplored if that explanation is
wrong.

SUMMARY OF THE ARGUMENT

The point of this chapter has been to make an argument by example. The
argument is that the archive of CPS files represents an important resource for the
construction of social indicator models. The advantage of the CPS files consists
in their inherent attention to comparability over time and the fact that
numerous "replications" are available at comparatively low cost.

I have tried to illustrate the importance of attention to comparability in the
details of data collection by counterexample; that is, by showing how a series of
"distinguished" cross-sectional surveys which appear marginally heterogeneous
as to method yield marked ambiguities in interpretation of the analysis
performed upon them by virtue of that heterogeneity.

I have tried to illustrate the advantage of numerous replications by choosing
to use a model which captures intercohort change. Short of having genuine panel
data, the capacity to deal in cohort change seems to me our primary hope for
the estimation of dynamic social models. This capacity, however, depends on
having several cross sections and its potentialities increase rapidly as more
replications are added. The reader should note that the force of this argument
depends neither on his agreement with the specific form of the cohort model
here used nor on the adequacy of the estimation methods I have used. Rather,
the point is that numerous replications permit specification and estimation of
some cohort model.

Illustration of the relative cost advantage of using CPS files is perhaps the most ambiguous argument made here. My work was performed at an average cost of perhaps $10,000 while OCG II, reported on elsewhere in this volume, will cost over a million dollars for a simple replication. The comparison is, of course, unfair because the kinds of information to be collected in OCG II are not to be had in any other way but by replication and the value of having that information is high indeed. However, the information potentially available in the CPS also has a high value.

There is also another way in which the above cost comparison is unfair. Although the average cost of my work was relatively small, it was accomplished in the context of a research facility within the Center for Demography at the university (supported by a "Centers Grant" from NICHD) which is designed to minimize the time and money cost of just this kind of work. Without these facilities, the average costs would have been increased manyfold. To routinely and economically investigate social indicator models using CPS data would require design of a facility even more specialized than the one available to us at Wisconsin. Because I believe investment in such a facility would yield high returns to our knowledge of social change, I will conclude this chapter with some observations on what I think would be required.

OBSERVATION ON A FACILITY TO PRODUCE INDICATORS FROM CPS FILES

Let me begin this section by recounting briefly the data-processing and computation strategy employed in estimating parameters of the model previously described. As we began—about the beginning of April—it was unclear how many of the surveys we would actually be able to use. The 1968 and 1970 CPS person files were due to arrive shortly from the Rand Corporation. We had ordered from the Census Bureau material from the 1964 CPS. We had never used our copy of the 1966 SEO. I chose, therefore, a computing strategy which allowed us to begin with those data at hand and "add on" additional periods as they became available. Therefore, for each of the surveys on hand—the 1960 1/1,000 Sample, the OCG, and the 1966 SEO—we began selecting cases in the universe and constructing tables of age by education by race. We accumulated the number of observations in each cell, the sum of log income, and the sum of log income squared. All of these operations used the weighting scheme of the specific survey. As each of these tables were made they were stored on disk in a common format. At the same time, we designed a program to produce the required $X'X$ and $X'Y$ matrices from the tables. This program has the capacity to expand the number of periods fairly freely. Finally, we wrote a program to do the estimation itself. This program selects rows and columns from the previously constructed matrices. (It thereby permits some modification of the basic model and also will accommodate new surveys.) It then solves the equations under the constraint required and takes care of transforming these estimates into usable form.

In general, I think this computing routine is similar to one which would be chosen by a facility designed to estimate models from CPS files—producing a new set of estimates with each new relevant survey. If I am right, two points in our experience deserve special attention.

First, the expensive part of the job was the data-processing task. Of course, that task was less amenable to a generalized procedure in our work than would be a sequence of CPS files because most of our tapes were in different formats. On the other hand, we were dealing with only 5 files whereas between March 1960 and March 1970 there are extant 120 files of CPS surveys. Managing and processing that volume of data would be quite expensive. It would require a heavy personnel investment to keep track of the abundance of riches and very large computer bills would be generated as well.

Indeed, designing a data management system to retrieve information from the sequence of CPS files oriented to experiments in social modeling is a rather complex task. Such a system should keep track of rotation groups and primary sampling units (to facilitate estimating standard errors of parameters) as well as periods. A master code book is required to indicate in which periods and for which rotation group a given set of questions were asked. Ideally, this code book should itself be a machine readable file—one which could be efficiently and accurately updated—and should contain pointers to the data file. Overall, then, our experiment suggests that data management and data processing are difficult nonsubstantive tasks to be faced in designing a facility to experiment with models of social indicators using CPS files.

A second kind of computing problem which deserves comment arose in the course of our experiment. In the course of parameter estimation we encountered fairly difficult numerical analysis problems. Specifically, our $X'X$ matrix contained numbers of widely varying magnitude. This fact, which seems endemic in work with files of the kind under discussion, can lead to a considerable problem with round-off and accumulation errors. The estimation procedure for our model, for example, is very sensitive to an indexing error which will produce a matrix whose determinate is zero. We found that round-off errors can interact with this kind of program error in fiendish ways—ways which lead to indications of the difficulty designed to drive one out of his mind. At one point, we found ourselves dealing with a matrix whose determinate should have been positive but was in fact negative. To explore the difficulty, we computed eigenvalues for the matrix. Some of them were negative (none of them should have been), and we thought we had a clue to our difficulty. However, since we had computed a negative determinate, we expected an odd number negative eigenvalue and in fact we found an even number.

We believe we have uncovered all the "bugs" in our programming and dealt with the round-off and accumulation errors in a fashion comparable with the state of the art. Our experiment suggests, nonetheless, that a facility designed to do such work routinely should include skilled numerical analysts who are well versed in the adequacies and difficulty of the locally available package of programs for matrix algebraic computation.

The burden of these observations is that, presuming a decision were made to release CPS files for public use, the next problem would rapidly become that of designing and supporting a facility to make them usable. Our experience is that such a facility will require a rather high level of skill in both data management and numerical analysis.

REFERENCES

Coale, Ansley, and Melvin Zelnick.
  1963   New Estimates of Fertility and Population in the United States. Princeton, N. J.: Princeton University Press.
Duncan, Otis Dudley.
  1969   Toward Social Reporting: Next Steps. (Social Science Frontiers, No. 2.) New York: Russell Sage Foundation.
Keyfitz, Nathan.
  1972   "Oscillations in a demographic-economic model." Paper presented at the Conference on Population Dynamics (June), sponsored by the Mathematics Research Center, University of Wisconsin.
Scheffe, Henry.
  1959   The Analysis of Variance. New York: Wiley.
Thurow, Lester.
  1968   "The occupational distribution of returns to education and experience for whites and Negroes." In Federal Programs for the Development of Human Resources, Volume I. Washington, D. C.: Subcommittee on Economic Progress of the Joint Economic Committee, Congress of the United States.
  1969   Poverty and Discrimination. Washington, D. C.: Studies in Social Economics, The Brookings Institution.
Winsborough, H. H., and Peter Dickinson.
  1971   "Components of Negro-white income differences." Proceedings of the Social Statistics Section, American Sociological Associations:6–8.

9

DESIGN FOR A REPLICATE STUDY OF SOCIAL MOBILITY IN THE UNITED STATES*

David L. Featherman and Robert M. Hauser

In the early 1960s Professors Peter M. Blau and Otis Dudley Duncan initiated a major sample survey of the extent and sources of social mobility in the United States. Entitled "Occupational Changes in a Generation" (OCG), their survey was carried out as an adjunct to the monthly Current Population Survey (CPS), which in March of 1962 elicited data on fertility, education, income, and employment. Using a two-page mail-back questionnaire from which supplementary details about socioeconomic origins, residential background, and spouse characteristics were ascertained, Blau and Duncan were able to carry out an extensive analysis of the processes of status attainment and social mobility in an unusually large (by social science standards) cross-section sample of the American population.

We are presently engaged in a replication and extension of the 1962 OCG survey for which the field work will be carried out in 1973. In this chapter our purpose is to present the major features of our study design and, in so doing, to give particular attention to problems in achieving a strict replication. Our concept of a strict replication is taken from Duncan (1969, 1970) and denotes a

*The paper was prepared for the Conference on Social Indicator Models, Russell Sage Foundation, under a grant from the National Science Foundation (Grant No. GI-31604X). Support was received from the College of Agriculture and Life Sciences and the Center for Demography and Ecology, University of Wisconsin, Madison. The authors wish to thank the numerous colleagues and critics in universities and governmental agencies, particularly the Bureau of the Census, who have been instrumental in the development of our research design.

reapplication of the same measurement instruments, according to the same techniques of sampling, to an equivalently defined population as in a base-line study; we differentiate a strict replication from a restudy, in which one or more elements of the original design has been compromised. The idea of replicating the OCG survey has received some attention in the recent literature on social reporting, not only because of the quality and importance of the base-line measurements, but also because the model-building strategy employed in analyses of the 1962 data seems especially likely to yield useful social indicators (see Land, 1971, and his introductory chapter of this volume). In an agenda on "Social Reporting for the 1970s" prepared for the Commission on Federal Statistics, Sheldon, Land, and Bauer recommend "the replication of the Occupational Changes in a Generation survey in 1972 and the repetition of the survey on at least a decennial basis" (1971:418). In arguing for a replication Sheldon et al. observe:

> First of all, the survey was conducted in 1962 which makes the data nearly a decade old. Second, this has been a decade of broadened governmental activities to influence the distribution of opportunities throughout the society, particularly with regard to racial and ethnic minorities. Therefore, it is a matter of considerable urgency to ascertain the effects, if any, of such activities on social mobility. Finally, excellent though the survey was by comparative standards, it could certainly be improved in both its execution and analysis if repeated today.

With regard to the feasibility of replicating the OCG survey in order to measure trends in stratification, Otis Dudley Duncan has written (1968:716):

> We are now in a position to argue that any real change in the degree of stratification, or in correlations between variables implicated in the process of stratification, provided the change is large enough to be interesting, can be detected by repeated surveys, provided there is rigorous standardization of concepts, scales, and survey techniques. Thus, I would urge that high priority be given to a replication of the OCG survey in 1972 (to take advantage of the convenience of a ten-year interval). In all relevant particulars, the survey should repeat the procedures used ten years earlier. This would not preclude experimentation with new questions, alternative measures of occupational status and so forth, provided that these are handled as additions to the replication and not as substitutes for it.

While the time is already past when we might have enjoyed the convenience of replication at a ten-year interval, in other respects we are hopeful of fulfilling the recommendations just cited.

THE 1962 SURVEY: DESIGN

The target population in the 1962 OCG survey was males 20 to 64 years old in the civilian noninstitutional population in March 1962 (including as eligible about 900,000 Armed Forces personnel living in families on military posts in the

United States or off posts in civilian quarters). Details of the design and procedures of the CPS in 1962 have been described elsewhere (U. S. Bureau of the Census, 1963, 1967). Suffice it to say that the stratified, multistage cluster sample included more than 35,000 occupied dwelling units or households which contained about 25,000 eligible males. By March of 1973 the design of the CPS sample will have changed in several respects. Major changes include a substantial increase in the size of the sample, reduction in the size of sample segments, and use of 1970 census materials in the selection of new primary sampling units, the preparation of lists of households, and the weighting of sample data to represent the estimated current age-sex-color composition of the population. Since the primary effects of these changes are to improve the efficiency of the survey and to update procedures for adjusting the data to reflect changes in the composition of the population, they are not expected to affect replicability. Other changes in CPS procedures, discussed below, present greater obstacles to comparability.

CPS interviewers left behind a two-page questionnaire for each eligible male, and of these 83 percent were returned. The 20,700 respondents represented about 45 million males in the eligible population. Two items in the supplement (father's occupation and son's first full-time occupation) were subjected to a field edit, and the entire supplement was reviewed when the response to either of these items was deficient. Mail and personal follow-up calls were made, and in addition to the weights usually applied in the CPS to reduce sampling variability, the data were weighted to compensate for the effects of failure to return the supplement.

THE 1962 SURVEY: SUMMARY OF MAJOR FINDINGS

Analyses of the 1962 OCG data advanced the ability of students of stratification to describe and analyze the processes of inter- and intragenerational mobility.[1] We have learned, for example, that the flow of manpower from social origins to social destinations (father to son occupational mobility), for the 45 million males represented in these data, was comprised primarily of small upward and downward movements (in terms of the status ranking of occupations). Despite a large amount of upward mobility, the patterns of recruitment to occupations in adulthood and of the supply from origin sectors were not random. Independent professionals, proprietors, and farmers in 1962 displayed a marked tendency to "inherit" the self-employed occupations of their fathers. On the other hand, the three lowest (status) white-collar occupational groups (clerical, retail sales, and service) and the two

---

[1] These selected conclusions drawn from the OCG data are reported in Blau and Duncan (1967) and elaborated in Duncan et al. (1972). Other generalizations are documented in the bibliographic citations appended hereto.

lowest blue-collar categories (both nonfarm labor) both recruited extensively from other occupational statuses in the paternal generation and were sources of supply (from the paternal generation) to other (destination) statuses in the filial generation. Patterns of intergenerational supply and recruitment appeared to be reflecting shifts in the structure of the labor force, as for example in the expansion of the lower white-collar occupational sector.

On balance, the net upward direction of intergenerational mobility was a function of short-distance movements (in the socioeconomic space of rank-ordered occupational statuses) induced in part by structural expansion and supported by semipermeable boundaries between the farm and the manual labor sectors and between the blue-collar and white-collar sectors. These semipermeable boundaries between "classes" permitted upward mobility from one sector to another but inhibited downward mobility. Whether the pattern and degree of upward mobility is a function of historical trends (viz., period-specific differential fertility rates and farm to nonfarm migration rates) is a matter for future study; this is an example of the type of trend issue to which our research is designed to speak.

Although the OCG research is important for its description of intergenerational mobility for the selected age cohorts as of 1962, perhaps the more fundamental contribution to the study of stratification (and indirectly to public policy) follows from the Blau and Duncan analysis of the process of status attainment. The latter is differentiated from mobility analysis in that the process of status attainment focuses the analyst's attention on the degree to which the status attainments of the son depend upon the statuses of his father, and on the variables which intervene between origin and destination statuses to explain the effect of paternal on filial achievements. Mobility analysis, on the other hand, does not typically decompose the movement between statuses into its constituent elements, thereby limiting the understanding of how vertical circulation is facilitated or thwarted by events and conditions in one's social past and throughout the life-cycle.

With regard to the decomposition of paternal on filial occupational achievement, Blau and Duncan specified a causal model of the process of intergenerational status attainments by ordering status events in the life-cycle as in Figure 9.1 and by estimating the dependence relationships through a series of recursive regression equations. These methods provided for a quantitative assessment of the antecedent conditions of socioeconomic status achievements and of the relative importance of social origins and of later achieved statuses (viz., education) for these socioeconomic attainments.

From their basic model, Blau and Duncan concluded that years of formal schooling accounted for nearly all of the direct effects of paternal occupational status and education on son's occupational standing as of 1962. Moreover, son's education and the number of siblings in his family of origin explained virtually

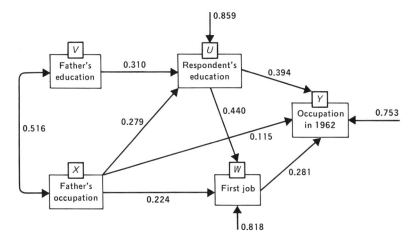

Figure 9.1. Basic Causal Model of the Process of Status Attainment

Source: Blau and Duncan (1967:170); coefficients on straight, one-headed arrows are net regression coefficients in standard form; coefficient on curved, two-headed arrow is a coefficient of correlation.

all of the variance in occupational status between the farm and the nonfarm background subgroups (since those of farm origin attained fewer years of schooling, an outcome, but only in part, of higher levels of fertility in the parental generation and the lower socioeconomic background statuses associated with the farm residential sector).

Aside from education, another intervening variable between social origins and social destinations (see Figure 9.1) was first full-time job after the completion of schooling (the measurement of this variable proved to entail knotty problems and possible reporting errors). Holding constant social background statuses, education was more influential in determining 1962 occupational statuses for each of the selected age cohorts than was first job, although there was some fluctuation in the net regression coefficients across cohorts. Ignoring distortions owing to differential reporting and measurement errors, these fluctuations in the cohorts models reflected both historical aspects of the respective cohort experiences and differential durations of full-time labor force tenure. In the 1962 cross-section these effects could not be separated directly, but in the proposed trend data, such an issue becomes tractable.

The OCG data permitted an examination of ethnic and minority group achievements based on the Blau and Duncan model of the process of status attainment. First and second generation immigrants to the United States differed (in 1962) in the degree to which their national origin backgrounds accounted for the variance in their respective socioeconomic attainments in their adopted country. For native sons of foreign parentage, national origin was less a factor in educational and occupational status attainment than for their fathers. Still, among these native white males of nonfarm background (determined by paternal employment in farm or nonfarm occupations while son was about age 16), the Russian-Americans surpassed all other ethnic subgroups, while the Latin Americans fell below all others in educational and occupational attainments. By and large the variance between these white ethnic groups could be attributed to social origin differentials and subsequent achievements, leaving little support for pervasive discrimination in the distribution of education and occupation on grounds of national ancestry. Moreover, that both sons of immigrants and native males who had migrated from their regions of birth enjoyed greater social mobility than natives who had remained in their natal environs attested to the possibility of achievement and assimilation for white males, irrespective of national origins.

However, there was no similar evidence for the operation of vertical circulation based on universalistic criteria in the OCG data for nonwhites (hereafter, blacks). Neither background characteristics (paternal statuses and southern natality) nor educational differentials were capable of accounting for the relative socioeconomic underachievements of blacks vis-à-vis whites of similar characteristics; these differences were greater at the higher levels of completed schooling. While for white minorities there was not abundant evidence for a "cycle of poverty," there was greater plausibility for such a condition among the black population in 1962: for each of the achieved statuses of education, occupation, and income, there remained proportions of black-white differences which could not be explained by regional, social background, intellectual, and prior achieved status. In short, in the 1962 data there was evidence for cumulative racial (but not national origin) discrimination over the life-cycle.[2]

POLICY IMPLICATIONS

Following Sheldon and Land (1972:139) we may say that social indicators derived from OCG data (past and future) are mainly "analytic" or "descriptive," rather than "problem oriented or directly policy-oriented." That is, they "serve as components of explicit conceptual and causal models" of segments of the social system and are "intended primarily to describe the state of society and changes taking place within it," while their utility for "direct use in policy and program decisions" is limited.

This is not merely a euphemistic way of saying that OCG data are irrelevant

---

[2] Excluded from this brief summary of the OCG findings are the socioeconomic effects of the internal structure of the family of origin (sibling position; data on R's brother), stability of family of origin, migration, and marriage and fertility.

in policy formation. Like Blau and Duncan (1967:1), we believe that our findings "will be helpful to policy-makers and the interested public in formulating appropriate action programs and clarifying public controversy." We think that our findings will be useful to policy makers and others by helping them to assess the opportunities which are available to major population subgroups and the factors which limit or enhance those opportunities. Such assessments are not presently available from any other source with the scope and detail made possible by the combination of the original and replicated OCG surveys, and we believe they can be an important input to processes of setting goals and strategies for the enhancement of opportunity.

At the same time we do not wish to oversell the utility of our research in the formation of policy. Other large-scale social researches have engendered great disappointment by claiming more immediate relevance to the formation of policy than was justified by the facts, and we do not propose to repeat such claims. For example, we think it most unlikely that our work will lead directly to the implementation of specific social programs with predictable cost and effectiveness. The major policy value of our research lies in its potential contributions—substantive and methodological—to the construction of a time-series of indicators (both descriptive and analytic) of the distribution of social and economic opportunity in the United States. Specifically, there are five areas in which we think our study can contribute to policy formation:

1. *In the assessment of widespread beliefs about equality of opportunity and factors affecting it.* We think that the "debunking" function of OCG findings should not be underrated. For example, findings from the 1962 study cast a great deal of doubt on the utility of concepts of a "cycle" or "culture" of poverty, and more specifically on the suggestion that family instability was the major source of white-black achievement differentials. Other pertinent 1962 findings include the fact that excess fertility in the family of orientation is not a major factor in black-white occupation and income differentials in adulthood and that discrimination in the labor market is a source of a larger share of white-black occupation and income differentials than is differential educational attainment. We expect our replication to further validate and refine these findings and to produce new findings about specific variables in the process of achievement which are relevant to public policy. For example, we shall obtain measurements of the role of military service, union membership, and interruptions in schooling on the inheritance of social status across generations. In a sense such measurements provide "cost-free" estimates of the possible value of successful intervention in the achievement process.

2. *In locating and defining the problems of specific population subgroups.* We think that our measurements on women and on ethnic-racial groups— especially on blacks and on the Spanish-speaking—and on rural out-migrants will be especially pertinent here. From a policy perspective the outcome of these

measurements in younger cohorts will be especially interesting inasmuch as their experiences incorporate recent trends.

3. *In providing an overall model of the process of social and economic achievement which can serve as a frame of reference for discussions about specific aspects of that process.* We expect to refine and elaborate the "basic" model of occupational achievement proposed by Blau and Duncan. We think the value of operating within that kind of explicit model is amply illustrated by findings like those cited under no. 1 above, and at a more general level, by other examples of social indicator models in this volume.

4. *In providing a set of current trend estimates on major features of the process of social achievement.* We think that trend measurements will be of value in the process of policy formation, even where the allocation of responsibility for specific changes (or the lack thereof) is a matter of judgment, rather than proof. It has been our impression that the value of single-time measurements, like the survey undertaken for *Equality of Educational Opportunity*, is lower because many policy judgments must rest on inherently unsupportable assumptions about what earlier surveys might have shown. Fortunately, the design of OCG permits us to obtain implicit trend measurements in a single-time survey, to replicate and validate earlier trend measurements of the same kind, to obtain bench-mark trend measurements on additional variables, and to extend the existing "stock" of trend measurements by one more point in time.

5. *In improving the measurement of processes of social and economic achievement.* We think that our investment in improved measurement techniques—and also in new techniques of data reduction and analysis—will be quite as important for the policy applications of our findings as for their purely academic uses. We think our proposed innovations can contribute both to the quality and legitimacy of the information we can supply and to the development of methods for future replications and other related studies.

For example, the questions of poverty and its possible transmission between generations are interesting research issues for the student of American society and of its distribution of rewards, services, and life changes. OCG data bearing on these issues can also serve as a base-line for a series of social reports on the trends of opportunity and socioeconomic well-being in this country. Knowing that as of 1962, growing up in an intact (rather than a broken) family provides from 0.6 to 1.0 year more of schooling for young boys, that increasing their fathers' occupational statuses by 10 Socioeconomic Index (Duncan, 1961:Chap. 6) units adds another 0.3 years, and that limiting the number of their potential siblings by one would increase their formal education by yet another 0.2 years is at least potentially useful for those whose function is to write public policy. Being able to calculate the costs of discrimination in the distribution of education and occupational status (among men of different skin colors but otherwise equivalent) in terms of dollars of earnings not only speaks to the credibility of academic arguments regarding the pervasiveness of a "culture of poverty" for all of "the poor" (regardless of skin color), but it provides statistical estimates of the cost (*ceteris paribus*) of being black. Moreover, the latter estimates could be used to calculate the probable gains to black citizens, and to the nation as a whole, of ameliorative programs and of alternative interventions in the processes of status attainment.

A detailed analysis of cohort-specific attainment processes for whites and blacks during the past decade would constitute an important input to social policy formulation. After all, one could argue that the social legislation of the late 1950s and the 1960s should by now be producing effects on the distribution of statuses and life chances between racial and ethnic minorities, at least for selected age cohorts. Although the effects of specific programs are unquestionably difficult to disentangle, one would expect *prima facie* the effects of discrimination to be less costly on younger cohorts of minorities in 1972 than in 1962. If, when compared with the OCG base-line, replication data were to indicate no diminution in the cost to younger cohorts of being black, one might regard this as a relevant datum for the evaluation of current public policies. Regardless of the outcome of a replicate study, we argue that such an undertaking is policy related, at least to the degree that the maximization of opportunity for all Americans is still a viable societal goal.

In this context, we feel that an intergenerational focus is an appropriate framework for estimating the degree of opportunity (alternatively, the degree of status inheritance). We argue that attention directed at the mechanisms by which statuses (including "poverty") are transmitted between generations captures the essence of the process of stratification, or social mobility, as this process is experienced differently by various age cohorts or subpopulations. By calculating cohort- and period-specific data for intergenerational status transmission, the relationships of cause and effect, of policies and social conditions, and of events and populations are rendered more tractable. We would argue further that data so derived are more useful in assessing our abilities to reach societal goals (i.e., equality of opportunity) than are aggregate income and family labor force statistics for short-term movements into and out of "poverty."

Our replication of the 1962 OCG study will provide a valuable cross-sectional survey of these issues (and others) for the new decade, and both cross-sections will be a rich resource for information concerning the stratification of American society, as experienced by specific age cohorts of males. For example, if we accept the basic causal model adduced in Figure 9.1, we can construct tables of statistical estimates like Table 9.1 (containing estimates of coefficients in the basic model of achievement for four age cohorts of nonfarm men in 1962) for both 1962 and 1972. Our replication is designed so changes in the coefficients over the decade indicate real shifts in the processes of status attainment. Changes in coefficients for the age group 25–34 in both years will

Table 9.1. Regression Coefficients for Recursive Model Relating Achieved Statuses to Family Background Factors, by Age, for Non-Negro Men with Nonfarm Background, in Experienced Civilian Labor Force: March 1962

Age and Dependent Variable[a]	Independent Variables					Coefficient of Determination
	Y	U	T	X	V	
25–34						
U			−0.2211	0.0352	0.1889	0.263
Y		4.8333	−0.1889	0.0833	0.4520	0.436
H	0.0452	0.0785	−0.0813	0.0152	(−0.0151)	0.126
35–44						
U			−0.2281	0.0384	0.1707	0.269
Y		4.3767	−0.4633	0.1352	(0.0485)	0.431
H	0.0704	0.1998	−0.0374	0.0114	0.0712	0.216
45–54						
U			−0.2057	0.0471	0.1493	0.260
Y		3.7994	−0.3960	0.1533	−0.1513	0.372
H	0.0918	0.2394	(0.0182)	0.0395	(0.0109)	0.222
55–64						
U			−0.2028	0.0399	0.1672	0.208
Y		3.1965	−0.6454	0.1366	0.3094	0.342
H	0.0768	0.2281	(0.0214)	(0.0076)	(0.0212)	0.159

Source: Duncan et al., 1972:Tables 3.1 and 3.2.

Notes: Parentheses enclose each coefficient whose value is less than its standard error in absolute value.

[a] V: Father's educational attainment.
X: Father's occupational status.
T: Respondent's number of siblings.
U: Respondent's education.
Y: Respondent's occupational status, March 1962.
H: Respondent's income in 1961.

be indicative of interperiod shifts in the parameters of stratification for persons at equivalent stages of the life-cycle; associated with fluctuations in the coefficients for an aging cohort (say one ages 25–34 in 1962 and ages 36–45 in 1973) will be the effects of maturation and its location in history. In short, our replication will allow a duplication of the types of analyses summarized above from the OCG study in a second cross-section, but in conjunction with the 1962 OCG, the 1972 data will introduce new capacities for the assessment of trend over the decade.

We understand the net result of our replication to be the estimation of a set of parameters for the processes of stratification which have the status of social indicators. These indicators, be they single coefficients such as those in Table 9.1 or entire systems of equations (or their graphic counterparts, as in Figure 9.1), delineate social states in the two cross-sections, define lingering and new social problems, and trace social trends over the decade in the intergenerational mobility processes, "which by social engineering may hopefully be guided toward social goals formulated by social planning [paraphrase of Stuart Rice's (1967) definition of social indicators from the form cited in Duncan, 1969:2]." We concur with Duncan (1969) that replication studies of the sort permitted by the OCG cross-section and the provision of analytic indicators of states and trends are important "next steps" for the social sciences. It is our view that replications of base-line studies of the variety proposed here not only enrich the context wherein a system of social accounts (social reports) is possible, but these endeavors also serve to consolidate, integrate, and advance our social science *qua* science. The latter functions ensue from the demands imposed by the goal of social accounting—demands for the standardization of measurement, for reference to clearly defined populations and subpopulations, and for the storage of archival data in accessible forms for the myriad purposes of secondary analysis—as well as from the sheer accumulation of knowledge so derived.

THE 1973 STUDY: DESIGN[3]

Three major data collection operations are included in the design of the 1973 replication and extension of OCG (hereafter, OCG-II). The first is a national survey, carried out in conjunction with the March 1973 CPS, which will be comparable to the March 1962 CPS and OCG survey, except blacks and persons of Spanish origin or descent will be oversampled. The second phase of the field work is a statewide survey in Wisconsin, also carried out in the

---

[3]While our text is cast in the past tense, certain statements of "fact" about the survey (e.g., the exact number of completed interviews) remain as educated guesses at the time we completed this draft, in late January. While details of design had become firm in late December after our pretest, the OCG field work had not begun nor were the March CPS and state of Wisconsin surveys underway.

spring of 1973. The third phase comprises several efforts to ascertain response validity and reliability, which uses subsamples of both the national and statewide surveys. We shall describe these three phases of data collection in the order just listed.

The National Survey: Data Collection

In the national survey we aim to achieve a strict replication of the 1962 study within the limits of desirability and feasibility. We have sacrificed comparability grudgingly where the design could be improved, and the 1962 design is so defective that replication did not seem worthwhile (as in the measurement of first job); where we had evidence that failure to replicate exactly had no effects on comparability (see Duncan, 1968:715); and where the alternative was not to do the study at all. In some ways failure to replicate is inevitable. For example, given identical procedures, the upward intercohort trend in educational attainment would be expected to improve the reporting of both contemporaneous and retrospective items. Likewise, while the field work again was carried out by the U. S. Bureau of the Census, it will be impossible to replicate 1962 procedural and organizational conditions exactly (see Thompson, 1970; Shapiro and Thompson, 1972). With one important exception, the coding of occupation, we could not expect to exercise any control over procedures in the March CPS which have changed in the past eleven years.

One major change in the method of data collection in the national survey which has been dictated by changes in the CPS design was that items in the OCG-II supplement were ascertained by means of a mail-out, mail-back questionnaire in late August or early September of 1973, rather than by a leave-behind mail-back operation in March. While we should have preferred to retain the 1962 procedure, the Bureau of the Census assured us that a mail-out survey of experienced respondents with telephone and personal follow-up by CPS interviewers would yield data of coverage and quality comparable to that obtained in the 1962 survey. Our pretest experience substantiates this confidence.

In addition to the usual labor force information the March CPS household interview contains a supplement in which a variety of socioeconomic information is ascertained; e.g., educational attainment, work experience, and the several components of income. It is this supplementary information in the household record which makes the March CPS so attractive as a sample frame. Because of the pattern of rotation into and out of the CPS sample, according to which each selected housing unit is in the sample for the same four months during each of two consecutive years, there is a 75 percent overlap from month to month in the composition of the CPS sample. In principle the linkage of household records from month to month permits the construction of lengthy records without placing the burden of a lengthy interview on respondents. However, in order to produce a larger volume of linked records, the length of the March interview has been increased, and supplements to interviews in adjacent months have been eliminated. Thus, the Bureau of the Census is concerned about demands already placed on respondents by March interviews and is understandably reluctant to burden them with additional questionnaires at that time.

With the OCG field operation carried out in August and September, no respondent was contacted for the first time within two months of his rotation out of the CPS sample or within two months of his rotation back in. Thus, one advantage to the new design was a lessening of concern within the Bureau of the Census about the possible effects of the OCG questionnaire on returning members of the CPS sample. An attendant disadvantage to the revised design was that the bureau could not undertake a personal follow-up of movers between March and September who leave their March primary sampling unit of residence (usually a county or a large metropolitan area). We gauge this to be a relatively minor problem because telephone and mail follow-ups were made, and most movers remained in the same primary sampling unit.

The National Survey: Sample Design

Changes in the sample design for the 1973 OCG were dictated by changes in the CPS design over the past decade, to which we have already referred, and also by our interest in oversampling blacks and persons of Spanish origin or descent. Because the CPS sample has been expanded to include 45,000 household interviews, which yield an average of about one eligible respondent per household, we obtain about 37,500 completed supplements (if 1962 response rates to the supplement are maintained). The larger total sample will permit us to undertake detailed analyses which could not be contemplated even with a sample as large as that obtained in 1962. For example, we shall be able to use a more detailed occupational classification than the 17-category scheme used in 1962 for basic occupational mobility analyses. We will be able to talk with more confidence about cohorts defined by five-year age intervals, and we will be able to make some intercohort comparisons within population subgroups defined by region of origin, nativity, national origin, race, and other variables.

Of these possibilities the most important may be that of producing accurate estimates of parameters of the stratification process for cohorts within the black population. The interpretation of 1962 OCG data was frustrated at many points by the large sampling errors of estimates pertaining to the black population. We thought it especially important that accurate estimates for cohorts of blacks be obtained because of the possibility that the parameters of the stratification process for blacks may have changed within the past decade. While the expansion of the CPS sample increases the number of black respondents from about 2,000 to 3,500, we thought that estimates of sufficient accuracy could be obtained only by increasing the sample of blacks to the point where we will have at least 1,500 respondents per ten-year age group, that is, by again doubling the size of the black sample. Our plan for supplementing blacks was to draw about 4,000 persons from the October 1972 CPS sample, from households where the head is Negro. In March of 1973, CPS interviewers visited about 5,000 such households as were identified in October to screen for eligible black males and to elicit personal (or telephone, where necessary) interviews, on the substance of the March CPS schedule and the OCG supplement.

Because of the widespread belief (supported by some presumptive evidence in the 1962 data, viz., Duncan and Duncan, 1968) that persons of Spanish origin face obstacles to social achievement which are similar to those faced by blacks, we increased the number of such persons in the sample up to about the number of blacks, 2,000, included in the 1962 sample. Households of Spanish origin were identified from the October 1972 CPS and added to the March 1973 CPS sample; these households were contacted for CPS labor force, income, and work experience information as part of the regular CPS survey in March. Along with the basic sample from the March CPS frame, eligible males of Spanish origin were mailed the OCG questionnaire in late August or September. We gained an additional 2,000 men of Spanish origin by this means.

The National Survey: Procedural Changes and Replication

An opportunity to measure the aggregate effect of procedural changes follows from the fact that most cohorts covered in the 1962 study also appear in the replication. By ascertaining occupation in March 1962 we will be able to replicate the findings as of 1962 for three of the ten-year cohorts covered in 1962, subject only to the effects of procedural change, cohort attrition and differential recall. As to errors of recall of occupations five or ten years in the past, we have obtained one measurement which suggests that such errors are not large in comparison with errors affecting contemporaneous reports of occupations. For employed men 19 years and older in 1968 who recalled having an occupation in July 1963, the correlation coefficient between recalled occupation and actual CPS report of occupation in 1963 was 0.80, when major occupation categories were scored using Duncan's (1961) index of socioeconomic status (calculated from Walsh and Buckholdt, 1970). This may be compared with a correlation of 0.86 reported by Siegel and Hodge (1968) for all males in a census-CPS match.

Our capacity to achieve replication will be enhanced by our access to the 1962 unit record tapes. We shall be able to improve comparability by changing tabulation specifications for the 1962 data, as well as by choosing those for the 1973 data. Our access to both sets of unit record tapes will also make it possible to use new coding and scaling systems, like the prestige scores for all occupations developed at NORC (Siegel, 1971).

Our effort to achieve comparability is inconvenienced in one minor respect because the replication was carried out in 1973, rather than in 1972 as we had originally hoped. Because each cohort is ten years older ten years later, a 1972 replication would have permitted us to use the same age-breaks for purposes of intercohort, interperiod, age-constant comparisons as for intracohort interperiod comparisons. In order to make both kinds of comparisons with the 1973 replication, we will have to use two sets of age-breaks and extend the coverage of the survey by one year. For example, to compare the achievements of men aged 55–64 in the two periods, we need only to use the same age-breaks in both samples. However, men aged 45–54 in 1962 will be 56–65 in 1973, so to make true intracohort comparisons we have to shift the age-breaks and to include 65-year-olds in the eligible population.

Our twin goals of extension and replication of the substance of Blau and Duncan's bench-mark survey have lengthened the OCG questionnaire (described subsequently). The pretest draft comprised eight legal-sized pages, compared to the two pages of the 1962 OCG supplement. We share with the Bureau of the Census some concern about the effect of questionnaire length on response rates and quality. Consequently, the pretest was designed to test two forms of the questionnaire—the long form, which we designed, and the original 1962 instrument. The pretest, conducted in Chicago, Houston, and San Antonio in the fall of 1972, provided limited comparisons of the two instruments with regard to effects of length, layout formats, and deliberate changes in selected items which had been regarded as defective in the 1962 (short) form. These issues of departure from strict replication are reported below in the section, "Questionnaire Design."

As noted in a previous section, the supplement items on father's occupation and son's first job after leaving school were edited in the field in 1962. Questionnaires where either of those items were left blank or did not permit coding at the level of major occupation groups were rejected and assigned to interviewers for follow-up during April. Exact replication of these procedures should present no difficulty.

Another procedural source of noncomparability is change in methods for allocating values for missing data on March CPS items. The Bureau of the Census uses a "hot deck" technique to allocate responses for items with missing data (Levine, 1967). This procedure involves the creation of a matrix whose cells represent subpopulations likely to differ in respect to the item for which values are to be allocated. After a "cold start," in which average values are entered in the matrix and substituted for missing data for persons in the cell, an observed value for the first person in a cell with data present is recorded, and that value is substituted for missing data for persons in the same cell until another record with a response is processed, at which point the new value becomes the proxy for missing data. The procedure has some tendency to distort analytical results, because variables assigned by the method are related to other measured variables only through their mutual relations with variables used to construct the matrix. While this procedure will be followed in 1973 as it was in 1962, the variables entering the matrixes have changed, with effects on the data which are presently unknown to us. One bright element in this picture is that the 1973 tape will have allocated items "flagged," so we shall be able to assess some of the effects of allocation on our findings.

Changes in concepts or questions relating to March CPS items which will be used extensively in OCG-II analyses present an especially difficult problem. For example, the wording of the income questions has been changed significantly, and work experience in the preceding year, which is used in the allocation of income nonresponses, now is ascertained in March, rather than in February. We can think of no remedy for differences in the measurement of income between the two surveys beyond reliance on professional opinion as to the extent and character of those differences.

In the case of occupation, which we view as the most important concept in our research design, the problem of establishing comparability is superficially greater than in the case of income, but we think we have achieved a satisfactory resolution of it. In the period since 1962 there have been a couple of minor changes in the series of questions used to ascertain occupation, industry, and class of worker. For example, the category "government" under class of worker has been split into local, state, and federal categories. More importantly, persons reporting self-employment are asked whether their own business is incorporated, and, if so, they are reclassified as private wage and salary workers. One major change in the series is the addition of the question, "What were . . . 's most important activities or duties?" Responses to this question are reported to have a large effect on the classification of self-employed craftsmen, who are frequently misclassified as managers but will not be classified in the appropriate craft category unless their major activity actually is management. In addition to these changes occupations are now being coded in the 1970 census classification, which represents a substantial departure from that used in 1960, and in the March 1962 CPS (Greene et al., 1969; Bregger, 1971).

After considering a variety of alternatives we decided to have each occupation item presented in its up-to-date form and coded twice: once to 1970 specifications by the regular CPS coders; a second time to 1960 specifications, ignoring the item on major duties and activities, by a staff of coders specially trained to use 1960 census materials. By this device we achieve replication of procedures employed in the base-line study, insure consistency in the classification of occupations between those ascertained in the March 1973 CPS and those in the OCG-II supplement, and ease replication of current (1970) measurement procedures in the next OCG survey.

The Wisconsin Survey

The state of Wisconsin survey was fielded in March–April 1973 through the University of Wisconsin Survey Research Laboratory. We conducted telephone interviews of about 40 minutes' duration with 1,200 whites in the age range 20–65, and personal interviews of about an hour's length with 800 black males in the same age range. Because of the nearly complete concentration of the state's small black population in Milwaukee, virtually all of the black respondents were drawn from that area. White respondents were sampled in accordance with a stratified random sampling of telephone numbers from throughout the state. One function of the state survey was to update and improve a time series on socioeconomic achievement in Wisconsin which began in 1961 and to make possible state-national comparisons (say) of labor force participation and returns to education. To accomplish this end, the state questionnaire contained all relevant items from the March 1973 CPS interview, in addition to items constituting the national OCG supplement. In this survey we could ascertain religious affiliation, index social participation, and measure attitudes which were either practically or politically infeasible in the context of the national study design. Finally, the statewide survey provided excellent opportunities for the assessment of data quality, especially the quality of proxy reports of parental statuses, as discussed subsequently.

In its own way the state of Wisconsin survey is a bench-mark study, owing to its concurrence with and its replication of our national survey. These data are a "splice" between the national time series and what could become a statewide one. The items unique to the state questionnaire were chosen to enrich our understanding of nonstatus or nonsocioeconomic consequences of social mobility. We included consequences such as mobility ideology, work ethic, alienation, voting and social involvements, and psychological well-being; clearly some of these "consequences" may be "causes" of mobility. Our purpose, in any event, is to integrate two types of analytic indicators: (1) those which describe the process of stratification in structural terms (e.g., Figure 9.1) and which can be normed against national parameter estimates for the same models, and (2) those indicator models which portray social and psychological processes. Such an integration of models enriches our knowledge of how opportunities for social mobility are related to both social and psychological integration.

Measurement of Response Error

One of the criticisms made of the 1962 OCG was that estimates of the rigidity of the stratification system were biased downward by virtue of random measurement error, particularly in respect to parental characteristics (Bowles, 1972). While we are not inclined to agree with Bowles' estimates of the extent of the problem, we think that it will be useful to assemble a variety of data on the extent and character of measurement error and to make use of it in the course of our analyses.

One incidental check on reliability will be provided by the ascertainment of educational attainment in the OCG supplement (as part of the series to ascertain first job after leaving school) as well as in the March CPS. More important, we shall obtain a work tape from the regular CPS reinterview program following the March CPS, and the Bureau of the Census will reinterview samples of 500 whites and 500 blacks on selected CPS and OCG items following completion of the field work for the supplementary survey. Approximately a dozen variables will be included in the reinterview schedule.

In connection with the Wisconsin survey we validate son's reports of parents' statuses using a match to decennial census records. A similar exercise was carried out in 1962 using data from the Chicago pretest (Blau and Duncan, 1967:Appendix D), but the validity estimate obtained there for father's occupation was clearly a lower bound because of the time lead or lag between the son's sixteenth birthday (the temporal referent of father's occupation) and the nearest census data. We asked respondents to report the name, address, and occupation of their fathers (or heads of family) as of the census date nearest their sixteenth birthday, and we validate those reports against the census records. Matches are effected by census personnel in order to preserve confidentiality, and for the same reason identifying information will be removed from our tape before it is returned to us for analysis. The census match may be used to validate education and income as well as occupation. Finally, for younger cohorts in the Wisconsin sample it is possible to validate reports of parental occupation and income against state income tax records, which are accessible for legitimate research purposes.

QUESTIONNAIRE DESIGN

In its original draft, our pretest questionnaire was more than four times the length of the less than two-page form used in 1962. Greater length followed naturally from two factors: first, our desire to ascertain more details on family of origin (e.g., mother's education, family income, education in the sibship), education (e.g., name of last school attended, major field of study, interruptions in schooling), and other career contingencies (e.g., active service in military); second, our inability (for logistical reasons cited previously) to administer the OCG supplement until some five or six months after the March CPS survey. The latter delay recommended our inclusion of some items which were redundant, given the CPS interview, but which we employed to filter respondents properly through the OCG questionnaire [e.g., current (March) school enrollment and years of school completed (in March) vis-à-vis first full-time civilian job after regular schooling]. Greater length in the questionnaire, especially a mail-out and return instrument, represented a potential compromise of comparability. To assay effects of this procedural change, we compared the pretest performances of the long (OCG-II) and short (OCG-I) forms described in a previous section.

We learned several things from the pretest. First, analysis reponse rates to the long and short forms indicated a 9 percent difference—82 percent short and 73 percent long. Virtually all of this difference was attributable to refusals—5.7 percent short and 12.9 percent long—and the overall difference in rates remained constant over the course of follow-up phases. Consequently we eliminated some dozen items from the pretest draft and shortened the final questionnaire to just under eight pages of regular-sized (contrasted to legal-sized) paper.

Second, there were some few instances of "forms effects" between the long and short versions. For example, one item which appeared on both forms elicited whether or not the respondent was living with both parents most of the time up to age 16. The only difference between the items was in the manner of display on the printed pages. For whatever reason, more (statistically significant) respondents reported living in intact families to the long form (90 percent) than to the short form (84 percent), and the latter more closely corresponded to the estimate of this characteristic for March 1962. With some other variables which appeared on both forms (e.g., father's education), we found no significant forms effects. In any case, we were unable to secure a restoration of questionnaire format according to the 1962 layout.

Third, we observed a low incidence of certain events and characteristics and an impressive high stability and certainty in the reports of selected background characteristics; these observations assisted us in identifying items to delete. While we would have liked to ascertain the effects of nonregular schooling (e.g., business, technical, vocational, on-the-job formal training) on socioeconomic achievements, we were unable to justify the inclusion of these items on the basis of the relatively few respondents who had such training (fewer than 25 percent of all men on any single item). On the other hand, a question eliciting parental income at the time respondents were about 16 years of age yielded substantial variance and a credible distribution over 14 dollar intervals. Further, there was only a single refusal, and the other unclassifiable responses were just over 11 percent of total responses, a rate which is comparable to those on other retrospective survey items. Another datum encouraged us to keep this item, and this information came from the 36 reinterviews taken about two months after the completion of the pretest. Of 34 respondents answering the parental income item, 28 reported exactly the same response in the mail survey and in the reinterview. Instances of "inconsistency" were reconciled in the context of reinterviews. One of the "inconsistent" respondents returned to his original report, three reconciled to categories adjacent to the original report, and two differed by two categories. When asked how certain the respondent was when he recorded his original report, 21 were "very certain," 4 were "mostly certain," and 9 were "mostly uncertain."

Our final questionnaire draft was eight pages of standard-sized paper. In order to overcome the remaining handicap of length, relative to our ability to achieve a response rate of about 83 percent, we reorganized follow-up procedures and statements of introduction of the study both to interviewers and to respondents. Following the pretest, our optimism about the final response rate to a visually more compact eight-page booklet was not too shaken. A 1964 CPS-NORC study of young male veterans and nonveterans (Klassen, 1966) replicated several OCG supplement items and used similar data-collection procedures. With an eight-page questionnaire this survey achieved a response rate of 82.2 percent—essentially the same as that in the 1962 OCG—and correlations among original and achieved statuses in the 1964 sample were virtually identical to those in the relevant cohort in the 1962 study (Duncan, 1968:715). Still, we shortened to one week the interval between the initial OCG-II mailing and the first follow-up, a reminder postcard. After a second week, another questionnaire was mailed, followed a week later by an attempted telephone interview or personal interview for those without phones. Four weeks after initial mailing, not contacted nonrespondents were visited by a CPS interviewer. In cases where the respondent had moved to another PSU, materials were forwarded to an updated address or a telephone interview was attempted. Finally, the cover letters which introduced the study and the interviewer training manuals for the supplement were redesigned so as to state more clearly the objectives and values of the project and to differentiate it from regular CPS monthly labor surveys. The latter seemed important to the cooperation of sample cases which had just completed the rigors of the 4:8:4 CPS rotation. In short, the departure of our final draft from the length of the 1962 questionnaire was problematic, and we strove to overcome the potential negative effects of greater length on comparability.

The OCG-II questionnaire replicates all but three of the 1962 items. Auspices of schooling (e.g., public or private) demonstrated no significant effects in the analysis of the 1962 data and was deleted. (The reader is directed to tabulations of this schooling variable: see U. S. Bureau of the Census, 1964; and Duncan, 1965). The 1962 item on first full-time civilian job held after the respondent "left school" proved defective, inasmuch as a tabulation of age at first job by years of school completed identified a substantial ·minority of reports which could not have been first jobs but probably were jobs held prior to completing the highest grade of regular school (see Duncan et al., 1972:Chap. 8). While retaining the concept of first job in the replicate study, we expanded the series of questions on education and the timing (dates) of schooling so as to eliminate respondents who would not appropriately be asked the first-job question (e.g., those currently enrolled in school) and to assist in the reconstruction of events surrounding the transition from school to work. Additionally, we rephrased the defective first-job item in consonance with greater clarity. Finally, we modified the concept of "older brother's education" to "oldest brother's and youngest brother's educations" so as to increase the numbers of sibships for which we could calculate within-family variance in achievement.

New items on the OCG-II questionnaire were drawn usually from a pool of extant items which had appeared in census questionnaires or in the context of large-scale sample surveys. Our intent was to employ items as instruments of our purpose only if we were aware of their performances in similar populations. In the absence of useful replicates, we designed our own items. Table 9.2 lists the items appearing on the March 1973 CPS (using the most current information available at this writing) in comparison to the March 1962 CPS instrument; similar item comparisons describe the coextensiveness of the OCG supplements. (Copies of the OCG-II questionnaire and descriptions of the sources from which items were drawn are available upon request.)

Finally, it is necessary to emphasize the important way in which the information on occupation obtained in the OCG replication precludes comparability, short of special efforts to avert this outcome. All occupation items on the OCG-II questionnaire (e.g., occupation, industry, and class of worker) are consistent with the current (1973) practices of the Bureau of the Census. While the phrasings of items are substantially identical to corresponding items from the 1962 study, the new regime collects additional, clarifying details (e.g., "What are your most important activities and duties?") and classifies on the basis of expanded information into categories which cannot be reconciled to 1960 (1962) classifications. (The reader can find partial documentation of these technical and procedural changes in Greene et al., 1969; Bregger, 1971; and Shapiro and Thompson, 1972.) Therefore, the 1962 study and the 1973 replicate would ordinarily not be comparable with respect to reports of occupation and industry, despite the apparent similarities of corresponding questionnaire items. This difficulty is remedied by our strategy of employing two sets of coders, each trained in different classification systems. When classifying into the 1960 scheme, coders will be instructed to disregard (to physically cover over) all items of clarifying information which would not have appeared as part of the 1962 reports. In large measure, the success of our efforts to replicate hinges on our ability to reproduce the 1960 (1962) treatment of occupation reports.

ANALYSIS PROSPECTUS

Anyone familiar with the Blau and Duncan bench-mark study can anticipate our major plan for analysis. Our first efforts will summarize the new cross-section as a series of descriptive and analytic indicators. We shall reestimate all the models for the process of stratification which appeared in *The American Occupational Structure*, and the inter- and intrageneration mobility matrices by

Table 9.2. Variables in the March Current Population Survey* and the OCG Supplement by Question Numbers

Source	Item	March 1962	Replication 1973
CPS	*Identification, geographic location, housing unit, type of interview and noninterview data*	Q.1–17	Q.1–17
	Persons 0–13 years old		
	Age (by month in 1962, year in 1972)	29–29a	27
	Race (white, Negro, other)	31	29
	Sex	32	30
	Relation to head	28	26
	Civilian household members aged 14 and older		
	Labor force status, unemployment	19–20, 22, 24–25a	19–20, 21–22
	Hours worked	21	20A, 20E
	Reason for part-time work	21A–21C	20C
	Employer	26A	23A
	Industry	26B	23B
	Occupation	26C	23C
	Class of worker	26D	23E
	Most important activities or duties	—	23D
	Duration of unemployment	23	22C
	Job search behavior	—	22A–22F, 24A–24E
	All household members aged 14 and older		
	Population status	27a	25a
	Relation to head	28	26
	Age (by month in 1962, year in 1972)	29, 29a	27
	Marital status	30	28
	Race	31	29
	Sex	32	30
	Veteran status (males, WW II in 1962; all, in 1972)	32	30
	Education (attended, completed)	33, 34	31, 32
	Married more than once	35	

Table 9.2 Variables in the March Current Population Survey* and the OCG Supplement by Question Numbers (cont.)

Source	Item	March 1962	Replication 1973
	Date of first marriage	36	—
	Live births (married women only)	37	—
	Income		
	Wage and salary	38	45
	Self-employment	39	46
	Farm	40	47
	Nonearned income	41	—
	Social Security, veterans' payments, private pensions	41a	—
	Dividends, interest, annuity	41b	—
	Rental	41c	—
	Other	41d	—
	Social Security, railroad retirement	—	48a
	Estates, trusts, dividends interest on savings bonds, net rental income	—	48b
	Welfare payments or other public assistance	—	48c
	Unemployment compensation, workmen's compensation, government employee pensions, veterans' payments		
	Private pensions and annuities, alimony, regular contributions from persons not in same household, other	—	48d
			48e
	Weeks worked in previous year	—	34
	Nonwork activity	—	35–42
	Longest job in previous year	—	43–44E
	Origin or descent	—	52

Table 9.2 Variables in the March Current Population Survey* and the OCG Supplement by Question Numbers (*cont.*)

Source	Item	March 1962	Replication 1973
OCG Supplement	Birthplace		
	Respondent	1	1[A]
	Father	2	2[A]
	Mother	3	3[A]
	Number of sisters	4a	5[A]
	Older sisters	4b	5[A]
	Number of brothers	4c	5[A]
	Older brothers	4d	5[A]
	Older brothers live at age 25	4e	—
	(Any brothers live to age 25)	—	6[D]
	Educational attainment, oldest brother	5	6[B]
	Size of place of origin, age 16	6	7[A]
	Auspices of schools (parochial, private, public)	7	—
	Age at first job	8a	18f[B]
	First full-time civilian job	8b–8d	18a–18e[B]
	Living with both parents	9	8a[A]
	Other head of household	9a	8b[A]
	Father's occupation, son's age 16	10	11a–11e[B]
	Father's educational attainment	11	12[A]
	Marital status	12	28[A]
	Wife's siblings	13a, 13b	30a, 30b[A]
	Wife's father's occupation	14	32a–32e[B]
	Original nationality, father's side	—	4[C]
	Educational attainment, youngest brother	—	6c[D]
	Family annual income, age 16	—	9[D]
	Year of father's birth	—	10[D]

Table 9.2 Variables in the March Current Population Survey* and the OCG Supplement by Question Numbers (cont.)

Source	Item	March 1962	Replication 1973
	Father(head) usually work, R's age 16	—	11f[D]
	Mother's educational attainment	—	13[D]
	School enrollment status, March	—	14[D]
	Education completed, March	—	15[D]
	Name and address of college last attended	—	16a[D]
	Field of specialization	—	16b[D]
	Month and year when completed highest grade	—	17[D]
	Never worked; no civilian full-time job	—	18[D]
	Discontinue school for six months	—	19a[D]
	Highest grade at first school interruption	—	19b[D]
	Month and year first school interruption	—	19c[D]
	Ever serve in active military service	—	20[D]
	Highest grade completed before first entered military service	—	21[C]
	Date first entered military	—	22[C]
	Date last military separation	—	23[C]
	Occupation, March 1962	—	24a–24f[C]
	Labor union membership	—	25[D]
	Ever married	—	26[D]
	Date first married	—	27[C]
	Current marriage is first marriage	—	29[C]
	Wife living with both parents, age 16	—	31a[D]
	Other head of wife's household	—	31b[D]
	Wife's father(head) usually work,		

Table 9.2 Variables in the March Current Population Survey* and the OCG Supplement by Question Numbers (*cont.*)

Source	Item	March 1962	Replication 1973
	wife's age 16	—	32f[D]
	Wife's father's education	—	33[D]
	Wife's mother's education	—	34[D]

Note: Dash indicates that item does not appear.

*Content of the March 1972 CPS was used as a guide for anticipating that of March 1973, unless we were aware of a Bureau of Census decision to exclude an item from the 1973 schedule (e.g., one-year migration). Question numbers refer to those on the 1972 schedule.

[A]Replicate OCG-I item on OCG-II questionnaire.

[B]Parallel item to OCG-I, but modified in wording of question.

[C]New item on OCG-II, borrowed verbatim from another survey or census, or whose format has been borrowed and focused for our purpose.

[D]New item on OCG-II, constructed by principal investigators.

cohort and color will be scrutinized to describe the patterns of supply and recruitment as of 1973.

Naturally, our second major thrust will be into the data on trends—or changes in mobility regimes (e.g., inter- and intrageneration outflow matrices) and parameters of the process of stratification (e.g., coefficients in models such as Figure 9.1 of this chapter). We are most eager to analyze these data, inasmuch as we have detected trends in mobility matrices for men in the experienced civilian labor force in the period 1940—1970 (Hauser and Featherman, 1973) and for blacks and whites in the period 1962—1972 (Hauser and Featherman, 1972). To cite only the most dominant trend, there has been a shift away from self-employment in professional occupations and as proprietors. Concurrently, employment in salaried professional, managerial, and administrative occupations has increased. The greatest bulk of these changes in intergeneration mobility has been effected in the transition probabilities linking first full-time jobs to current jobs, and not in (a) the outflow matrices joining social origins (father's occupation) with son's first full-time job, or (b) the composition of social origins, as given by the vector of sons by fathers' occupations.

While we have confidence in these trend estimates, we know only the most gross details. Our method of estimation employed the 1962 OCG mobility matrices and origin vectors for selected age cohorts. Applying the outflow matrix of men aged 35—44 in 1962 to the origin vector of men aged 25—34 in 1962 generated an expected destination vector for the younger men in 1972, when they were age 35—44. By comparing this expected vector with an observed occupation distribution of men aged 35—44, as published by the Bureau of Labor Statistics from the March 1972 CPS, we estimated change in the outflow matrix. On the assumption of no change in outflow or transition matrices, there would be no difference between observed and expected distributions. Since we could not observe the 1972 matrices directly, we ascertained change indirectly by this technique. When we can analyze the cells of our March 1973 mobility matrices, we shall know more about trends, as for example, if the exit from self-employment is linked to entrance into the salaried class of worker, by men leaving proprietorships to become salaried managers and executives.

Our third analysis phase refocuses on the 1973 cross-section, elaborating the models of phase one by including new measurements and estimating new models which incorporate assumptions about errors in variables. An important aspect of this phase is our effort to establish both base-line and trend estimates for married women for a basic model of the process of stratification (see Figure 9.1). The Bureau of the Census will supply us with a unit-record tape for 1962 which merges all information elicited by the March CPS for males eligible for the OCG supplement (including all information on employment, income, labor force experience, and education for spouses living with these men) with the data derived from the OCG supplement itself. For married women living with spouses aged 20–64 in the civilian noninstitutional population in March 1962, we can calculate basic regression models linking social statuses of parents to a woman's education, occupation, and earnings. The same (and slightly more elaborate) models of achievement can be calculated for the population defined above but from the 1973 cross-section. In addition to trend analyses, we anticipate examining the means by which the attainments of women depend upon the careers of their husbands, and vice versa, although this is a topic of our investigation in other and more detailed data files. Perforce, the OCG analyses of stratification for females will be limited; they do promise to be important analytic indicators, however, and critical first steps in a long-needed time series.

SUMMARY

Replication of the bench-mark survey, "Occupational Changes in a Generation," will make possible the measurement of trends in numerous indicators of social stratification. This chapter has outlined the design of a replication and extension and discussed aspects of study design, questionnaire construction, field operations, and data processing which bear on the problem of comparability.

In the initial survey, carried out in conjunction with the March 1962 Current Population Survey, interviewers left behind a two-page supplementary questionnaire to be mailed in by males aged 20–64 in the civilian noninstitutional population of the United States. The supplement asked about socio-economic and structural characteristics of the respondent's family of orientation and that of his wife; nativity and size of place of origin; and first job and age at first job. Returns were obtained from 20,700 respondents, 83 percent of those eligible, and responses on the supplement were linked with selected items in the March CPS record. Analyses of the 1962 data have yielded measurements of occupational recruitment and supply; the causal nexus linking family background, educational attainment, and occupational achievement; and the sources of color and ethnic differentials in education, occupation, and earnings. Numerous trend measurements were obtained within the cross-section survey by means of intercohort comparisons.

The 1973 survey also is linked to the March CPS, but changes in the respondent workload precluded use of a leave-behind instrument: a mail-out, mail-back questionnaire was sent out in August of 1973. Because the CPS sample has increased, the total number of respondents has more than doubled, and Negroes and persons of Spanish origin are oversampled by about a factor of two. A separate but parallel survey of men in the state of Wisconsin measures additional variables, including some which are thought to be politically sensitive by the Bureau of the Census.

The selection and construction of supplement items has required hard choices. Changes in CPS procedures have made verbatim replication problematic. Multitudes of potential new items were evaluated in terms of relevance to social theory and policy, validity, and feasibility of measurement and effect on the quality of replicated items and on overall response rates.

Numerous checks on the quality of data were built in the study design. These include reinterviews on selected March CPS and supplement items and record checks to be carried out in connection with the Wisconsin survey.

Conditional on the achievement of a true replication, the new OCG survey presents rich possibilities for measuring trends in stratification and for improving the quality of indicators of stratification. Whether we shall attain strict replication hangs heavily upon our ability to implement successfully the proposed design and to educate ourselves about the technical and procedural changes instituted by the Bureau of the Census which, at least in some measure, will affect comparability of our study and the 1962 bench mark.

REFERENCES

Blau, Peter M., and Otis Dudley Duncan.
  1967   The American Occupational Structure. New York: Wiley.
Bowles, Samuel.
  1972   "Schooling and inequality from generation to generation." Journal of Political Economy (June):S219–S251.
Bregger, John E.
  1971   "Revisions in occupational classifications for 1971." Employment and Earnings (February):5–8.
Duncan, Beverly.
  1965   Family Factors and School Dropout: 1920–1960. Final Report, Cooperative Research Project No. 2258, U. S. Office of Education. Ann Arbor: University of Michigan.
Duncan, Beverly, and Otis Dudley Duncan.
  1968   "Minorities and the process of stratification." American Sociological Review 33 (June):356–364.
Duncan, Otis Dudley.
  1961   "A socioeconomic index for all occupations." Pp. 109–138 in A. J. Reiss, Jr. (ed.), Occupations and Social Status. New York: Free Press.
  1968   "Social stratification and mobility: problems in the measurement of trend." Pp. 675–720 in Eleanor Bernert Sheldon and Wilbert E. Moore (eds.), Indicators of Social Change: Concepts and Measurements. New York: Russell Sage Foundation.
  1969   Toward Social Reporting: Next Steps. (Social Science Frontiers, No. 2.) New York: Russell Sage Foundation.
  1970   Indicators of Social Change from Replication Studies. A research proposal to the Russell Sage Foundation. Ann Arbor: University of Michigan.

Duncan, Otis Dudley, David L. Featherman, and Beverly Duncan.
   1972   Socioeconomic Background and Achievement. New York: Seminar
           Press.
Greene, Stanley, John Priebe, and Richard Morrison.
   1969   "The 1970 Census of Population occupation classification system."
           Statistical Reporter (December):77–84.
Hauser, Robert M., and D. L. Featherman.
   1972   "Black-white differentials in occupational mobility among men in the
           United States, 1962–1970." Meetings of the Research Committee on
           Social Stratification, International Sociological Association, Rome.
   1973   "Trends in the occupational mobility of U. S. men, 1962–1970."
           American Sociological Review 38 (June):302–310.
Klassen, Albert D.
   1966   "Military service in American life since World War II: An overview."
           (Report No. 117.) Chicago: National Opinion Research Center,
           University of Chicago.
Land, Kenneth C.
   1971   "On the definition of social indicators." The American Sociologist
           6 (November):322–325.
Levine, Daniel B.
   1967   "February work experience supplement: specifications for allocation
           of nonresponse entries." Unpublished memo, Bureau of the Census.
Rice, Stuart A.
   1967   "Social accounting and statistics for The Great Society." Public
           Administration Review 27 (June):169–174.
Shapiro, Gary M., and Marvin M. Thompson.
   1972   "Revisions in Current Population Survey." Employment and Earnings
           (February):6–9.
Sheldon, Eleanor Bernert, and Kenneth C. Land.
   1972   "Social reporting for the 1970's: A review and programmatic
           statement." Policy Sciences 3 (Summer):137–151.
Sheldon, Eleanor Bernert, Kenneth C. Land, and Raymond A. Bauer.
   1971   "Social reporting for the 1970's." Pp. 403–435 in Report of the
           President's Commission on Federal Statistics, Volume II. Washington,
           D. C.: U. S. Government Printing Office.
Siegel, Paul M.
   1971   "Prestige in the American occupational structure." Doctoral
           dissertation, University of Chicago.
Siegel, Paul M., and Robert W. Hodge.
   1968   "A causal approach to the study of measurement error." Pp. 28–59 in
           H. M. Blalock and A. Blalock (eds.), Methodology in Social Research.
           New York: McGraw-Hill.
Thompson, Marvin M.
   1970   "March CPS–past and future." Mimeographed manuscript. U. S.
           Bureau of the Census, Series DSD-R-2.

U. S. Bureau of the Census
  1963   "The Current Population Survey: A report on methodology."
          Technical Paper No. 7.
  1964   "Educational change in a generation, March 1962." Current
          Population Reports. Series P-20 No. 132 (September 22).
  1967   "Concepts and methods used in manpower statistics from the Current
          Population Survey." Current Population Reports. Series P-23 No. 22
          (June).
Walsh, Thomas C., and Paula J. Buckholdt.
  1970   "Accuracy of retrospectively reporting work status and occupation
          five years ago." Unpublished manuscript, U. S. Bureau of the Census,
          PA-(75).

APPENDIX: Bibliography of Publications from the 1962 OCG Survey

Blau, Peter M.
  1965   "The flow of occupational supply and recruitment." American
          Sociological Review 30 (August):475–490.
Blau, Peter M., and Otis Dudley Duncan.
  1961   "Eine Untersuchung beruflicher Mobilitaet in den Vereinigten
          Staaten," Koelner Zeitschrift fuer Soziologie und Sozialpsychologie
          5:171–188.
  1967   The American Occupational Structure. New York: Wiley.
  1969   "Some preliminary findings on social stratification in the United
          States." Acta Sociologica 9:4–24. Reprinted in C. S. Heller (ed.),
          Structured Social Inequality. New York: Macmillan, 1969.
Duncan, Beverly.
  1965   "Dropouts and the unemployed." The Journal of Political Economy
          73 (April):121–134.
  1965   Family Factors and School Dropout: 1920–1960. (Final Report,
          Cooperative Research Project No. 2258, U. S. Office of Education.)
          Ann Arbor: University of Michigan.
  1967   "Early work experience of graduates and dropouts." Demography
          4:19–29.
  1967   "Education and social background." American Journal of Sociology
          4 (January):363–372.
  1968   "Trends in output and distribution of schooling." Pp. 601–672 in
          Eleanor Bernert Sheldon and Wilbert E. Moore (eds.), Indicators of
          Social Change: Concepts and Measurements. New York: Russell Sage
          Foundation.
Duncan, Beverly, and Otis Dudley Duncan.
  1968   "Minorities and the process of stratification." American Sociological
          Review 33 (June):356–364.
  1969   "Family stability and occupational success." Social Problems
          16 (Winter):273–285.

Duncan, Otis Dudley.
  1965   "Farm   background   and   differential   fertility."   Demography
          2:240–249.
  1965   "Social origins of salaried and self-employed professional workers."
          Social Forces 44 (December):186–189.
  1965   "The trend of occupational mobility in the United States." American
          Sociological Review 30 (August):491–498.
  1966   "Occupational trends and patterns of net mobility in the United
          States." Demography 3:1–18.
  1967   "Discrimination against Negroes." The Annals of the American
          Academy of Political and Social Science 371 (May):85–103.
  1968   "Ability and achievement." Eugenics Quarterly 15 (March):1–11.
  1968   "Patterns of occupational mobility among Negro men." Demography
          5:11–22.
  1968   "Social stratification and mobility: Problems in the measurement of
          trend." Pp. 675–720 in Eleanor Bernert Sheldon and Wilbert E.
          Moore   (eds.),   Indicators   of   Social   Change: Concepts   and
          Measurements. New York: Russell Sage Foundation.
  1969   "Inheritance of poverty or inheritance of race?" Pp. 85–110 in Daniel
          P. Moynihan (ed.), On Understanding Poverty. New York: Basic
          Books.
Duncan, Otis Dudley, and James D. Cowhig.
  1966   "Social   backgrounds   and   occupational   commitment   of   male
          wageworkers   in   agriculture."   Agricultural   Economics   Research
          18 (October):129–135.
Duncan, Otis Dudley, Ronald Freedman, J. Michael Coble, and Doris Slesinger.
  1965   "Marital   fertility   and   size   of   family   of   orientation."   Demography
          2:508–515.
Duncan, Otis Dudley, David L. Featherman, and Beverly Duncan.
  1968   Socioeconomic   Background   and·   Occupational   Achievement:
          Extensions of a Basic Model. Ann Arbor: University of Michigan.
  1972   Socioeconomic Background and Achievement. New York: Seminar
          Press (revision of Duncan, Featherman, and Duncan, 1968).
Hauser, Robert M., and David L. Featherman.
  1972   "Black-white differentials in occupational mobility among men in the
          United States, 1962–1970." Meetings of the Research Committee on
          Social Stratification, International Sociological Association, Rome.
  1973   "Trends in the occupational mobility of U. S. men, 1962–1970."
          American Sociological Review 38 (June):302–310.
Rhodes, Lewis.
  1971   "Socioeconomic correlates of fertility in the metropolis: Relationship
          of   individual   and   areal   unit   characteristics."   Social   Biology
          18 (September):296–304.
U. S. Bureau of the Census.
  1964   "Lifetime   occupational   mobility   of   adult   males.   March   1962."
          Current Population Reports. Series P-23 No. 11(May 12).

1964   "Educational change in a generation, March 1962." Current
       Population Reports. Series P-20 No. 132 (September 22).
Wanner, Richard, and E. M. Beck.
1972   "Least-squares estimation of effects on inter- and intra-generational
       occupational transition probabilities." Annual meetings of the Social
       Statistics Section, American Statistical Association, Montreal, Quebec.
Warren, Bruce L.
1966   "A multiple variable approach to the assortative mating
       phenomenon." Eugenics Quarterly 13 (December):285-290.

10

TRANSITION AND ADMISSION MODELS IN SOCIAL INDICATOR ANALYSIS

Richard Stone

INTRODUCTION

When I was invited to contribute a chapter to this volume it was suggested to me that I might concentrate on extending my work on the application of demographic models to the educational system; and this idea is reflected in what follows. But when I came to put something down on paper, a number of other thoughts came into my mind. In the end what I have done is to attempt to unify the analysis of social structure and social change at different levels of generality, ranging from the total population of a country, through various social subsystems such as the educational sequence or the sequence of health and medical care, to individual organizations or specific diseases. My unifying tools are a matrix framework and a few simple models based on either outflow or inflow coefficients. While most of what I have to say concerns the assignment of individuals to different categories or states and the movements that take place between states, I also show how this kind of information can be related to economic information on costs or gains and how economic or other variables can be used to maintain a balance between the supplies generated by organizational practices and the demands generated by sociodemographic pressures.

The arrangement of the chapter is as follows. The second section begins with a closed model of population change based on the reproduction and survival characteristics of a community and goes on to consider an open model in which new entrants, whether by birth or immigration, are treated as exogenous. The sociodemographic models of the third section are simply an elaboration of this open model; two main variants are considered, one based on outflow coefficients

253

(or transition proportions) and the other on inflow coefficients (or admission proportions). In the fourth section these models are applied to the educational system of England and Wales. The fifth and sixth sections are concerned with projections based on a matrix of transition proportions (the C-matrix); first, when these proportions are fixed and, second, when they change through time. The seventh section gives two interpretations of the C-matrix, one based on input-output analysis and the other on probability theory. The second of these interpretations, in particular, places restrictions on the acceptable definition of states; and some examples of these difficulties and the ways in which they can be resolved are given in the eighth, ninth, and tenth sections. The eleventh section takes up the question of age as an element in the definition of states, describes the difficulty that is likely to arise if it is not an element, and shows what can be done in such cases. The twelfth section begins a discussion of the problems that may arise if movements are governed by rigid rules and gives as an illustration a well-known example of marriage and descent rules which, while superficially acceptable, would not enable any community that adopted them to survive. The discussion is continued in the thirteenth section, where the rules governing recruitment and promotion in an individual organization are analyzed in terms of outflow coefficients, and in the fourteenth section, where the pattern of admissions and vacancies is analyzed in terms of inflow coefficients. The fifteenth section discusses balance and control in terms of regulating the supply and demand of teachers in the branches of an educational system. The sixteenth section describes the cost equation corresponding to the model based on outflow coefficients. Finally, the last section is devoted to conclusions and is followed by a list of references.

2. DEMOGRAPHIC TRANSITION MATRICES

Matrix methods appear to have been introduced into demographic analysis nearly a generation ago by writers such as Bernadelli (1941) and Leslie (1945, 1948). They have been developed by many writers, in particular by Keyfitz (1964a, 1964b) and, more comprehensively (1968). The last-mentioned volume provides endless elaborations and numerical examples and shows that the matrix approach is consistent with traditional forms of demographic analysis.

An analysis of the evolution of a population usually starts off from a description of its reproduction and survival characteristics. These can be summarized in two matrices, B and C say, which relate respectively to age-specific surviving birth rates and survival rates. If we denote the age-composition vector of the population by n and the shift operator by Λ, $(\Lambda^\tau n(\theta) \equiv n(\tau + \theta))$, and if we distinguish the male and female parts of the population by the suffixes m and f then we can write

$$
\begin{aligned}
\Lambda n_f &= B_f n_f &+ C_f n_f \\
&= A_f n_f
\end{aligned}
\tag{10.1}
$$

where $A_f \equiv B_f + C_f$, and

$$\Lambda n_m = B_m n_f + C_m n_m \tag{10.2}$$

if we relate the birth of males to the female age-composition vector. If the B and C matrices remain constant over time, the age-composition vectors τ years hence are given by

$$\begin{aligned} \Lambda^\tau n_f &= A_f^\tau n_f \\ &= C_f^\tau n_f + \sum_{\theta=0}^{\tau-1} C_f^{\tau-\theta-1} B_f A_f^\theta n_f \end{aligned} \tag{10.3}$$

and

$$\Lambda^\tau n_m = C_m^\tau n_m + \sum_{\theta=0}^{\tau-1} C_m^{\tau-\theta-1} B_m A_f^\theta n_f \tag{10.4}$$

In the second row of Equation (10.3) and in (10.4) the age-composition vectors consist of two terms, the first of which shows the survivors from the initial stock and the second of which shows the surviving new entrants from all later periods. Since the C-matrices are lower-triangular, the first terms of (10.3) and (10.4) are zero for all values of τ which exceed the human life span.

It is important to be clear about the nature of the A, B, and C matrices and so I shall now give an example relating to the female population of England and Wales around 1961 (Table 10.1). The table itself is simply the A-matrix; the B-matrix consists of the three entries in the first row and zeros everywhere else; and the C-matrix consists of the six entries in the leading subdiagonal and zeros everywhere else.

In this example the population is condensed into 15-year age groups, so that the entry in the first row and the first column, 0.339, when multiplied by the number of girls aged 0–14 in 1961 gives the number of girls born to them in the ensuing 15 years, who will still be alive in 1976 when, of course, they will all be in the age group 0–14. Similarly, the entry in the second row and the first column, 0.994, when multiplied by the number of girls aged 0–14 in 1961 gives the number of survivors from this group in 1976 when, of course, they will all be in the age group 15–29. The numbers in the top left-hand corner of Table 10.1 are taken from Keyfitz (1968:42). Keyfitz was not interested in the entire female population but only in that part of it which had not reached the end of the reproductive span. In this table the small number which might be expected in the first row and the fourth column has been merged in the number in the first row and the third column to enable illustrative calculations to be made as simply as possible.

Table 10.1. A Condensed Births and Survival Matrix
England and Wales, Females, 1960-1962

Age Range	0-14	15-29	30-44	45-59	60-74	75-89	90-104
	(1)	*(2)*	*(3)*	*(4)*	*(5)*	*(6)*	*(7)*
0- 14	0.339	0.843	0.131	0	0	0	0
15- 29	0.994	0	0	0	0	0	0
30- 44	0	0.988	0	0	0	0	0
45- 59	0	0	s_{43}	0	0	0	0
60- 74	0	0	0	s_{54}	0	0	0
75- 89	0	0	0	0	s_{65}	0	0
90-104	0	0	0	0	0	s_{76}	0

Table 10.1 illustrates the matrices required to make projections, as in Equation (10.3). For practical purposes this model is too simple and can easily be criticized. For instance: (1) the model is female-dominated, that is to say, births are related to the female age-composition vector without any reference to the male population, whereas it is possible to devise a more symmetrical treatment of the two sexes; (2) the model takes no account of the formation and dissolution of marriages whereas it could; (3) it would be desirable to distinguish marital status, since age-specific birth rates are strongly influenced by it and there has been a general tendency in recent years for marriages to take place at younger ages; (4) allowance should be made for so-called parity, that is, the number of children to which a woman has already given birth, since this factor also influences age-specific birth rates; and (5) survival rates tend to increase over time but not uniformly for all ages or for men and women.

But there are other factors for which it is more difficult to make allowance. For instance there are migration, war and pestilence, and the attitudes of the public and of religious and political leaders to birth control, abortion, family allowances, and so on.

Of such factors, migration is perhaps the only one we can hope for the time being to handle quantitatively. In some countries it cannot be ignored and so we may prefer to replace the closed model by an open model. In this case, we can write, ignoring the distinction between the sexes,

$$\Lambda n = Cn + b \tag{10.5}$$

where the vector b either includes net immigrants as well as births; or, if it is to include gross immigrants, allowance is made for the loss by emigration in the elements of C.

3. THE INTRODUCTION OF SOCIAL CATEGORIES

As we have seen, the matrix C in Equation (10.5) is square and nonnegative and has positive elements only in its leading subdiagonal. Clearly the individuals

Table 10.2. A Demographic Matrix Connecting the Opening and Closing Stocks of Year θ with the Flows during Year θ

State at New Year $\theta + 1$	State at New Year θ	Outside World	Our Country: Opening States	Closing Stocks
Outside world		α	d'	
Our country: closing states		b	S	$\wedge n$
Opening stocks			n'	

in any age group could be classified into categories appropriate to their progression through some part of the social system, say the system of full-time formal education. If this were done, each scalar element of the C-matrix in (10.5) would be replaced by a matrix and the elements of the population vector would relate not simply to age but to educational status as well; in other words, the states of the enlarged system would be defined by combining categories of age and of educational status. A stock-flow matrix appropriate to this system, whatever the categories may be, and so to the purely demographic system as well, is set out in Table 10.2.

The symbols in this table have the following meaning:

α, a scalar, denotes the total number of individuals who both enter and leave "our country" in the course of year θ and so are not recorded in either the opening or the closing stock of that year. An example is a baby born during the year who dies before the end of it.

b, a column vector, denotes the new entrants into "our country," namely the births and immigrations of year θ, who survive to the end of the year. Individuals in this group are recorded in the closing stock but not in the opening stock.

d', a row vector (the prime superscript indicates transposition), denotes the leavers from "our country," namely the deaths and emigrations of year θ. Individuals in this group appear in the opening stock but not in the closing stock.

S, a square matrix, denotes the survivors in "our country" through year θ, and these are recorded in both the opening and the closing stock. They are classified by their opening states in the columns and by their closing states in the rows.

n', a row vector, denotes the opening stock in each state.

This form of presentation is quite general; the information we can obtain from it depends on the classifications used to define states. For many purposes we should wish to treat males and females separately and to record individuals by year of birth or by age group. Apart from these general criteria of classification, additional specific criteria would depend on the aspect of life we were studying. For instance, if we were interested in the flow of students through the educational system, the specific criteria might be type of establishment attended, level of work (for example, 0 or A level work in secondary school), subject of study, and qualifications obtained at different stages of the educational progression; if we were interested in the changing conditions of health over the life-cycle, the specific criteria might be conditions predisposing to some disease, presence of the disease, method of treatment, and degree of incapacity; and if we were interested in the movement of employees through an organization, the specific criteria might be occupation and grade.

The framework shown in Table 10.2 can be used to organize transversal (cross-section) data as well as longitudinal (time-series) data. In the first case, age may or may not be a criterion of classification. In all cases, states may be defined either in terms of the present characteristics of individuals or in terms of a mixture of present and past characteristics.

Equation (10.5) can be derived from this table as follows. From the row for our country, we can write

$$\Lambda n \equiv Si + b \tag{10.6}$$

where i denotes the unit vector, so that Si denotes the row sums of S. If we derive C by dividing the elements in the columns of S by the corresponding element in the opening stock, n, we obtain

$$C = S\hat{n}^{-1} \tag{10.7}$$

where the circumflex accent indicates that the vector n is spread out to form a diagonal matrix. If we substitute for S from (10.7) into (10.6) we obtain

$$\begin{aligned} \Lambda n &= C\hat{n}i + b \\ &= Cn + b \end{aligned} \tag{10.8}$$

which is the same as (10.5).

The elements of C are usually called transition proportions and, provided they remain constant (or their future movements can be estimated), Equation (10.8) can be used, as we shall see in the section on "Projections" below, for making projections contingent on a knowledge of the future values of the exogenous vector, b.

It is important to realize that Equation (10.8) is not the only set of difference equations that can be derived from Table 10.2 and that we can form another set by concentrating on the column rather than the row for "our country" in that table. Thus we can see that

$$n \equiv S'i + d \tag{10.9}$$

where the prime superscript indicates transposition. If, now, we define a coefficient matrix, G' say, based on the rows of S, then

$$G' = S'\hat{n}^{-1} \tag{10.10}$$

and if we substitute for S' from (10.10) into (10.9) we obtain

$$n = G'\hat{n} + d \tag{10.11}$$

The elements of G' can be called admission proportions, and by using Equation (10.11) instead of (10.8) we can project backward instead of forward. We shall see the point of doing this in the following section.

4. APPLICATIONS TO EDUCATION

Before proceeding, let me illustrate the use of Equations (10.8) and (10.11) by means of an educational example. This study is concerned with the flow of students through establishments of full-time formal education in England and Wales in 1964—1965 and 1965—1966. It treats males and females separately and covers the first 20 years of life, ages 0 through 19. The primary criterion of classification is year of birth; the secondary criterion is type of educational establishment attended, including a category for "not in full-time formal education"; and the tertiary criterion is level of work, work at secondary schools up to 0-level being distinguished from A-level work. The combination of these classifications leads to 114 states, so that the S-matrix is of order 114. The matrix framework is not identical with that set out in Table 10.2 above: the flows, instead of connecting the opening and closing stocks, connect the leavers from two successive years. This alternative framework appears in Stone (1971) as Table IX.1; and the matrices S, C and $(I - C)^{-1}$ based on it, and relating to males in 1964—1965, are set out in Table X.1, X.2, and X.3. Since in Stone (1971) the flow matrix is presented as the transpose of the matrix in Table 10.2, the notation has some obvious differences from that adopted in this chapter.

I shall now use this material to answer two questions relating to the five years of age, 15 through 19, which begin with the school-leaving age of 15. In the first place, how are these years likely to be allocated, on average, to different activities by a group of children who have just come into the world and how does the expected allocation change as these children progress through the school system? In the second place, how are these years likely to have been allocated, on average, by people who in their twentieth year, that is at age 19, find themselves in any particular activity?

The first question can be answered from a variant of Equation (10.8) which is restricted to survivors. Let us define a matrix, D say, as

$$D = S(\hat{n} - \hat{d})^{-1} \tag{10.12}$$

On rearranging (10.12) and postmultiplying by $\hat{n}^{-1}$, we obtain

$$D(I - \hat{d}\hat{n}^{-1}) = S\hat{n}^{-1} \tag{10.13}$$

whence

$$(I - D)^{-1} = \left[I - C(I - \hat{d}\hat{n}^{-1})^{-1}\right]^{-1} \tag{10.14}$$

Table 10.3 is obtained from two matrices, one for males and one for females, of the form of $(I - D)^{-1}$. Each column of these matrices relates to one of the 114 states; and rows 60 through 114 show the expected time spent, on average, in the various activities during the five ages 15 through 19. Table 10.3 is formed by adding up over the five ages the time spent in each activity.

The first entry in columns 1 and 2 shows that, at birth, children can expect to spend nearly three and a half of the five years outside the system of full-time formal education and one and a half years inside it. The entries contained in rows 2 and 3 relate to average experience and do not, of course, imply that individual children pass through a succession of secondary schools. If we add up all the entries relating to secondary schools in the first two columns, we obtain 1.267 for boys and 1.202 for girls, indicating that at birth the expectation for girls is 5 percent less than expectation for boys. There are minor changes at age 11 but nothing very striking.

At age 13, separate tabulations are made for children at secondary modern schools and at grammar schools, the former being the least and the latter the most academic type of secondary school. Children who go to secondary modern schools can expect less than 1 year inside the system of full-time formal education from ages 15 through 19 while those who go to grammar schools can expect over 3 years. Of this period, the grammar school boys spend 2.620 years at school whereas the girls spend only 2.318 years; so the gap is now 12 percent. This figure, however, does not fully reflect the disadvantage of girls in the matter of preparing for university entrance since for this purpose success in at least two A-level examinations is needed. The expected time to be spent on average in such work is 1.334 years for boys and 0.962 years for girls, indicating a gap of 28 percent. This gap is associated with, but does not altogether account for, the sex

Table 10.3. Years Expected to Be Spent in Various Activities from Age 15 Through Age 19 by Survivors from Four Selected Initial States (Based on transition proportions for England and Wales in 1965–1966)

State / Activity	Age 0 Preschool		Age 11 Primary		Age 13 Secondary Modern		Grammar	
	Males	Females	Males	Females	Males	Females	Males	Females
	(1)	(2)	(3)	(4)	(5)	(6)	(7)	(8)
0 Not in full-time formal education	3.414	3.455	3.351	3.456	4.090	4.124	1.775	1.967
2 Secondary schools: up to 0-level								
a) Secondary modern	0.270	0.261	.0.243	0.248	0.566	0.549	0	0
b) Grammar	0.273	0.319	0.294	0.303	0	0	1.249	1.299
c) Comprehensive	0.216	0.214	0.265	0.262	0.068	0.070	0.037	0.057
d) Other normal	0.096	0.086	0.088	0.074	0.012	0.012	0	0
3 Secondary schools: A-level								
a) Secondary modern	0.006	0.005	0.005	0.005	0.012	0.011	0	0
b) Grammar	0.289	0.228	0.310	0.218	0.004	0	1.311	0.935
c) Comprehensive	0.090	0.076	0.110	0.091	0.036	0.030	0.021	0.026
d) Other normal	0.027	0.013	0.025	0.012	0.007	0.005	0.002	0.001
4 Special schools	0.023	0.011	0.004	0.001	0	0	0	0
5 Further education n.e.s.	0.163	0.175	0.163	0.172	0.173	0.165	0.190	0.271
6 Colleges of education	0.021	0.101	0.023	0.102	0.009	0.029	0.055	0.258
7 Universities	0.110	0.057	0.119	0.055	0.020	0.006	0.360	0.187
Total	5.000	5.000	5.000	5.000	5.000	5.000	5.000	5.000

Note: Components do not always add up to totals because of rounding-off errors.

differential in the expectation of university entrance apparent in row 7 and columns 7 and 8 of the table.

The second question can be answered from a variant of Equation (10.11) in which G' is replaced by another matrix, H' say, just as C was replaced by D in the example just given. Table 10.4 is obtained from two matrices, one for males and one for females, of the form of $(I - H')^{-1}$.

The extremes illustrated in Table 10.4 are those not in full-time formal education at age 19 (columns 1 and 2) and those at university at that age (columns 7 and 8). As we should expect, their educational history from the school-leaving age onward is very different and a numerical measure of this is provided in the table.

If we compare Tables 10.3 and 10.4 we can see that those at secondary modern schools at age 13 could expect to be in the educational system for a shorter time than those who were outside it at age 19, since some of the latter group will have had a slightly more extended education. On the other hand, those at university at age 19 spent less time out of the system than could be expected by the average grammar school child at age 13, since those who enter university are only a proportion of those who have had an extended education at school.

The figures in Tables 10.3 and 10.4 are hypothetical in the sense that they relate to people who live their lives under the conditions of 1965–1966. In fact, of course, conditions change and so, when I have described the method of making projections on the basis of fixed coefficients, I shall go on to consider, in the section on "Changes in the C-Matrix," the problem of changing coefficients. Some of the difficulties of measuring changes in coefficients are described and illustrated in Stone (1971 and 1973).

The analyses given above only make use of classifications available in British educational statistics and not even all of these. For a better understanding of educational careers we should have to consider not only criteria like sex and type of school attended but also criteria like social class, parental interest, family size, and ability. In Britain, thanks to the longitudinal study of Douglas (1964) and Douglas et al. (1968), allowance can be made for the effects of sex, ability, social class, and type of school on educational performance. On this type of analysis reference should be made to the work of Tuck (1973), an early version of which was described in Stone (1973), and of Orr (1972).

5. PROJECTIONS BASED ON FIXED TRANSITION PROPORTIONS

If we apply the operator Λ to Equation (10.8), we obtain

$$
\begin{aligned}
\Lambda^2 n &= C\Lambda n + \Lambda b \\
&= C^2 n + Cb + \Lambda b
\end{aligned}
\tag{10.15}
$$

Table 10.4. Years Estimated To Have Been Spent in Various Activities from Age 15 through Age 19 by Those in Four Final States at Age 19 (Based on admission proportions for England and Wales in 1965–1966)

State / Activity	Age 19 Not in Full-Time Formal Education		Further Education N.E.S.		Colleges of Education		Universities	
	Males	Females	Males	Females	Males	Females	Males	Females
	(1)	(2)	(3)	(4)	(5)	(6)	(7)	(8)
0 Not in full-time formal education	3.944	3.981	1.523	1.545	0.835	0.597	0.464	0.347
2 Secondary schools: up to 0-level								
a) Secondary modern	0.339	0.324	0.279	0.232	0.188	0.127	0.084	0.051
b) Grammar	0.222	0.246	0.578	0.679	0.751	0.911	0.959	1.134
c) Comprehensive	0.071	0.070	0.068	0.063	0.059	0.066	0.052	0.040
d) Other normal	0.099	0.099	0.104	0.122	0.115	0.110	0.075	0.048
3 Secondary schools: A-level								
a) Secondary modern	0.003	0.001	0.004	0.001	0.075	0.040	0.003	0.001
b) Grammar	0.137	0.084	0.803	0.781	1.329	1.302	1.667	1.645
c) Comprehensive	0.007	0.005	0.055	0.036	0.073	0.095	0.073	0.053
d) Other normal	0.011	0.004	0.064	0.002	0.143	0.141	0.089	0.056
4 Special schools	0.018	0.013	0.010	0.007	0.005	0.003	0.003	0.001
5 Further education n.e.s.	0.146	0.174	1.508	1.534	0.030	0.027	0.017	0.016
6 Colleges of education	0	0.001	0	0	1.395	1.579	0	0
7 Universities	0.002	0.001	0	0	0	0	1.514	1.606
Total	5.000	5.000	5.000	5.000	5.000	5.000	5.000	5.000

Note: Components do not always add up to totals because of rounding-off errors.

on substitution form (10.8) for Λn. If we continue in this way, we can write in general

$$\Lambda^\tau n = C^\tau n + \sum_{\theta=0}^{\tau-1} C^\theta . \Lambda^{\tau-\theta-1} b$$

$$= C^\tau n + \sum_{\theta=1}^{\tau-1} C^\theta \Lambda^{\tau-\theta-1} b + \Lambda^{\tau-1} b \qquad (10.16)$$

where the alternative form shown in the second row is given for comparison with the second row of Equation (10.23) below.

Ignoring the lack of sex distinction, Equation (10.16) can be compared with (10.3). Each equation contains a term $C^\tau n$ which relates to the survivors from the initial stock. The second terms in the two equations are equivalent. For instance, if we put $\theta = 0$ in (10.3), then $\Lambda^0 n \equiv n$ is the initial age-composition vector; Bn is the vector of new entrants (births) in the 12 months that follow; and $C^{\tau-1} Bn$ is the vector of these new entrants subjected to $\tau-1$ transformations by the C-matrix, that is the component of $\Lambda^\tau n$ resulting from the new entrants in the year succeeding the initial date. Similarly, if we put $\theta = \tau - 1$ in (10.16), $\Lambda^0 b \equiv b$ and this too is subject to $\tau - 1$ transformations by the C-matrix to give, again, the component of $\Lambda^\tau n$ resulting from the new entrants in the year succeeding the initial date.

The general form of the projection equation given in (10.16) can be simplified if the population is initially in a state of stationary equilibrium and the $\Lambda^\theta b$ take some simple form for all relevant values of θ. The first of these conditions amounts to saying that

$$n_0 = Cn_0 + b_0$$
$$= (I - C)^{-1} b_0 \qquad (10.17)$$

If $\Lambda^\theta b = b_1$ for $\theta > 0$, then Equation (10.16) simplifies to

$$\Lambda^\tau n = C^\tau n_0 + \sum_{\theta=0}^{\tau-1} C^\theta b_1$$

$$= C^\tau n_0 + (I - C^\tau)(I - C)^{-1} b_1$$
$$= C^\tau n_0 + (I - C^\tau) n_1 \qquad (10.18)$$

As we have seen, $C^\theta = 0$ for all values of θ which exceed the human life span, and so we can see from (10.18) that a single, sustained step in b will completely work itself out in one human life span, during which time the population vector will be a changing weighted sum of the elements of the initial and final population vectors, n_0 and n_1.

A second case which is of some interest arises if, at the end of the period of stationary equilibrium, b grows in geometric progression at an annual rate of ρ. In this case, writing $C^* \equiv C/(1 + \rho)$, we can see that

$$\Lambda^\tau n = C^\tau n_0 + (1 + \rho)^{\tau - 1} \sum_{\theta = 0}^{\tau - 1} C^{*\theta} b_0$$

$$= C^\tau n_0 + (I - C^{*\tau})(I - C^*)^{-1}(1 + \rho)^{\tau - 1} b_0 \qquad (10.19)$$

If, from an initial value of b_0, the elements of b are to move along sigmoid paths, it does not seem possible to obtain simple expressions like Equations (10.18) and (10.19). However, from a computational point of view, this complication presents little difficulty. For instance, if the elements of b are all to grow along logistic curves, then we can write

$$\Delta b = \hat{r} \, (\hat{b}^* - \hat{b}) \, b \qquad (10.20)$$

where $\Delta \equiv \Lambda - 1$ denotes the first difference operator, r is a vector of constants and the elements of b^* are the upper bounds of the corresponding elements of b. From (10.20)

$$\Lambda b = [I + \hat{r} \, (\hat{b}^* - \hat{b})] \, b \qquad (10.21)$$

Starting with $b = b_0$, we can work out Λb from this expression, insert it in (10.15) and continue.

6. CHANGES IN THE C-MATRIX

In most practical applications it will be found that some of the elements of the C-matrix change over time. For instance, in the last generation more children have tended to stay on at school after the school-leaving age and to stay on for longer; and more of them enroll in teacher-training colleges, universities, and the like.

Let us suppose that we have some means of projecting the elements of C and let us denote this matrix β periods from now by $\Lambda^\beta C$. Then the series $C, C^2, C^3,$ ... will have to be replaced by $C, \Lambda C.C, \Lambda^2 C.\Lambda C.C, \ldots$. In this notation, Equations (10.15) and (10.16) become

$$\Lambda^2 n = \Lambda C \, \Lambda n + \Lambda b$$
$$= (\Lambda C.C)n + \Lambda C \, b + \Lambda b \qquad (10.22)$$

and

$$\Lambda^\tau n \;=\; \overset{\tau-1}{\underset{\beta=0}{\Pi}} \; \Lambda^\beta Cn + \overset{\tau-1}{\underset{\theta=1}{\Sigma}} \left[\overset{\tau-\theta}{\underset{\beta=\tau-1}{\Pi}} \; \Lambda^\beta C \right] \Lambda^{\tau-\theta-1} b + \Lambda^{\tau-1} b$$

$$=\; \bar{\bar{C}}^\tau n \;+\; \overset{\tau-1}{\underset{\theta=1}{\Sigma}} \; \Lambda^{\tau-\theta} \, \bar{\bar{C}}^\theta \, \Lambda^{\tau-\theta-1} b + \Lambda^{\tau-1} b \qquad (10.23)$$

where Π denotes the operation of forming a product and

$$\bar{\bar{C}}^\theta \;=\; \overset{\theta-1}{\underset{\beta=0}{\Pi}} \; \Lambda^\beta C \qquad\qquad (10.24)$$

In (10.16) the multiplier of $\Lambda^{\tau-\theta-1} b$ is C^θ and in (10.23) this multiplier is replaced by $\Lambda^{\tau-1} C.\Lambda^{\tau-2} C \ldots \Lambda^{\tau-\theta} C$.

Let us donote by $(I - \bar{C})^{-1}$ the expression which, with changing coefficients, is comparable to $(I - C)^{-1}$ with fixed coefficients. Then just as

$$(I - C)^{-1} \;=\; I + \overset{\infty}{\underset{\theta=1}{\Sigma}} \; C^\theta \qquad\qquad (10.25)$$

so

$$(I - \bar{C})^{-1} \;=\; I + \overset{\infty}{\underset{\theta=1}{\Sigma}} \; \bar{\bar{C}}^\theta \qquad\qquad (10.26)$$

where $\bar{\bar{C}}^\theta$ is defined by (10.24). From (10.26) it follows that

$$\bar{C} \;=\; {}^\cdot I \;-\; \left[I + \overset{\infty}{\underset{\theta=1}{\Sigma}} \; \bar{\bar{C}}^{\vec{\theta}-1} \right] \qquad\qquad (10.27)$$

The summations in (10.25) and (10.26) do not extend beyond the number of years in the human life span, since, for higher values of θ, C^θ, and $\bar{\bar{C}}^\theta$ are identically zero.

The effect of using $\bar{C}$ in place of C can readily be described. If we work with $(I - \bar{C})^{-1}$ based on data for, say, 1965, the babies born in that year implicitly have the same expectations at, say, age 18, that is in 1983, as had the 18-year-olds of 1965; whereas, if we work with $(I - \bar{C})^{-1}$, these expectations are updated to 1983, bearing in mind the changes at intermediate ages that now seem likely to take place between the two dates.

7. INTERPRETATIONS OF THE C-MATRIX

For a population in stationary equilibrium, $\Lambda^\theta n = n$ and $\Lambda^\theta b = b$ for all relevant values of θ and so, as we saw in Equation (10.17),

$$n = Cn + b$$
$$= (I - C)^{-1}b \qquad (10.28)$$

Despite its unconventional symbolism, an economist would immediately recognize (10.28) as the equation of an open input-output system, C as Leontief's matrix of input-output coefficients, and $(I - C)^{-1}$ as the matrix multiplier of the system, a term introduced by Goodwin (1949) to describe the generalization to many sectors of the scalar multiplier of Keynesian income analysis. Formally this is correct but, whereas in economics b would represent a vector of final demands for commodities and n would represent a vector of total outputs of commodities, in the present case b represents a vector of new entrants and n represents a vector of the total numbers in different categories of the population. Thus our economist could fairly describe b as a vector of primary inputs and n as a vector of total inputs, meaning the survivors from all the new entrants of the past. If, despite this reversal of the roles of outputs and inputs, the economist were assured that the variables in Equation (10.28) were quantities, he would reply that, if so, there must be a similar equation, with C' in place of C, which had something to do with costs and prices. This is indeed the case, as we shall see in the section on "Prices and Quantities," below.

The significance of the economist's interpretation is that it provides a link between sociodemographic data on the numbers in different states and economic data on costs, prices, gains, losses, income, benefits, and the like associated with the same set of states.

A probability theorist confronted with Equation (10.28) would say that if C could be interpreted as a probability matrix, then $(I - C)^{-1}$ must be the fundamental matrix of an absorbing Markov chain so that the equation must be descriptive of a Markov process. This interpretation is also correct but it puts severe restrictions on the definition of states, that is, on the classifications used in n, b, and C. The essential requirement is that states must be so defined that the probability of movement from a state is independent of the path along which that state has been reached. In other words, each state must be so defined that all its members are homogeneous in the sense that they have the same probabilities of staying in that state or of moving to other states, probabilities that will be measured by the transition proportions of which C is composed.

Let us now look at some of the circumstances which make it impossible to interpret a C-matrix as a probability matrix. The examples in the three sections which follow can be regarded as instances of the aggregation problem, referred to by Kemeny and Snell (1960) as the problem of lumpability.

8. SOCIAL MOBILITY IN A COMMUNITY MADE UP OF DISTINCT GROUPS

Social mobility is frequently studied by relating the occupations of sons to the occupations of their fathers. Consider a transition matrix (a type of D-matrix in this case) in which the rows relate to the class of the son and the columns to the class of the father. Suppose the community is divided into two classes, upper and lower, denoted by the suffixes 1 and 2 in the matrix, and into two distinct groups, denoted by the symbols * and **. Then we might find that

$$D^* = \begin{bmatrix} 0.9 & 0.9 \\ 0.1 & 0.1 \end{bmatrix} \tag{10.29}$$

whose stable vector, n^* say, is proportional to

$$n^* = \{9 \quad 1\} \tag{10.30}$$

whereas

$$D^{**} = \begin{bmatrix} 0.1 & 0.1 \\ 0.9 & 0.9 \end{bmatrix} \tag{10.31}$$

whose stable vector, n^{**} say, is proportional to

$$n^{**} = \{1 \quad 9\} \tag{10.32}$$

Each group in this community is perfectly mobile in the sense that the probability of a son being in a particular class is independent of the class of his father (Prais, 1955); and, under stable conditions, 90 percent of the families in the * group will be in the upper class and 90 percent of the families in the ** group will be in the lower class.

If an attempt is made to analyze this community with the help of a pooled matrix, D say, it is obvious that the outcome will depend on the relative importance of the two groups. For instance, if the * group accounts for 99 percent of the population, then

$$D(99{:}1) = \begin{bmatrix} 0.8991 & 0.83 \\ 0.1009 & 0.16 \end{bmatrix} \tag{10.33}$$

whose stable vector is proportional to

$$n(99{:}1) = \{892 \quad 108\} \tag{10.34}$$

On the other hand, if the two groups are of equal importance, then

$$D(1:1) = \begin{bmatrix} 0.8902 & 0.5 \\ 0.1098 & 0.5 \end{bmatrix} \tag{10.35}$$

and

$$n(1:1) = \{82 \quad 18\} \tag{10.36}$$

The mean staying time in a class is $1/(1 - d_{jj}), j = 1,2$; and the transition matrix of a perfectly mobile society has a vector, whose elements sum to one, proportional to the stable vector repeated in each of its columns. The degree of mobility can be measured by considering the ratio of the actual mean staying time in each class to the time in the corresponding perfectly mobile society. From Equations (10.29), (10.31), (10.33), and (10.35) we can set out these measures as in Table 10.5.

Since we know that the community is made up of two distinct groups we realize that the pooled analyses are invalid; but if we did not have this knowledge and did not realize the need for it, we might easily carry them out. If the mix of the groups was as in $D(99:1)$ we should probably conclude that the community was almost perfectly mobile, as indeed it is; but we might not realize that this almost perfect mobility was compatible with a tiny "culture of poverty" in which 1 percent of the families, those in the ** group spend 90 percent of their time in the lower class.

The moral of this example is that if a community is made up of groups with different transition matrices, conclusions based on pooled data are likely in some

Table 10.5. Measures of Social Mobility

Class				Generations and Ratios		
	D^*			D^{**}		
	Actual	Perfectly Mobile	Ratio	Actual	Perfectly Mobile	Ratio
1	10	10	1	1.$\dot{1}$	1.$\dot{1}$	1
2	1.$\dot{1}$	1.$\dot{1}$	1	10	10	1

Class	$D(99:1)$			$D(1:1)$		
	Actual	Perfectly Mobile	Ratio	Actual	Perfectly Mobile	Ratio
1	9.91	9.26	1.07	5.$\dot{5}$	2	2.$\dot{7}$
2	1.20	1.12	1.07	5.$\dot{5}$	2	2.$\dot{7}$

respects to be misleading. In the present case we need to treat the two groups separately or, equivalently, to work with four states rather than two.

9. REFERRALS IN A SYSTEM OF MEDICAL CARE

By a system of medical care I mean a collection of hospitals, clinics, aftercare organizations, specialists, and practitioners of all kinds which cater to the needs of a community in some branch of medical diagnosis and treatment. If such a system is divided into branches, a patient from outside the system will enter it by being referred to a particular branch; and, from there, he may either be referred out of the system or be referred to another branch (or a succession of branches) within it before he finally gets out. If the states of the system are equated to its branches, then for a valid analysis on the foregoing lines, the probabilities of movements from any branch must be independent of the way in which that branch was reached.

An example of this kind can be based on the data presented by Baldwin (1971:Table 8.1) relating to the movement of patients in the psychiatric service system of northeast Scotland in 1965. The system is divided into nine branches and the information on flows is reproduced in Table 10.6.

From Table 10.6 we see that 2,260 referrals were made to the branch "out patients," of which 1,989 were from outside the system; and that 2,213 referrals were made from the branch "outpatients," of which 1,628 were to the outside world. The remaining rows and columns provide similar information for the other branches.

By dividing the entries relating to the nine branches in each column by the grand total for the column, we can form a C-matrix and from it derive the usual inverse, $(I - C)^{-1}$, as set out in Table 10.7.

On the assumption that C can be interpreted as a probability matrix, Table 10.7 shows the direct and indirect consequences of 1,000 referrals from outside into any branch of the system. A matrix inverse $(I - C)^{-1}$ can always be decomposed into three terms $I + C + C^2(I - C)^{-1}$ which, in the present context, relate to initial, direct, and indirect referrals. Thus the entry of 1,033 in row 1 and column 1 of Table 10.7 can be decomposed into $1,000 + 9 + 24 = 1,033$. This means that the initial referral of 1,000 individuals to branch 1 of the system from outside generates 9 additional referrals directly and a further 24 referrals indirectly. Similarly, the entry in row 2 and column 1 can be decomposed into $0 + 205 + 49 = 254$, so that the initial referral of 1,000 individuals to branch 1 leads to 205 direct referrals and 49 indirect referrals to branch 2. By summing the entries in column 1 of Table 10.7 we obtain a figure of 1,440, which indicates that if 1,000 patients are referred into the system at branch 1, 440 additional referrals will be made before the 1,000 patients have all left the system. The same interpretation can be put on the entries in the other columns of the table.

Table 10.6. Movements of Patients Into, Within and Out of the Psychiatric Service System of Northeast Scotland in 1965

To \ From	Outside World	The System								Referrals Totals		
		(1)	(2)	(3)	(4)	(5)	(6)	(7)	(8)	(9)	Totals
Outside world		1,628	1,486	38	115	123	256	19	491	1	
The Sys-tem 1 Outpatients	1,989	20	7	89	46	10	87	1	2	9	2,260
2 Inpatients	1,159	453	136	44	248	20	197	17	113	23	2,410
3 Day-patients	7	72	63	3	7	0	4	0	10	1	167
4 Domiciliary visits	405	0	0	0	0	1	0	0	0	0	406
5 Domiciliary treatments	9	39	83	3	7	0	6	0	35	1	183
6 Hospital consultations	565	1	0	0	1	0	1	0	1	0	569
7 Other emergencies	61	0	0	0	0	0	0	0	0	0	61
8 Inpatient follow-up	4	0	729	0	0	0	0	0	0	1	734
9 Other psychiatric	0	0	1	0	0	0	0	0	0	0	1
Total		2,213	2,387	177	424	154	551	37	652	36	

Note: Components do not always add up to totals because of rounding-off errors.

Table 10.7. Initial, Direct and Indirect Referrals per 1,000 New Entrants Into Each State of the Psychiatric Service System of Northeast Scotland in 1965 $1,000 (I-C)^{-1}$

To \ From	(1)	(2)	(3)	(4)	(5)	(6)	(7)	(8)	(9)
1 Outpatients	1,033	27	537	138	72	178	40	20	293
2 Inpatients	254	1,149	423	711	170	456	534	216	819
3 Day-patients	42	37	1,048	44	8	27	18	23	64
4 Domiciliary visits	0	0	0	1,000	6	0	0	0	0
5 Domiciliary treatment	32	60	49	57	1,010	38	29	66	78
6 Hospital consultations	0	0	0	2	0	1,002	0	1	0
7 Other emergencies	0	0	0	0	0	0	1,000	0	0
8 Inpatient follow-up	78	350	129	217	52	139	163	1,066	278
9 Other psychiatric	0	0	0	0	0	0	0	0	1,000
Total	1,440	1,624	2,186	2,169	1,318	1,841	1,784	1,391	2,533

Note: Components do not always add up to totals because of rounding-off errors.

Starting again from Table 10.6, if we divide the entries relating to the nine branches in each row by the grand total for the row, we can form a G'-matrix and from it derive $(I - G')^{-1}$ as set out in Table 10.8.

On the assumption that G' can be interpreted as a probability matrix, Table 10.8 shows the average experience within the system of 1,000 leavers from any branch of it. The nature of these entries can be seen most easily from column 7. Since we know from Table 10.6 that no one is referred to branch 7 from within the system, it follows that those who leave from branch 7 have not been

Table 10.8. Final, Direct and Indirect Referrals per 1,000 Exeants from the Psychiatric Service System of Northeast Scotland in 1965 $1,000 (I-C')^{-1}$

From \ To	(1)	(2)	(3)	(4)	(5)	(6)	(7)	(8)	(9)
1 Outpatients	1,035	235	560	1	382	3	0	233	235
2 Inpatients	34	1,152	534	2	763	2	0	1,144	1,154
3 Day-patients	43	31	1,051	0	46	0	0	31	31
4 Domiciliary visits	26	125	111	1,000	127	2	0	124	125
5 Domiciliary treatment	5	10	7	2	1,008	0	0	10	10
6 Hospital consultations	44	105	91	0	112	1,002	0	104	105
7 Other emergencies	0	8	4	0	5	0	1,000	8	8
8 Inpatient follow-up	6	60	91	0	233	2	0	1,059	60
9 Other psychiatric	5	12	13	0	14	0	0	12	1,012
Total	1,198	1,738	2,462	1,005	2,690	1,011	1,000	2,725	2,740

Note: Components do not always add up to totals because of rounding-off errors.

admitted, directly or indirectly, into any other branch. In contrast, the 1,000 who leave from branch 1 have made 198 moves within the system before they finally return to the outside world. Many of them will have gone straight in and straight out but others may have entered the system from any branch and moved around in it until they finally emerge from branch 1. The average experience of these people results in the numbers in column 1.

I must emphasize that the flow matrix, reproduced here as Table 10.6, was originally compiled to indicate the connectedness of the system and not to enable the kind of analyses set out in Tables 10.7 and 10.8 to be made. It is very likely that the nine branches into which the system is divided do not define states with probabilities of movement independent of the paths along which they have been reached. However, the kind of record system which makes possible the construction of Table 10.6 would also make it possible to check the suitability of any proposed set of states. My point here is that this checking would have to be carried out before the results in Tables 10.7 and 10.8 could be regarded as of more than methodological interest.

10. DEPENDENCE ON THE PAST: THE ANALYSIS OF AN IMAGINARY DISEASE

The assumption that movements from a given state are independent of past states is a strong one and will only be warranted if states are appropriately defined. If they are defined wholly in terms of present characteristics, the definitions will often not be appropriate. For instance, in the matter of social mobility, the grandfather's class may exert an influence on the son's class beyond that which is transmitted through the father. If this were so, separate *D*-matrices, of the type of Equation (10.29), tabulated according to the class of the grandfather, would be different and the father-son tabulation of (10.29) would have to be set up for each class of grandfather.

Influences from the past are also important in other areas. For instance, in many medical applications it seems unlikely that the probability of entering different medical categories at the next stage of life can be inferred from the medical category at the present stage without reference to the individual's medical history. This kind or problem for which individual longitudinal records would be needed, could be handled as follows.

Suppose that the life span is divided into τ age groups or stages, and that at each stage individuals are classified to μ medical categories. In the simplest case the medical categories might consist of the dichotomy well or ill. There would in this case be two states at the first stage. At the second stage, those who were well at the first stage would be classified according as they were now well or ill, and those who were ill at the first stage would be classified in the same way. Thus, at the second stage there would be μ^2 states and at stage τ there would be μ^τ states.

If we think in terms of a period of one year between the opening and closing stocks and of a stage length of ten years, then in any period an individual can: (1) remain in the stage and, as far as this chapter is concerned, also the state in which he was recorded at the beginning of the period; (2) move to one of the states characteristic of the next stage; or (3) move into the absorbing state, that is die or emigrate.

With this method of recording, the C-matrix takes a very special form: the diagonal submatrices are diagonal (corresponding to the fact that changes of state within a stage are not recorded); and the only other nonzero submatrices are those immediately below the diagonal ones (corresponding to the fact that individuals can only go from one stage to the next and can neither skip a stage nor go backward). Thus, in the case of three stages, C takes the form

$$C = \begin{matrix} \hat{c}_{11} & 0 & 0 \\ C_{21} & \hat{c}_{22} & 0 \\ 0 & C_{32} & \hat{c}_{33} \end{matrix} \qquad (10.37)$$

whence

$$(I - C)^{-1} = \begin{bmatrix} (I-\hat{c}_{11})^{-1} & 0 & 0 \\ (I-\hat{c}_{22})^{-1}C_{21}(I-\hat{c}_{11})^{-1} & (I-\hat{c}_{22})^{-1} & 0 \\ (I-\hat{c}_{33})^{-1}C_{32}(I-\hat{c}_{22})^{-1}C_{21}(I-\hat{c}_{11})^{-1} & (I-\hat{c}_{33})^{-1}C_{32}(I-\hat{c}_{22})^{-1} & (I-\hat{c}_{33})^{-1} \end{bmatrix}$$

$$(10.38)$$

Thus, while the C-matrices tend to be large, the inverse matrices can be built up by taking reciprocals and by systematic matrix multiplication.

I am not aware of any data which would enable me to illustrate this scheme and so I shall have to make use of a constructed example. In it, life is divided into three stages, each of 10 years' duration, so that the life span is 30 years. Individuals are recorded either as well or as suffering from the one identified disease which I shall refer to as Stone's disease since, as far as I know, there is no real disease of this name. Stone's disease may strike at any stage of life and there are two methods of treating it. The first is an operation which either kills or cures but which, if successful, effects a lasting cure so that, after it, an individual cannot contract the disease again. The second is a regime of drugs which prevents the patient from dying of the disease but cannot cure him and keeps him alive with some measure of disability.

Every year a thousand babies are born into the community we are studying. There is a certain probability that they will enter stage 1 with the disease and, if they do, that they will choose either of the two treatments. Similar probabilities exist for the later stages; and to each state there corresponds a state-specific mortality rate. If we were able to observe this community from one year's end to the next, we might be able to draw up a matrix of stocks and flows as set out in Table 10.9.

Table 10.9. A Stationary Population Subject to Stone's Disease

Columns 1–3 are Stage 1; columns 4–9 are Stage 2; columns 10–19 are Stage 3.

	Outside world	1 W	2 I_1	3 I_2	4 WW	5 WI_1	6 WI_2	7 I_1W	8 I_2I_1	9 I_2I_2	10 WWW	11 WWI_1	12 WWI_2	13 WI_1W	14 WI_2I_1	15 WI_2I_2	16 I_1WW	17 I_2I_1W	18 $I_2I_1I_1$	19 $I_2I_2I_2$	Totals
Outside world		800	100	100																	1000
1. W	8	7128			634	58	100														7928
2. I_1	50		450					50													550
3. I_2	10			810					10	80											910
4. WW	34				5400						480	30	90								6034
5. WI_1	35					207								23							265
6. WI_2	15						765								5	80					865
7. I_1W	3							423									47				473
8. I_2I_1	2								36									4	4		46
9. I_2I_2	16									612										64	692
10. WWW	480										3888										4368
11. WWI_1	30											81									111
12. WWI_2	90												648								738
13. WI_1W	23													189							212
14. WI_2I_1	5														9						14
15. WI_2I_2	80															576					656
16. I_1WW	47																378				425
17. I_2I_1W	4																	36			40
18. $I_2I_1I_1$	4																		9		13
19. $I_2I_2I_2$	64																			451	515
Totals	1000	7928	550	910	6034	265	865	473	46	692	4368	111	738	212	14	656	425	40	13	515	24955

In this table, the 24,955 individuals who make up the population are distributed among the 19 possible states of the system as members of both the opening and the closing stock. In the body of the table we find the movements between states, which take place over a single annual period. The states are indicated in a mnemonic notation obtained by combining in order the symbols W (well), I_1 (ill and opting for treatment 1) and I_2 (ill and opting for treatment 2). Thus WI_2I_1 indicates an individual who is well at the first stage, is ill and opts for treatment 2 at the second stage and is still ill and opts for treatment 1 at the third stage. It might be supposed that with $\tau = 3$ stages and $\mu = 3$ medical categories at each stage, there would be ω states, where

$$
\begin{aligned}
\omega &= \sum_{\theta=1}^{\tau} \mu^\theta \\
&= \frac{\mu(\mu^\tau - 1)}{\mu - 1} \\
&= 39
\end{aligned}
\tag{10.39}
$$

but reflection will show that many of these states, in fact 20 of them, cannot exist. For instance, at the second stage nobody can be in state I_1I_2 because an individual who is operated on at the first stage is either killed or cured.

By dividing the numbers in the columns (other than the first) of Table 10.9 by the column totals and by discarding the entries in the first row (which relate to deaths), we obtain the C-matrix as set out in Table 10.10. Apart from rounding-off errors (effective only in column 1 of the table) all column sums are less than one since there are some deaths from each state.

The fundamental matrix derived from this C-matrix is set out in Table 10.11.

The following statements can be made about the entries in Table 10.11:

(a) The diagonal entries measure the mean time spent in a state by an individual about to enter that state. For instance, the figure of 9.91 at the intersection of row 1 and column 1 indicates that on average an individual entering state 1 spends 9.91 years in it (out of a potential 10 years). Apart from a small rounding-off error, this checks with the fact that the state-specific mortality rate assumed in this case is 1 percent.

(b) The off-diagonal entry in row j and column k measures the mean time spent in state j multiplied by the probability of reaching state j from state k. For instance, the figure of 9.52 at the intersection of row and column 4 corresponds to the fact that the state-specific mortality rate for state 4 is assumed to be 5 percent; and the ratio $7.54/9.52 = 0.8$ indicates that 80 percent of the survivors from state 1 are assumed to go next into state 4 (that is to remain well at the second stage) rather than into states 5 or 6.

(c) The column sums of the table measure the expectation of life of an

Table 10.10. The Matrix of Transition Probabilities, C, Based on Table 10.9.

		Stage 1			Stage 2						Stage 3									
		1	2	3	4	5	6	7	8	9	10	11	12	13	14	15	16	17	18	19
		W	I_1	I_2	WW	WI_1	WI_2	I_1W	I_2I_1	I_2I_2	WWW	WWI_1	WWI_2	WI_1W	WI_2I_1	WI_2I_2	I_1WW	I_2I_1W	$I_2I_2I_1$	$I_2I_2I_2$
Stage 1	1. W	0.90																		
	2. I_1		0.82																	
	3. I_2			0.89																
Stage 2	4. WW	0.08			0.89															
	5. WI_1	0.01				0.78														
	6. WI_2	0.01					0.88													
	7. I_1W		0.09					0.89												
	8. I_2I_1			0.01					0.78											
	9. I_2I_2			0.09						0.88										
Stage 3	10. WWW				0.08						0.89									
	11. WWI_1				0.00							0.73								
	12. WWI_2				0.01								0.88							
	13. WI_1W					0.09								0.89						
	14. WI_2I_1						0.01								0.64					
	15. WI_2I_2						0.09									0.88				
	16. I_1WW							0.10									0.89			
	17. I_2I_1W								0.09									0.90		
	18. $I_2I_2I_1$									0.01									0.69	
	19. $I_2I_2I_2$									0.09										0.88

Table 10.11. The Fundamental Matrix, $(I - C)^{-1}$, Based on Table 10.10.

		Stage 1			Stage 2						Stage 3									
		1 W	2 I_1	3 I_2	4 WW	5 WI_1	6 WI_2	7 I_1W	8 I_2I_1	9 I_2I_2	10 WWW	11 WWI_1	12 WWI_2	13 WI_1W	14 WI_2I_1	15 WI_2I_2	16 I_1WW	17 I_2I_1W	18 $I_2I_2I_1$	19 $I_2I_2I_2$
Stage 1	1. W	9.91																		
	2. I_1		5.50																	
	3. I_2			9.10																
Stage 2	4. WW	7.54			9.52															
	5. WI_1	0.33				4.57														
	6. WI_2	1.08					8.65													
	7. I_1W		4.73					9.46												
	8. I_2I_1			0.46					4.60											
	9. I_2I_2			6.92						8.65										
Stage 3	10. WWW	5.46			6.89						9.10									
	11. WWI_1	0.14			0.18							3.70								
	12. WWI_2	0.92			1.16								8.20							
	13. WI_1W	0.26				3.66								9.22						
	14. WI_2I_1	0.02					0.14								2.80					
	15. WI_2I_2	0.82					6.56									8.20				
	16. I_1WW		4.25					8.50									9.04			
	17. I_2I_1W			0.40					4.00									10.00		
	18. $I_2I_2I_1$			0.13						0.16									3.25	
	19. $I_2I_2I_2$			5.15						6.44										8.05
	Totals	26.48	14.48	22.16	17.75	8.23	15.35	17.96	8.60	15.25	9.10	3.70	8.20	9.22	2.80	8.20	9.04	10.00	3.25	8.05
Well	I	23.66	14.48	0.99	16.59	8.23	0.14	17.96	8.60	0.16	9.10	3.70	0	9.22	2.80	0	9.04	10.00	3.25	0
	III	2.82	0	21.17	1.16	0	15.21	0	0	15.09	0	0	8.20	0	0	8.20	0	0	0	8.05

individual entering the state to which the column refers. For instance, the sum of the entries in column 1 is 26.48 years and this, accordingly, is the expectation of life at birth of a child born into the category well. As can be seen from columns 2 and 3, the position is very different for children born with Stone's disease and, moreover, the expectation is greatly affected by the choice of treatment.

By assumption, 80 percent of children are born well and, of those born ill, one-half opt for each alternative treatment. We can see that (0.8×26.48) + (0.1×14.48) + (0.1×22.16) = 24.948 gives the average expectation of life at birth. This number can be compared with the ratio of population to births, namely 24.955. The two numbers are the same apart from rounding-off errors.

(d) The entries in the columns enable us to divide life expectancies between years of healthy and years of unhealthy life. In the formulation given, it is necessary to assume that all events take place at the outset of the stages, though this restriction could probably be removed by a more general formulation of the system. As it is, the probable time spent in, let us say, WI_1, is to be counted as a healthy period since it relates to time spent by surviving, and therefore healthy, patients who undergo treatment 1 at the outset of stage 2. Proceeding in this way, we can see that of the 26.48 years which a healthy baby can expect to live, 23.66 years will, on average, be in the category well and 2.82 will, on average, be in the category ill.

By comparing the figures in columns 2 and 3 we can see the probable consequences of the choice of treatment for those born with Stone's disease. Those who choose treatment 1 have a comparatively short average expectation of life, 14.48 years, but it is all healthy. If, on the other hand they choose treatment 2, their average life expectancy is increased to 22.16 years but, of these, an expected 21.17 are years of ill health. A choice of treatment would presumably be influenced in any particular case by the patient's valuation of a year of good health as against a year of bad health. If λ, $0 \leqslant \lambda \leqslant 1$, represents the valuation of a year of bad health compared with a year of good health, then it is clear from the totals of columns 2 and 3 that the break-even point between the two treatments in terms of initial life expectancy occurs when $\lambda = 0.64$. On this criterion, anyone for whom $\lambda < 0.64$ should opt for treatment 1 and anyone for whom $\lambda > 0.64$ should opt for treatment 2. That babies are not capable of weighing such arguments is a fact that need not detain us here. Their parents or their doctor will have to take the decision on their behalf, and at later stages in life the individual may have a little more say about his own destiny.

(e) In applications in which medical categories do not appear, we can find, with the help of a life table, the age at which any column sum of Table 10.11 is the expectation of life. In the present application we cannot speak of a single life table: the relevant life table depends on the state. It is clear, however, that those entering stage 1 are aged 0, those entering stage 2 are aged 10, and those entering stage 3 are aged 20.

Since Table 10.9 was constructed, it is a simple matter to write down the assumptions needed to construct it. These are of five types, as follows:

1. The number of births in the period of observation which is assumed to be a year. This is a purely arbitrary number.
2. The number of stages and the length of each stage in years. This length need not be the same for all stages.
3. The probability of entering a stage in the category well. This is likely to vary from stage to stage and, generally speaking, to diminish at later stages.
4. The probability of opting for treatment 1. This is likely to vary from state to state. If living with the disease is unpleasant, an individual with experience of it may be more likely to opt for treatment 1 than would an individual with no experience of it.
5. The state-specific mortality rates.

These five types of assumption are clearly of very different kinds. Type 1 would normally be given, the period of observation being chosen in relation to the particular problem under investigation. Type 2 is at the choice of the investigator, subject to any restriction imposed by the contribution of this choice to combinatorial escalation. Types 3 and 5 relate to the state of health of a population and could only be ascertained in practice by collecting data. Type 4 could also, doubtless, only be ascertained by collecting data but, in the language of control, these choices are, in fact, control of policy variables and depend, ultimately, on the attitudes of doctors, patients, and administrators. These attitudes may remain unchanged over long periods or alter radically in response to changes in medical knowledge and technology, in personal feelings on medical matters, and in financial and other practical conditions which inevitably weigh with administrators. It would be a simple matter to reformulate Table 10.9 so that the dependence of the flows on these policy variables was shown explicitly. This explicitness can be carried into the fundamental matrix so that many of its entries become a function of policy variables. It would therefore be possible to calculate from the points of view of the different interested parties the consequences of changing any of these variables.

11. DISPENSING WITH AGE IN THE DEFINITION OF STATES

In practice we rarely, if ever, encounter populations in stationary equilibrium and so we must ask what effect this has on our ability to construct meaningful *C*-matrices. The answer would seem to be that it has comparatively little effect if age is the primary criterion of classification and is not too broadly grouped. For instance, if age is defined by year of birth, all the numbers entered in a column of a *C*-matrix relate to individuals born in a single year and are not likely to be much affected by the distribution of births within that year. On the other hand, if age is not a criterion of classification, then the entries in a given column of a C-matrix may be drawn from vintages of very different years and, therefore, of very different sizes. This can easily be seen if one of the states of the system relates to the gainfully occupied. Those who remain in this state from one year to the next may have been born anywhere from, say, 15 to 65 years ago; those who temporarily return to some branch of further education will mostly have been born between 20 and 30 years ago; and those who retire from employment will mostly have been born some 60 to 65 years ago. If the population has been growing, the vintage size around the age of retirement will be quite different from the vintage size around the age of returning to the educational system. As a consequence, the elements in the columns of a C-matrix will depend on the rate at which the population has been growing and so will be of very limited use. The question arises, therefore: What, if anything, can be done with information of this kind?

As an example, I shall outline an analysis of the active sequence, by which I mean the progression from inactivity in infancy through learning and earning activities in youth and middle age to inactivity again in old age. A part of this sequence, covering the first 20 years of life, was discussed in the section "Applications to Education" above. With the existing information it is not possible to complete the lifespan with year of birth as the primary criterion of classification, and even the use of age groups would present great difficulties. Accordingly, I decided to abandon age altogether and to set up a flow matrix in which states are defined in terms of activities without reference to age. This had the advantage that it was now possible to introduce additional information; for instance, the final year at secondary school could be treated as a separate category and pupils could be classified by the qualification they obtained at the end of their school career. A matrix relating to males in England and Wales in which 43 states are distinguished was constructed for 1965-1966 and a version in which these were combined to give 22 states is set out in Stone (1972).

These matrices are large and I shall not reproduce them here. They relate like the tables in "Applications to Education," leavers from two successive years and are disaggregations of Table 10.12.

In order to get over the difficulty of unequal vintage sizes, an attempt was made to adjust the elements of the matrix to what they would have been had the population not been growing over the human life span ending in 1965-1966. This adjustment was carried out in two parts. First, an estimate was made of the age range relevant to each element and the element was multiplied by the ratio of the life-table number in this age range to the actual number in it. Second, since this procedure did not bring the row and column totals into equality, the elements were further adjusted to ensure this equality by means of a biproportional method usually known as RAS technique (see Bacharach, 1970; Cambridge, Department of Applied Economics, 1963; and Stone, 1962).

From the adjusted flow matrix, a C-matrix and a matrix inverse, $(I - C)^{-1}$,

Table 10.12. The Active Sequence as a Whole—England and Wales, Males, 1965–1966

| | State on Leaving 1965 | | | | | | | | | | Thousands |
State on Leaving 1966	(0)	(1)	(2)	(3)	(4)	(5)	(6)	(7)	(8)	(9)	Total
0. Outside world		10.9	1.1	0.5			˙0.1	1.2	89.8	178.6	282.3
1. Preschool	435.6	1,603.2									2,037.8
2. Nursery and primary schools	−4.0	411.8	2,055.9								2,463.7
3. Secondary and special schools	−1.5	8.3	325.4	1,327.9							1,660.1
4. Further education	0.2			24.7	43.7		0.9		43.6		113.1
5. Teacher-training colleges				4.4	0.7	13.5	0.2	1.4	5.5		25.7
6. Universities	1.5			23.8	2.2		75.8		12.3		115.6
7. Teachers					0.3	7.6	4.1	192.9	0.6		205.5
8. Other employment	18.2			274.8	56.7	1.2	23.5	0.6	14,414.5		14,789.5
9. Home and retirement				0.1				2.1	162.4	2,191.9	2,356.5
Total	450.0	2,033.2	2,382.4	1,656.2	103.7	22.3	104.6	198.2	14,728.7	2,370.5	24,049.8

Table 10.13. Alternative Estimates of the Expectation of Life at Birth and Its Main Components—England and Wales, Males, 1965–1966

				Years
	Individual Ages	*All-Age*		
		Fully Adjusted	*Partially Adjusted*	*Unadjusted*
Preschool	4.6	5.1	4.5	4.7
School	11.3	12.4	11.4	11.9
Further education	. . .	0.7	1.0	1.1
Economic activity	. . .	44.5	47.2	56.6
Home and retirement	. . .	6.6	6.8	7.9
Total	68.5[a]	69.2	71.0	82.3

[a]The official estimate for 1964-1966 taken from U. K. General Register Office (1966). Components do not always add up to totals because of rounding-off errors.

were calculated. *Mutatis mutandis* the interpretation of the entries in this inverse is as set out under (a) through (e) of the preceding section.

With the data and methods used, the results, as described in Stone (1972), are interesting but not in all respects reliable. For instance, the expectation of life at birth based on the fully adjusted table works out at 69.2 years, which can be compared with the official estimate of 68.5 years in respect to 1964-1966. But in this table the amount of time spent, on average, in the preschool and school states is so large as to imply that the amount spent in later states is too small. Alternative estimates based on individual ages, as indicated in "Applications to Education" above, and on the fully adjusted, partially adjusted, and unadjusted tables in the present study are set out in Table 10.13.

From Table 10.13 we can see the importance of adjusting an all-age table. We can also see that partial adjustment is an unmixed blessing, since it improves both the total and its components, and that the mechanical stage of the adjustment further improves the total but distorts the components.

Many more examples could be extracted from the inverse derived from the all-age table. Thus, in the first place, the expectation at birth is of 6.59 years of retirement while the expectation on entering retirement is of 11.05 years. These numbers imply that the expectation at birth of reaching retirement is 6.59/11.05 = 0.6 and that the average age on entering retirement is 66. In the second place, the average age on entering employment (other than in teaching) is 16, which seems plausible, but the average age of entry into school teaching is 33, which is absurdly high. Finally, the expectation at birth of going to a university is 0.08 but this number drops to 0.02 for school leavers without 0-levels and rises to 0.57 for leavers with two or more A-levels.

12. VIABILITY

In societies that have no rigid rules governing marriage and descent, people may worry about social mobility or the lack of it but they are not very likely to worry about the possibility that their society will one day cease to exist because of a lack of suitable marriage partners. However, societies with rigid rules of marriage and descent may find themselves in difficulty on this score. The case of the Natchez Indians, which was analyzed by R. R. Bush and is described by Goldberg (1958), provides an example.

This society was divided into two broad classes which I shall call upper and lower. The upper class was composed of three strata which I shall call royalty, nobility, and gentry; and the lower class was composed of a single stratum which I shall call peasants. The marriage rule required that at least one partner in any marriage should be a peasant. The rules of descent laid down that: (1) if the mother were upper class, any child would belong to her stratum; (2) if the father were upper class, any child would belong to the stratum or class below his; and (3) if both parents were peasants any child would be a peasant.

To make possible an analysis of these arrangements, Bush made the following assumptions: (1) in each generation, each class has an equal number of men and women; (2) each individual marries once and only once; and (3) each marriage gives rise to exactly one son and one daughter. On these assumptions it is possible to relate the numbers in each category in the next generation to the number in the present generation. For instance, every royal mother, and no other mother, will have one royal son and so the number of royal males will not change over the generation. In this way, we can describe the evolution of this society by the relationship

$$\Lambda^\tau n = A^\tau n \tag{10.40}$$

where

$$A = \begin{bmatrix} 1 & 0 & 0 & 0 \\ 1 & 1 & 0 & 0 \\ 0 & 1 & 1 & 0 \\ -1 & -1 & 0 & 1 \end{bmatrix} \tag{10.41}$$

so that

$$A^\tau = \begin{bmatrix} 1 & 0 & 0 & 0 \\ \tau & 1 & 0 & 0 \\ \tau(\tau-1)/2 & \tau & 1 & 0 \\ -\tau(\tau+1)/2 & -\tau & 0 & 1 \end{bmatrix} \tag{10.42}$$

from which we reach the somewhat surprising conclusion that this society will eventually die out for lack of peasants if: (1) there are some members of each of the four categories to start with; (2) they maintain their marriage and descent rules unchanged; (3) our auxiliary assumptions are satisfied; and (4) the society is not continually increasing its supply of peasants by foreign conquest. We can also see that if the gentry and peasantry decide at some point to massacre all the royalty and nobility, their numbers will remain unchanged to eternity.

This peculiar example shows that rigid rules may be dangerous. Let us now look at their consequences in a different context, that of governmental or business organizations.

13. RECRUITMENT AND PROMOTION

The grade structure of an organization depends on recruitment and promotion and on the losses from different grades, which are not very easy to control except, perhaps, in the case of losses due to retirement. A large organization is likely to develop rules in these matters, partly to replace losses which experience teaches it to expect, partly to ensure prospects of advancement which are acceptable to its employees, and partly to ensure a balanced staff of adequate size. However, rules have indirect consequences, as well as the direct ones by which they are usually judged, and they too must be taken into account if the organization is not to run into difficulties.

The elements I have described—recruitment, promotion, wastage—are the very elements, with slightly different names, that we have encountered in the various models described in earlier sections. In particular, Equation (10.8) seems suitable to the present case.

Let us consider an organization with five grades, in which an individual in any grade can, in the following year: (1) remain in that grade; (2) be promoted to the next highest grade; or (3) leave the organization. A C-matrix, which reflects conditions that one might expect to find in a typical management hierarchy, is given by Bartholomew (1967:45). It takes the form

$$C = \begin{bmatrix} 0.65 & 0 & 0 & 0 & 0 \\ 0.20 & 0.70 & 0 & 0 & 0 \\ 0 & 0.15 & 0.75 & 0 & 0 \\ 0 & 0 & 0.15 & 0.85 & 0 \\ 0 & 0 & 0 & 0.10 & 0.95 \end{bmatrix} \qquad (10.43)$$

from which we see that, of those in the first grade at the beginning of a year, 65 percent are still in that grade at the end of it, 20 percent are promoted to the second grade in the course of the year, and the remainder, 15 percent, leave the organization in the course of the year. From C, which in the form shown in Equation (10.43) is what I have called an all-age matrix since age does not enter into the definition of the five states, we can form the mátrix multiplier, $(I - C)^{-1}$, namely

$$(I - C)^{-1} = \begin{bmatrix} 2.8571 & 0 & 0 & 0 & 0 \\ 1.9048 & 3.\dot{3} & 0 & 0 & 0 \\ 1.1429 & 2 & 4 & 0 & 0 \\ 1.1429 & 2 & 4 & 6.\dot{6} & 0 \\ 2.2858 & 4 & 8 & 13.\dot{3} & 20 \end{bmatrix} \qquad (10.44)$$

The entries in this matrix can be interpreted as follows. The column sums indicate the number of years which an individual who enters the grade to which the column refers can be expected, on average, to remain with the organization; and this period is divided into the time he may be expected to spend in each grade. These sums are

$$i'(I - C)^{-1} = [9.33 \quad 11.33 \quad 16 \quad 20 \quad 20] \qquad (10.45)$$

approximately and so we see that the higher up an individual is in an organization characterized by (10.43) the longer he is likely to remain with it.

The diagonal elements in Equation (10.44) indicate the number of years which an individual entering a grade will, on average, spend in that grade. We cannot, however, add up these elements to find the length of time an individual who passes through all the grades will spend with the organization because the numbers relate to leavers as well as to stayers. Thus in the lower grades in particular, the numbers are much reduced by the high wastage rates in these grades.

We can divide the elements in each row of (10.44) by the diagonal element in the row and obtain the probability that an individual who enters the grade indicated by the column will eventually enter the grade indicated by the row. If we denote this matrix by P, then, from (10.44),

$$P = \begin{bmatrix} 1.00 & 0 & 0 & 0 & 0 \\ 0.57 & 1.00 & 0 & 0 & 0 \\ 0.29 & 0.50 & 1.00 & 0 & 0 \\ 0.17 & 0.30 & 0.60 & 1.00 & 0 \\ 0.11 & 0.20 & 0.40 & 0.67 & 1.00 \end{bmatrix} \qquad (10.46)$$

Thus 57 percent of those who enter the first grade will enter the second grade $[0.20/(0.20 + 0.15) = 0.57$ approximately] and 11 percent of those who enter the first grade will eventually enter the fifth grade. Not surprisingly, the chance of further progression increases as progress is made.

Let us now ask to what stable grade structure this pattern of promotion and wastage tends. As is evident if we think back to what was said in the section on projections above, the answer to this question depends on the organization's recruitment policy and the rate of growth at which it aims. Suppose that its aim is to keep its initial staff of 10,000 constant and that its recruitment policy is to place 75 percent of its new recruits in any year into the first grade and 25 percent into the second grade. Let us further assume that its initial staff, n_0, is divided by grades as follows.

$$n_0 = \{4000 \quad 3000 \quad 1500 \quad 1000 \quad 500\} \tag{10.47}$$

In order to ensure an equilibrium staff of 10,000, with constant recruitment numbers, the organization will find that annually the vector of new entrants, b_1, will have to be

$$b_1 = \{763 \quad 254 \quad 0 \quad 0 \quad 0\} \tag{10.48}$$

but with this constant vector the equilibrium grade composition vector, $n_1 = (I - C)^{-1} b_1$, is

$$n_1 = \{2179 \quad 2300 \quad 1380 \quad 1380 \quad 2760\} \tag{10.49}$$

which bears no relation to Equation (10.47) and indicates a hopelessly top-heavy organization. Yet, inescapably, this is the consequence of the organization's recruitment and promotion policies, making allowance for losses from the different grades which, by assumption, cannot be controlled.

Before we go on to consider what might be done to improve the situation, three points should be noted. The first is that, although the staff as a whole is the same size in the stable state as it was initially, it will not, in general, remain constant during the transient period; in the present instance, ten years after the initial date it will number about 9,100 people. The second point is that the final outcome, n_1, does not depend on the initial position, n_0, but on the recruitment and promotion policies of the organization, coupled with the inevitable wastage rate. A different value of n_0 would affect two things: the size of the staff during the transient period; and the speed at which the numbers in the different grades approached their equilibrium. The third point is that if the organization, instead of aiming at a stationary state, were expanding, the outcome would be different and could be calculated by the methods described in Section 5 above.

Given that a stationary state is the aim of our organization, there are several policy changes that might be tried in order to avoid the imbalance that we have seen to be inevitable under the existing policy.

To begin with, we might see what could be done by changing the recruitment policy since if this course provided a solution the upheaval caused in the organization would be small. If we ignore transient problems, it is easy to calculate the recruitment vector, b^* say, which will preserve n_0 as the stable grade-composition vector. Evidently,

$$b^* = (I - C)n_0 \qquad (10.50)$$

but in the present case the solution is not a very happy one since it leads to

$$b^* = \left\{1400 \quad 100 \quad -75 \quad -75 \quad -75\right\} \qquad (10.51)$$

or, in words, 225 senior people would have to be fired every year. It is hard to imagine that an organization that tried to put such a policy into practice could ever operate successfully.

This being the case, we might try to learn something from the calculations that have just been made and find out whether by changing the promotion rules as well as the recruitment rules we might achieve a viable policy. With this in mind, let us first set out, on the lines of Table 10.2, the stable state achieved by changing only the recruitment rules. This is done in Table 10.14, our country being replaced by our organization.

If we accept the figure of 475 for those remaining in grade 5 throughout the year, and if we assume that the losses in each grade are independent of the promotion policy, then the simple structure of this example will dictate a unique set of promotions from grades 2, 3, and 4 and require corresponding changes in the numbers remaining in those states. The argument runs as follows: If we are to have 500 individuals in grade 5 at the end of the year and if new entrants into that grade are to be zero, then we can only have 25 promotions from grade 4 to grade 5 in place of the 100 shown in Table 10.14. Since there were 1,000 in

Table 10.14. A Stock-Flow Matrix for Our Organization

State at New Year θ / State at New Year $\theta + 1$		Outside World	Our Organization: Opening States					Closing Stocks
			(1)	*(2)*	*(3)*	*(4)*	*(5)*	
Outside world			600	450	150	50	25	
Our	1	1,400	2,600	0	0	0	0	4,000
organi-	2	100	800	2,100	0	0	0	3,000
zation:	3	−75	0	450	1,125	0	0	1,500
closing	4	−75	0	0	225	850	0	1,000
states	5	−75	0	0	0	100	475	500
Opening stocks			4,000	3,000	1,500	1,000	500	

Table 10.15. A Revised Stock-Flow Matrix for Our Organization

State at New Year θ / State at New Year θ + 1		Outside World	Our Organization: Opening States					Closing Stocks
			(1)	*(2)*	*(3)*	*(4)*	*(5)*	
Outside world			600	450	150	50	25	
Our	1	1,275	2,725	0	0	0	0	4,000
organi-	2	0	675	2,325	0	0	0	3,000
zation:	3	0	0	225	1,275	0	0	1,500
closing	4	0	0	0	75	925	0	1,000
states	5	0	0	0	0	25	475	500
Opening stocks			4,000	3,000	1,500	1,000	500	

grade 4 at the beginning of the year and the losses are only 50, it follows that 925 rather than 850 must remain in this grade throughout the year. If this is so and if the new entrants into grade 4 are to be zero then the promotions from grade 3 must be reduced to 75; and so those remaining in grade 3 must be increased to 1,275. This argument can be continued until we come to the promotions from grade 1. In the following example these are compatible with no new entrants into grade 2, so that all the 1,275 new entrants needed to balance the losses are recruited to grade 1. The outcome of these revisions to Table 10.14 are set out in Table 10.15.

These arrangements will certainly keep the size and grade composition of the staff constant; but what other effects will they have? We can answer these questions by calculating from Table 10.15 the various vectors and matrices set out in (10.43) through (10.46) above.

First, the C-matrix is

$$C = \begin{bmatrix} 0.68125 & 0 & 0 & 0 & 0 \\ 0.16825 & 0.775 & 0 & 0 & 0 \\ 0 & 0.075 & 0.85 & 0 & 0 \\ 0 & 0 & 0.05 & 0.925 & 0 \\ 0 & 0 & 0 & 0.025 & 0.95 \end{bmatrix} \qquad (10.52)$$

By comparison with (10.43) we see that in the first four grades the diagonal elements have been increased and the subdiagonal elements progressivley reduced.

Second, the matrix multiplier, $(I - C)^{-1}$, is

$$(I - C)^{-1} = \begin{bmatrix} 3.1373 & 0 & 0 & 0 & 0 \\ 2.3529 & 4.\dot{4} & 0 & 0 & 0 \\ 1.1765 & 2.\dot{2} & 6.\dot{6} & 0 & 0 \\ 0.7843 & 1.4815 & 4.\dot{4} & 13.\dot{3} & 0 \\ 0.3922 & 0.7407 & 2.\dot{2} & 6.\dot{6} & 20 \end{bmatrix} \qquad (10.53)$$

By comparison with (10.44), the mean time which an individual can expect to spend in each of the first four grades is increased, quite sensationally so in the case of grade 4. Further, starting from any grade, the time an individual may expect to spend in higher grades falls off uniformly with the height of the grade; whereas this was not the case in (10.44).

Third, the expected time spent with the organization, $i'(I - C)^{-1}$, by those entering each grade is

$$i'(I - C)^{-1} = [7.84 \quad 8.\dot{8} \quad 13.\dot{3} \quad 20 \quad 20] \qquad (10.54)$$

which for the first three grades represents a shorter time than was shown in (10.45).

Fourth, the matrix showing the probabilities of entering higher grades, P, is

$$P = \begin{bmatrix} 1.00 & 0 & 0 & 0 & 0 \\ 0.53 & 1.00 & 0 & 0 & 0 \\ 0.18 & 0.33 & 1.00 & 0 & 0 \\ 0.06 & 0.11 & 0.33 & 1.00 & 0 \\ 0.02 & 0.04 & 0.11 & 0.33 & 1.00 \end{bmatrix} \qquad (10.55)$$

By comparison with (10.46) it can be seen that the numbers in the columns fall off very rapidly, indicating, as we should expect, that the chances of getting to the top, or even near the top, have been greatly reduced.

Having reached this point, we might reflect that, while we have succeeded in working out a viable policy, it is only one out of many and that it does considerable violence to the policies which the organization's establishment department had wished to pursue. That these policies are no good in the long run is not the only consideration; it may also be true that for quite other reasons our policy is no good. For one thing, it completely upsets career prospects in the organization and, for another, it concentrates all recruitment in the first grade. It would not be easy to deal with the first point and, while we could do something about the second, we could never get back to the position in which 25 percent of the new entrants were recruited to the second grade.

Let us, therefore, try another tack. Let us ask the question: What are the minimal changes to the original policy which will ensure a policy that is viable in terms of maintaining the desired numbers and grade structure? If we find that the changes are not very big, neither we nor the establishment department will have much to worry about.

A method suitable for this purpose is the RAS method of adjustment which was referred to in Section 11 on "Dispensing with Age..." above. This method can be described, in general terms, as follows. An initial matrix, A, when postmultiplied by a diagonal matrix, $_q$, constructed from a known vector, q, leads to a vector of row totals. $Aq \neq u$, where u is a known vector, and to a vector of column totals $_q A'i \neq v$, where v is also a known vector. A matrix $A^* = {}_r A_s$, where r and s are vectors to be calculated, is to be found such that $A^* q = u$ and $_q A^{*'}i = v$. It is possible, in practical cases, to calculate A^*, and A^* is always fairly "close" to A, if not demonstrably the "closest" matrix that satisfies the constraints.

Reflection will show that in the present instance the scope of this method is limited. This is because there is only a single element in the fifth column of A, as can be seen from (10.52). This feature of the example, which would not be present if it were possible to be promoted to grade 5 from grade 3 as well as from grade 4, forces us to make exactly the adjustments we have already made until we get back to the top left-hand corner of the matrix, comprising rows 1 and 2 and the columns for the outside world and grade 1. Here, but only here, there is some scope for further adjustment.

This very limited application of the RAS method therefore runs as follows:

$$A = \begin{bmatrix} 0.75 & 0.65 \\ 0.25 & 0.20 \end{bmatrix} \tag{10.56}$$

$$q = \{1275 \quad 4000\} \tag{10.57}$$

$$u = \{4000 \quad 675\} \tag{10.58}$$

and

$$v = \{1275 \quad 3400\} \tag{10.59}$$

From these data we obtain

$$A^* = \begin{bmatrix} 0.848332 & 0.729594 \\ 0.151668 & 0.120406 \end{bmatrix} \tag{10.60}$$

This is the nearest we can get to (10.56) if the system is to produce the desired stable grade composition vector. In terms of the expressed wishes of the establishment department it is an improvement on the corresponding matrix, A^{**} say, implicit in Table 10.15, since

$$A^{**} = \begin{bmatrix} 1 & 0.68125 \\ 0 & 0.16875 \end{bmatrix} \tag{10.61}$$

However, it will be noticed that (10.61) offers better promotion prospects, 16.9 percent a year, to those in grade 1, than does (10.60) with its 12 percent a year. In this example, the desired 20 percent in (10.56) is simply unattainable.

14. ADMISSIONS AND VACANCIES

We have seen from Equation (10.11) and elsewhere that we can form a coefficient matrix, G', from the rows rather than the columns of the stock-flow table. If we do this with the data in Table 10.15, we obtain

$$G' = \begin{bmatrix} 0.68125 & 0.225 & 0 & 0 & 0 \\ 0 & 0.775 & 0.15 & 0 & 0 \\ 0 & 0 & 0.85 & 0.075 & 0 \\ 0 & 0 & 0 & 0.925 & 0.05 \\ 0 & 0 & 0 & 0 & 0.95 \end{bmatrix} \tag{10.62}$$

whence

$$(I - G')^{-1} = \begin{bmatrix} 3.13725 & 3.13725 & 3.13725 & 3.13725 & 3.13725 \\ 0 & 4.\dot{4} & 4.\dot{4} & 4.\dot{4} & 4.\dot{4} \\ 0 & 0 & 6.\dot{6} & 6.\dot{6} & 6.\dot{6} \\ 0 & 0 & 0 & 13.\dot{3} & 13.\dot{3} \\ 0 & 0 & 0 & 0 & 20 \end{bmatrix} \tag{10.63}$$

We have met these numbers before: they are the mean staying times in the different grades, that is the diagonal elements of (10.53). In commenting on that equation I said that these mean times were not necessarily applicable to individuals who had spent their whole career with the organization, and this is true. But since I have not distinguished between movers and stayers, the analysis cannot do so either and provides only mean times for all individuals passing through the system of grades. Thus, according to (10.63), the average leaver from grade 5 must have spent 47.58 years with the organization, made up of times spent in the different grades as shown in the final column.

If $(I - G')^{-1}$ is postmultiplied by the stable vector of leavers, d, where

$$d = \{600 \quad 450 \quad 150 \quad 50 \quad 25\} \tag{10.64}$$

we obtain the stable grade composition vector, (10.47).

From what has been said it is evident that the stable vector of new entrants is related to the stable vector of losses by the transforming matrix $(I - C)(I - G')^{-1}$. For the system set out in Table 10.15, this matrix

$$(I - C)(I - G')^{-1} = \begin{bmatrix} 1 & 1 & 1 & 1 & 1 \\ -0.52941 & 0.47059 & 0.47059 & 0.47059 & 0.47059 \\ 0 & -0.\dot{3} & 0.\dot{6} & 0.\dot{6} & 0.\dot{6} \\ 0 & 0 & -0.\dot{3} & 0.\dot{6} & 0.\dot{6} \\ 0 & 0 & 0 & -0.\dot{3} & 0.\dot{6} \end{bmatrix} \quad (10.65)$$

If (10.64) is premultiplied by (10.65) the result is the column vector for the outside world in Table 10.15.

The G-matrix of admission probabilities is given a different interpretation by White (1970) in his book on chains of opportunities where attention is directed to the movement of vacancies rather than to the movement of men. For a stationary organization in which existing posts are not destroyed and new posts are not created, the flow of men in one direction is matched by a flow of vacancies in the opposite direction. In particular, the retirement of a man is accompanied by the appearance of a vacancy; and the recruitment of a man is accompanied by the disappearance of a vacancy. Thus, the whole system is driven by d, interpreted as a vector of vacancies in different grades, and the Q-matrix used by White is equivalent to the matrix here denoted by G.

I shall conclude my discussion of recruitment, promotion, and vacancies at this point. A more adequate treatment would require the introduction of additional criteria of classification, in particular length of service, which has a strong effect on wastage rates, and probably age as well. A systematic account of these matters is given in Bartholomew (1967), from which many useful insights can be gained.

15. BALANCE AND CONTROL

Let us now consider the problem of keeping supply and demand in balance. I shall take as my example teachers, who are a special case inasmuch as they are both supplied and demanded by the educational system. To begin with, let us concentrate on a single-stage system and then go on to see what additional difficulties arise when this is replaced by a multistage system in which the earlier stages require teachers but cannot themselves produce them.

The primary input into the single-stage process consists of teachers, t, and the final output consists of graduates, g. One teacher can turn out α graduates per unit of time and so the technology of the system can be expressed by the simple relationship

$$g = \alpha t \quad (10.66)$$

where, for the moment, g and t denote scalars, although the same symbols will be used to denote the corresponding vectors later on.

The rate of change, $\dot{t}_s$, in the supply of teachers, t_s, is made up of two parts: (1) a positive part consisting of the proportion, β, of graduates who take up teaching; and (2) a negative part consisting of the proportion, γ, of the existing stock of teachers lost through change of job, retirement or death. Thus

$$\begin{aligned} \dot{t}_s &= \beta g - \gamma t_s \\ &= (\alpha\beta - \gamma)\, t_s \end{aligned} \tag{10.67}$$

on substituting for g from (10.66). Thus the supply of teachers will grow at the rate of $\alpha\beta - \gamma$.

Let us suppose that the rate of growth of the demand for teachers, $\dot{t}_d/t_d$, is simply the rate of growth, ν say, of the population. If supply and demand are initially equal, so that $t_{s0} = t_{d0}$, continued equality requires that

$$\alpha\beta - \gamma = \nu \tag{10.68}$$

How are we to ensure the equality of these growth rates? A simple mechanism can be formulated by recognizing that the proportion of new graduates attracted to teaching is not necessarily constant but is likely to respond to the relative net advantages, ω say, enjoyed by teachers. If the relationship of β to ω were hyperbolic, β would approach zero as ω declined to some positive value and would approach an upper limit as ω increased. In this case

$$\beta = \beta_0 - \frac{\beta_1}{\omega} \tag{10.69}$$

from which we can see that (10.68) will be satisfied if

$$\omega = \frac{\alpha\beta_1}{\alpha\beta_0 - \gamma - \nu} \tag{10.70}$$

Thus, in this simple case, the two growth rates could be equalized by fixing ω at an appropriate level.

It is not difficult to show that if the population were to grow along a logistic rather than an exponential curve, then the equilibrium value of ω, now a function of time, could be calculated by replacing ν by $\mu(\sigma^* - \sigma)/\sigma^*$, where σ denotes the size of the population, σ^* its saturation level, and μ the speed of adjustment of the logistic process. More complicated but essentially similar expressions would result if we allowed for: (1) logistic growth in the proportion of the population intending to graduate; and (2) logistic growth in the teachers required per graduate.

Let us now see what happens if these ideas are applied to a multistage educational system. Suppose that there are three stages, denoted by the suffixes 1, 2, and 3, and that while teachers are needed in appropriate numbers at each stage, they are only produced at stage 3. Then, corresponding to (10.67), we can write

$$\begin{matrix} \Delta t_1 \\ \Delta t_2 \\ \Delta t_3 \end{matrix} = \left\{ \begin{bmatrix} 0 & 0 & b_{13} \\ 0 & 0 & b_{23} \\ 0 & 0 & b_{33} \end{bmatrix} \begin{bmatrix} a_{11} & 0 & \\ 0 & a_{22} & 0 \\ 0 & 0 & a_{33} \end{bmatrix} - \begin{bmatrix} c_{11} & 0 & t_1 \\ 0 & c_{22} & 0 \\ 0 & 0 & c_{33} \end{bmatrix} \right\} \begin{bmatrix} t_1 \\ t_2 \\ t_3 \end{bmatrix} \quad (10.71)$$

or, more compactly

$$\Delta t = (B\hat{a} - \hat{c}) \, t \qquad (10.72)$$

where $\hat{a}$, B, and $\hat{c}$ are the matrix analogues of α, β, and γ in (10.67) and the suffix s has now been dropped. The matrix in round brackets in (10.72) takes the form

$$B\hat{a} - \hat{c} = \begin{bmatrix} -c_{11} & 0 & b_{13}a_{33} \\ 0 & -c_{22} & b_{23}a_{33} \\ 0 & 0 & b_{33}a_{33} - c_{33} \end{bmatrix} \qquad (10.73)$$

From (10.72)

$$\Lambda^\tau t = (I + B\hat{a} - \hat{c})^\tau t \qquad (10.74)$$

and so

$$\Lambda^\tau t_1 = (1 - c_{11})^\tau t_1 \; + \; \sum_{\theta=0}^{\tau-1} (1 - c_{11})^\theta (1 + b_{33}a_{33} - c_{33})^{\tau-\theta-1} b_{13}a_{33}t_3 \qquad (10.75)$$

$$\Lambda^\tau t_2 = (1 - c_{22})^\tau t_2 \; + \; \sum_{\theta=0}^{\tau-1} (1 - c_{22})^\theta (1 + b_{33}a_{33} - c_{33})^{\tau-\theta-1} b_{23}a_{33}t_3 \qquad (10.76)$$

and

$$\Lambda^\tau t_3 = (1 + b_{33}a_{33} - c_{33})^\tau t_3 \qquad (10.77)$$

The control variable, originally a scalar, ω, is now a vector, $w = \{w_1 \; w_2 \; w_3\}$, and so, in principle at any rate, we can set the elements of w to ensure the desired supply and distribution of teachers.

With regard to the demand for teachers, we are essentially back at Equation (10.16), with a C-matrix that distinguishes educational stages. This expression would have to be premultiplied by a diagonal matrix to allow for the needs for teachers at each stage in relation to the number of students. If the educational structure were changing, it would be necessary to replace (10.16) by (10.23). If all this were done it would be possible to calculate the changing future demand for teachers in the different stages of the educational system. Given these demands, we could then try to manipulate the parameters in (10.72) to ensure the necessary supply. So far I have only considered the manipulation of B, but in case of need, which is always liable to arise in transient situations, it would be possible to increase a, the student-teacher ratios, and also to effect a temporary change in c either by allowing retirement to be postponed or by persuading more married women to return to teaching than would do so of their own accord.

In what I have just said, I have indirectly emphasized the importance of activities in defining states: being, for instance, at a particular stage of the learning process and so requiring a particular type of teacher. As is fairly obvious, but perhaps worth demonstrating, more than this is needed: the states of the transition matrix must be so defined that they relate to a common interval of time. Either we can set out to calculate demands and supplies year by year, in which case year of birth must enter into the definition of states; or we can content ourselves with calculating the position at, say, five-year intervals, in which case states must be so defined that they all take five years, on average, to pass through.

What happens if the age dimension is not used? Suppose we have five states: preschool being 1; primary, secondary, and tertiary education being 2, 3, and 4; and posteducation being 5. Now suppose that

$$C = \begin{bmatrix} 0.80 & 0 & 0 & 0 & 0 \\ 0.19 & 0.85 & 0 & 0 & 0 \\ 0 & 0.15 & 0.80 & 0 & 0 \\ 0 & 0 & 0.02 & 0.68 & 0 \\ 0 & 0 & 0.18 & 0.32 & 0.98 \end{bmatrix} \tag{10.78}$$

then

$$(I - C)^{-1} = \begin{bmatrix} 5 & 0 & 0 & 0 & 0 \\ 6.\dot{3} & 6.\dot{6} & 0 & 0 & 0 \\ 4.75 & 5 & 5 & 0 & 0 \\ 0.296875 & 0.3125 & 0.3125 & 0.3125 & 0 \\ 47.5 & 50 & 50 & 50 & 50 \end{bmatrix} \tag{10.79}$$

from which we can see that people spend on average 5 years before going to school, 6.6 years in primary education, 5 years in secondary education, and 3.125 years in tertiary education. What happens after that can be neglected. But the uneven intervals up to the end of education mean that we cannot interpret C as relating to any single time interval. It is intended to relate to years, hence the interpretation of the numbers in (10.79). But in this case, newly born children get into primary education in the following year; first-year students contribute to the number of graduates in the following year, and so on. To avoid such absurd results, we must either combine year of birth with other criteria in defining states; or we must change the C-matrix to allow for the fact that it relates to, say, five-year age groups. For instance, in five years time far more than 15 percent of the children now in primary school will be in secondary school.

16. PRICES AND QUANTITIES

I mentioned in the section "Interpretations of the C-Matrix" that if (10.28) is an equation connecting quantities, which of course it is, there must also be an equation connecting costs, or prices, which is based on C' rather than on C. This equation can be derived as follows.

Let m denote a vector whose elements measure the educational costs, say, that must be incurred this year to educate an individual now in a given state of the system. On the assumption that m remains fixed in the future the total cost to be incurred from now on to educate, or complete the education of, an individual now in a given state is an element of a vector, k say, where

$$
\begin{aligned}
k &= m + C'm + C'^2 m + \dots \\
&= m + C'k \\
&= (I - C')^{-1} m
\end{aligned}
\tag{10.80}
$$

The terms on the right-hand side of the first row of (10.80) relate to the successive years in which educational costs will be incurred. The elements of these vectors relate to the present states of individuals multiplied by the probable educational costs they will incur this year, next year, and so on.

If it is expected that unit costs will change so that, in year θ, m will be replaced by $\Lambda^\theta m$, then (10.80) becomes

$$
\begin{aligned}
k &= m + C'\Lambda m + C'^2 \Lambda^2 m + \dots \\
&= m + C'\Lambda k \\
&= (I - C'\Lambda)^{-1} m
\end{aligned}
\tag{10.81}
$$

Thus if we can estimate $\Lambda^\theta m$ for the relevant values of θ, we can allow for changing costs.

If it is also expected that the C-matrix will change, C^θ must be replaced by $\bar{C}^\theta \equiv \Lambda^{\theta-1} C. \Lambda^{\theta-2} C \dots C$, and so (10.81) becomes

$$
\begin{aligned}
k &= m + \bar{C}'\Lambda m + \bar{C}'^2 \Lambda^2 m + \dots \\
&= (I - \bar{C}'\Lambda)^{-1} m
\end{aligned}
\tag{10.82}
$$

where $\bar{C}$ is defined as in Equation (10.27). Thus if we can estimate $\Lambda^{\theta}C$ for the relevant values of θ, we can allow for changing transition probabilities.

If ρ denotes the rate of interest, then $\sigma \equiv 1/(1 + \rho)$ denotes the discount factor; and if the states of C are separated by annual intervals (as would be the case if year of birth were the primary criterion of classification) it is easy to calculate the discounted streams of future costs corresponding to (10.80). If $\tilde{k}$ denotes the vector of discounted accumulated costs and if $\tilde{C} \equiv \sigma C$, then (10.80) is replaced by

$$\tilde{k} = (I - \tilde{C}')^{-1} m \tag{10.83}$$

If we have calculated the inverse in (10.80), we can readily calculate the inverse in (10.83) since

$$(I - \tilde{C}')^{-1} \equiv \hat{s}(I - C')^{-1} \hat{s}^{-1} \tag{10.84}$$

where the elements of s are descending powers of σ, a power being repeated for states reached in the same number of time intervals from a fixed point in time. For instance, consider a system of four states which is spread over three time intervals such that the first two states occur respectively in the first and second time intervals and the last two states are alternatives which occur in the last time interval. In this case

$$s = \{\sigma^2 \quad \sigma \quad 1 \quad 1\} \tag{10.85}$$

17. CONCLUSIONS

The conclusions I should like to draw in this chapter are as follows.

Models based on linear difference equations provide a good starting point for the study of social processes.

Care is needed in the definition of states since otherwise the basic Markov assumption which usually lies behind the use of these equation systems will not be satisfied. For instance, the trouble with (10.78), as we have seen, is that an infant does not have the same transition probabilities as has a four-year-old, nor a freshman as has a student in his final year.

As a consequence, thought must be given to the detail demanded in any representation of the real world because, with many criteria of classification, the number of states rapidly becomes large and statistically unmanageable. It is important in any classification to keep the number of categories down to a minimum.

The methods I have described are much better for handling steady states than for handling transient states. They do, of course, enable the transients to be calculated but they do not ensure that desirable features, such as constancy of relative grade size, will be realized under transient conditions.

For this reason it seems desirable to think in terms of control variables which can be used to improve balance under transient conditions, as indicated in the section "Balance and Control" above.

Although the literature goes far beyond what I have attempted here, there are great difficulties in an analytical treatment of the problems encountered in transient states. As long as this is so, the best policy would seem to be a computational approach to these problems.

In many fields, such as education and health, the cost of any proposed program is likely to be of great importance. An attempt is made in the preceding section to show how cost data could be linked to data on the stocks and flows of human beings passing through some sequence of life.

It is not worth trying to enumerate all the things this chapter does not try to do, with one exception. Nowhere is there any discussion of optimizing. The point of view is that of an observer who would like to know the probable outcome of present tendencies and, if he happens to be an administrator, would like to deal with them to the best of his ability but cannot even envisage the ideal solution.

REFERENCES

Bacharach, Michael.
   1970   Biproportional Matrices and Input-Output Change. London: Cambridge University Press.
Baldwin, J. A.
   1971   The Mental Hospital in the Psychiatric Service: A Case-Register Study. London: Oxford University Press for the Nuffield Provincial Hospitals Trust.
Bartholomew, D. J.
   1967   Stochastic Models for Social Processes. New York: Wiley.
Bernadelli, Harro.
   1941   "Population waves." Journal of the Burma Research Society 31, part 1:1-18.
Cambridge, Department of Applied Economics.
   1963   Input-Output Relationships, 1954-1966. No. 3 in A Programme for Growth. London: Chapman & Hall.
Douglas, J. W. B.
   1964   The Home and the School. London: MacGibbon and Kee.
Douglas, J. W. B., J. M. Ross, and H. R. Simpson.
   1968   All Our Future. London: Davies.

Goldberg, Samuel.
   1958   Introduction to Difference Equations. New York: Wiley.
Goodwin, R. M.
   1949   "The multiplier as matrix." The Economic Journal 59, No. 236:
               537-555.
Kemeny, John G., and J. Laurie Snell.
   1960   Finite Markov Chains. New York: Van Nostrand Reinhold.
Keyfitz, Nathan.
   1964a   "Matrix multiplication as a technique of population analysis." The
               Milbank Memorial Fund Quarterly 42, no. 4, part 1:68-84.
   1964b   "The population projection as a matrix operator." Demography 1, no.
               1:56-73.
   1968   Introduction to the Mathematics of Population. Reading, Mass.:
               Addison-Wesley.
Leslie, P. H.
   1945   "On the use of matrices in certain population mathematics."
               Biometrika 33, part III: 183-212.
   1948   "Some further notes on the use of matrices in population mathe-
               matics." Biometrika 35, parts III and IV: 213-245.
Orr, Lea.
   1972   "The dependence of transition proportions in the education system on
               observed social factors and school characteristics." Journal of the
               Royal Statistical Society, Series A (General) 135, part 1: 74-95.
Prais, S. J.
   1955   "Measuring social mobility." Journal of the Royal Statistical Society,
               Series A (General) 118, part 1: 56-66.
Stone, Richard.
   1962   "Multiple classifications in social accounting." Bulletin de l'Institut
               International de Statistique 39, no. 3: 215-233.
   1971   Demographic Accounting and Model Building. Paris: Organization for
               Economic Cooperation and Development.
   1972   "The fundamental matrix of the active sequence." In Input-Output
               Techniques. Amsterdam: North-Holland.
   1973   "A system of social matrices." The Review of Income and Wealth 10,
               no. 2: 143-166.
Tuck, Mary G.
   1973   "The effect of different factors on the level of academic achieve-
               ment." To be published in Social Science Research.
U. K. General Register Office.
   1966   Registrar General's Statistical Review of England and Wales. part II.
               London: H.M.S.O.
White, Harrison C.
   1970   Chains of Opportunity. Cambridge, Mass.: Harvard University Press.

11

MODELS AND INDICATORS OF ORGANIZATIONAL GROWTH, CHANGES, AND TRANSFORMATIONS

Judah Matras

INTRODUCTION

Though kinship groupings, residential and local community enclaves, and organizations may be identified in a broad range of societies, a characteristic feature of modern urban-industrial societies is the increasing dominance of organizations as settings in which social interaction and individual social integration take place. Employment, education, politics and community participation, and religious observance are all typically carried out in organization settings. More generally both access to social rewards, and exchange and conversion of social resources tend increasingly to take place in organizational settings in modern societies.

The current flowering of attention to organizations, to analysis of their types and purposes, size and composition, recruitment and stratification, and to the behavior of individuals and subgroups within organizations reflects recognition by social scientists of the importance of organizations in social life and social structure. At the same time, many of our measures of social and industrial development, of social and industrial change, and of social and economic well-being are in fact statements about organizations: their sizes, their distributions among social and industrial categories, their relationships to the total population and its sectors, and changes in these. Accordingly exploration of approaches and methodologies for studying and analyzing organizational growth, changes, and transformations may be useful in the analysis of societal change generally.

In this chapter I try to explore the applications to study of organizations of concepts and styles of problem formulation drawn from demography and

301

population studies. The first section consists of a brief review of the central concepts of demographic analysis and population studies. The sections which follow consider (1) the individual organization as a population, (2) organizational networks as population systems, and (3) populations of organizations.

The central variables of demography and population studies are size, territorial distribution, and density of populations, their composition by sex, age, marital status, and various social and economic characteristics, and the components of change in all of the above—births and entrances into populations; deaths and departures from populations; and geographic or "social locational" movements within populations. Following the Hauser-Duncan (1959:2-3) convention, I use the name "demographic analysis" to connote the study of internal reciprocal relationships between variables within this set of "central variables," while the term "population studies" is used to indicate the study of relationships between demographic and "nondemographic" variables. A marriage, of sorts, between "demographic analysis" and "population studies" is effected in the application of the notion of "population transformations" or "sequences of population transformations." Because the notion of "population transformation" is both fairly novel *and* central to the discussion in the rest of the chapter, I reproduce here an extract from an earlier discussion (Matras and Winsborough, 1969):[1]

> We understand by "population transformation" any process in time (a) involving aggregates of (1) entrances or births into, (2) exits or deaths out of, and (3) changes of social or demographic statuses or characteristics, or of geographic or social locations, in a population and (b) whose net effect is to alter in time the size and composition of the population. If we consider an initial population of given size and composition or distribution with respect to any specified single characteristic or combination of characteristics, we may see that the sum total over a time interval of births or entrances, deaths or departures, and changes with respect to attributes of the characteristics in question *transforms* the initial population rendering it different in size and composition or distribution at the close of the interval. It is the set of rates of births (entrances), deaths (exits), and movements (changes of attribute) that we denote "population transformation."
>
> If we represent the initial population by an n-dimension vector, say π_0, the population transformation by an $n \times n$ matrix of rates, say, T_1, then the population at the end of the interval can also be represented by an n-dimensional vector, π_1, and in the interval the change in population size and composition is exactly described by the matrix equation,

$$T_1 \pi_0 = \pi_1 \tag{11.1}$$

---

[1] A very brief statement appears in Hirschman and Matras (1971) and an extensive discussion appears in Matras (1973a).

The general form of population transformation takes account *both* of the "openness" of populations—i.e., of the fact that in any interval there may be migration or births into a population or migration or deaths out of the population—*and also* the possibility of change or movement among geographic or social states, attributes, or locations. Thus the "intergenerational" change in the occupational distribution of a population involves *both* differential fertility and labor force entrance and participation patterns *and also* patterns of intergenerational and intragenerational occupational mobility, and, hence, is appropriately viewed as a population transformation.[2] Similarly processes of internal migration and population redistribution likewise involve *both* entrances into and departures from the total population *and also* geographic movements within it, so that they may also be treated as population transformations. Both types of processes, occupational mobility and changing occupational distribution of populations, have been represented and studied in the form of equation (11.1) above [see Matras, 1967; Rogers, 1968].

Ordinary natural increase is a population process in time involving births, deaths, and aging only, no attention necessarily being paid to other changes in status, attributes, or locations. However, it may nevertheless be viewed as a special case of population transformations in which *only* entrances, departures, and time-in-the-system considerations are involved; and the projection matrix format used to represent and study natural increase, population growth, and change in the composition of the population by sex and age [Keyfitz, 1968] may be viewed as a special case of equation (11.1). Similarly mobility and migration within closed populations can also be viewed as a special case of population transformations in which *no* entrances or departures are involved; and the Markov Chain or similar formats used to represent mobility and changing distributions of closed populations[3] may also be viewed as special cases of equation (11.1)....

We can associate a *sequence* of population transformations with a sequence of time intervals. The general representation of the sequence of population transformations and changing population size and composition is

---

[2] This very terminology is used by Duncan (1965) in showing why the usual inflow or outflow tables as obtained from most surveys of intergenerational mobility are inadequate representations of the transformations undergone by real populations. Unfortunately this point of view leads Duncan and his collaborator Blau to separate analyses of mobility and of changing occupational structure (see Blau and Duncan, 1967). For a different view of the use of outflow tables to portray the occupational transformation, see Ramsoy (1965).

[3] For a recent summary of these formulations , see Bartholomew (1967: Chap. 2); Boudon (1973); and White (1970: Chaps. 8, 9).

$$T_1 \pi_0 \quad = \pi_1$$
$$T_2 \pi_1 \quad = \pi_2$$
$$\cdot$$
$$\cdot$$
$$\cdot$$
$$T_k \pi_{k-1} = \pi_k \qquad\qquad (11.2a)$$

or, alternatively,

$$T_k T_{k-1} \cdots T_3 T_2 T_1 \pi_0 = \pi_k \qquad\qquad (11.2b)$$

There are both formal and empirical questions to be cast in terms of population transformations and sequences of populations. The formal questions are of two general kinds:

1. Where can a population, π_i, "go" in time, under different assumptions about the sequence of population transformations, $T_1, T_2, T_3, \ldots T_{k-1}, T_k$? Where a population "can go" may be considered in terms of its size, rate of growth, or composition. Thus, for example, stable population theory tells us that, under a *fixed* fertility and mortality regime, the age composition and growth rate become fixed, i.e., $\pi_{i+1} = c\pi_i$

2. What, if any, are the constraints upon the population transformations, T_i, imposed by any initial population, π_{i-1}? What are the ways in which population transformations are dependent upon the populations upon which they operate, and to what extent are they transferable or interchangeable among different populations? Also, what are the constraints upon population transformations imposed by any specified *net change* in a given population, i.e., when *both* π_{i-1} and π_i are given? Thus, for example, a given change in occupational distribution generates *minimum* amounts of occupational mobility, but an infinite number of alternative sets of mobility rates will generate the same distributional change.

The empirical questions on sequences of population transformations are the heart of "population studies":

1. What are the characteristic sequences of population transformations, and what is the range of their variation?
2. What are the correlates, causes, and consequences of variations in sequences of population transformations?

The outstanding example of a widely identified and studied characteristic sequence of population transformations is that usually called the "demographic transition," a sequence of population transformations involving (in order):

1. High mortality and high fertility ("high balance")
2. Declining mortality and high fertility
3. Declining mortality and declining fertility
4. Low mortality and declining fertility

5. Low mortality and low fertility ("low balance")

Discussion around the correlates, causes, and consequences of this type of sequence of population transformations enjoys that status of "theory" among demographers.

Other characteristic sequences of population transformations which have been identified include urbanization, suburbanization, overseas movements, frontier settlement, and other recurring sequences of population redistribution processes; changing labor force participation and structure; processes of social, occupational, residential segregation and concentration; changing marriage regimes, marriage "squeezes" and their resolutions; and intragenerational and intergenerational social mobility sequences. By and large, however, these kinds of sequences have less frequently been identified as such, have been less extensively compared, and represent more "frontiers" of population theory compared to the relatively well-developed theory of demographic transitions. A further frontier of population theory is the study of sequences of joint population transformations—e.g., the demographic transition simultaneously with an urbanization-migration sequence (see Friedlander, 1969), social mobility and social class transformation sequences simultaneously with a differential fertility sequence (see, e.g., Boudon, 1973), or marriage market, marriage squeeze, and mate-selection transformation sequences simultaneously with educational attainment transformation sequences or with immigration sequences (see, e.g., Matras, 1973a and 1973b).

To summarize, then, the business of demography and population studies is:

1. To describe and measure population size, composition, distribution, changes, and transformations
2. To discover factors influencing or connected to variations in these population variables, and to plot their connections
3. To discover consequences of these population variables and their variations, and to plot these connections.

THE ORGANIZATION AS A POPULATION

Viewing the individual organization as a population of its members obviously entails description and characterization of the organization in terms of the size and composition of its membership, and also in terms of the change process affecting membership size and composition: recruitment, separation, and intraorganizational mobility. The organizational analog of "age" is "duration of membership," and the analog to "age composition" is composition by duration of membership, seniority, or other expression of "time in the system." Other compositional axes in organizations might be by broad categories of organizational roles and by rank in the organizational hierarchy.

The elements of changing size of the organization are recruitment and separation. The elements of changing composition are differential growth (recruitment less separations) of the respective components *and* various types of intraorganizational mobility: transfers, promotions, election to office, or other changes of organizational roles or status. These can all be measured in ways more or less analogous to their measurement in population studies.

The literature dealing with the size and composition of organizations, with recruitment and mobility patterns, and with the effects of variations in organizational size, composition, and change patterns upon other facets of organizations: e.g., authority structures, efficiency, autonomy, communication arrangements, formal and informal structures, line and staff components, functional differentiation, etc., is voluminous and defies summary.[4] However, one summary observation which can be advanced is the following: my impression is that, in these studies and discussions, both organizational *size* and organizational *growth* tend to be cast in an undifferentiated way. There is no reason to assume that all seniority categories, all role categories, all functional categories of an organization's membership grow at the same rate—indeed there is every reason to suppose that they grow at different rates, and the questions are: what differences, and why? Nevertheless, the concept of "organizational growth" cast as an independent variable typically ignores this differentiation. An analog from population studies would be asking, say, the effects of population growth upon total or per capita output, consumption, and savings. Clearly, the effects are different if the "growth" consists entirely of babies, of adults, of males, of females, of clever persons, or of inept persons. Just as a current age distribution reflects past fertility, mortality, and migration, the composition of an organization reflects past recruitment, separation, and mobility; and just as current differential fertility, mortality, and migration affect future population composition, so current differential recruitment, separation, and mobility affect future organizational composition.

In other words, instead of asking if and why "growth" *entails* changing proportions in the different organizational sectors and components, we may as well understand that organizational growth *is* differential growth; only the quite special situation in which rates of recruitment, separation, and mobility are all *fixed* indefinitely over time can result in "nondifferential" organizational growth. Thus, the "finding" that organizational growth, or variations in organization size, are correlated with changes or variations in line/staff or production/administration ratios or proportions seems, to a demographer, tautological. More to the point, it would seem, would be the study of correlates,

---

[4] The "standard" summary statement appears to be that of Starbuck (1965). More recently, Blau (1970) has offered a set of propositions relating size, growth, and structural differentiation in organizations as a "formal theory." Other recent discussions, which also contain brief summaries of previous works, include Klatzky (1970), and Hendershot and James (1972).

causes, and consequences of the individual components of growth in the various organizational sectors.

A more novel application of demographic reasoning to analysis of organizations and organizational change is that which focuses upon the organizational transformation. Consider the number of persons in an organization, $P(x)$, who have belonged for x years, and suppose that the annual rate at which they leave the organization is $1 - s(x)$, where $0 \leqslant s(x) \leqslant 1$, and the rate at which new members are recruited is proportional to the total membership, say $R\Sigma P(x)$. Then, if the initial size and duration of membership composition of the organization is given by the row vector, $\alpha_0 = (P(O), P(1), P(2), \ldots P(n))$, the annual recruitment and separation conditions outlined above can be summarized in an $n \times n$ matrix:

$$
M_1 \;=\;
\begin{bmatrix}
R & s(0) & 0 & 0 & \ldots\ldots 0 \\
R & 0 & s(1) & 0 & \ldots\ldots 0 \\
R & 0 & 0 & s(2) & \ldots\ldots 0 \\
\cdot & \cdot & \cdot & \cdot & \ldots\ldots \\
\cdot & \cdot & \cdot & \cdot & \ldots\ldots \\
\cdot & \cdot & \cdot & \cdot & \ldots\ldots \\
R & 0 & 0 & 0 & \ldots\ldots s(n-1) \\
R & 0 & 0 & 0 & \ldots\ldots s(n)
\end{bmatrix}
$$

The size and duration of membership composition of the organization at the close of the year are, then

$$\alpha_1 = [P'(0), P'(1), P'(2), \ldots P'(n)]$$

where

$$P'(0) = \sum_x RP(x) = R \sum_x P(x)$$

and $\quad P'(x) = P(x - 1)S(x - 1) \quad$ for $x \neq 0, x \neq n$

$$P'(n) = P(n - 1)S(n - 1) + P(n)S(n)$$

since n is an open-ended category, and this is equivalent to

$$\alpha_0 M_1 = \alpha_1$$

as in the population transformation. In the following interval, the organizational transformation is

$$\alpha_1 M_2 = \alpha_2$$

so that over the two years, the initial organization is transformed

$$\alpha_0 M_1 M_2 = \alpha_2$$

and over k years, the organization is transformed

$$\alpha_0 M_1 M_2 M_3 \ldots M_{k-1} M_k = \alpha_k$$

as in the sequence of population transformations.

Such a formulation leads us directly to the question of the relationship of the seniority-composition of the organization to recruitment: Is the recruitment associated with the number of persons of x seniority different from that associated with persons of y seniority, i.e., is $R(x) \neq R(y)$? If yes, why should this be so? If not, how *does* recruitment vary with internal organizational composition? What factors affect levels of recruitment? We return to this problem later.

Consider now the members of an organization, $P(i)$, with organizational role i. Assume that during the year there are neither accessions nor separations in the organization and denote the proportion of those initially having role i who change to organizational role j is a_{ij}. Then if

$$\beta_0 = [P(1)\, P(2)\, P(3) \ldots P(m)]$$

represents the initial composition of the membership by organizational roles, and if

$$A_1 = \begin{bmatrix} a_{11} & a_{12} & \cdots & a_{1j} & \cdots & a_{1m} \\ a_{21} & a_{22} & \cdots & a_{2j} & \cdots & a_{2m} \\ \vdots & & & & & \\ a_{i1} & a_{i2} & \cdots & a_{ij} & \cdots & a_{im} \\ \vdots & & & & & \\ a_{m1} & a_{m2} & \cdots & a_{mj} & \cdots & a_{mm} \end{bmatrix}$$

is the set of proportions of persons initially in role i and subsequently in role j

$$(\textstyle\sum_j a_{ij} = 1 \; ; 0 \leqslant a_{ij} \leqslant 1)$$

and

$$\beta_1 = [P'(1)\, P'(2)\, P'(3) \ldots P'(m)]$$

represents the subsequent composition of the membership (at the end of the year) by organizational roles, then

$$\beta_1 = \beta_0 A_1$$

in which

$$P'(j) = \sum_i P_i a_{ij}$$

represents the organizational transformation by role categories during the year. Similarly in the following year

$$\beta_2 = \beta_1 A_2$$

and over k years the sequence is

$$\beta_0 A_i A_2 A_3 \ldots A_k = \beta_k$$

The two kinds of transformations outlined above can readily be combined in a single transformation representing *both* recruitment and separations *and* changes in role categories. If the initial organizational membership is

$$\gamma_0 = (P_{0,1}, P_{0,2}, \ldots P_{0,i}, \ldots P_{x,1}, P_{x,2}, \ldots P_{x,i}, \ldots P_{n,m})$$

the final size and composition is

$$\gamma_1 = (P'_{0,1}, \ldots P'_{x,i}, \ldots P'_{n,m})$$

There is a matrix, T_1, representing both kinds of changes simultaneously, which effects the organizational transformation[5]

$$\gamma_0 T_i = \gamma_i$$

In the T-matrix, rates of recruitment to the different role categories appear separately, as do rates of separation. Thus, the T-matrix transformation is a direct representation of differential growth and changing composition of the organization.

Consider, finally, the sequence of organizational transformations,

$$\gamma_0 T_1 T_2 T_3 \ldots T_{k-1} T_k = \gamma_k$$

We can address the same kinds of formal and empirical questions to this sequence as were addressed to the population transformation sequences:

---

[5] The format of the T-matrix is shown in Matras (1967). It is developed and elaborated considerably in Boudon (1973: Chap. 4).

1. Where "can the organization go" under different assumptions on the transformation sequence?
2. What are the constraints upon the possible organizational transformations imposed by the initial organizational structure, or by any specified change, γ_0 to γ_1, in the organization's size and structure?
3. What are the characteristic sequences of organizational transformations, and what is the range of their variation?
4. What are the correlates, causes, and consequences of variations in sequences of organizational transformations?

Two ideas familiar in population analysis, that of *strong ergodicity* and *weak ergodicity* (for an extensive treatment see Lopez, 1961, and Keyfitz, 1968), are suggestive of kinds of answers possible to the first formal question: "Where can an organization go?" The *strong ergodicity* principle may be applied to a transformation sequence in which the rates of recruitment, separation, and mobility are all fixed, i.e., $T_1 = T_2 = T_3 = \ldots = T$, and it says that—if they are fixed over an indefinite number of time intervals—organizational transformations generate organizations which are stable with respect to their annual rates of growth and with respect to their duration-of-membership and other compositional facets. The *weak ergodicity* principle applies when two or more organizations undergo the *same sequence* (but not necessarily fixed) of transformations: the compositions and growth rates of two or more such organizations tend to converge in time. Both principles highlight the fact that sequences of organizational transformations in time—rather than the initial membership structure—determine the ultimate size and composition of organizations at sufficiently distant subsequent points in time. Thus, two corporations whose recruitment, separation, and transfer and promotion patterns are identical year after year, will ultimately be identically structured and characterized by the same growth rate, regardless of their initial differences in membership composition and structure.

The strong and weak ergodicity considerations provide an alternative way of looking at the relationships between the date of invention of organization types and their present social structures. Stinchcombe (1965) has observed that the chronologies and origins of organizational forms and types are associated with their social structures throughout their existence, and he suggests that this connection is due (1) to the dependence of organizational inventions made at a particular time and with a particular purpose upon the "social technology available at the time," (2) the initial effectiveness with which the organizations functioned under those conditions, and (3) the institutionalization of the organizational forms developed in that particular constellation of social-historical exigencies.

The strong ergodicity idea tells us that organizations with fixed patterns of differential recruitment, separation, and mobility quickly become stable, irrespective of their efficiency, traditionalizing forces, vesting of interest, etc., or of the absence of these factors. Similarly, the weak ergodicity idea tells us that organizations undergoing similar sequences of changing patterns of differential recruitment, separation, and mobility fairly quickly come to resemble one another structurally, regardless of their initial differences and irrespective of their efficiency, traditionalizing forces, and vesting of interests, etc. Thus strong or weak ergodicity of sequences of organization (recruitment, separation, and mobility) transformations, may account in part for correlations between date of invention and present social structure of organizations.

Changing the number or proportion having a given organizational role—e.g., adding more vice-presidents in a corporation—is an example of a specified change in the organization's structure. The implications of such a change are examples of the question of constraints upon the possible organizational transformations. Thus, if vice-presidents may be recruited only from within the ranks of organization membership, restriction of recruitment to *given* origin categories actually entails a greater total volume of movements, shuffles, and mobility than would opening of recruitment to all origin categories in the organization. Similarly, opening of recruitment to vice-presidencies from *outside* the organization diminishes intraorganization mobility.

An example of a characteristic sequence of organizational transformations is the sequence involving foundation, growth, zenith, decline, and disappearance of organizations. Such sequences are probably characteristic of businesses, voluntary organizations, political movements, churches, *landsmannschaften,* gangs, and other organizations. We might very well inquire about parameters, similarities and differences between such sequences, and seek explanations and interpretations of their variation.

ORGANIZATIONAL NETWORKS AS POPULATION SYSTEMS

Consider, now, two organizations whose initial sizes and compositions are represented respectively by Φ_0 and Ψ_0. Each such organization may undergo an organizational transformation, in the sense of the previous section, say,

$$\Phi_0 A_1 = \Phi_1 \quad \text{and} \quad \Psi_0 B_1 = \Psi_1$$

involving recruitments, separations, and intraorganizational mobility. In addition, however, the two organizations may recruit from one another, *exchange* members, or share members. To deal with these movements jointly, we need a definition of an organizational network, say

$$T_0 = \Phi_0 \cup \Psi_0$$

the union of the two organizations, representing the roles and duration of membership in the two respective organizations *and* the intersection between them—the set of joint roles and durations in the two organizations.

A matrix of recruitment, separation, mobility (including exchange, and joint incumbency) rates or probabilities, say V, can represent the organizational network transformation over time,

$$\tau_0 V_1 = \tau_1$$

As before, the sequence of such transformations is

$$\tau_0 V_1 V_2 V_3 \ldots V_k = \tau_k$$

and we may address the same kinds of queries to such sequences. Characteristic sequences of network transformations might include growth and merger sequences, or, conversely, growth and specialization sequences, "raiding" of membership in certain role categories, "springboard" relationships among organizations, or "big league-little league" relationships between organizations. Obviously the approach can be generalized for three or more organizations, or for organizational networks of any size or complexity.

Consider, again, our first organization whose initial size is represented by ϕ_0. Suppose now that ψ_0 represents not a second organization as previously, but rather the entire population by initial age, sex, and social class or location. The union,

$$\tau_0 = \phi_0 \cup \psi_0$$

now represents the roles and duration of membership in the organization, the sociodemographic categories in the population, and *their* intersection. The matrix, V, in the network transformation

$$\tau_0 V_1 = \dot{\tau}_1$$

now represents differential recruitment into and separation from the organization in the various sociodemographic categories in the population. If ϕ_0 represents a voluntary organization, the V- transformation has elements reflecting the rates of joining, retaining membership, and extent of participation in the organization over an interval of time for those in the different age-sex-social class categories of the population (see recent summaries by Hyman and Wright, 1971; Curtis, 1971). If we extend the approach to two, three, or k voluntary organizations, then the elements of the τ vector show multiple memberships at different ages and for different social groups, and the V matrix shows *changes* in membership profiles in a standardized format (see Babchuk and Booth, 1969).

Whether organizational growth is spontaneous or a consequence of decisions (see Starbuck, 1965), the relationship between population structure and growth itself and organizational growth and change seems inherently worth investigating.

I have argued elsewhere that population growth generates expansion of boundary systems, as well as division of labor—individual and organizational differentiation—and adoption of innovations (Matras, 1973a). But how are organizational size and patterns of recruitment and separation related to population size and composition? The

$$\tau_0 V_1 = \tau_1$$

equation is a standardized way of representing this relationship, so that discovery or estimation of its elements can provide answers to this type of question. In particular, the sequence of such transformations, $\tau_0 V_1 V_2 \ldots V_k = \tau_k$ shows how *changing* population size and composition affect individual organizations and networks of organizations.

POPULATIONS OF ORGANIZATIONS

Consider, next, a population of organizations comprising a total of, say, $\Sigma G(x)$ organizations, including $G(0)$ organizations less than a year old; $G(1)$ year-old organizations; . . . and $G(x)$ x-year-old organizations. If an initial set of such organizations is represented by

$$G_0 = [G(0), G(1), G(2), \ldots G(x), \ldots]$$

then a set of rates of organization founding, organization survival, and organization mortality can be represented by a matrix, say S_1, such that the equation

$$G_0 S_1 = G_1$$

represents the transformation of the population of organizations and a new age distribution of the organizations. Thus, it seems reasonable to suppose that such foundation-survival-mortality transformations vary among populations of organizations: i.e., that the voluntary organization population, the retail store population, the university population, the church population, or the industrial conglomerate population foundation-survival-mortality transformation differ from one another.

As written here, the S-matrix includes entries representing both probabilities or rates of survival of x-year old organizations, *and* rates of foundation of new organizations. This suggests that foundation of new organizations—of new retail stores, universities, churches, or factories—may be related to the number and "age distribution" of the existing organizations, a type of connection which may hold for some types of organizations, but not for others. Stinchcombe's (1965) discussion suggests that young newly founded organizations beget other new organizations in a "threshold" situation, while surviving and established "old" organizations inhibit competition and foundation of new organizations.

As in the case of human populations, we can amend the question of organizational survival rate to take account of rates of survival *and* change or nonchange in characteristics—e.g., size of the organization, structural character-istics, or organizational activities or outputs. The modified transformation, then

$$G_0^* S_0^* = G_1^*$$

plots the change in:

1. The number of organizations (the size of the population of organizations)
2. The distribution of the organizations by age or age groups
3. The distribution of the organizations by size or size categories
4. The distribution of the organizations by structural or activity characteristics

For example, if the G^* vector represents industrial organizations of different branches or sectors, of different sizes, and of different ages, the S^* matrix plots *both* survival and growth of existing industrial organizations *and* foundation of new organizations. Again: the S^* matrix represents foundation of new organizations as dependent upon the numbers of existing industrial organizations of various ages and size in *both* the same *and* in different industrial sectors. Study and comparison of such rates of organization foundation is, then, a direct and standardized approach to analysis of the effect of social structure on the rate of foundation of new organizations.

Again, we may posit a sequence of organization population transformations,

$$G_0^* S_1^* S_2^* \ldots S_k^* = G_k^*$$

and address our formal and empirical questions to such sequences, as before. The question of indefinite *stability and recurrence* or organizational foundation, survival, mortality, and change processes is probably more of hypothetical than of practical interest. However, the question of *constraints* on such transforma-tions imposed both by present social exigencies and by conditions on future organizational distributions and composition, e.g., connected to ideologies, planning and social engineering, etc., is of more practical interest. So, too, are some obvious examples of characteristic sequences of transformations in populations of organizations, e.g., "industrialization" sequence, or the "social and political modernization" sequence.

Indeed, it is appropriate to remark that the central hypothesis of the current research and theory of "modernization" seems to be that *there are* characteristic and recurring sequences of organizational transformations, that these can be observed and studied, and that generalizations about such sequences and their variations can be formulated and tested (see, e.g., Eisenstadt, 1966: Chap. 1, and Goldscheider, 1971: Chap. 4).

Consider, finally, *two* populations of organizations, say, U_0^*, the universities, and C_0^*, the military-industrial organizations. The union of these, say $X_0^* = U_0^* \cup C_0^*$, represents the distribution of universities, military-industrial organizations, and combined university-military-industrial enterprises by age, by size, by structural characteristics, etc. This network or organization population is, in turn, subject to the change processes summarized in a matrix, say, H_1, such that

$$X_0^* H_1^* = X_1^*$$

In this formulation, the X^* vector comprises *both* universities *and* military-industrial organizations of different branches, sizes, and ages. The H^* matrix represents foundation of new organizations—say, of new universities—as dependent upon the numbers and composition of existing military-industrial organizations as well as upon the existing size and composition of the population of universities. Similarly, the rates of foundation of new military-industrial organizations are connected to numbers, types, sizes, and ages of universities in the H^* matrix. Lastly, there is a sequence of such transformations,

$$X_0^* H_1^* H_2^* \ldots H_k^* = X_k^*$$

over time. Again, the directions possible for the union of universities and military-industrial organization populations, the constraints on changes in this union, and the characteristic sequences of such transformations are areas for analysis and study.

In particular, in this formulation we can plot the effect upon the university population of changes in the industrial-military organization population, and vice versa. The approach generalizes, of course, to 3, 4, or k populations of organizations.

CONCLUDING REMARKS

In this chapter I have suggested viewing organizations as population càtegories or subgroups. This approach is, essentially, a generalization of long-standing procedures for analyzing population subgroups such as the labor force, the school population, the farm population, the armed forces, or other population categories wherein both entrance into and departure from them are possible. Just as the changing size and composition of the labor force, the school population, and other population subgroups are important social indicators, so the changing parameters of organizational participation, and of numbers and composition of organizations, are significant social indicators.

The distinctive attribute of organizations is that they are population subgroups in explicitly purposive interaction. This attribute is not directly reflected in the models suggested here. But comparison of patterns of recruitment and participation, and of growth and transformation among organizational types, classified from the point of view of their purposes and functions, should be suggestive both of explanations of variations in growth and transformation sequences and of hypotheses concerning the bearing of such changes on organizational activity and effectiveness. Thus information on changing participation in—or exclusion from— community organizations as compared to, say, participation in religious organizations, and patterns of recruitment and mobility of industrial unions as compared to those of agricultural workers unions, should be both important kinds of social indicators as well as suggestive of hypotheses concerning the relationship between organization type and their participation, size, growth, and transformation patterns. For the time being, at least, it would seem that imaginative comparison of standardized representations and indicators of the changes and transformations in organizations of different types, rather than development of specialized, organization-type-specific, models is the more promising path.

REFERENCES

Babchuk, N., and A. Booth.
   1969   "Voluntary association membership: A longitudinal analysis." American Sociological Review 34, no. 1 (February):31-45.
Bartholomew, D. J.
   1967   Stochastic Models for Social Processes. New York: Wiley.
Blau, Peter M.
   1970   "A formal theory of differentiation in organizations." American Sociological Review 35, no. 2 (April):201-218.
Blau, Peter M., and Otis Dudley Duncan.
   1967   The American Occupational Structure. New York: Wiley.
Boudon, R.
   1973   Mathematical Structures of Social Mobility. San Francisco: Jossey-Bass.
Curtis, J.
   1971   "Voluntary organization joining: A cross-national comparative note." American Sociological Review 36, no. 5 (October):872-881.

Duncan, Otis Dudley.
1965 "Methodological issues in the analysis of social mobility." In N. J. Smelser and S. M. Lipset (eds.), Social Structure and Mobility in Economic Development. Chicago: Aldine.

Eisenstadt, S. N.
1966 Modernization: Protest and Change. Englewood Cliffs, N. J.: Prentice-Hall.

Friedlander, D.
1969 "Demographic responses and population change." Demography 6, no. 4 (November):359-382.

Goldscheider, C.
1971 Population, Modernization, and Social Structure. Boston: Little, Brown.

Hauser, R. M., and Otis Dudley Duncan (eds.).
1959 The Study of Population. Chicago: University of Chicago Press.

Hendershot, G. E., and T. F. James.
1972 "Size and growth as determinants of administrative-production ratios in organizations." Americal Sociological Review 37, no. 2 (April): 149-153.

Hirschman, C., and J. Matras.
1971 "A new look at the marriage market and nuptiality rates, 1915-1958." Demography 8 (November):549-569.

Hyman, Herbert, and C. R. Wright.
1971 "Trends in voluntary association memberships of American adults." American Sociological Review 36, no. 2 (April):191-206.

Keyfitz, Nathan.
1968 Introduction to the Mathematics of Population. Reading, Mass.: Addison-Wesley. Chaps. 3 and 4.

Klatzky, S. R.
1970 "Relationship of organizational size to complexity and coordination." Administrative Science Quarterly 15 (December):428-438.

Lopez, A.
1961 Problems in Stable Population Theory. Princeton, N. J.: Office of Population Research.

Matras, J.
1967 "Social mobility and social structure: Some insights from the linear model." American Sociological Review 33 (August): 608-614.
1973a Populations and Societies. Englewood Cliffs, N. J.: Prentice-Hall.
1973b "On changing matchmaking, marriage, and fertility in Israel: some findings, problems and hypotheses." American Journal of Sociology 79 (September):364-388.

Matras, J., and H. H. Winsborough.
1969 "On the empirical study of population transformations." Paper presented at Second Conference on Mathematical Demography, Berkeley and Asilomer, Calif. (August).

Ramsoy, Natalie Rogoff.
   1965   "Changes in rates and forms of mobility." In N. J. Smelser and S. M. Lipset (eds.) Social Structure and Mobility in Economic Development. Chicago: Aldine.
Rogers, André.
   1968   Matrix Analysis of Interregional Population Growth and Distribution. Berkeley: University of California Press.
Starbuck, W. H.
   1965   "Organizational growth and development." In J. G. March (ed.), Handbook of Organizations. Chicago: Rand McNally.
Stinchcombe, A. L.
   1965   "Social structure and organizations." In J. G. March (ed.), Handbook of Organizations. Chicago: Rand McNally.
White, Harrison C.
   1970   Chains of Opportunity. Cambridge, Mass.: Harvard University Press.

12

ANALYSIS OF OCCUPATIONAL MOBILITY BY MODELS OF OCCUPATIONAL FLOW

James S. Coleman

The analysis of continuous work history data or more generally continuous life history data creates opportunities for data analysis and resynthesis which are unusual in social science. I want to discuss here a kind of analysis that appears fruitful for the development of social accounting.

The data assumed by this analytical approach consist either of continuous records for a sample of persons which record the times of each shift from one state to another, or of frequent and equally spaced observations which record the state each person is in at that time. The states may be residential locations that can be classified in some way (e.g., by size of place or by type of residence), or they may be full-time occupational states, or perhaps another kind of state. The only requirement is that they be mutually exclusive and exhaustive, so that an individual may be located in one and only one state at each point in time. Thus if they are occupational states, there must be as well states which describe the individual's activity when he is not in an occupation (for example, is in education, military service, jail, hospital, unemployed, etc.). There can, of course, be residual states which lump together several states that are not in themselves of interest and are infrequently occupied.

The data I will use in an example are taken from a study carried out by Peter Rossi, Zahava Blum, Aage Sørensen, myself, and others (see Coleman, Blum, Sørenson, and Rossi, 1972; Blum 1972; and Coleman, Berry, and Blum, 1972). They consist of two samples of men, interviewed in 1968, who turned 30 to 39 in that calendar year. One is a national probability sample of Negro men, and another is a national probability sample of non-Negro men, nearly all Caucasian.

They will be referred to as the "black" and "white" samples respectively. Sample sizes are 738 and 851. The men provided retrospective histories of their full-time educational and occupational activities from age 14 to their current age, reporting the month at which any change in status occurred. The methodological problems and points involved in obtaining and preparing such data for analysis have been described elsewhere (Blum et al., 1969), and will not be repeated here, except for one point: it was necessary to locate individuals in a "major activity" at each point in time. In a few cases, individuals appeared to be in two full-time activities simultaneously, for example, in full-time education and a full-time job. These were resolved by arbitrarily giving one activity priority over the other, in this case, education priority over job. I will call the activities "occupations" in the present chapter, by which I intend to include activities such as education and military service as well.

Before proceeding further in discussion of these data, I will describe the model which is to be used in their analysis. The model was suggested by an application by Richard Stone (1966) of a birth and survival matrix, used in population mathematics. Stone used this matrix, together with a vector that orders the in-school population by ages, to describe the entry into the educational system and movement through those ages in which they may be in school.

The birth and survival matrix is a matrix of probabilities of birth and survival which carries the population forward for one year. In this matrix, which I will call H, the first row, with typical entry h_{oj}, is the probability that a person of age j gives birth to a child (of course, age o) during that year.[1] For the matrix beyond the first row, the typical entry is h_{ij}, the probability of surviving to age i, given that one was age j one year earlier. Thus $h_{j+1,\,j}$ is the probability of survival for one year, for persons aged j. All entries other than $h_{j+1,\,j}$ (excluding the first row) are zero. Thus the matrix consists of zero entries except for some nonzero entries in the first row, and nonzero entries in the diagonal below the main diagonal.[2]

There is in addition a column vector representing the expected or observed numbers of persons in age i at time t, $N(t)$, with typical entry $n_i(t)$. If at time $t =$ o, the number of persons observed in the population at each age is $N(o)$, the expected number at time 1 is

---

[1] The matrix is specified for a single sex, so the birth probability is a probability of giving birth to a child of the same sex.

[2] The usual notation for stochastic matrices has the first subscript representing the state at the later time. However, the standard convention by demographers of birth and survival matrices is the reverse of this, and I will maintain that notation here. The maximum age in the matrix is the age beyond which it can be assumed no one survives. This will be labeled r, so that $h_{r,\,r-1}$ is nonzero, but it is assumed that if the matrix were extended, $h_{r+1,\,r} = 0$. In practice, a number of ages are lumped together at the end.

$$N(1) = HN(0) \tag{12.1}$$

and the expected number at time t is

$$N(t) = H^t N(0) \tag{12.2}$$

In my adaptation of this formulation, there are *several* states at a given age, each state representing a major activity, an occupation, in which a person may be found.[3] In addition, the total population considered is the population between ages 14 and 80, the age period within which most occupational activities take place. Thus men are born into this population at chronological age 14.

The existence of several states at each age means that every element of $N(t)$ is itself a column vector of states. For age j, I will label this $n_{jk}(t)$ for each state k, the expected number of persons at age j in occupation k. Each element $h_{j+1\,j}$ of the matrix H is itself a matrix, with elements $h_{j+1\,g,j,k}$, the probability that a man who is in occupation k at age j is in occupation g at age $j + 1$. Except for death and emigration, that is, leaving the occupational system, the sum of $k_{j+1\,g,j,k}$ over all states g is 1.0. In the application to be made here, death and emigration cannot be estimated, since the probabilities were calculated on the basis of all men in the system at the terminal age (39 in our case). The element h_{oj} is a matrix with elements $h_{o,g,j,k}$, representing the probability that a man of age j in occupation k will have a son at age 0 (chronological age 14) in occupation g. Recall that the generalized use of the term "occupation" here includes education. This "birth rate" is of course not a birth rate into the live population, as in the use of birth-and-survival matrices in population mathematics, but is a birth rate into the population of males 14 to 80, since the population defined by the matrix is that population. Table 12.1 shows an expanded submatrix and subvector, showing birth rates into four occupational statuses of men of chronological ages 36 (22 + 14). Table 12.1 assumes that at age 14, no son is in occupation 3 or 4, but all are in states 1 and 2. For example, states 1 and 2 might be a college preparatory course in high school, and a

Table 12.1. An Expanded Birth Submatrix and Subvector

$$
\begin{bmatrix}
h_{0,1,22,1} & h_{0,1,22,2} & h_{0,1,22,3} & h_{0,1,22,4} \\
h_{0,2,22,1} & h_{0,2,22,2} & h_{0;2,22,3} & h_{0,2,22,4} \\
0 & 0 & 0 & 0 \\
0 & 0 & 0 & 0
\end{bmatrix}
\begin{bmatrix}
n_{22,1}(t) \\
n_{22,2}(t) \\
n_{22,3}(t) \\
n_{22,4}(t)
\end{bmatrix}
$$

---

[3] Similar formulations for describing mobility may be found in Rogers (1968) and Feeney (1970).

noncollege preparatory course, respectively. The entries, h_{og22k} are the result of several processes; birth into the live population, survival rate up to age 14, and selection rate into the two educational streams. The rates will vary as men of different occupations have different birth rates (at each age), and as their sons go differentially into educational streams.

There are, of course, difficulties in estimating such "birth rates" by occupational group, but that problem I will set aside for the present. It is useful, however, to consider some of the assumptions implicit in the model up to this point. First, the specification of a matrix $H_{j+1\,j}$ or $h_{o\,j}$ as independent of t implies that the age-specific transition probabilities among occupations are the same for all cohorts. Although that assumption is not strictly valid, it may be reasonable over a relatively small period of time. Second, the transition probabilities of which $h_{j+1\,j}$ is made up and the birth rate of which $h_{o\,j}$ is made up are conditional probabilities of the state at time $t + 1$ given state at time t. Thus the probability is not conditional upon any earlier history of the individual. This is the standard assumption of Markov processes, that previous history does not affect future movement.

This model gives a dynamic system in which there is an input of new members of the population, in various statuses, at age 0, and then an exit after an arbitrarily high age (say 80), or if death-and-emigration is included as an absorbing state, until a cutoff age at which all or nearly all men are in the absorbing state. The submatrices in the first row of H describe intergenerational mobility, and the submatrices below the main diagonal describe intragenerational mobility, that is, mobility from year to year throughout a man's occupational career.

Before moving to a specific application of the model to the data at hand, I will mention a minor modification of it which may make it more accurately describe intergenerational mobility. The problem with the formulation discussed above is that by starting at an arbitrarily early age, such as age 14, when everyone is still in education, the effect of the father's occupation on the son's future occupation may be obscured. This danger would be less great in a country with a highly differentiated educational system in which the son's position is highly related to father's occupation; but it is severe in a undifferentiated system.

Consequently, the model should more accurately capture the father's effect on the son by not requiring all births to be at age 0 of the system, but by taking the first year out of the educational system or the last year in it as the starting point. Then in some cells of the upper right half of the matrix, there would be nonzero entries, h_{ij}, where j is the father's age (minus 14) and i is the son's (minus 14). The probability h_{igjk} is the probability that a father of age j and occupation k has a son enter occupation g (i.e., enter the population) at age i. In this way, persons would be born into the population at whatever chronological age they first entered the labor force (or were last in school).

This model describes, for the data from which the coefficients of H were calculated, the allocation and birth processes through which men move from one job to another through a career, and give birth to sons at particular ages throughout that career. When applied to varying initial distributions of individuals among ages and statuses at time 0, then it predicts the expected new status distribution at future times as a function of the age and status distribution at time 0, and of the matrix of coefficients, H, which are assumed constant. That would show, for example, the predicted number of persons at time t in different educational streams at each age (assuming the supply of places is not constrained), as a function of birth rates of men at each age and occupational status, distribution of the sons of those men among educational streams, and the movements of men through occupations during their work career. It would show also the predicted size at time t of each occupational group in the labor force, again assuming that the same coefficients hold. This would be given by $\sum_{j=0} n_{jk}(t)$, where $N(t) - = H^t N(0)$.

IMPLEMENTATION OF THE MODEL

The model as described above can be partly implemented by data from a cohort of men such as those from the samples described earlier. Continuous work history data provide the necessary information for estimating the matrices $h_{j+1,j}$, below the main diagonal, for all those ages up to the age of interview. There is one omission by use of such retrospective data: men who have died or emigrated before time of interview never enter the system. The parameters for birth of men into the system, for submatrices h_{oj}, could not easily be esitmated from such data, unless the cohort is old enough at time of interview to have all their sons in the labor force—an age that would probably be too old on other grounds. Ideally, the data for estimating parameters would not derive from retrospective data at all, but from contemporaneous data. Such data are approximated by a question in the British census, which asked not only a man's present job, but his job one year ago. Another question, about whether he had had a son leave education for the first time in the past year, and if so, what activity did he enter, would have been sufficient for estimating the birth rates.

However, the model will be only partially applied, using the retrospective data on career histories. In this application, only four states will be used, both for ease of illustration and because of the small sample sizes. The states are:
1. Education (any full-time)
2. White-collar job (professional, managerial or proprietary, clerical and sales)
3. Blue-collar job (craftsman, operative, labor, farm, service)
4. Military

The black sample and the white sample will be characterized by the proportion of men in each of these states, from age 14 to 39. At age 13, all men in both samples are assumed to be in education.

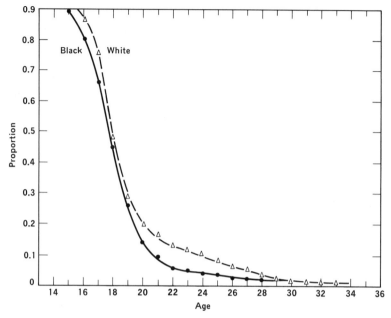

Figure 12.1. Proportion in Education

The data available include ten cohorts, men born between 1929 and 1938. It will be treated, however, as if it were only a single-year cohort. This means, in terms of the model presented above, that data represent a portion of the N vector, $n_{j1}(t)$, $n_{j2}(t)$, $n_{j3}(t)$, $n_{j4}(t)$, for a particular correspondence between j and t. If we measure t according to the calendar, and j with $j = 0$ at chronological age 14, then the age group that is age 39 in 1968 (the last age of the cohort in this sample) would be denoted by $n_0.$ (1943), $n_1.$ (1944), and so on with the progression of years to $n_{25}.$ (1968), and since no death or migration processes are included, all these values are equal. Thus this is a four-element portion of the

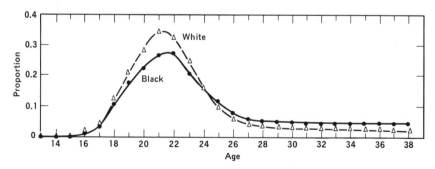

Figure 12.2. Proportion Military

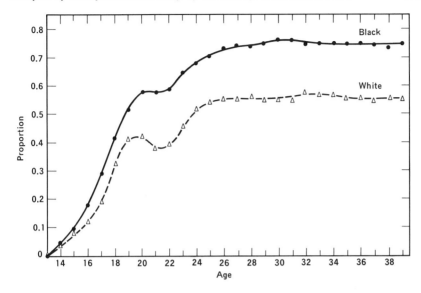

Figure 12.3. Proportion Blue Collar

vector which moves progressively down the vector from position $i = 0$ in 1943 to position $i = 25$ in 1968.

The functioning of this system of movement into and through the labor force can be seen in Figures 12.1-12.4. These figures show the proportions in each status at each age, for blacks and whites. The values from which Figures 12.1-12.4 are plotted have been found by first creating all elements in the H matrix except the top row of submatrices representing birth into the system, estimating $h_{j+1,g,j,k} = n_{j+1,g,j,k}/n_{jk}(t)$. Then the values in Figures 12.1-12.4 are a certain portion of the vector $N(1943 + t)$, found as:

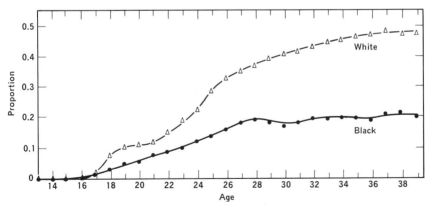

Figure 12.4. Proportion White Collar

$$N(1943 + t) = H^t N(1943) \qquad (12.3)$$

for $j = 0,\ldots,25$, with calculations made only for the portion of the vector that is $n_{0k}(1943)$, $k = 1,2,3,4$.[4] The figures show the vector of numbers divided by the sample size, so they represent the porportions of the cohort in each of the four statuses.

As Figure 12.1 shows, education is, of course, a state of origin from which evacuation occurs. The evacuation is somewhat more rapid for blacks than for whites. Figure 12.2 describes how military service is a temporary state beginning in the late teens and ending in the early twenties. For blacks compared to whites, it is skewed slightly to the right, and continues at a slightly higher level in later ages. The major long-term differences occur, of course, in the occupational states where blacks and whites end up, after these transient states are evacuated. Figure 12.3 shows that a majority of both blacks and whites are in blue-collar jobs at age 39, though about 20 percent fewer whites than blacks. The kink in the two curves from ages 19 to 23 is caused, as Figure 12.2 shows, by military service.

Over 45 percent of whites end up in white-collar occupations at age 39, Figure 12.4 shows, while only about 20 percent of the blacks do so, with the remainder in blue-collar occupations (which includes service workers and farmers, the latter small in number).

There is also an important assumption: that this cohort's transition probabilities at each age are like those of all the other cohorts for which the data are to be used.

USE OF THE MODEL FOR HYPOTHETICAL EXPERIMENTS

The graphs provided in Figures 12.1-12.4 constitute nothing more than a description of the proportions of this cohort in each state at each age. This description would have been possible merely from the observed values without all the apparatus that has been introduced here. However, the existence of the H matrix makes further analysis possible. If the "birth rates" of the matrix were estimated as well, it would be possible to use the model to move the population through time, that is, over generations. Such a matrix, rather than the usual intergenerational mobility matrix, is the appropriate means for doing this, for it allows for differential birth rates, different ages of birth by occupation of father, different ages of entry into the labor force, different periods of time in the labor force—none of which is possible in the simple father-son occupational mobility tables.

---

[4] Since the values for H are calculated from the overserved numbers of $n_{j+1,g,j,k}$ for the single cohort, the values in $N(1943 + t)$ are simply the observed quantities, with Equation (12.3) being an identity. In general, H would have been calculated from data in other cohorts, and $N(1943 + t)$ would be an expectation.

The specific analysis I want to carry out is somewhat different. If we want to compare black and white career mobility, it would appear that the most straightforward way of doing so is through comparing transition probabilities in the matrices. However, there is another way, which can be regarded as a "hypothetical experiment": this is to combine certain columns of the black matrix with other columns of the white matrix, to obtain a mixed system.

A first example is to construct a new *H* matrix with one column for each age from the white matrix, giving the proportions going from white-collar occupations into school, military, and blue collar, and the remaining columns at each age from the black matrix. This newly constructed *H* matrix includes proportions characteristic of whites, going *from* white-collar occupations, and proportions characteristic of blacks going from other statuses *into* white-collar occupations. A second *H* matrix may be constructed in exactly the reverse way. With these matrices we can ask the question: What would the proportion white collar among blacks at age 39 be, under two possible conditions—first, if the rates of movement *from* white-collar jobs (to blue-collar or education or military) were changed to be like that of whites; and second, if the rates of movement *into* white-collar jobs from these other states were changed to be like that of whites?

Figure 12.5 shows, from age 17, the hypothetical condition in which white rates of movement *into* white collar are used in a matrix otherwise like that of blacks. Under these conditions, the blacks' occupational positions would be about the same as those of whites up to age 26, but would level off after that, due to the greater departure rates for blacks from white-collar jobs into blue-collar jobs. Still, the blacks' proportion in white-collar occupations under these conditions would hold at about 15-18 percent above the actual blacks.

In contrast, a hypothetical condition in which the rates of movement from other occupations to white-collar jobs stays like that which blacks already have, while the rates of movement *from* white-collar jobs are like those of whites, does

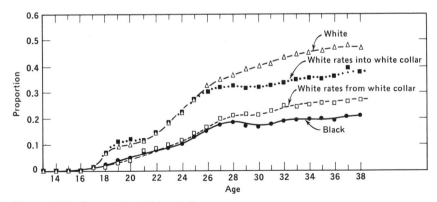

Figure 12.5. Proportion White Collar

not deviate from the all-black curve until about age 26. From this age onward, the lower rate for whites of leaving white-collar jobs is apparent, resulting in blacks having about 5 percent more white-collar jobs by age 32, an increment that maintains itself through age 39.

This comparison shows that the greatest bottleneck for blacks is in the movement into white-collar jobs. Once there, the curve for black rates of movement from white-collar jobs shows that they remain there reasonably well, staying about 15-18 percent above the actual blacks. However, the curve for blacks with white rates of movement from white-collar jobs shows that unless they somehow get into these jobs, an improvement of their retention rate to equal that of whites will only make about a 5 percent difference.

Figure 12.6 shows the consequences of a different kind of hypothetical change. Only one thing is changed from the black situation: school leaving is changed to correspond to that of whites, both in the overall rates of leaving, and in the various statuses to which school leavers go. The graph shows that the total effect is accomplished in two years at age 18 and 19, resulting in about 4 percent more white-collar jobs than currently exists among blacks. But that increment does not even maintain itself; it slowly declines through age 39. Not even the reentry of whites into education, and their reemergence as white-collar workers, has any noticeable impact after age 20.

Figure 12.7 shows again the consequences of a single change from the blacks' current condition: proportions going from blue-collar jobs to school, military service, or white-collar jobs are changed to be like those of whites. The graph shows that this indeed does make a large difference, reducing the black-white difference in proportion white collar to about half its actual value.

Part of the reason this change shows so much greater effect than the comparable change in rates of leaving white-collar jobs (Figure 12.5) is that it begins so much earlier. By age 19, the white rates of movement out of blue-collar jobs have begun to feed additional men into white-collar jobs. This

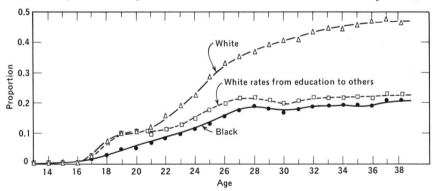

Figure 12.6. Proportion White Collar

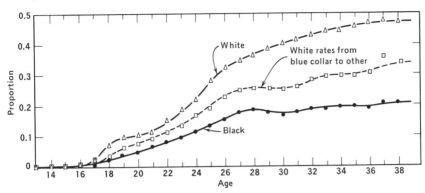

Figure 12.7. Proportion White Collar

effect continues to cumulate, with the gap growing throughout the twenties and thirties. This contrasts sharply to the effect of changes in rates of movement into other statuses from education, shown in Figure 12.6, for that effect took place only at ages 18 and 19, and was diminished later.

The effect of changes in the destination of blacks who leave the military is shown in Figure 12.8, comparing it with the effect of education. The scale is doubled here, and only ages 16-26 are shown, since education and military have all their effects in that period. Figure 12.8 shows the big bulge in white-collar occupations for whites leaving school at ages 18-19, but then continuing in a path that is parallel to current blacks. White destinations on leaving military service have their effects on members holding white-collar jobs several years later, in ages 23-25. Perhaps the most interesting point is that the long-term effect is nearly the same. The curve for white movement out of military service (not shown here) is parallel and very close to the curve for white movement out of education, all the way to age 30.

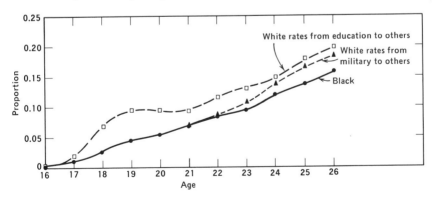

Figure 12.8. Proportion White Collar

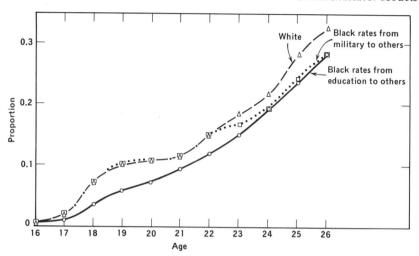

Figure 12.9. Proportion White Collar

This similar but delayed effect of changing blacks' destinations after military service to correspond to whites can be seen by a reverse experiment, giving whites exit rates from military service into other statuses that correspond to those of the blacks. This is shown in Figure 12.9, which also includes a curve showing whites with black movement from education to other statuses. Again the difference shows up at age 18 and 19 for education, but not until ages 23 and 24 for military service, yet with the same result. The curves are almost identical from age 26 on.

It is important to be clear about the interpretation of this result. It does not mean that military service is as "effective" for obtaining white-collar jobs as is education, but in fact almost the opposite to that. It means that the occupational differences between blacks and whites that show up before military service still remain at the end of military service. The difference in profiles of jobs obtained by whites and blacks after military service is enough like the difference in profiles of jobs obtained after education that the long-range effect of changing the movement from military service is nearly identical to that of changing the movement from education.

MODIFICATION OF THE MODEL

The model as discussed above has certain defects. One of these is that if the hypothetical experiments are to be taken seriously, the changed occupational distribution for one population group has implications for that of the other. If there is a fixed number of white-collar jobs then any increase in white-collar jobs for blacks means a decrease for whites. The fact that blacks make up less than 15 percent of the labor force means that the impact of the 1 percent increase in white-collar jobs for them is only about 1/8 of 1 percent for the whites' occupational distribution. However, in some applications, where the two population groups are nearer the same size, the effect is large. Consequently, it is useful to modify the model to take this into consideration. A simple way of correcting the direct effect is to recombine the populations, in their correct proportions, and to calculate transition probabilities for the combined population. Then a hypothetical experiment may ask what is the effect in occupational distribution of blacks and whites of their having the *same* rates and directions of movement from white-collar occupations. That question is answered by taking a column from the combined matrix, to replace the white-collar column in both the white and black matrices. This would lower the proportion of whites in white-collar occupations as it raised the proportion of blacks.

This, however, would correct only the direct effects. The proportions of men in each occupation would still not be that found in the original population. For example, by decreasing the flow of blacks from white collar jobs and proportionally increasing that of whites, the effect is to move into blue-collar jobs a group which will more quickly move out—since there will be a larger portion of whites (who move out more quickly than blacks) in blue-collar jobs than there is in the actual population. I see no way at the moment for solution of this second-order effect.

A MODEL THAT INCORPORATES EFFECTS OF INDEPENDENT VARIABLES

The model presented above has certain further defects if used for hypothetical experiments in the ways discussed above. The hypothetical experiments constitute a direct change in transition probabilities, but not a change in the factors that are determinants of those transition probabilities. I want to outline here a revised model that will do so. The virtues of this approach stem from the fact that it is able to combine a system of flows among occupations with a causal model that makes these flows functions of variables characterizing the individual.

The idea is first of all to replace the discrete-time model by a continuous-time model with transition rates that are a function of age. What this means is that rather than to obtain a separate estimate for each year, as in the case of transition probabilities, one may obtain a single estimate over all years, but letting the transition rate vary continuously with age.

In the process of estimating the transition rate as a function of age, it is possible to let it be a function of other characteristics of the individual and the job he is in. With continuous data, the total transition rate from a state may be estimated from the fact that in a Markov process, the expected time of residence in a state is the inverse of the transition rate. For state k

$$E(t_k) = \frac{1}{q_k} \ h \tag{12.4}$$

Thus the total transition rate from occupational state k for a given individual may be estimated as the inverse of the time he spends in this state. If we envision q_k as a function of various characteristics of the person and the job, then it is possible to estimate, as Sørensen (1972) has done, the sizes of those effects. The assumed functional relation is

$$q_k = exp \ (a + b_1 x_1 + \ldots + b_n x_n) \tag{12.5}$$

for characteristics of jobs and individuals $x_1, \ldots, x_n$. This leads to a linear relation between log q_k as the dependent variable and $x_1, \ldots, x_n$ as independent variables. But q_k is estimated by the inverse of the duration of the job, so that the empirical analysis is a regression at the individual level of $-$log (duration) on $x_1, \ldots, x_n$.

This regression, for each occupational state, gives the total transition rate from the state as a function of the independent variables. It does not, however, give the fraction of that flow which goes into state g. Since that fraction can be expected to vary independently of q_k, it should also be seen as a function of age and other independent variables. If for all moves from occupational state k, we define a variable y_{gk} (g = 1,2,3,4) to be zero if the move was to a state other than g, and 1 if the move was to state g, this variable can be a dependent variable in an individual-level regression analysis,[5]

$$y_{gk} = a_{gk} + b_{1gk} x_1 + \ldots + b_{ngk} x_n \tag{12.6}$$

The results of these analyses give q_k and y_{gk} as functions of various independent variables. For persons characterized by certain values on those variables, a matrix of transition rates Q, consisting of elements q_{gk}, may be constructed by the product $q_k \ y_{gk}$. This gives the transition matrix for a population group characterized by particular values of $x_1, \ldots, x_n$. From that transition matrix (which changes with age), it is possible to calculate a set of transition probabilities for each year, like the matrix $h_{i+1,i}$ which was estimated in the earlier model.

But now, something more can be done. Since these transition probabilities are functions of characteristics of the individual and jobs, it is possible to carry out hypothetical experiments of a more sophisticated sort than with the earlier model. It is possible to construct, for example, transition rates for blacks that

---

[5] The use of an 0-1 dependent variable in least-squares estimation is not desirable on statistical grounds, but appears to be the least undesirable method of estimating the required parameter.

are like their present rates except that the average level of education is higher by a given amount (perhaps made equal to that of whites).[6]

The hypothetical experiment now becomes a different one: rather than a direct change in the transition rates (carried out by some unknown means), the implied policy change is a change in certain underlying variables, like education, which have an impact on the transition rates among jobs. Note that this is quite different from the substitution carried out earlier, of a white vector of transition probabilities out of education for the black vector. That substitution did not capture the effects of education on transition probabilities from one occupation to another, but only changed the rates and directions of movement out of education itself. That, of course, is why its effect dampened out quickly. Here, however, its effect continues to the degree that education has an effect on the movement among jobs after one is in the labor force.

CONCLUSION

In this chapter I have attempted to develop a model to describe the birth of persons into a system of occupations, and their movement from one occupation to another while they are in that system. Such a model lends itself to "hypothetical experiments," in which transition probabilities are directly modified (as I have done in the earlier part of this chapter), or in which characteristics of the individual that affect the transition probabilities are modified (as I have outlined in the last section).

The usefulness of the model itself, apart from the hypothetical experiments, lies in the general area of social accounting. The model constitutes simply an accounting scheme for tracing members of a population's birth into and progression through a system of states. Certain assumptions, such as constancy of the transition matrix (assuming that H is independent of t), and the ahistoricity assumption of Markov processes (that H^t can be used to describe the probability of being in state g at time t given occupancy of state k at time o) make the model more than descriptive, and able to make predictions about future distributions in the system.

I believe that such a social accounting framework, similar in its structure and assumptions to economic accounting and its offspring, input-output analysis, will be the mature form that social indicators will take. One of the principal reasons for this belief is the kind of hypothetical experimentation described in this chapter. When one has an accounting system with parameters that govern the flow of persons through states in the system, then policy

---

[6] This can be done also for transition rates from only one occupational state (such as white-collar occupations), although the interpretation of this hypothetical experiment in terms of actual changes is less straightforward.

questions can be asked about changes in these parameters. In some cases, the changes can be direct, as for example, when government in a state-supported system of higher education determines the number of places in higher education for a given year. In other cases, the changes are indirect, through changing some factor which is one of many determinants of a transition probability. In either case, application of the model as an accounting system with modified parameters can predict the effects on the system of the proposed policy changes: effects on the distribution of persons in different states, effects on the expected time for an individual to get from one state to another, and other properties of the system. Whether the system is, as in the present application, occupational states, or regional states, or educational states, or health states, or household composition states, or different states in the system of criminal justice, or still a different system, the general approach is the same, and the kinds of policy questions that can be asked through hypothetical experiments, like those I've discussed, are similar.

REFERENCES

Blum, Zahava D.
   1972   "White and black careers during the first decade of labor force experience. Part III: Income differences." Social Science Research 1, no. 3 (September): 271-292.
Blum, Zahava D., Nancy L. Karweit, and Aage B. Sørensen.
   1969   "A method for the collection and analysis of retrospective life histories." Report no. 48 (July). Baltimore, Md.: Center for Social Organization of Schools, The Johns Hopkins University.
Coleman, James S., Zahava D. Blum, Aage B. Sørensen,. and Peter H. Rossi.
   1972   "White and black careers during the first decade of labor force experience. Part I: Occupational status." Social Science Research 1, no. 3 (September): 243-270.
Coleman, James S., Charles C. Berry, and Zahava D. Blum.
   1972   "White and black careers during the first decade of labor force experience. Part III: Occupational status and income together." Social Science Research 1, no. 3 (September): 293-304.
Feeney, Griffith M.
   1970   "Stable age by region distributions." Demography 7:341-348.
Rogers, A.
   1968   Matrix Analysis of Interregional Population Growth and Distribution. Berkeley: University of California Press.
Sørensen, Aage B.
   1972   "The occupational mobility process: An analysis of occupational careers." Ph.D. dissertation, Johns Hopkins University, Baltimore, Md.
Stone, Richard.
   1966   Mathematics in the Social Sciences and Other Essays. London: Chapman & Hall.

13

GROWTH IN OCCUPATIONAL ACHIEVEMENT: SOCIAL MOBILITY OR INVESTMENT IN HUMAN CAPITAL*

Aage B. Sørensen

INTRODUCTION

The term "occupational achievement" is used here to refer to the occupational prestige and income an individual has obtained at a point in time. Although it is of interest to explore differences in the processes that generate prestige and income respectively, the common elements in these processes should be specified first. This chapter focuses on what are believed to be such common elements in the processes that result in the attainment of a certain level of prestige and income at a given point in time.

The objective of the analysis of the occupational achievement process presented here is to contribute to the development of appropriate indicators of the process. We shall be concerned with the development of analytic indicators (Sheldon and Land, 1972), i.e., indicators that constitute parameters in a model of the process. We shall argue for a model that shows the outcome of the achievement process as a result of several forces that may vary independently from each other. This model therefore implies that alternative policies for affecting the process are possible. Evaluation of these alternative policies needs indicators that can separate the operation of the various forces that affect the achievement process. One must use analytic indicators, rather than descriptive ones.

*The research reported here was supported by funds granted to the Institute for Research on Poverty at the University of Wisconsin by the Office of Economic Opportunity pursuant to the provisions of the Economic Opportunity Act of 1964. The conclusions are the sole responsibility of the author.

Research on occupational achievement has been carried out both in economics (mostly on income) and in sociology (mostly on status or prestige). The conceptualizations of the process have been quite different in the two fields. The two approaches are not mutually exclusive, however, and a comprehensive theory of achievement needs elements from both approaches. Such a theory, we will argue, can fruitfully be based on an analysis of job shifts since the achievement process can be considered as a result of a succession of job shifts.

The following sections will briefly review some of the most relevant features of the conceptualization of occupational achievement in economics and sociology. The review is followed by an analysis of the outcome of job shifts carried out by a cohort of 30–39-year-old males from their entry into the labor force until time of interview. The data are obtained from the Hopkins Life-History Study.[1] A discussion follows that will attempt to clarify what the estimated parameters indicate and what are the policy implications of the various interpretations.

OCCUPATIONAL ACHIEVEMENT AS SOCIAL MOBILITY

The sociological research on achievement process originates in research on social mobility. Social mobility and occupational achievement are closely related phenomena. The main problem posed in traditional mobility research is however not the question of what makes a person achieve a certain level of prestige and income, but what makes a person's achievement differ from the achievement of his father. However, given a certain origin, the factors that determine the distance from that origin are of course those that determine occupational achievement.

Traditional mobility research seems most interested in establishing only the magnitude of the difference between origin and current status—that is, the amount of mobility. The amount of mobility in turn indicates the "openness" of a society, an important social indicator in a society concerned with equal opportunity. The concern with mobility is for what it tells about social systems rather than what it tells about individual achievement.

Mobility is the movement of individuals among positions in a social structure. Most often these positions are jobs organized in occupations. Individuals differ with respect to characteristics that affect their probability of moving between a given set of positions; that is, mobility depends on individual ability, values, and motivation. Also, in order for an individual to move there must be a vacant position for him to occupy. Hence, mobility is also a function of the distribution of opportunities given by the occupational structure. This

---

[1] The life history study was conducted as part of the Social Accounts Program at the Center for Social Organization of Schools, The Johns Hopkins University. The Social Accounts Program was initiated by James S. Coleman and Peter H. Rossi.

definition and the conceptualization of social mobility as an interplay between structural and individual characteristics is accepted in most mobility research. Consequently, much effort has been directed toward separating individual and structural contributions to mobility.

The most ambitious attempt to separate the various sources of mobility is probably the one made by Kahl (1957), who tried to separate out the contribution of technological change, demographic factors, migration, and individual characteristics to mobility. The result is unsatisfactory; the information contained in a father-son mobility table cannot be linked to structural changes in society. As argued by Duncan (1966), the generation of fathers is not a cohort which represents occupational structure at any point in time. It might be added that mobility between father and son is the result of a career mobility process that cannot be located precisely in time with cross-sectional data, and therefore cannot be linked to observed structural changes. Despite continued ingenuity in the development of measures and models of mobility for intergenerational data it seems doubtful that such data will ever enable a separation of various sources of mobility. Instead, intragenerational mobility data are needed since such data will at least permit a more precise time-anchoring of the mobility process and therefore may allow a more detailed analysis of the process.

A major recent development in the analysis of mobility with the emphasis on structural sources of movement uses data that represent intragenerational mobility. The data are, however, only indirectly data on individual mobility as they are measures of the movement of vacancies in organizations (White, 1970). Individuals are seen to move in response to the creation of vacancies, that is opportunities, and this generates chains of moves that will end only with the elimination of jobs or the entrance of new individuals to the system. Vacancy chains in this way generate careers of individuals by offering opportunities for gains in achievement without changes in individual characteristics.

White's models are an important contribution to our understanding of how structural opportunities may create mobility and represent a major advance over the many unsatisfactory models and measures that have been proposed for conventional mobility tables. The initiative is, however, completely in the hands of vacancies in White's models. There is no attempt to specify the interplay between individual and structural characteristics for generating mobility.

The analysis of the importance of specific individual attributes for mobility is difficult to carry out within the context of traditional mobility tables. This point is well documented in the critique of Anderson's (1961) analysis of the importance of education for mobility given by Blau and Duncan (1967). A reformulation of the basic question was needed. Thus, rather than asking what is the importance of, for example, education, for the distance between origin and current status, the status attainment literature asks what is the importance of individual characteristics for occupational achievement. The origin is seen as one of those characteristics, and the status attainment literature thus gives a more appropriate formulation of the problem for the analysis of occupational achievement. This most important reorientation of mobility research of which the monograph by Blau and Duncan (1967) is the most prominent example, also represents a change in emphasis away from the study of mobility as a system characteristic to the focus on mobility as an individual process.

The origin of the status attainment literature in research on intergenerational mobility is visible in the concern for the influence of origin variables both directly and indirectly through the achievement of education and first job. In other words, it is an analysis of the transmission of resources from one generation to the next (Duncan, 1966). The origin in mobility research is, however, not reflected in a concern for structural sources of variation in occupational achievement. On the contrary, there is no attempt to specify structural opportunities as a source of variation in occupational achievement in the status attainment literature. But if changes in occupational structure influence the degree of departure of sons' status from fathers', as the traditional conceptualization of mobility dictates, then structural characteristics certainly will affect occupational achievement in general and therefore the relation between background variables and achievement.

From a largely descriptive concern for the measurement of the mobility between father and son, in order to establish mobility as a system characteristic, research, in sum, has turned to the analysis of the sources of individual processes of mobility. However, recent research has diverged into two unrelated activities with respect to implementing the conceptualization of mobility as an interplay between structural and individual characteristics. One activity, status attainment literature, focuses exclusively on individual attributes. The second activity, White's models, show an exclusive concern for structural sources or mobility and careers.

Status attainment research concerns itself with individual attributes that directly or indirectly influence a person's occupational achievement. Although the term is not universally used in the literature, it seems reasonable to subsume those individual characteristics under the term "personal resources." Family background and education do not determine a fixed level of resources throughout an individual's lifetime, although sociological literature is only concerned with these characteristics. A person may undertake additional training and in other ways add to his resources at any point in the life-cycle, and in this way influence his achievement. We must turn to the economic literature, and more specifically, to the so-called human capital theory for a concern for the change and development of personal resources over time.

OCCUPATIONAL ACHIEVEMENT AS INVESTMENTS IN HUMAN CAPITAL

Sociological research on occupational achievement is not grounded in any well-specified theory about the achievement process. Apart from the distinction between structural and individual sources of mobility there is little concern for the mechanisms that produce occupational achievement. A comprehensive conceptual scheme that will justify the choice of variables and interpret their interrelations does not exist. This contrasts to the economic approach, where human capital theory offers a rather elaborate conceptual apparatus developed mainly analogous to standard economic concepts.

The basic idea in the human capital theory is that the resources of an individual can be regarded as a stock of capital that determines the individual's productivity and hence his earnings. This stock can be augmented by investments in training and education. These investments in human capital increase productivity and hence earnings, and the earnings increase constitutes a return on the investments.

Investments are undertaken at a cost: a direct one in the form of tuition and material, and an indirect one that are earnings foregone. The indirect costs are present even if training takes place on the job, since general training (that may be transferred to another job) must be financed by the individual. Otherwise, such training would reduce the competitiveness of the firm that gives on-the-job training (Becker, 1964).

The increase in earnings subsequent to the investment, that is the return on the investment, is compared to the cost of the investment. Individuals are assumed to be rational beings who maximize their achievement. Investment in human capital will therefore only be undertaken if the predicted increase in the sum of future earnings due to the investment, discounted back to the time of the decision, exceeds the cost of the investment.

Human capital theory is first a theory about the conditions under which a person will decide to increase his education or undertake other forms of training. However, it is also a theory about the process through which individuals increase their income and thus their occupational achievement.

The total stock of personal resources determines earnings. As long as there are no changes in resources, earnings are assumed to be constant. This is a crucial assumption, since it implies that the occupational achievement process is seen as a question of changes only in a person's level of resources. Becker (1964) thus uses the observed flat earnings profiles of unskilled workers as an indication of their lack of investments in themselves. Of course, human capital analysis would admit to factors other than resources as determinants of earnings, but the theory does not relate such factors to systematic variations in earnings over age.

Generally, investments do take place after entry into the labor force and the resultant age profile will be concave to the age axis with a gradually declining slope. The shape of the curve is due to a tendency to concentrate investments at younger ages. There are several explanations for this pattern (See Becker, 1964; Ben-Porath, 1967). First, the remaining time in the labor force will determine the total return on an investment, so the investment is therefore more profitable the younger the individual. Second, investments at older ages are more costly since earnings foregone will be larger as a result of earlier investments. Finally, the rate of return may decline with age as a result of a decline in a person's ability to learn. This tendency to accumulate investments at younger ages is counteracted by upwardly sloping marginal costs of investments (Mincer, 1970), so that there will be a tendency to spread out investments.

In order to calculate the precise return on investment activities it is necessary to separate out that amount of an earnings differential which is due to the investment activity as such, and the amount due to "ability." Ability is somewhat nebulously treated in the literature, but Becker's (1964) definition is probably acceptable to most. He defines ability as whatever produces earnings differences holding constant all investments. Since ability will be correlated with investment activities, especially education, it may be difficult to assess whether it is the schooling as such or the ability differences associated with schooling that produce earnings differentials.

The concept of ability as defined by Becker is very similar to the sociological concept of ascribed status determinants. The origin variables that loom so large in the status attainment literature may be seen as indirect measures of characteristics that would be subsumed under "ability" in the economic literature. The effect of parental education and father's status on occupational achievement thus would be explained by most as reflecting the differences in IQ, motivation, and values associated with these background variables. The linear models (path models) developed in sociology thus may be seen as an attempt to specify the interrelationship between "ability" as measured by background variables, and one crucial investment, education, in producing occupational achievement. Griliches (1970) has in fact argued for the formation of such models in the economic literature in order to overcome some of the difficulties encountered when attempts are made to take ability into account.

Although the status attainment literature and human capital theory are similar in the distinction between ability and investment and achieved and ascribed individual characteristics, the two research traditions tend to focus on different attributes of occupational achievement. Human capital theory focuses on earnings, the status attainment literature on status or prestige. This difference however seems to be mostly a difference in tradition. It is difficult, if not impossible, to argue that propositions for attainment of income developed in human capital theory are not as valid for prestige. Similarly the models developed in status attainment literature for the interrelationship of ascribed and achieved characteristics should be as valid for income as for prestige.

The two approaches complement each other in that the status attainment literature primarily deals with the development of resources up to the entry into the labor force, while human capital theory's concern for on-the-job training and the like focuses on how the achievement process develops after entry into the labor force. The concern for age variations in achievement is an important one. First a systematic age variation in achievement is an important phenomenon in itself and a comprehensive theory of achievement should of course address itself to the explanation of change in achievement over time. Second, even if the explanation of age change is not deemed essential, as the sociological literature will have it, the existence of such change will make the parameters in models of the achievement process dependent on the age distribution of the population. This, of course, adds to the difficulty in making comparisons over time or between places and therefore hinders the development of satisfactory social indicators.

Human capital analysis shares with the status attainment approach a lack of concern for structural sources of variation in occupational achievement. The only systematic source of variation in achievement is changes in personal resources, according to human capital theory. If no such change takes place, the earnings profile will be flat. As in status attainment literature, individual characteristics are the only ones deemed relevant for achievement.

It would be futile to deny that a person may increase his prestige and income by undertaking additional training and education. Human capital analysis provides a theory about how such additions to a person's level of resources come about. As a theory about the achievement process it is only partial since it seems equally futile to deny that at times a person may experience a gain in prestige and income because an opportunity for advancement presented itself as a result of the creation of a new job or the retirement of the incumbent of an old job. Also, at times people are fired or pressured out of their job without an apparent change in resources but with losses in prestige and income as probable consequences. In these instances there are structural sources to the variation in achievement. A comprehensive theory of occupational achievement should take both individual and structural influences on the achievement process into account. We will in the next section try to carry out an analysis that fulfills this demand.

A MODEL FOR JOB SHIFTS

We have seen that the answer to the problem of what determines occupational achievement is given by human capital analysis as well as by the status attainment literature in terms of individual characteristics—achieved or ascribed resources. The human capital approach goes further than the status attainment literature in one crucial respect: the economic approach does attempt a specification of the mechanisms that produce growth in achievement, these mechanisms being acts of investments. In the investment approach the occupational achievement process clearly is conceived of as an age-dependent process. Earnings profiles or careers are therefore important variables on which data are needed in order to apply the theory.

The attempt to relate mobility to the formation of vacancies by White (1970) uses a data base that indirectly stems from the intragenerational mobility of individuals. We have argued, in general, that if more successful attempts to specify the structural sources of variation in mobility are to be made, data on the careers of individuals are needed, as intergenerational data do not give enough information to identify the structural sources of variation. It is apparent, then, that a more comprehensive approach to the achievement process that incorporates the analysis of structural mechanisms as well as mechanisms for change in resources, will need to rely on repeated observations of individuals' careers. Such data are available in the form of a set of retrospective life histories, that are occupational, familial, educational, and residential experiences, on a sample of 30–39-year-old men.[2]

The data available give us detailed information on every change in the respondents' occupational careers. We shall argue that the best way to utilize all this information is to analyze the outcomes of the job shift undertaken by the respondents. This will enable us both to make most efficient use of the information available, and also to identify individual as well as structural sources of variation in careers.

The analysis of job shifts is the most efficient use of the information on careers if all major variations in achievement take place through job shifts. This is certainly true for variations in prestige, as prestige is an attribute of an occupational category; and we believe it is the case for earnings, too. Every change in the individual's duties, tasks, or firm in which he was employed was supposed to be registered as job shifts in the life history data. It follows that except for general increases in wages—real and inflationary—that can be controlled for, no major change in earnings should occur within a job.

The analysis of job shifts may enable us to identify the influence of structural forces on the achievement process since job shifts are elementary acts of mobility. They are the response of individuals either to opportunities for

---

[2] The universe for the life history study is the total population of males 30-39 year of age, in 1968, residing in the United States. Two samples were drawn: (a) a national sample; and (b) a supplementary sample of blacks. The total number of interviews obtained was 1,589: 738 blacks and 851 whites. The completion rates were 76.1 percent for sample (a) and 78.2 percent for sample (b). The 973 cases constituting the national sample are used in the analysis here.

gains in achievement or to pressures to leave their job; that is, job shifts represent an interplay between structural and individual characteristics. By making some simple assumptions about individual behavior we hope to be able to specify this interplay.

As already indicated, we shall use the term resources in the following discussion to label all individual characteristics that have a bearing on a person's value in the job market. We shall characterize every job by its level of achievement, measured by prestige or income. A job shift will ordinarily produce a change in achievement, and we may form this outcome as the difference between the new and the old level of achievement. The simplest model for this outcome is a linear difference equation:

$$\Delta X_1 = b_1 X_{11} + b_2 X_2 \tag{13.1}$$
$$\Delta X_1 = X_{12} - X_{11}$$

where X_{11} stands for the achievement of the job left
$\qquad X_{12}$ is the achievement of the job entered
and $\quad X_2$ stands for an (assumed) comprehensive measure of a person's level of resources

It will be crucial in the following analysis to distinguish between the situation where the job shift is preceded by an increase in resources obtained during the job left, and the situation where resources remain at a constant level. The former case will be one where the job shift is a result of an investment activity, the latter is a case of "pure" mobility—the job shift is a response to an opportunity for a better job and is not preceded by an increase in personal resources. The notation of Equation (13.1) is only correct if resources remained unchanged prior to the job shift. If the job shift is a response to increments in resources only, then X_2 should be replaced by a term $\Delta X_2 = X_{21} - X_{20}$, where X_{20} is the level of resources at the time of entry into the job, and X_{21} the level of resources when the job shift occurs.

Whether the job shift is a response to opportunity or to an increase in resources is crucial for the interpretation of b_2. If the job shift is strictly a response to opportunities ($\Delta X_2 = 0$), then b_2 measures the *increment in return on resources*. If the job shift is a response to increased resources, then b_2 measures the *return on an increment in resources*.[3] This difference in interpretation is of major importance when we want to distinguish between the relative importance of investment activities to mobility as a source of variation in occupational achievement. We shall proceed with a theoretical analysis of the

---

[3] If there are earnings and prestige foregone in the job left due to training then there will also be an increment in return on the level of resources at entry into the job (X_{20}).

case where resources did not change prior to the job shift, since a model for the career pattern in that case may be developed from Equation (13.1). In the empirical analysis, to follow, the different interpretations of b_2 become important, however. The parameter b_1 of Equation (13.1) measures the effect on the gain, usually a negative one, of the achievement already obtained. This parameter will be determined partly by negative feedback through unmeasured variables, and partly by measurement error in X_1 that will produce a regression toward the mean (Coleman, 1968).

The magnitude of b_1 and b_2 can be shown to be determined by structural characteristics, i.e., such factors as the distribution of job opportunities and the level of employment. To see this, let us assume that individuals maximize occupational achievement. They will undertake job shifts whenever they can obtain a gain in achievement. However, individuals may also undertake a job shift when they cannot obtain a gain—they may be forced out of their job. Individuals are more likely to be forced out of their job when there is a high level of unemployment. The level of employment thus may be seen to determine a person's *control* over the decision to leave. When the level of employment is high and there are many job opportunities we will expect that job shifts are likely to be undertaken voluntarily. When the level of employment is low, and there are few opportunities, most job shifts may be expected to take place when the job holder has little or no control over the decision to leave.

Suppose that a person, in fact, has full control over the decision to leave. If a job shift is undertaken, the new level of achievement should at least equal the old level of achievement plus an increment determined by the level of resources:

$$X_{12} = X_{11} + a_2 X_2 + a_0$$

or   (13.2)

$$\Delta X_1' = a_2 X_2 + a_0$$

where a_2 is the maximum increment in return on his resources a person may obtain, or the maximum return on the increase in resources if the job shift is a response to a gain in resources prior to the job shift. Suppose now instead that a person was forced out of his job, that is, he had no control over the decision to leave. He will then be expected to suffer a loss, since he should have left his job before getting forced out, if a gain was available. The loss will constitute a fraction of the achievement of the job left, and the increment in return on resources will be zero:

$$\Delta X_1'' = -d_1 X_{11} + 0 \cdot X_2 + d_0$$

or   (13.3)

$$X_{12} = (1 - d_1) X_{11} + 0 \cdot X_2 + d_0$$

The parameter d_1 measures how far down the occupational ladder a person will have to go in order to find a vacant job. This parameter then is determined by the distribution of vacancies according to occupational achievement.

In the general situation a person will have some degree of control, c, that may be assumed to vary between 0 and 1. The expected outcome of the job shift can now be written as:

$$\Delta X_1 = (1 - c) \Delta X'^L + c \Delta X'$$

or (13.4)

$$\Delta X_1 = (1 - c)(d_1 X_{11} + d_0) + c(a_2 X_2 + a_0)$$

that may be written as:

$$\Delta X_1 = b_1 X_{11} + b_2 X_2 b_0 \tag{13.5}$$

where $b_1 = (1 - c) d_1 \leqq 0$

and $b_2 = c \cdot a_2 \geqq 0.$

As a person gains control over the decision to leave his job the coefficient b_1 gets closer to zero and the coefficient b_2 approaches its maximum a_2. In this way characteristics of the occupational structure will have an impact on the outcome of the job shift and therefore on the achievement process that is a succession of job shifts.

Those who responded to the life history study were asked about every job in their employment history whether they left it voluntarily or not. This information offers an opportunity to test the above ideas, although the validity and the reliability of the item may be less than desirable. First we may test whether job shifts where the individual had control, result in a gain, as argued above.[4] All job shifts undertaken by all respondents in the national samples were divided into two groups according to stated control,[5] to produce Table 13.1.

The overall gain in achievement is obtained by weighting prestige and income gains by canonical weights obtained from an analysis of simultaneous gains in prestige and income (see Sørensen, 1972b, for detail). This measure of

---

[4] Prestige is measured by a three-digit score on all census occupations obtained from the NORC Study (Siegel, 1971). Income is monthly earnings in the job price adjusted to the base 1957-1959 = 100.

[5] Deleted from the analysis were job shifts into and out of unemployment, and job shifts where there were periods of full-time schooling or military service in between the job left and the job entered. The 4,203 job shifts analyzed give an average of 4.3 shifts per respondent.

Table 13.1. Mean Prestige and Income and Mean Gains in Prestige and Income According to Stated Control over the Decision to Leave

	Own Decision	*Not Own Decision*
Mean prestige	336.59	388.35
Mean gain prestige	20.26	1.47
Mean income	397.96	378.79
Mean gain in income	28.39	-11.96
Mean occupational achievement	369.83	325.40
Mean gain in achievement	24.66	-5.80
N	3,179	689

Note: Occupational achievement computed as a weighted average of income and prestige with weights obtained from a canonical analysis.

achievement clearly shows the expected difference between those who said they had control and those who did not so claim.

The data also enable a test of the predictions concerning the behavior of b_1 and b_2 according to amount of control. A reformulation of Equation (13.1) is advantageous:

$$X_{12} = (1 + b_1) X_{11} + \sum_{i=2}^{n} b_i X_i + b_0 \qquad (13.6)$$

The reformulation permits us to have a set of independent variables rather than a single comprehensive one. Also, the parameter $(1 + b_1)$ will vary as b_2 according to control over the decision to leave. This means that we may use the amount of variance explained by Equation (13.6) to test our predictions, i.e., as $(1 + b_1)$ and b_2 increases with amount of control so will the amount of variance explained by X_{11} and resource variables X_i's increase[6] (see Table 13.2).

The test seems satisfactory: there is a clear difference in R^2's between the two groups.

Table 13.2. Amount of Variance Explained (R^2) by Prestige and Income of Job Left and Resources, by Stated Control over the Decision To Leave Job

	Prestige Equations	*Income Equations*
Own decision	0.467	0.504
Not own decision	0.366	0.416

---

[6] The resource variables are those presented in Tables 13.3 and 13.4.

CAREER PATTERNS

We have shown how the outcome of job shifts is a function of a person's level of resources and the impact of structural characteristics that affect the level of control a person has on job transitions. Successive outcomes of job shifts constitute a person's occupational career. How the structural and individual characteristics determine the career through their impact on the outcome of job shifts can be seen by solving the difference Equation (13.1).[7] This is possible if we assume that a person's level of resources does not change over time, that is, we assume that job shifts are a response to only opportunity. The solution depends on the value of b_1. If $b_1 = 0$ we get

$$X_{1r} = X_{10} + r(b_2 X_2) \tag{13.7}$$

when X_{1r} is the achievement of job number r and X_{10} is the achievement of the first job. If $b_1 \neq 0$ we get

$$X_{1r} = (1 + b_1)^r \left(X_{10} + \frac{b_2}{b_1} X_2\right) - \frac{b_2}{b_1} X_2 \tag{13.8}$$

The form of the resulting career pattern[8] depends on the value of b_1. A value of $b_1 > 0$ is unreasonable since it implies that every job shift results in a greater gain than the achievement of the job left. A value of $b_1 < -1$ is also unreasonable since the resulting career line will be oscillating. In the situation $-1 < b_1 < 0$ the career line will be a concave curve gradually approaching an equilibrium (see Figure 13.1). The equilibrium value equals

$$X_{1e} = -\frac{b_2}{b_1} X_2 \tag{13.9}$$

The approach to equilibrium is faster, the closer b_1 is to -1. If $b_1 = -1$ the career line will be flat, parallel to the X-axis; no increase in achievement takes

---

[7] The model for careers that is given as a solution to Equation (13.1) is the topic of another paper (Sørensen, 1972b) and more fully treated there.

[8] Equation (13.8) gives the career as a function of job number. There is a remarkable regularity in the relationship between age and frequency of job shifts. This regularity may be embodied in an expression that gives the relation between job number and age (see Sørensen, 1972b, for detail). The career in age will be given as:

$$X_{1t} = (1 + b_1)^{\frac{1}{\gamma}(1 - e^{-\gamma t})} \left(X_{10} + \frac{b_1}{b_2} X_2\right) - \frac{b_1}{b_2} X_2$$

where γ is a parameter that measures the impact of age on the frequency of job shifts. There will still be an approach to equilibrium in age, although more complicated, and the age profile will have the same general form as that produced by Equation (13.8).

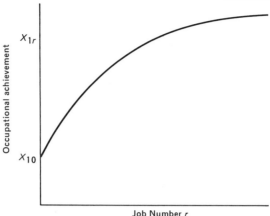

**Figure 13.1. Expected Occupational Achievement by Job Number for the
Situation When b_1 of Equation (13.8) is Less than Zero and Greater than -1.**

place. This contrasts to the other extreme when $b_1 = 0$ and every job shift
produces a gain in achievement.[9]

The impact of b_1 on the career pattern corresponds well to what should be
expected from the interpretation of b_1 given earlier. If $b_1 = 0$ every job shift
produces a gain. This would be a situation where there, in fact, are unlimited job
opportunities. Unlimited opportunities would mean many vacancies with little
demand for them. There would therefore be no pressure on individuals to leave
jobs, and people would have full control over their decision to leave. Estimates
of b_1 from job shifts taking place in such an occupational structure would
therefore give the expected value $b_1 = 0$.

The situation where $b_1 = -1$ is one where there are no opportunities for
gains in achievement. This implies that nobody should undertake job shifts
voluntarily. Job shifts that do take place in such a structure are therefore a result
of being pushed out of jobs and b_1 would be estimated as -1.

The general situation $-1 < b_1 < 0$ means that there are some opportunities
for improvement in achievement, but that they are finite. As the respondent
takes advantage of these opportunities his career will stabilize. The form of the
resulting career line is exactly as predicted by human capital theory, but for very
different reasons.

Human capital theory, it will be recalled, predicts career curves concave to
the X-axis as a result of investments after entry into the labor force—these

---

[9] Even when $b_1 = 0$, there still will be an approach to an equilibrium but produced by age
only. Inserting the relationship between age and the frequency of job shifts used in footnote
(8) into Equation (13.7) we get:

$$X_{1t} = X_{10} + \frac{1}{\gamma}(1 - e^{-\gamma t}) b_2 X_2$$

investments being undertaken at a declining rate as the individual gets older. It is argued that if there are no investments and hence no additions to a person's level of resources, the curve would be flat. Human capital theory in fact assumes an occupational structure that could be characterized by a $b_1 = -1$. All variations in achievement are caused by changes in levels of resources; the human capital theory does not allow for opportunities to improve achievement without changes in resources.

Empirically observed career curves have the general concave form (shown by Blum and Coleman, 1970, for the life history data). This would be explained by the career model developed here as a reflection of the existence of opportunities for gains in achievement without preceding changes in resources. The human capital theory on the other hand would explain it as a reflection of changes in resources only, that takes place in an efficient job market. The existence of concave curves clearly is no indication of which theory in fact is the valid one—the same pattern can be predicted from both theories on very different grounds.

It may be admitted that human capital theory would allow for other factors in addition to individual resources that influence earnings. What they do ignore is that the existence of structurally created opportunities, rather than being a random influence on achievement, will have a systematic impact on the age variation in achievement. This impact, furthermore, is identical to the one predicted as due to investments in on-the-job training and the like.

This section and the preceding one have attempted to develop a model for the occupational achievement process that embodies some of the features that are necessary for the development of a comprehensive theory of the occupational achievement process. A simple difference equation that gives the outcome of a job shift as a function of the achievement of the job left and a person's level of resources, is the fundamental equation of this model. The interplay between structural characteristics and individual attributes can be specified in this equation, as the magnitude of the coefficients of this equation is determined by a person's level of control over the job shift. The level of control in turn may be seen as reflecting the impact of structural constraints caused by the level of employment and the distribution of job opportunities.

The job shift may be a response to either a prior increase in the level of personal resources through additional training or education; and it may be a response to a structurally given opportunity for an increase in resources without a prior change in resources. Assuming that resources in fact remain constant throughout the individual's career it was possible to solve the fundamental difference equation to give the career line as a function of a person's job number. As just shown, the behavior of the solution reflects the interplay between structural characteristics and individual attributes in a way consistent with the interpretation given to the fundamental equation.

The career line predicted from the job shift model under the assumption of unchanged resources is the same form as the career line predicted from a human capital theory that explains all changes in achievement with changes in resources. It is therefore not fruitful to use the overall career patterns as data in an analysis that would attempt to specify the extent to which structural opportunities rather than changes in resources are responsible for the achievement process. To carry out such an analysis we need to return to the basic difference equation and analyze the outcome of the job shifts carried out by our sample. The next section will give an analysis of the outcome of job shifts using the basic Equation (13.6) in an attempt to establish what in fact are the mechanisms that produce career lines.

ANALYSIS OF RETURNS TO JOB SHIFTS

The life history data provide us with a variety of data on respondents' background and achievements. From these data variables may be formed that can act as independent variables in Equation (13.6), and with income and prestige of the job entered as dependent variables. A detailed analysis of all job shifts, irrespective of when they occur is carried out elsewhere (Sørensen, 1972b). The result of this analysis shall be briefly summarized in the first part of this section in order to give a background for an analysis that more directly relates to the problem discussed in this paper.

The average job shift produces a gain of 18 prestige points or 5.5 percent of the average prestige of the job left, 325 points. The standard deviation of the prestige of the job left is 134 points; for the prestige of the job entered it increases to 138 points. For income, the mean monthly income of the job left is $391.84 with a standard deviation of $220. The average job shift causes this income to increase by $19.23 or 4.9 percent, and the standard deviation is increased by $12 to $232. Taken together this means that as a person passes through job shifts, the achievement level will increase on the average and the variance between persons in achievement will increase, especially the variance in income. The variance in achievement is a measure of inequality in achievement so that we find that as our cohort gets older the level of achievement increases, but also the inequality of prestige and income increases.

The gains in achievement are related to a person's background and achievements as shown in Table 13.3.

Education is the dominant resource variable for gains in both prestige and income. The other variables all have a relatively modest contribution that should, however, be evaluated in light of a substantial collinearity among the variables. The collinearity is highest among the three variables, calendar year, labor-force experience, and age. Labor-force experience is measured as the amount of time spent in the labor force before the job shift occurs and may be

Table 13.3. Summary of Regression of Gains in Prestige and Income on Characteristics of the Job Holder

		Standardized Regression Coefficients		
Independent Variable		*Prestige t-Value*		*Income t-Value*
Prestige of job				
left (X_{11})	0.396	27.97	0.577	48.59
Education	0.224	12.13	0.079	5.03
Labor-force experience	0.061	2.23	0.053	4.22
Father's prestige	0.067	5.01	0.050	3.48
Verbal ability	0.075	4.82	0.032	2.50
Marital status	0.049	3.69	0.027	2.08
Race	0.054	3.52	0.020	1.67
Mother's education	−0.012	−0.81	−0.010	−0.79
Number of siblings	−0.011	−0.74	−0.007	−0.48
Father's education	−0.008	−0.55	−0.001	−0.05
Age	0.017	0.46	0.025	0.77
Calendar year	0.050	1.83	0.089	5.03
R^2		0.454		0.491
N = 4,203				

interpreted to reflect skills and experiences acquired in jobs. Calendar year is the year in which the job shift took place. Its effect reflects the impact of an overall expansion of the economy in the period lived through by our cohort, insofar as this expansion is linear. Age in itself does not appear to have an impact on the outcome of the job shift. What might be observed as aħ effect of age if this variable had been alone in the equation is thus due to experience and the economic conditions when the job shift took place (especially for income gains).

The partial effect of marriage means that married respondents (*ceteris paribus*) gain more in job shifts than unmarried respondents. This may signify the blessings of marriage but probably also reflects unmeasured ability differences not picked up by other individual characteristics. The effect of verbal ability reflects ability not translated into educational attainments; the same interpretation may be given to the effect of family background as measured by father's prestige. This is the only family background variable that is significant, but the collinearity among these variables again is of importance.

Race has only a modest effect on prestige gains and no significant effect on income gains. This is in contrast to the finding in an analysis of the determinants of the frequency of job shifts when it was found that black-white differences were substantial (Sørensen, 1972a). While blacks are less likely to shift jobs than whites (*ceteris paribus*), the outcome of these shifts is not much affected by a unique effect of race.

The effect of the prestige and income of the job left measures the term $(1 + b_1)$ in Equation (13.6). The parameter b_1 is hence -0.59 for prestige and -0.39 for income. According to the model for job shifts presented above, the size of b_1 reflects the amount of control and the distribution of job opportunities [d_1 of Equation (13.3)]. Measurement error producing a regression toward the mean is also of importance for the size of b_1. It is not possible to identify precisely these three sources of variation. The difference between prestige and income in the size of b_1 is therefore difficult to interpret.[10] However, the overall magnitude does indicate some control over the decision to leave in the average job shift.

The coefficients to the various resource variables, except labor-force experience, represent increments in returns on these resources. They are different from the returns dealt with in human capital theory. Returns could be measured by the regression coefficients to the resources with the *level of achievement*, that is the prestige and income at a point in time, not the growth in these quantities, as the dependent variable. The coefficients presented in Table 13.3 in contrast are increases in the rates of returns. Increments in returns are not dealt with in human capital analysis; rather all growth, as described above, is attributed to changing resources.   .

The increments in returns on resource variables can be explained by the model for job-shifts as reflecting the existence of career opportunities that enable a person to increase the return on his resources. If the coefficients in Table 13.3 are constant in age, and if the level of resources is unchanged after entry in the labor force, we would predict the career line shown in Figure 13.1. This career line would be the same as the one predicted by human capital analysis, but there predicted under the assumption of changing resources. Changing resources would produce positive coefficients to resource variables proportional to the amount of change in these variables. But we have observed significant coefficients to resource variables such as family background, education, and ability that do not change after entry into the labor force. The results presented in Table 13.3 thus seem to indicate that at least a substantial part of the increase in prestige and income after entry into the labor force cannot be explained by the human capital theory. The exception is the contribution of labor force experience to gains in achievement that best can be interpreted as reflecting an increase in experience and training between job shifts. Labor force experience is however far from being the dominant resource variable.

---

[10] It can be argued with support in Table 13.3 that there is a systematic bias in the income reporting so that earnings are given as too consistent across jobs. This explanation would account for the smaller amount of variance explained by resources for income gains and for the difference in b_1's (see Sørensen, 1972a, for details).

The above conclusion is based on the analysis of all job shifts irrespective of the age at which they occur. The result may conceal an age variation in the increments of return that would modify the above conclusion. If the effect of labor-force experience increases with age, while the increment in return on the resources determined before entry into the labor force decreases, this would be evidence that investment behavior is of increasing importance for the career. Table 13.4a and 13.4b therefore gives an analysis of gains in job shifts in three age groups determined from the age of the job holder when engaging in the shifts.

To enable comparisons across age groups, unstandardized regression coefficients are given. For prestige gains an increase in the coefficients of resource variables can be detected from the youngest to the middle age group, while the coefficients remain constant from the middle to the oldest age group. The exception to the general pattern is race. The difference between blacks and whites in prestige gains per job shift decreases with age. As mentioned above, the frequency of job shifts is lower for blacks, and we are dealing with a difference in *gains* so this result does not imply a decreasing difference in average

Table 13.4a. Regression of Gains in Prestige per Job Shift on Individual Characteristics in Three Age Groups

Independent Variable	Raw Regression Coefficients Age Group		
	I	*II*	*III*
Prestige of job left	0.261[a]	0.372[a]	0.515[a]
Education	12.21[a]	22.59[a]	20.39[a]
Verbal ability	2.72[a]	5.74[a]	5.40[a]
Labor-force experience	−0.01	0.04	0.25[a]
Father's prestige	0.65[a]	0.81[a]	0.65[a]
Marital status	2.07	17.79[a]	15.25[a]
Age	0.39[a]	0.21[a]	−0.16[a]
Race	27.43[a]	18.15[a]	11.42[a]
Size of household	−3.15[a]	−0.28	0.18
Number of siblings	0.35	−1.35[a]	−1.25[a]
Mother's education	0.22	5.92[a]	3.67[a]
Father's education	2.69	−0.78	−2.72[a]
Calendar year	0.24	0.40	0.05
Mean gain in prestige	18.88	18.95	14.52
R^2	0.24	0.39	0.53

Note: Mean age in age groups 20, 25, and 33 years, respectively.

[a]Significant at 0.05 level.

Table 13.4b. Regression of Gains in Income per Job Shift on Individual Characteristics in Three Age Groups

Independent Variable	Raw Regression Coefficients Age Group		
	I	II	III
Income of job left	0.372[a]	0.655[a]	0.628[a]
Education	7.004[a]	8.015[a]	13.080[a]
Verbal ability	0.870	4.195[a]	11.401[a]
Labor-force experience	0.498	0.090	0.592[a]
Father's prestige	0.196	0.148	1.323[a]
Marital status	11.340[a]	25.209[a]	44.145[a]
Calendar year	1.267	3.591[a]	5.155[a]
Race	17.182[a]	22.882[a]	−1.188
Age	0.015	0.028	−0.023
Size of household	−1.278	1.294	7.151[a]
Number of siblings	2.094[a]	−0.536	−1.680
Mother's education	2.843	−2.315	3.267
Father's education	1.940	1.102	6.108[a]
Mean gain in Income ($)	15.84	16.32	27.36
R^2	0.22	0.43	0.50

[a]Significant at 0.05 level.

achievement level. Quite to the contrary, the implication is that the difference in prestige level is increasing.

The increase of the coefficients to resources for income gain continues through all three age groups. The increase is substantial for the three major resource variables—education, fathers' prestige, and verbal ability. The increment in return on education is thus almost twice as large in the oldest age group as in the youngest.

The change in coefficients presented in Table 13.3 does not conform to the pattern one would expect if investment behavior was the major source of growth in achievement. We do not find a reduction in the increments in return on such resource variables as education, ability, and family background that are determined prior to entry into the labor force. The exception is a constant (for income gains) or increasing (for prestige gains) coefficient to labor-force experience that can be interpreted as reflecting investment behavior. However, inspection of the standardized regression coefficients (not presented) shows that labor-force experience never attains a dominant influence on the gain. Unfortunately, the high collinearity between the three time measures does depress the coefficients to all of them. It does not seem likely however that the above conclusion would be altered had this collinearity not existed. Collinearity seems responsible for the somewhat irregular pattern for the various measures of family background.

The overall gain for job shift is roughly constant for prestige and increasing for income. Had all coefficients been constant in age we would have expected a decrease in the overall gain since job holders would be approaching their equilibrium value of achievement as they get older. The fact that the gains are not decreasing might reflect investment behavior as job shifts then would occur only after a certain increment in resources. However, the above results concerning the behavior of the coefficients to resources and the pattern of the overall gain can both be explained by the model for job shifts without recourse to an explanation in terms of investment behavior. It will be noted that R^2's increase with age for both prestige and income gains. According to our model this can be interpreted as indicating an increase in the amount of control for job transitions. Also the pattern of the coefficients to the achievement of the job left [equal to $1 + b_1$ of Equation (13.6)] supports this conclusion. Hence, although we will not deny that an increase in resources may have contributed to the increase in gains, an increase in the amount of control appears operative and to be the most parsimonious explanation.

The above results are obtained on job shifts and could lead to misleading conclusions if interpreted as reflecting age variation in increments of returns per unit time. The frequency of job shifts is strongly dependent on age and Table 13.5a and 13.5b therefore gives the increment in returns for unit time. Thus,

Table 13.5a. Increment in Returns in Prestige per Month in Three Age Groups

Independent Variable	Raw Regression Coefficients Age Group		
	I	*II*	*III*
Prestige of job left	0.019	0.017	0.015
Education	0.907	1.022	0.593
Verbal ability	0.202	0.260	0.157
Labor-force experience	−0.007	0.002	0.007
Father's prestige	0.048	0.037	0.019
Marital status	0.154	0.805	0.444
Age	0.029	0.010	−0.005
Race	2.038	0.821	0.332
Size of household	−0.235	−0.013	0.005
Number of siblings	0.026	−0.061	−0.036
Mother's education	0.016	−0.268	0.107
Father's education	0.199	−0.037	−0.079
Calendar year	0.018	0.018	0.001
Average gain in prestige	1.40	0.86	0.42
Average duration of job (in months)	13.46	22.16	34.38

Table 13.5b. Increments in Returns in Income per Month in Three Age Groups

Independent Variable	Raw Regression Coefficients Age Group		
	I	*II*	*III*
Income of job left	0.028	0.030	0.018
Education	0.520	0.362	0.380
Verbal ability	0.065	0.189	0.332
Labor-force experience	0.037	0.004	0.017
Father's prestige	0.015	0.007	0.038
Marital status	0.843	1.138	1.284
Calendar year	0.094	0.162	0.150
Race	1.276	1.033	−0.035
Age	0.001	0.001	−0.001
Size of household	−0.095	0.058	0.208
Number of siblings	0.156	−0.024	−0.049
Mother's education	0.211	−0.104	0.093
Father's education	0.144	0.050	−0.177
Average gain in income ($)	1.18	0.736	0.796

coefficients are obtained simply by dividing the increments per job shifts by the average duration of jobs.

As would be expected there is an overall decrease in the increments per unit time for the returns on a person's resource. This result is still consistent with our previous analysis. It indicates a gradual approach to an equilibrium level of occupational achievement that is produced by an exhaustion of opportunities for gains as predicted by the career model of Equation (13.8) in combination with the impact of age on the frequency of job shift.

We have shown that throughout the part of the career covered with our sample, a major portion of the increase in achievement can be explained as a result of increments in return on resources rather than by increases in levels of resources brought about by investments in human capital. The increments in return we explain by the existence of career opportunities that are created by the structure of the labor market. One might object to this conclusion that we have only rather poor measures of investments after entry into the labor market. It is argued in human capital theory that the frequency of investments correlate with ability since returns are higher for those with greater ability (Becker, 1964). Unmeasured investment would therefore show up as increasing returns on measured resource variables conforming to our results. Also part of the increments in return could be explained as due to earnings and prestige foregone in the job left and as a result of training. These are possible alternative explanations, but it seems unlikely that we would have to completely reject the previous analysis as a result. Further research with direct measurement of investment behavior is needed. We shall however proceed and discuss some implications of the previous results assuming that the parsimonious explanation given in terms of the model for job shifts will retain its validity as a model for one important mechanism in the achievement process.

CONCLUSION

We have presented two alternative, although not mutually exclusive, viewpoints, on the growth in occupational achievement after entry into the labor force. Human capital theory explains such growth as resulting from changes in a person's level of resources due to on-the-job training experience and so forth. The social mobility approach sees changes in achievement as a result of job opportunities which allow for gains in prestige and income without changes in levels of personal resources. We have shown through a model for career lines that the structural opportunities will have a systematic impact on the age profile of earnings and prestige as the person gradually approaches his equilibrium level of achievement. This age profile has the same form as the one predicted in human capital theory. The age variation in prestige and income therefore cannot in itself be taken as evidence for investment in human capital after entry into the labor force, nor can it of course be used to claim the exclusive operation of structural opportunities.

The empirical analysis of the outcome of job shifts gave evidence for the operation of changes in level of resources and opportunity as a source of variations in achievement. Furthermore, although definite evidence has not been given due to our rather poor measure of change in resources after entry into the labor force, our result strongly indicates that a major part of the age variation in achievement is due to mobility to better jobs that increases the return on a given level of resources rather than being a result of increases in resources. Returns on a person's background, ability, and major investment (education), are therefore obtained gradually through age; that is, we have shown that in all age groups there is a positive *increment* in the returns on a person's major resource variables.

The increments in returns on major resource variables signify that the assumption of an efficient labor market made in human capital analysis is an unrealistic one. More important it is a misleading assumption. Labor market inefficiencies have a systematic impact on the career pattern that results in an age pattern the same form as the one predicted from human capital theory by investments in on-the-job training. Our result thus points to a necessary modification of human capital theory.

Structural opportunities also produce increments in return on the background characteristics that are such an important topic in the status attainment literature. This means that the estimates of effect of background variables on achievement obtained from cross-sectional data will be influenced by the age distribution of the sample as well as by characteristics of the occupational-industrial structure in the periods in which respondents achieved their status. The confounding of the effects of age and structure in cross-sectional data obviously do present difficulties in identifying sources of variation in the parameters of the status attainment models.

Our analysis points to two alternative policy instruments for affecting the occupational achievement of a population group. A policy that affects the distribution of personal resources is one such instrument and the existence of education and training programs obviously testifies to the recognition of such an instrument. However our analysis indicates that the results of such programs are determined by structural forces that determine the return on training, education, and other personal resources. Evaluation of a policy to affect resource distribution therefore needs to take into account the labor market conditions that determine the result of these programs. Policies that affect the structure of the labor market are themselves alternatives to those affecting resource distributions. Such policies may affect the occupational achievement resulting from a given level of personal resources.

That policies that affect the occupational structure as well as policies that affect individual characteristics are possible instruments for affecting occupational achievement is of course well known. The contribution of an analysis like the one given here lies in its attempt to specify the interplay between structural and individual characteristics in producing achievement. The model for job shifts presented above is a step toward obtaining measures of the influence of the occupational structure on the return on personal resources. The model should be extended to take explicitly into account changing resources.[11] The parameters of such a revised model would constitute indicators of the occupational achievement process that seem superior to the simple return rates that are obtained from the status attainment literature and human capital theory.

Measures of the extent to which job shifts are a response to prior increases in personal resources or responses to structural opportunities, and measures of the extent to which individuals have control over their job shifts, would constitute social indicators of both analytic and policy relevance. Such measures have been obtained in this analysis using retrospective life history data. For the systematic and continuous collection of such indicators, the use of life history data covering many years of a person's existence may present a number of problems. Fortunately, however, it is not necessary to collect retrospective

---

[11] By adding an equation to Equation (13.1) that gives the change in resources as a function of the job left and then try to solve this system of equations.

life histories that cover many years of a person's existence to obtain the desired measures.

We have analyzed every job shift undertaken by the respondents as a separate event. Hence, there is in fact no need to have a data base that consists of continuous observations on the same individuals. Only information on a job shift is needed. Such data could be obtained from a cross-sectional sample survey where respondents were asked to report on the job shifts they might have undertaken, say within the last year. Information on the outcome of the job shift, the level of resources prior to the shift, and the possible changes in these resources (through additional training and education) would enable us to give the desired measures.

We regularly obtain detailed information on the employment situation for different population groups, for different regions, and for different industries and occupations. This information has a variety of uses, but in itself it only constitutes measures on one particular "job shift," the shift to unemployment. Data on job shifts in general could provide a much more comprehensive picture on the workings of the labor market in determining individual control on their careers and hence the returns they obtain on their ability, schooling, and other investments.

REFERENCES

Anderson, C. Arnold.
  1961   "A skeptical note on the relation of vertical mobility to education." American Journal of Sociology 66.
Becker, Gary S.
  1964   Human Capital. New York: National Bureau of Economic Research.
Ben-Porath, Yoram.
  1967   "The production of human capital and the life cycle of earnings." Journal of Political Economy (August).
Blau, Peter M., and Otis Dudley Duncan.
  1967   The American Occupational Structure. New York: Wiley.
Blum, Zahava D., and James S. Coleman.
  1970   "Longitudinal effects of education on the incomes and occupational prestige of blacks and whites." Report No. 70. Baltimore, Md.: Center for Social Organization of Schools, The Johns Hopkins University.
Coleman, James S.
  1968   "The mathematical study of change." In H. M. Blalock, Jr., and A. B. Blalock (eds.), Methodology, in Social Research. New York: McGraw-Hill.
Duncan, Otis Dudley.
  1966   "Methodological issues in the analysis of social mobility." In N. J. Smelser, and S. M. Lipset (eds.), Social Structure and Mobility in Economic Development. Chicago: Aldine.

Griliches, Zvi.
1970   "Notes on the role of education in production functions and growth accounting." In W. Lee Hansen (ed.), Education, Income and Human Capital. New York: National Bureau of Economic Research.
Kahl, Joseph A.
1957   The American Class Structure. New York: Holt, Rinehart and Winston.
Mincer, J.
1970   "Distribution of labor incomes: A survey." Journal of Economic Literature, 8:1-26.
Sheldon, Eleanor Bernert, and Kenneth C. Land.
1972   "Social reporting for the 1970's." Policy Sciences (Summer).
Siegel, Paul M.
1971   "Prestige in the American occupational structure." Ph.D. dissertation, University of Chicago.
Sørensen, Aage B.
1971   "The occupational mobility process: An analysis of occupational careers." Ph.D. dissertation, The Johns Hopkins University, Baltimore, Md.
1972a   "The organization of activities in time." Center for Demography and Ecology, The University of Wisconsin-Madison, Working paper 72-1, Madison, Wis.
1972b   "A model for occupational careers." Paper presented at the session on Mathematical Sociology, at the 1972 meeting of the American Sociological Association, New Orleans, August 28-30.
White, Harrison C.
1970   Systems Models of Mobility in Organizations. Cambridge, Mass.: Harvard University Press.

14

MODELS INVOLVING SOCIAL INDICATORS OF POPULATION AND THE QUALITY OF LIFE

David D. McFarland

The word "model" is an ambiguous one, with many different meanings, as has been pointed out by Brodbeck (1959). Unfortunately, instead of clearing up the resulting confusion, she managed only to exacerbate it somewhat by introducing yet another usage of "model" to accompany the various usages she had identified in previous literature. The fact that Land (1971a) considered it worthwhile to write a paper on the definition of "social indicators" seems to suggest the existence of terminological confusion in that area as well.

Perhaps then it is not surprising that a conference on "social indicator models" would bring together authors holding several different notions of what is a social indicator model. Thus it may be useful to begin by specifying how we shall use the term "social indicator models" and how our usage differs from that of some other authors in this volume or in the related literature.

A "social indicator model" might be a type of social indicator which is a model for social indicators in general, in the sense of being prototypical or exemplary. Davis, in Chapter 4 of this volume, seems to view the various indices of political tolerance, and change over time therein, in this manner.

A "social indicator model" might be a set of schematic plans about how social indicators should be developed, in much the same sense that a collection of miniature houses and trees in an architect's studio constitutes a model of an as yet unbuilt housing development. Land's paper (1971a) on social indicators as components of social system models and Duncan's work (1969; and for this volume) on social reporting via replication of base-line studies are both of this type.

A "social indicator model" might be a contentless general purpose data analysis procedure such as the general linear model (which includes regression and analysis of variance) or, as a multiplicative variant thereof has come to be called, the log linear model which is useful among others for manipulating raw data to yield social indicators. Chapter 4 by Davis and Chapter 6 by B. Duncan and Evers, in this volume, both include this usage of the term "model."

Or, finally, a "social indicator model" might be a type of mathematical model which warrants the modifier "social indicator" because it is a model of some phenomenon of social concern and, hence, of some phenomenon whose progress or lack thereof ought to be monitored by social indicators. Land (1971a), in his paper on the definition of social indicators, was concerned with this usage, citing as examples mathematical models of population growth (Keyfitz, 1968), divorce (Land, 1971b), and occupational attainment (Blau and Duncan, 1967), and mentioning the parameters of these models as possible social indicators.

The latter is the usage of "social indicator model" which will be followed herein. We shall consider some mathematical models of phenomena of social concern and set forth, in a tentative manner, some suggestions as to how these models might possibly benefit the development of social indicators for these phenomena.

However, although this constitutes some acceptance of Land's (1971a) position, that acceptance is only partial. One can certainly think of sociological variables which may be of interest as "social indicators" quite irrespective of their roles in any mathematical models. For example, no mathematical model comes to mind which incorporates "attitude toward women's work" as one of its parameters, but that in no way reduces its importance in any accounting of the state of our society. Nevertheless, since the present author is a specialist in mathematical models of social phenomena, the discussion below will almost entirely exclude those social indicators which are not related to mathematical models.

POSSIBLE BENEFITS FROM MATHEMATICAL MODELS

The uses to which mathematical models have been put in the social sciences, and the benefits to be obtained therefrom, are both numerous and varied, as they relate both to the collection and interpretation of data and to the development of theory (Charlesworth, 1963; Coleman, 1964: Chap. 1; Keyfitz, 1971; McFarland, 1971a). Mathematical models are used for systematically keeping track of and properly combining various numbers; for clarification of concepts; for demonstration that certain concepts are of limited utility; for axiomatic construction of indices; to demonstrate that certain indices do not in fact accomplish what they are purported to do; for clarification of substantive questions by showing that, as initially formulated, they do not have unique answers; to enable investigators to ask more complicated questions than could readily be formulated verbally; to provide guidance during the planning which precedes data collection; to aid in the discovery of structure in the empirical world; to help systematize comparisons between places or over time; to help distinguish between definitional relationships and empirical regularities; to deduce empirical propositions from substantive axioms, for either forecasting or testing purposes; for study of nonobvious relationships where the logic is tricky and strictly verbal treatment is prone to go astray; in lieu of experiments, to study the effect of changes in one variable with others held constant; to infer the values of quantities which are inconvenient, difficult, time consuming, or costly to measure directly; for relating observed data to latent or unobserved, and possibly unobservable, variables found in theories; to reveal formal analogies between apparently dissimilar phenomena; for checking the logic of the deductions in verbally formulated theories; to determine the viability of hypothetical social systems; to demonstrate that certain unobserved entities cannot possibly exist as hypothesized; and as a language for the statement of social science laws.

Although each of these uses to which mathematical models have been put is of some importance in sociology more generally, most of them have no immediately apparent bearing on issues concerning social indicators, and hence will not be considered herein. Those uses whose relevance to social indicators are most apparent are those concerned with concept formation and index construction, guidance in the planning of empirical studies and aid in the formulation of substantive questions, extraction of the effect of one variable from those of contaminating factors, and relating observed data to latent or unobserved variables.

It would be of benefit to the social indicators field if, on the negative side, the use of mathematical models should help to prevent the use of indices which are misleading, either in the sense of being prone to misinterpretation, or in the sense of not in fact doing what they are purported to do. As an example of the former, we shall use a mathematical model as an aid in arguing that for some purposes divorce rates are misleading. As an example of the latter, Blau and Duncan (1967: 90-97) demonstrated that a certain type of mobility index intended to "remove the effects of" the marginal totals in various origins and destinations did not in fact succeed in doing so. In this regard, however, as both these examples illustrate, a mathematical model may be more useful in pointing out the existence of a problem than in pointing out a way in which it may be resolved.

On the positive side, the use of mathematical models might suggest indicators one would not be likely to think of in the absence of a model, or those he might think of in a vague sense but would be at a loss to operationalize in the absence of a model. As an example of the former, we shall consider below various characteristics which pertain not to the observed population but to the population which would eventually develop were the observed vital rates to be continued indefinitely into the future; such concepts simply would not be thought of in the absence of a model to specify how the future population is affected by vital rates. As an example of the latter we shall consider isolating the effect of a single variable by removing the effects of contaminating factors; while this can easily enough be expressed in verbal form, it cannot be operationalized without a model, since one cannot remove the effects of contaminating factors in the absence of a model which tells the nature and magnitude of those effects. But models very frequently relate observed data to unobserved or unobservable "latent" or "intrinsic" parameters which are more easily interpreted than the observed data in that the effects of various contaminating factors, as specified in the model, have been removed.

With these preliminaries completed, we turn now to a discussion of mathematical models of several social processes which seem to be of social concern and which may be important for public policy considerations. In each case consideration will be given as to whether and how the model might be helpful in designing a social indicator which would be preferable to those which might be designed in the absence of the model.

POPULATION GROWTH

Population growth is certainly a process of social and policy concern, sufficiently so that we recently saw the completion of an extensive study by a presidential commission. It even approaches satisfaction of the very restrictive requirement in the Department of Health, Education, and Welfare (1969:97) definition, which states that a social indicator "is in all cases a direct measure of welfare and is subject to the interpretation that, if it changes in the 'right' direction, while other things remain equal, things have gotten better, or people are 'better off' "—although there is still somewhat less than complete consensus on the proposition that the "right" direction is that of decreasing population growth. Indeed, population growth is one of the specific social indicator content areas listed by Sheldon and Land (1972).

Demography is concerned with counts of vital events, such as births and deaths; and in the absence of migration, growth is simply the difference between those two. But mathematical models, ranging from the extremely simple to the quite complex, tell the demographer how to interpret such data, how to study relationships between variables, etc. The basic demographic model (see Stinchcombe, 1968) is one which decomposes the number of events occurring in a particular group as the product of the number of persons in that group and the rate of occurrence applicable to persons in that group; for the i-th group,

$$E_i = P_i R_i \tag{14.1}$$

where E denotes number of events, P denotes number of persons, and R denotes rate of occurrence, the subscript i denoting the i-th group in each case.

Ordinarily the number of people, P_i, and the number of events, E_i, will be directly observed, and Equation (14.1) serves as a definition of the rate, R_i. As a definitional statement, the decomposition in Equation (14.1) is neither true nor false; but it may be of greater or lesser usefulness depending upon the substantive context.

Specifically, such a decomposition will be of little use except in substantive contexts where it makes sense to assume that R_i and P_i vary independently; i.e., that the value of either may change without affecting the value of the other. In the case of demographic events, births and deaths, it usually makes substantive sense to assume that the vital rates vary independently of the numbers of persons at risk. (Exceptions include the sort of situation considered by Malthus, among others, where population size has increased to the limits of available resources and further increase in population would result in increased death rates.)

When it makes sense to assume that R_i and P_i vary independently, one can ask and answer questions about how the number of events would change if either the number of people or the applicable rate were to change while the other remained constant, thus performing a computation in lieu of an experiment. If, for example, a representative sample of group members were to leave the group by migration (the requirement of representativeness being redundant if groups were chosen so as to be internally homogeneous in the first place), this would affect the number of events (births, say, or deaths) solely through a change in the number of persons at risk without any changes in the rate. Thus if P_i' persons were to remain in the group while the others left, the number of events, instead of E_i, would then be:

$$E_i' = P_i' R_i \tag{14.2}$$

On the other hand, the availability of a new contraceptive technique or a new cure for a disease would bring about changes in the number of events (births and deaths respectively) solely through changing the rates, say from R_i to R_i'', without any changes in the number of persons at risk, P_i. The number of events, instead of E_i, would then be:

$$E_i'' = P_i R_i'' \tag{14.3}$$

The total number of events occurring to all groups is, from Equation (14.1):

$$E = \Sigma P_i R_i \tag{14.4}$$

and this, along with the total population size, $P = \Sigma\ P_i$, would constitute the raw data whose interpretation is required. The crude rate, $R = E/P$, is hardly ideal for policy considerations, since it is affected by migration in and out of the various groups:

$$R = E/P = \Sigma\ (P_i/P)\ R_i \qquad (14.5)$$

But this difficulty is overcome by reference to a hypothetical standard or base-line population whose distribution by groups is taken as a weighting, constant over time, applied to the changing rates:

$$R^* = \Sigma\ (P_i^*/P^*)R_i \qquad (14.6)$$

The choice of the P_i^*, the distribution among groups in the standard or base-line population, is somewhat arbitrary; but once they are selected they will be used repeatedly, in conjunction with differing sets of rates, to answer questions about the effects on the overall or crude rate of changes in or differences between regimes of group-specific rates.

This type of standardization is quite familiar to demographers, but perusal of the social indicators literature suggests that the sorts of things demographers take for granted are considerably more sophisticated than much of the discussion by others in the social indicators area, and that even demographers are at somewhat of a loss in dealing with "soft" concepts such as "people becoming better off."

But how should one go about choosing a particular hypothetical population for use as the standard of base-line? Again, a mathematical model is of some assistance. For some purposes one is interested in the effects which would be implied by continuation or a particular set of vital rates indefinitely into the future, and a mathematical model enables us to determine the stable distribution which would eventually result from continuation of the given vital rates indefinitely into the future, and the corresponding weights, P_i^*, to insert in Equation (14.6). The resulting standardized rate, R^*, is, in demographic terminology, an "intrinsic" rate.

Demographers commonly express the notion that intrinsic rates of birth, death, and natural increase [Equation (14.6), with weights according to the stable population which would result from indefinite continuation of current age-specific rates] are better than their crude rate counterparts [Equation (14.5), with weights according to the observed population]. The crude rates depend not only on prevailing fertility and mortality conditions, but also on a contaminating factor, namely the current age composition of the population. Intrinsic rates have that contamination removed.

This could not be done in the absence of a model of some sort: one cannot possibly "remove the effects of" a contaminating factor, in order to isolate the effects of primary concern, unless he has some sort of model which specifies just what those effects are—just how the contaminating factor interacts with the factors of interest to produce the observed data.

Stated differently, intrinsic rates, and stable populations which form their bases, are not the sorts of things which can be readily determined by scanning the observed data. On the contrary, they are obtained in a nonobvious manner by solving an integral equation, or by finding eigenvalues and eigenvectors of a matrix, the sorts of operations one would hardly think of performing on the data if he did not have a population growth model in mind.

One possible contribution mathematical models might make to the social indicators field is to get scholars in the latter field to begin thinking about developing social indicators which, like the intrinsic rates which arise in mathematical population models, have some of the contaminating factors removed from them.

But the jump from crude to intrinsic rates may turn out to be a premature and uncritical embracing of the results of mathematical models. The stable population, after all, is an *asymptotic* kind of entity, arising in the limit as *t*, time, approaches infinity. And even if convergence is rapid—a matter to be considered below—it might require the best part of a century to damp out most of the oscillations, since the lowest frequency oscillatory terms have a period of approximately the length of a generation (Keyfitz, 1972).

A number of serious scholars, and not just the crisis-mongers, have become impatient with asymptotic results. We will all be dead as *t* approaches infinity, while many population-related problems have come to have a sense of immediate urgency about them. And asymptotic results, including intrinsic rates, can be highly misleading if one's concern is mainly with the proximate future. The *immediate* effects of a change in rates from R_i to R_i' would be found by applying Equation (14.5) and not Equation (14.6), the appropriate weights being the current population numbers, not the numbers in some hypothetical, future, or asymptotic standard population.

If the argument in the preceding two paragraphs is valid, then we have found at least one instance where the investigator would be worse off studying parameters of elaborate mathematical models, and better off merely studying data which had been standardized in a much more straightforward manner. In any case, the argument has sufficient plausibility for us to exercise some caution when choosing parameters of mathematical models for use as social indicators.

OSCILLATIONS IN POPULATION GROWTH

The postwar baby boom has, at various life-cycle stages, met with a society which was unprepared to cope with its relatively large numbers. Public schools and colleges were caught first in a frantic rush to expand, followed by curtailment of growth or actual contraction, and this must be at least partially responsible for the current state of employment opportunities for teachers and professors, which is much less promising than that of a few years ago. The baby boom has played havoc in a similar manner with the labor market generally, and can be expected to affect various other institutions as it makes its way up through the various age categories.

The extent of the irregularity in the annual number of births over the past several decades in the United States is shown in Figure 14.1. Annual births rose steadily from around 2 million in 1930 to around 4¼ million in 1960, thereafter declining to the most recent figures of about 3¼ million in 1972.

Irregularities in the birth sequence, as shown in Figure 14.1, give rise to corresponding irregularities in the subsequent age distributions. Thus, for example, the 1970 census has a relatively large number in the 10-14 age group, the 1980 census will have a relatively large number in the 20-24 age group, etc., corresponding to the relatively large number of births between 1955 and 1960. Eventually such a relatively large cohort will disappear from mortality, but in the meantime it may produce another relatively large cohort of babies, an

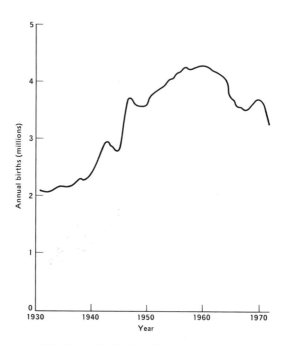

Figure 14.1. Annual Births in the United States since 1930.

"echo" of the original irregularity in the birth sequence. Indeed, the upturn in births during 1969 appears to be an "echo" of the sharp increase in births in 1947. The 1969 increase is not as steep as that of 1947, and such damping of irregularities is generally the case, since the fertility of any particular cohort, such as the one born in 1947, is spread over a number of years rather than being concentrated entirely at, say, age 22 (see McFarland, 1969).

While the prophets of doom have tended to concentrate solely on size and growth of population, it is coming to be recognized that at least some of the contemporary population problems stem not from size or growth per se, but from the irregular pattern according to which growth takes place, and from the resulting demands that our institutions alternate between rapid expansion and retrenchment (see Keyfitz, 1972).

In the remainder of this section we shall focus on the age distribution, rather than the birth sequence. We shall be interested in a method for assessing the degree of irregularity in an age distribution, and also the rapidity with which a regime of vital rates will damp out whatever age distribution irregularities it encounters.

Consider a population classified by age, ignoring the males in order to avoid complications which need not concern us here (McFarland, 1971b, 1972), letting P_i denote the number of persons (i.e., females) in the i-th age group at a particular point in time, written as $P_i(t)$ when clarity requires explicit mention of time. Let the unit of time be the same as the unit of age (e.g., five years), so that all the women who survive from one time point to the next also necessarily move from one age group to the next. Let s_i and f_i denote survival and fertility rates of the sort described in Equation (14.1), for events occurring between times t and $t + 1$. Then the recurrence relation between the population numbers at successive time points is conveniently expressed in terms of the Leslie matrix as follows:

$$
\begin{bmatrix}
P_1(t+1) \\
P_2(t+1) \\
P_3(t+1) \\
P_4(t+1) \\
\cdots
\end{bmatrix}
=
\begin{bmatrix}
f_1 & f_2 & f_3 & f_4 & f_5 & \cdots \\
s_1 & 0 & 0 & 0 & 0 & \cdots \\
0 & s_2 & 0 & 0 & 0 & \cdots \\
0 & 0 & s_3 & 0 & 0 & \cdots \\
\cdot\cdot & \cdot\cdot & \cdot\cdot & \cdot\cdot & \cdot\cdot & \cdots
\end{bmatrix}
\begin{bmatrix}
P_1(t) \\
P_2(t) \\
P_3(t) \\
P_4(t) \\
\cdots
\end{bmatrix}
\qquad (14.7)
$$

Note that the fertility rates. are all in the first row, since all babies will enter the youngest age group regardless of the ages of their mothers; and that the survival rates are directly below the main diagonal, thus taking account of the aging of those who survive. The same equation may be written in compact matrix notation as:

$$P(t + 1) = M P(t) \qquad (14.7a)$$

The matrix algebra of population projection is given extensive treatment in Keyfitz (1968: Chaps. 2-4); only a few essential concepts will be introduced here. Equations (14.7) and (14.7a) specify how the population projection matrix transforms an arbitrary vector, $P(t)$, whose entries are the numbers in the various age groups; but it is useful to consider the special case of a vector K whose numbers in the various age groups would all be changed by the same factor λ when it is transformed by the population projection matrix M, so that

$$M K = \lambda K \tag{14.8}$$

When Equation (14.8) holds we say that K is a right eigenvector of the matrix M and that λ is the corresponding eigenvalue.

With this notational machinery, we return to the substantive matter of demographic oscillations, and ask what sorts of social indicators might provide useful information about such oscillations. Two different questions come to mind: How far is the current population from one whose age distribution is such that it would grow in a smooth manner without oscillation? And how rapidly will current vital rates damp out the oscillations due to irregularities in the current age distribution?

The matrix M has exactly one positive real eigenvalue, λ_1, and its magnitude is no less than (and, in practice, strictly greater than) the magnitudes of the other eigenvalues, which are negative or complex. The corresponding right eigenvector, $K^{(1)}$, which is unique up to multiplication by a (real or complex) scalar, may be chosen in such a manner as to have only positive real entries. The eigenvalue and eigenvector may be interpreted as a growth ratio and as a vector giving the numbers in the various age groups for a population which would grow smoothly under the regime of vital rates specified in the matrix M. The remaining eigenvalues and eigenvectors, which generally involve negative or complex numbers, cannot be interpreted in such a manner, but instead pertain to oscillatory terms superimposed on the stable growth.

Consider now the possibility of defining a social indicator of the distance from the current population to one whose age distribution is such that it would grow in a smooth manner, "degree of irregularity" for short hereafter. My suggestion is that this involve a comparison between the current population vector $P(t)$ and one of the eigenvectors $K^{(1)}$ which would grow smoothly under prevailing vital rates. The latter is unique only up to multiplication by a scalar; and there exists a wide variety of alternative distance functions (McFarland and Brown, 1973); so there exists a certain amount of arbitrariness at this point.

Table 14.1 gives some numerical results for illustrative purposes, covering several different countries and years. In each case 12 age groups are considered (five-year intervals through age 54, plus a residual age group). Degree of

Table 14.1. Degree of Irregularity in Selected Age Distributions

Country, Year	Degree of Irregularity
United States	
1919-1921	19.3
1959-1961	19.5
1963	12.6
1964	10.0
Ireland	
1926	5.9
1960-1962	20.4
Honduras	
1959-1961	3.6
1965	7.1

Note: Observed and stable percentage distributions among age categories (five-year intervals through age 54, plus 55 and over) obtained from Keyfitz and Flieger (1968). "Degree of Irregularity" is calculated as sum of absolute values of discrepancies between corresponding percentages in the two distributions.

irregularity is calculated as the sum of absolute values of differences between corresponding entries of the current population vector and the appropriate eigenvector, with both converted to percentage distributions. Ireland in 1926, with a value of 5.9, had an age distribution quite similar to that which would grow smoothly under the then prevailing vital rates, with every age group growing by the same factor. By 1960-1962, however, both the observed and the stable age distributions (not shown here) had shifted, but in opposite directions, so that Ireland in 1960-1962 had too few under age 10 and too many over age 40 for the population to grow smoothly under the then prevailing vital rates, this discrepancy being reflected in the figure of 20.4 for the degree of irregularity. For the United States, the *degree* of irregularity is nearly the same in 1919-1921 and 1959-1961, but examination of the age distributions (not shown here) reveals that the nature of the irregularity had changed: in 1919-1921 there were too many young people for the population to grow smoothly, while in 1959-1961 there were too many older people for the population to grow smoothly.

Consider next the possibility of defining a social indicator of the rapidity with which prevailing vital rates would damp out any oscillations which did arise. (For an alternative approach to the same problem, based on the formulation in which time and age are continuous variables rather than discrete categories, see Keyfitz, 1972.) If the vital rates specified in the matrix M were to persist, the population after one time period would be determined by $M P(t)$, the population after two time periods would be determined by $M^2 P(t)$, and in general the population after n time periods would be determined by $M^n P(t)$. Thus the rapidity with which irregularities in the age distribution are damped out depends on what happens to the matrix M as it is raised to higher powers.

The answer comes from the spectral decomposition of higher powers of the population projection matrix (Keyfitz, 1968:63):

$$M^n/\lambda_1^n = K^{(1)}H^{(1)} + \sum_{i=2} (\lambda_i/\lambda_1)^n \, K^{(i)}H^{(i)} \tag{14.9}$$

From this decomposition it follows that after n time units, the population takes on an age distribution proportional to the dominant right eigenvector, $K^{(1)}$, except for oscillatory terms which are damped according to the factors $(\lambda_i/\lambda_1)^n$ These factors, as successively higher powers of quantities whose magnitudes are less than unity, converge to zero as n increases.

The damping for a particular term on the right of Equation (14.9) is slow or rapid depending on whether the ratio of magnitudes of the i-th and first eigenvalues, $|\lambda_i|/|\lambda_1|$, is near unity or substantially below unity. If the eigenvalues be indexed by decreasing magnitude, so that λ_2 is the second largest, then the ratio $|\lambda_2|/\lambda_1$ describes the damping rate of the most slowly damped terms on the right of Equation (14.9), and thus seems a prime candidate for a social indicator of the rate at which prevailing vital rates would damp out any age distribution irregularities they might encounter.

(Keyfitz considers an index which differs from ours, nor is his merely the continuous formulation analogue to our index which arose in the discrete formulation. The difference seems at least in part to be due to a difference in emphasis: he is concerned with damping of oscillations in the birth sequence, while we are concerned with damping of irregularities in the age distribution. See Keyfitz, 1972, for details on his index.)

Table 14.2 gives illustrative numerical values of the quantity we proposed as a social indicator of the rate at which prevailing vital rates would damp out any age distribution irregularities. Based on these few cases, it seems that the rapidity of damping differs from country to country much more than it differs from time to time within any one country. The vital rates of Honduras, in either year, are much more effective at damping out age distribution irregularities than are the vital rates of Ireland, while those of the United States are of intermediate effectiveness at damping out such irregularities.

We have suggested two different kinds of social indicators for describing two different aspects of oscillations in population growth, and have made some suggestions regarding the details of constructing each of them. In both cases, there has been a heavy reliance upon the mathematical model of population growth. Verbal discussion might suffice to propose that a particular phenomenon ought to be represented by a social indicator, and it also might suffice to interpret numerical values of the resulting social indicator. But the mathematical model seems indispensable at the intermediate stage, when one is trying to determine exactly how the desired social indicator should be constructed.

Table 14.2. Degree of Damping in Selected Vital Rates

Country, Year	Degree of Damping
United States	
1919-1921	0.771
1959-1961	0.768
1963	0.775
1964	0.776
Ireland	
1926	0.878
1960-1962	0.861
Honduras	
1959-1961	0.742
1965	0.742

Note: First two eigenvalues obtained from Keyfitz and Flieger (1968). "Degree of Damping" is calculated as the ratio of their absolute values. Notice that damping takes place most rapidly when "Degree of Damping" is considerably less than unity.

DIVORCE RATES AND CRIME RATES

There has been much public concern about an alleged "breakdown" of the family in general, a significant part of it addressed specifically to the observed increases in divorce rates. These matters have also received considerable attention from professional sociologists. Much of the writing in this area should be approached with skepticism if at all; for example, there is good reason to believe that what Goode has called the "Classical Family of Western Nostalgia" never actually existed in significant numbers (Coale et al., 1965; Goode, 1968:321-324). On the matter of divorces per se we are on rather more solid footing; empirical data from the United States and various other countries show significant increases in divorce rates over the past decade; in the United States the divorce rate has been steadily rising for 50 years, except for a dip during the midst of the depression and a sharp peak at the end of World War II (National Center for Health Statistics, 1970:Table 2, Figure 1). Thus this is a likely candidate for the development of social indicators.

Divorce is, in some respects, analogous to death. Married couples replace individuals as the units at risk, duration of marriage replaces age in the reckoning of time, and of course divorce replaces death as the event under consideration. The crude divorce rate, the ratio of the number of divorces during a year to the number of married couples at risk, is potentially misleading just as is the crude death rate. Divorces should be decomposed according to duration of marriage, just as deaths should be decomposed according to age.

Mathematical work along these lines has been carried out by Horvath and Foster (1963) and more recently by Land (1971b). Land's model treats different marriage cohorts separately, thus controlling for marriage duration. It incorporates two types of parameters, the transition intensity from marriage to divorce, and the proportion of the marriage cohort couples that will ultimately become divorced. These parameters could, as Land (1971a:324) states, in turn be related to various social processes, although it is not entirely clear that there would be any advantage in doing so. For example, one could relate these parameters to average age at marriage, as both vary from cohort to cohort; but there is no apparent reason to suppose that a change in average age at marriage would affect divorce frequencies solely through one of Land's parameters and leave the other unchanged, or that in some other respect such a change would relate more simply to his than to alternative parameterizations of the raw data on divorce frequencies by marriage cohort.

The analogy between divorce and death is by no means perfect. One difference, taken account of by Land, is that while all men—and women— are mortal, not all marriages end in divorce. One or other of the partners may die, thereby precluding the possibility of subsequent divorce. Thus divorce and death are "competing risks" as far as marital disruption is concerned, and I have suggested elsewhere that divorce might usefully be studied in terms of the models of deaths from various causes (Chiang, 1968), wherein a death from one cause deprives all the remaining causes of a potential victim.

The analogy suffers from a more fundamental defect, however, which relates to the Department of Health, Education, and Welfare (1969:97) definition of social indicators, which requires that if a social indicator changes in the right direction while other things remain equal, then people are better off. The expectation of life or some other suitably selected index summarizing mortality data would satisfy this definition, since it is an extremely rare individual who, given prevailing values, would be classified as "better off dead" in anything but a figurative sense. Herein lies the fundamental defect of the analogy between death and divorce: under currently prevailing values many couples *are* classified as "better off divorced."

In this regard the analogy is useful for the limited purpose of making the point that divorce, like death, plays a selection function, and is not solely a disruptive force. Mortality rates for infants are much higher than those for young children, and those for the first few hours or days after birth are particularly high. This does not mean that young children at home receive better care from their parents than the care which infants in a hospital receive from medical personnel; the key variable is the health of the children or infants, not the quality of the care they receive. The average child who survives past infancy is much healthier than the average newborn, precisely because the high death rate for infants has removed the weakest members of the cohort during their infancy.

A simplified mathematical argument will help to explain why this is the case. Consider a birth cohort composed of two types of babies, strong, n_s in number and each experiencing a monthly survival probability of p_s, and weak, n_w in number and each experiencing a monthly survival probability of p_w, with $p_w < p_s$. (The same conclusions will be valid if the strength variable admits more than two levels, but the exposition difficulty would be greatly increased without any corresponding improvements in insight into the substantive problem.) Initially the proportion of weak babies was

$$P_0 \text{ (weak)} = \frac{n_w}{n_w + n_s} \tag{14.10}$$

as a fraction of the total number of babies. Of these a fraction p_w survive the first month as do a somewhat larger fraction p_s of the strong babies. Thus after one month the proportion of weak babies is

$$P_1 \text{ (weak)} = \frac{n_w p_w}{n_w p_w + n_s p_s} = \frac{n_w}{n_w + k n_s} \text{ with } k = \frac{p_s}{p_w} > 1 \tag{14.11}$$

as a fraction of the total number of babies still alive after one month. This is a reduction in the proportion of weak babies, since the factor k makes the denominator of Equation (14.11) larger than that of (14.10) without any corresponding increase in the numerator.

In subsequent months mortality continues to reduce the ranks of the weak more than those of the strong, so that the average strength of those still alive increases as the cohort ages, although there is a deceleration in the rate of increase. It is in this sense that death provides a selection mechanism, whenever the initial population is heterogeneous (see McFarland, 1970, for a similar discussion of the effects of heterogeneity in social mobility).

The translation from deaths of babies to divorces of couples is straight-forward. Prevailing values admit the possibility of beneficial effects of divorce, although they are loathe to do so for death. But in that case, far from signaling the demise of the marriage institution, an increase in the number of divorces due to termination of marriages which are unhappy, or otherwise weak, would constitute a *strengthening* of the marriage institution by pruning its weaker parts.

Sociologists will recognize that there is some ambiguity in the definition which requires that "people" become better off when the value of a social indicator changes in the appropriate direction. "People" might mean individuals on whom data are aggregated to form an index; but "people" might alternatively mean the society in some collective sense which is not merely an aggregation of individual data. Indeed, one might argue that divorce is of no concern to the society, and hence not a proper subject for social indicators, except to the extent that it imposes costs on other members of society as well as imposing costs on the couples themselves. According to this viewpoint, it is these social costs, and not divorce rates per se, which should be summarized in social indicators.

But unhappy marriages as well as divorces impose costs on society: children from both unhappily married couples and divorced couples receive inadequate socialization in the home and create special problems for the schools, juvenile courts, etc; and society loses the productive efforts of a couple while they are preoccupied with their marital problems, whether or not the outcome is a divorce; etc. What we ideally should have is an index that summarizes the social costs arising from both types of marital difficulties, whether or not they lead to divorce.

Perhaps something can be learned here from an analogy with the social reporting of crime. Both crime and marital unhappiness are social problems whose measurement is problematic, although we would certainly be interested in knowing the magnitude, extent, and nature of each. But crime rates and divorce rates tell us about the *disposition* of these social problems—whether those involved decide to "report" the problems—and not about their magnitude or extent per se. The key to this methodological difficulty is that "changes in crime level may have been due in part to improved reporting procedures" (Biderman, 1966)—and analogously for the recent trend in divorce rates.

Here we can only conclude, along with Sheldon and Land (1972), that mathematical models, although sometimes helpful in clarifying the nature of the methodological difficulty, have little to offer toward its solution, and that the best way to proceed is to attempt to measure directly the extent of marital or criminal problems, as in crime victimization surveys, rather than in dealing with rates which depend upon both unmeasured magnitudes of the problems and unmeasured propensities to report these problems.

HEALTH, SICKNESS, HOSPITALIZATION, AND LONGEVITY

There is much more to "population and the quality of life" than can possibly be covered in a single chapter. Furthermore, many aspects of the quality of life have not yet been touched by mathematical modeling. Thus we shall omit amount of discretionary time, opportunities for travel, fine dining, etc., and numerous other aspects of "quality of life," and consider only one more, that having to do with such matters as health and longevity.

Mathematical models of competing risks (Chiang, 1968) have demonstrated that even age-specific or age-standardized mortality rates require some care in interpretation. An increase in deaths from heart disease or cancer at the older ages may indicate an *improvement* in health conditions, rather than a deterioration therein, since this result could be a consequence of decreases in the risk of mortality from infectious deseases at the younger ages.

Along similar lines, an increase in longevity is not necessarily an unmitigated blessing if it consists in part of artificially prolonging the lives, at least in the technical sense, of people who have degenerated to a state of illness from which the chance of recovery is negligible, or, at the aggregate level, if it increases the morbidity of the population with corresponding increases in both human misery and demand on the health care system.

Data on the health care system are, likewise, of ambiguous interpretation. An increase in the number of hospital patients may signal an increase in the amount of sickness, but it may be only the result of a Parkinsonian process whereby the definition of "need" is relaxed or tightened depending on the existence of slack in available resources.

The area of health and illness has not yet, at least to my knowledge, received much attention from mathematical model builders; for whatever reason, attention has focused more on deaths than on lives. One exception has been the mathematical study of epidemics (Bailey, 1957), but even there nothing like a comprehensive index of health is considered; the emphasis is on a single disease. Nevertheless, important problems of data interpretation exist in the area of health, and the development of mathematical models might turn out to be helpful in the attempt to design social indicators to monitor change in health conditions, as well as in other fields.

REFERENCES

Bailey, N. T. J.
  1957 The Mathematical Theory of Epidemics. London: Griffin.
Biderman, A. D.
  1966 "Social indicators and goals." In Raymond A. Bauer (ed.), Social Indicators. Cambridge, Mass.: Massachusetts Institute of Technology Press.
Blau, Peter M., and Otis Dudley Duncan.
  1967 The American Occupational Structure. New York: Wiley.
Brodbeck, M.
  1959 "Models, meaning, and theories." In L. Gross (ed.), Symposium on Sociological Theory. New York: Harper and Row.
Charlesworth, J. C. (ed.)
  1963 Mathematics and the Social Sciences. Philadelphia: American Academy of Political and Social Science.
Chiang, C. L.
  1968 Introduction to Stochastic Processes in Biostatistics. New York: Wiley.
Coale, A. J., L. A. Fallers, M. J. Levy, D. M. Schneider, S. S. Tomkins.
  1965 Aspects of the Analysis of Family Structure, Princeton, N. J.: Princeton University Press.
Coleman, James S.
  1964 Introduction to Mathematical Sociology. New York: Free Press.

Duncan, Otis Dudley.
   1969   Toward Social Reporting: Next Steps. (Social Science Frontiers, No. 2.) New York: Russell Sage Foundation.
Goode, W. J.
   1968   "The theory and measurement of family change." In Eleanor Bernert Sheldon and Wilbert E. Moore (eds.), Indicators of Social Change: Concepts and Measurements. New York: Russell Sage Foundation.
Horvath, W. J., and C. C. Foster.
   1963   "Mathematical theory of the dissolution of marriage by divorce." Unpublished manuscript, Mental Health Research Institute, University of Michigan.
Keyfitz, Nathan.
   1968   Introduction to the Mathematics of Population. Reading, Mass.: Addison-Wesley.
   1971   "Models." Demography 8:571-580.
   1972   "Population waves." In T. N. F. Greville (ed.), Population Dynamics. New York: Academic.
Keyfitz, Nathan, and W. Flieger.
   1968   World Population: An Analysis of Vital Data. Chicago: University of Chicago Press.
Land, Kenneth C.
   1971a   "On the definition of social indicators." American Sociologist 6 (November):322-325.
   1971b   "Some exhaustible poisson process models of divorce by marriage cohort." Journal of Mathematical Sociology 1 (July):213-232.
McFarland, David D.
   1969   "On the theory of stable populations." Demography 6:301-322.
   1970   "Intragenerational social mobility as a Markov process." American Sociological Review 35:463-476.
   1971a   "The role of mathematics in the recent development of sociology." Presented to the annual meeting of the American Association for the Advancement of Science, Philadelphia, December 26-31.
   1971b   "A model of the marriage market, with implications for two-sex population growth." Doctoral dissertation, University of Michigan.
   1972   "Comparison of alternative marriage models." In T. N. E. Greville (ed.), Population Dynamics. New York: Academic.
McFarland, David D., and Daniel J. Brown.
   1973   "Social distance as a metric." In Edward O. Laumann, Bonds of Pluralism. New York: Wiley-Interscience.
National Center for Health Statistics.
   1970   Increases in Divorces: United States, 1967. (Public Health Service Publication No. 1000, Series 21, No. 20.) Washington, D. C.: U. S. Government Printing Office.
Sheldon, Eleanor Bernert, and Kenneth C. Land.
   1972   "Social reporting for the 1970's: A review and programmatic statement." Policy Sciences 3 (Summer):137-151.

Stinchcombe, Arthur L.
   1968   Constructing Social Theories. New York: Harcourt Brace Jovanovich.
U. S. Department of Health, Education, and Welfare.
   1969   Toward a Social Report. Washington, D. C.: U. S. Government
          Printing Office.

15

FORECASTING SOCIAL EVENTS *

Seymour Spilerman

Current interest in social forecasting can be attributed to the confluence of a number of factors. Public concern regarding certain difficulties our country will encounter in the not too distant future—overpopulation, depletion of natural resources, excess production of scientific manpower—has created an awareness of the importance of specifying optimal rates for consumption and technological growth, and anticipating supply and demand levels in the advanced skills we provide our youth. Related to these issues, the complementary notions of social goals, social accounting, and social planning have been steadily acquiring legitimacy, even in a nation which still retains the patina of a laissez-faire ideology. Matters such as quality of health care, incidence of poverty, and educational attainment by minority children are now considered proper arenas for governmental intervention and manipulation; indeed, they may even require adjustment to levels which are politically acceptable.

The success that economists have achieved in constructing quantitative indicators and formal models of economic phenomena has also been a stimulant to social forecasting. In an age where "relevance" is upheld as a criterion for assessing the utility of research, and the funding it deserves, the adoption of econometric methods by many governmental agencies has spurred sociologists to investigate the applicability of these techniques to social processes. The

*The research reported here was supported by funds granted to the Institute for Research on Poverty at the University of Wisconsin by the Office of Economic Opportunity pursuant to the provisions of the Economic Opportunity Act of 1964. The conclusions are the sole responsibility of the author. This essay was originally presented at the Social Indicator Models Conference at Russell Sage Foundation, July 1972.

381

additional fact that economists are now routinely consulted by political influentials has not passed unnoticed among those sociologists who share an interest in policy formulation and believe that they can also contribute to the attainment of national objectives.

The attractiveness of econometric methods derives from their ability to forecast aspects of the future condition of the economy; indeed alternative futures, contingent upon the adoption of different policies, so that a choice can be made among competing programs. The importance of such a capability for an administrator is easily apparent: confronted with an array of complex programs, each ostensibly suitable for achieving the same economic objective—reducing the unemployment rate; stabilizing the price of farm commodities—he must be able to evaluate their relative effectiveness in terms of narrow cost/benefit ratios, as well as on the basis of secondary consequences which might be engendered (change in rate of inflation; effect on farm income). It is also evident that similar calculations would be desirable in choosing among *social* programs; for instance, selecting a strategy to increase educational attainment by minority youth, or one to combat street crime and delinquency.

To date, the activity of sociologists in this research area has been largely limited to subjects allied with social forecasting—social indicator construction, field experimentation—although the topic of forecasting has received some attention as well.[1] By a social indicator we mean a time series in an institutional or demographic variable. A useful indicator would relate to an issue of concern and either summarize some aspect of institutional performance (such as GNP measures economic output), lead some institutional condition (an increase in housing starts often signals an economic upturn), or be a variable in a temporal model. In the first instance the indicator charts progress so that we can assess how well the institution has performed; in the second it anticipates change, permitting an adaptive strategy to be prepared beforehand. The third use of a social indicator relates more directly to the construction of dynamic models appropriate for forecasting. A collection of time series would constitute the material from which the interrelations among social processes are derived and would also provide the initial conditions for priming the forecasting instrument. Validity of the model could be ascertained by comparing its projections with subsequent values of the empirical time series.[2]

---

[1] Some important early studies were by Hart (1945), Sorokin (1957), Bell (1964), and Moore (1964). More recent discussions, to some extent derivative of an interest in social indicators and social accounting, include de Jouvenel (1967), Duncan (1969), and Schuessler (1971).

[2] As an example, we might attempt to forecast rates for various kinds of criminal activities from trends in drug abuse, the age structure of the population, the high school drop out rate, and the age specific unemployment rate. Calculations of this nature are routinely performed by demographers in projecting changes in the size or composition of a population.

The participation of sociologists in field experiments such as the negative income tax studies, in which structural variables are artificially adjusted, has served to acquaint them with many of the component tasks in constructing complex models, especially dynamic models, of social processes. One purpose of experimentation is to supplement the natural variation in key variables when the institutional arrangements make for stable behavior or fail to exhibit the organizational forms which are of interest to investigators. Thus, since virtually no school system in the country offers concrete inducements to students— money and other valued commodities—to supplement the motivational impact of school grades, it becomes necessary to create this type of reward structure in order to assess the utility of a pedagogical arrangement which appears promising in light of theoretical argument (Spilerman, 1971). Another reason for experimenting is to separate among the effects of variables which are highly correlated in the normal operation of an institution. For example, a serious critique of the Coleman Report (Cain and Watts, 1970) stressed the point that it underestimated the importance of teacher competence for student performance, since teacher characteristics are highly correlated with SES measures of student background. Coleman used survey data and, being unable to separate between the effects of these two sets of variables, assigned their joint contribution to the latter factor.

A third use of experimentation is to provide information on the transient response of a social system to an exogenous manipulation, such as altering the level of a variable. How long it will take for change to begin, how much will result, and how long the effect will last, are the kinds of questions which the sponsors of field research typically want answered. In the process of addressing these issues, experimentation can constitute a powerful instrument in the repertoire of theory-testing techniques since competing explanations which are consistent with the same equilibrium conditions often predict divergent *transitory* effects. For example, the income maintenance experiments presently being conducted in New Jersey, Pennsylvania, and in other states, although undertaken for the narrow purpose of investigating the work effort response by families to the provision of income support, may enable us to compare the utility of cultural and situational explanations of poverty with respect to different aspects of behavior and different groups in the poverty population. The short-run adaptation to the experimental manipulation should vary according to whether a particular behavioral facet (e.g., poor school performance by children) is situationally determined or maintained by cultural forces such as values and peer pressure (Spilerman and Elesh, 1971).

For the above reasons the information that is obtained through experimentation, in addition to illuminating the probable consequences of adopting particular policies, should contribute to our modeling and forecasting capabilities in innumerable ways. By permitting statistical devices such as randomization, control groups, and different treatment levels to be employed, field experiments will permit important multivariate relationships to be estimated with greater accuracy than can be accomplished with survey data alone, and more complex dynamic models to be constructed than would be possible otherwise.

With the above introduction at hand, outlining the involvement of sociologists in topics relating to forecasting, I would like to discuss the likely rate of progress in developing actual forecasting capabilities for the trends and events which have interest for sociologists. My thesis is a simple one: Many social phenomena are not "well behaved" in the sense of having properties that would make them amenable to projection. In consequence, the techniques which are routinely employed in the prediction of economic trends are unlikely to be applicable to numerous social processes which, nonetheless, are very important. To lay the underpinnings for this thesis, I will first discuss some properties of time series data and, in this context, sketch the information requirements of different forecasting procedures. The central theme of the essay is then developed by considering the kinds of social phenomena which are likely to generate time series having certain properties. In the final section some of the difficulties inherent in conducting empirical analysis in particular subfields of sociology are reviewed from the vantage point of the preceding considerations.

EXPLANATION AND PREDICTION

While there is an intimate relation between the tasks of explaining and predicting, these two capabilities are not coincident. It is possible to explain the variation in a variable without being able to forecast its future levels. It is also possible to predict with considerable accuracy while understanding little about the causal processes involved.

Explanation versus a Capability to Predict

To simultaneously explain and forecast requires the availability of (a) a model of the determinants of the variable of interest at a single point in time, (b) a specification of expected shifts in the values of the determining factors, and (c) a specification of how the structural relationships, themselves, will change.

It is often possible to construct an adequate explanation of a phenomenon at a single instant in time without obtaining a corresponding capability to forecast, particularly when the causes of temporal change have no counterpart in cross-sectional data. For example, having devised an explanation of the determinants of anti-semitism from cross-sectional information, perhaps relating this psychological disposition to an individual's religious beliefs and occupational mobility experience, the model may be unsuitable for forecasting changes in the level of anti-semitism even though future values of the causal factors that were identified are known. The reason is that the most prominent determinants of the longitudinal variation in this disposition may be inherently constant in cross-sectional data—for instance, success or setback in international relations, economic recession or prosperity—and the contextual effects deriving from these conditions cannot be estimated from information at a single point in time. While we commonly infer developmental effects from cross-sectional data, in doing so we are implicitly assuming that the major determinants of longitudinal change also exhibit variation at one point in time.

In contrast, we can often forecast a variable without being able to explain why it should exhibit a particular time path. The most common instance involves the extrapolation of past trends by curve fitting, particularly when our interest is limited to the secular change and long cycles. When a variable is constant over time, or when its rate of change or rate of acceleration are invariant, we can forecast from this knowledge together with the initial conditions *without understanding the reasons for the behavior.* Such a situation is not infrequent, particularly for social processes which involve widely shared values that are culturally maintained (Spilerman and Elesh, 1971), technologies in which breakthroughs are now rare, or "sunk costs" in institutional arrangements. Thus, the year-to-year variation in desired educational attainment for children that is expressed by parents from a particular ethnic (cultural) group is likely to be small, as is the annual fluctuation in mean age of mortality in the United States, the latter being so despite the vast amount spent on medical research. Similarly, even though the metric standard constitutes a more rational measurement apparatus than the English system, owing to the costs of recalibrating machinery and reeducating adults which would accompany adoption of a new standard, we can forecast that the English system will continue in wide use in this country.

Our approach to explaining the variation in a time series must depend upon the time interval under consideration. As the interval is lengthened we expect the effect of the secular trend and long cycles to increase and dominate change; during brief durations small cycle fluctuations should account for the bulk of change. Whether the small cycle fluctuations are considered important or not depends on the consequences of cycles of different length for the social institutions of interest. In regard to this point, I would like to comment on one way in which the impact of cycles of brief duration is muted. This occurs when an institution can "store" the excess product from cycle peaks, drawing upon this supply in years of underproduction.

We are accustomed to such considerations in regard to agricultural produce; perishable crops can be obtained only in season while grains, by contrast, are available during all months and even in years of drought. Social institutions show analogous differences in sensitivity to cycle length. As an example, were the size of successive *one-year* age cohorts to exhibit greater variation than is presently the case, this variation probably would not be burdensome to the efficient functioning of industrial organizations. Individuals who are but a few years apart in age tend to be similar in their work relevant attributes—e.g., educational attainment, physical strength—and hence interchangeable in most economic roles. In this circumstance, one would *not* expect the age-specific unemployment rate, for instance, to exhibit variations corresponding to the relative sizes of the one-year age cohorts.

Were the cycles of longer duration, substitutability might break down and some institutional time series (such as the unemployment rate) would contain an age structure which parallels the variation in age-cohort size. A related way in which the impact of brief cycles is muted occurs when institutions are sensitive to the total stock of a factor, not to the new product alone. Thus, organizations which respond to total population size or to adult population size (such as marketing divisions of automobile manufacturers) would find the random fluctuations in one-year age cohorts to be of minor importance. In age-specific structures such as the university, by contrast, an increase in the magnitude of these annual fluctuations would present major problems and require extensive organizational restructuring to ensure efficient operation. What constitutes relevant cycle length for a given time series, then, is a specifiable matter, but only in conjunction with the requirements of particular social institutions.

It is of interest to note that contradictory requirements exist in being able to forecast by extrapolating trends, and in constructing structural or explanatory models. Forecasting by extrapolation requires that past relationships continue to operate unaltered and that levels, or manner of change in levels, of the determining variables be constant or nearly so. Explanation, by contrast, requires an abundance of variation so that the incidence of an event, or of different values of a variable, can be related to combinations of its suspected determinants. When we are able to forecast accurately by extrapolation we usually lack sufficient variation to construct adequate explanations. For instance, we can predict with some reliability that a revolution is unlikely in the United States next year, simply because this type of event has been so rare in our history. Yet, due to its infrequency, we are deficient in the information necessary for constructing an explanatory model of the determinants of political stability in the American context. It is not that we lack imagination in suggesting factors which might be pertinent; rather, it is that we are incapable of assigning weights to them indicative of their relative importance, because of the rarity of this type of governmental disruption.

A second example, from a study in which I am currently engaged, may also prove illuminating. I have collected data on lynching events in the South during the period 1882-1935. Except for some erratic behavior in the initial years of the time series (possibly reflecting inadequacies in early data collection procedures at Tuskegee Institute), there is a consistent secular decline. The annual rate for the five years beginning with 1891 is 188. The comparable rate for the concluding five years of the series is 17. Certainly we have here a systematic change which begs for explanation. Yet, if we were restricted to a single, regional-level time series, this pronounced decline *could not* be explained. There are too many other time series (rates of urbanization, mechanization of farming, professionalization of law enforcement) that are consistent with the noted secular decline and provide plausible explanations for it. Were it not for our ability to disaggregate the regional-level time series in lynching events and examine parallel time series for groups of counties having particular economic and demographic characteristics, we would be limited to addressing the variation about the secular trend. Only this aspect of the temporal change in the regional-level data has sufficient complexity to permit selection among competing explanations. Thus, in the absence of substantial variation our ability to comprehend is hampered; at the same time, though, there is little need for understanding in order to forecast.

Forecasting from the Unrestricted Reduced Form versus from a Structural Model

By the unrestricted reduced form we mean an equation in which the variable of interest is related only to exogenous factors, and parameter estimation has been carried out by a direct application of ordinary least squares. There are several advantages to forecasting from this formulation: (a) the dynamics of the process does not have to be delineated or fully understood; (b) estimation is a simple affair and identification problems do not arise; and (c) multicollinearity is not a difficulty since a collinear independent variable can be deleted with little effect on projections.

In terms of the degree of understanding that is required, forecasting from the unrestricted reduced form is intermediate between trend extrapolation and forecasting from a structural model, the latter representing an explicit theory of behavior. In trend extrapolation we assume the continuation of past history with respect to change in the variable of concern, and do not introduce explanatory variables. In forecasting from the unrestricted reduced form we do specify which exogenous variables are important, but not the dynamics of the process. If it is reasonable to assume that relationships among the variables are stable, and if we have knowledge about future values of the exogenous factors, this approach can yield satisfactory forecasts. Indeed, if the determinants are specified as lagged we can use their current values to predict future levels of the dependent variable. The hooker, however, is that if the structural relationships were to change, even in a simple fashion, the corresponding alterations in the reduced form coefficients could be exceedingly complex.

The importance of a structural model for forecasting when relationships are changing can be illustrated by comparing the mechanics of projection from structural equations (that is, from the *derived* reduced form) with projection from the unrestricted reduced form. By way of illustration consider the following model of shifts in vote intention during the course of an election campaign:

$$\left.\begin{array}{l} Y_{1t} = a_1 Y_{2t} + c_0 Y_{1t-1} + c_1 Z_{1t} \qquad\qquad\quad + c_3 + e_{1t} \\ Y_{2t} = a_2 Y_{1t} \qquad\qquad\qquad\qquad\qquad + c_2 Z_{2t} + c_4 + e_{2t} \end{array}\right\} \quad (15.1)$$

Y_{1t} and Y_{2t} are endogenous variables representing an individual's candidate preference (degree of leaning toward candidate A) and his expectation as to who will win the election during an interview in month t; Z_{1t} and Z_{2t} are exogenous variables that report the condition of the economy and candidate A's relative popularity from the latest opinion poll; e_{1t} and e_{2t} are disturbance terms.[3] In this model a respondent's candidate preference is therefore postulated to be a function of his expectation as to who will win, his preference in the preceding month, and the state of the economy. His expectation concerning who will be victorious is a function of current candidate preference and the published poll results.

Solving equation (15.1) for Y_{1t} and Y_{2t} in terms of the exogenous and lagged endogenous variables we obtain (providing $a_1 a_2 \neq 1$),

$$\left.\begin{array}{l} Y_{1t} = \dfrac{c_0}{1-a_1 a_2} Y_{1t-1} + \dfrac{c_1}{1-a_1 a_2} Z_{1t} + \dfrac{c_2 a_1}{1-a_1 a_2} Z_{2t} + \dfrac{a_1 c_4 + c_3}{1-a_1 a_2} + u_{1t} \\[3ex] Y_{2t} = \dfrac{c_0 a_2}{1-a_1 a_2} Y_{1t-1} + \dfrac{c_1 a_2}{1-a_1 a_2} Z_{1t} + \dfrac{c_2}{1-a_1 a_2} Z_{2t} + \dfrac{a_2 c_3 + c_4}{1-a_1 a_2} + u_{2t} \end{array}\right\}$$

$$(15.2)$$

which is the *derived* reduced form of the system and expresses the dependent variables in terms of the predetermined variables *after* the interdependency specified by (15.1) has been taken into account. These equations provide the most convenient way to forecast Y_{1t} and Y_{2t}, assuming the relationships specified by the structural model.

If we are interested solely in projecting candidate preference, and not in the explicit details of the dynamic process, we could proceed instead by estimating the *unrestricted* reduced form equation for Y_{1t} from observational data using ordinary least squares:

---

[3] The system (15.1) could be estimated most conveniently from data on a sample of individuals at two points in time. The first equation is just-identified and could be estimated using indirect least squares; the second equation is over-identified and would require a procedure such as two-stage least squares. See Kmenta (1971, pp. 531-573) for details on the estimation of simultaneous equations.

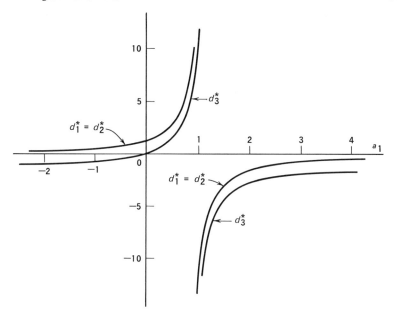

Figure 15.1. Coefficients of the Reduced Form Equation for Y_{1t} versus a_1.[†]

$$Y_{1t} = d_1 Y_{1t-1} + d_2 Z_{1t} + d_3 Z_{2t} + d_0 + u'_{1t} \qquad (15.3)$$

These coefficients will not be identical to the derived reduced form parameters in (15.2a) [which we denote by $d_1{}^*$, $d_2{}^*$, $d_3{}^*$, and $d_0{}^*$] unless all structural equations are just-identified. However, even when this is not the case, as in the present example, the unrestricted reduced form parameters often will not be very different from the derived ones and, so long as the coefficients in the structural equations remain constant, equation (15.3) permits a forecasting capability[4] without requiring a researcher to specify the linkages among variables in the dynamic process (Walters, 1970; pp. 188-190).

Suppose, now, being interested only in forecasting Y_{1t}, we have estimated equation (15.3) directly. Also assume that some structural parameter, say a_1, is changing in a simple manner, such as linearly. The effect on the reduced form equations will be that *all* coefficients $d_0{}^*$, $d_1{}^*$, $d_2{}^*$ and $d_3{}^*$ (and d_0 d_1, d_2, and d_3) will change, and this change will be non-linear. An illustration of how the reduced form parameters might vary as a result of a linear shift in a_1 is presented in Figure 15.1.

[†]The values of a_2, c_0, c_1, and c_2 have been set equal to one.

[4]To forecast from equation (15.3) [or from equation (15.2)] the researcher must make some assumption about the future values of Z_{1t} and Z_{2t}.

The essential point is that in situations of structural change, even simple structural change, it is vital to have available a behavioral model of the process. While structural relationships have a high degree of automony—few coefficients are affected by a particular alteration in the process—this property is not shared by the reduced form relationships. What would be a simple adjustment in a structural model becomes far more complex when only the reduced form coefficients are known.

Use of the unrestricted reduced form is therefore appropriate only where change is limited to the levels of the determinants. Yet, this situation is not an uncommon one for social processes. For example, in geographic migration, the effects of age, income, and length of stay at current residence on a decision to move are relatively stable through time, by comparison with changes in the values of these factors. Indeed, assuming constant relationships, the pattern of interregional migration for a population sample has been predicted fairly accurately through a 21-year interval (Spilerman, 1972). As a second example, consider projecting the distribution of black occupational status. It is likely that the return in occupational status from educational attainment will remain stable during the present decade, although mean school years completed by Negro youth should increase substantially. This suggests that the current relationship between these variables, together with extrapolations of the distribution of educational attainment among Negro youth, could be used to forecast the occupational status distribution of Negro males several years hence.

Selecting Variables for Explanation and Prediction

The factors which provide illuminating explanations often are not the ones which yield efficient predictions, and vice versa. For instance, it was reported in *The American Voter* (Campbell et al., 1960) that in the weeks before a presidential election the best predictor of an individual's partisan decision is his expressed vote intention. Important though this variable may be for predictive purposes, it is not very revealing for theorizing about the determinants of party preference. The task of explaining requires the use of theoretically significant variables, which are so distinguished because they relate particular aspects of social structure (such as organizational affiliations or class background in the present illustration) to the dependent variable (party preference). Typically, these variables are more distant temporally than are efficient predictors and explain less of the variation. This observation, incidentally, carries by implication a criticism of the excessive emphasis placed upon high R^2 values in the sociological literature, where the objective is traditionally one of explanation.

PROBLEMS IN FORECASTING VOLATILE SOCIAL PROCESSES

In the preceding section we have distinguished among time series according to their degree of continuity with past trends. This consideration was shown to be essential in selecting a forecasting procedure, as well as in determining our capability to explain a particular phenomenon. The following points were emphasized: (a) Where a time series is characterized by some manner of orderly trend, its future course can be predicted from its own past history. For the narrow purpose of forecasting, there is no need to consider causal or equilibriating factors that may affect the course of its development; (b) where the variation is more complex but a constant relationship can be assumed between the variable of interest and its determinants, the unrestricted reduced form will yield satisfactory projections and has the advantage of not requiring a comprehensive specification of the dynamic process; and (c) where change in relationships cannot be neglected we must forecast the nature of the alterations,[5] as well as shifts in the values of the independent variables. This makes the use of a structural model imperative.

By a volatile time series we mean one in which the amount of change between sample points is considerable. Thus, the very notion of volatility depends upon sampling frequency and on judgments of magnitude, the latter presumably reflecting the consequences of particular-sized variations for the institutions of concern. Some volatile phenomena present little in the way of forecasting problems, particularly when the variation largely stems from cyclical behavior such as might be generated by seasonal factors. A second category differs only in degree from the processes that have been already considered. While the values of the independent variables may change rapidly, and the relationships among factors might be subject to sizable alterations, in theory such a time series could be projected by the structural model formulation of the preceding section. The kind of volatility I want to discuss here concerns, instead, phenomena which have only tenuous historical antecedents.

Forecasting Underlying Conditions versus Forecasting Concrete Phenomena—Two-Stage Projection

Many social phenomena of considerable consequence can be viewed as concrete manifestations of more fundamental processes. Outbreaks of racial disorders in our ghettos may reflect the level of frustration among blacks, bomb plantings by radical youth have co-varied with the extent of U. S. engagement in Vietnam, and the intensity of anti-semitism is possibly related to the performance of the economy. A problem which we must consider in attempting to forecast such phenomena is that alternative expressions can arise from the same underlying conditions.

In order to predict the rate of occurrence of racial disorders, for instance, it

---

[5] In principle, this requires recognizing that any number of variables which might normally be ignored when the model is specified, either because they show little variation or have insignificant effects, could acquire importance at later times.

seems reasonable to first forecast the level of frustration in black neighborhoods and then consider the conditions under which high discontent will be translated into collective violence. Stated in this way, the procedure is formally one of constructing the requisite structural model. Nevertheless, the unusual difficulties encountered in modeling a volatile social process deserve special attention.

The task of forecasting a psychological state of a population, such as its frustration level, is exceptionally difficult because objective indicators of the attitude will serve this function only so long as the particular inequities which they tap continue to be invested with significance. Elaborating the preceding example, there are a great many injustices which Negroes suffer, any collection of which, potentially, could provoke extreme discontent and frustration. Negroes might respond to unsatisfactory housing conditions, to a lack of economic opportunity relative to the prospects of whites, to the segregated and inferior schools provided for their children, or to disappointment over the failure of improvements in these conditions to keep pace with expectations. Presumably all these factors contribute to frustration; yet, at any given time, some will be especially salient owing to scandals, news documentaries, or other reasons for receiving extensive media coverage. In attempting to forecast this collective psychological state one must therefore contend with shifts in emphasis upon the component deprivations—structural change, to be sure, but of a particularly volatile sort because of the ephemeral nature to the significance of a specific deprivation. Added to this difficulty is the powerful interactive role assumed by a quality such as "trust." With the same living conditions and economic opportunities for blacks, Robert Kennedy might have secured the calm ghettos which eluded Lyndon Johnson.

The second stage would also require elaborate theory, but of a more traditional kind. If alternative manifestations may arise from a single underlying condition, we must be able to predict which of the potential concrete expressions will occur. For instance, high levels of frustration in ghetto neighborhoods could foster the development of millennial movements or encourage organized political activity, as well as stimulate outbreaks of rioting. Because all these activities are possible manifestations of the same underlying discontent, if our interest is in forecasting a particular expression (such as the rate of riot outbreaks) we must have available theories which (a) identify the possible transformations of discontent and (b) suggest the conditions under which each manifestation will ensue.

We are not entirely ignorant on this score, although our theories are not very powerful. One type of literature relevant to this topic deals with the processing of frustration by persons from different class strata or with different socialization experience (Henry and Short, 1954; Bronfenbrenner, 1958). For instance, Henry and Short (1954, pp. 54-81) argue that loss of relative status leads to different types of aggressive acts according to social class—suicide among middle class persons, homicide by lower class individuals. Much analysis in political sociology has been concerned with the related issue of managing grievance and discontent. Examples may be found in the writings of William Kornhauser (1959) on the functions of secondary associations for maintaining political stability, in investigations by James S. Coleman (1957) concerning the consequences of particular organizational structures for the dynamics of community controversy, and in David Lockwood's (1958) analysis of some necessary conditions for collective action by members of a class stratum.

A different approach to predicting concrete manifestations involves the notion of "natural histories" of social movements and major societal transformations such as revolutions (Hopper, 1950; Brinton, 1952). Studies of this genre attempt to delineate developmental sequences or stages through which movements of protest, in particular, tend to progress and invoke conceptual mechanisms of the sort, "no enemies to the left,"[6] or "vulnerability of the social structure to rising expectations."[7] While these investigations are ordinarily deficient in identifying the causal forces responsible for the stage progression (Rule and Tilly, 1972), the perspective may have value in forecasting, much as trend extrapolation can be useful. It is not my intention at this point to consider in detail the merits of these contrasting research strategies, only to stress the importance of addressing transformational questions if we are to develop a capability to predict the course of particular expressions which emanate from more fundamental conditions. Interestingly, the problems we encounter in social forecasting compel us to revisit some of the more traditional topics in social theory.

A Single Activity Arising from Different Underlying Conditions

In addition to the difficulties that are posed when a single underlying process can give rise to multiple concrete expressions, certain activities, such as rioting, may constitute general expressive forms, able to serve as manifestations

---

[6] "We may say that in all our revolutions [England (1640), America, France (1789), Russia (1917)] there is a tendency for power to go from Right to Center to Left, from the conservatives of the old regime to the moderates to the radicals or extremists..... The details of this process vary naturally from revolution to revolution. Its stages are not identical in length or in their time sequence. In America power never got as far left as it did in the other countries" (Brinton, 1952; p. 130).

[7] Explanations of this type have been invoked in conjunction with the racial disorders of the 1960s. Typically, it is argued that the Civil Rights movement, by successfully challenging many discriminatory barriers, generated unrealizable expectations and created the preconditions for the subsequent upheavals. According to some (e.g., Rossi, 1971; pp. 421-425), the disorders, interpreted as revolts, have in turn produced enhanced self-esteem among blacks (evidenced by dress, hair styles, and interest in their African heritage), and this is a prerequisite for political organization of the ghetto along traditional ethnic lines, which Rossi foresees.

for a number of more basic conditions. This possibility was entertained in a limited version when it was noted that the frustrations which provide the preconditions for ghetto riots may derive from different combinations of objective conditions. More generally, riots may have causes apart from the level of deprivation or frustration. They could represent conspiracies—that is, intentional acts carried out for political purposes—or result from the behavior of criminals intent on vandalism and destruction. Indeed, in the weeks subsequent to the outbreak of large scale urban violence in the mid-1960s, both views were widely expressed in the media. The fact that they proved to be largely erroneous in light of later investigations does not alter the fact that rioting is capable of deriving from such factors.

Disorders may also be invested with symbolic significance and performed to acknowledge collective membership. Many of the student disturbances in the late 1960s were probably carried out as expressions of solidarity with demonstrators on other campuses. "We did our share" was a slogan of the period. This point is not intended to downgrade the importance of the war in Vietnam as an instigating factor in the campus disorders, but rather to stress the fact that this particular act of protest, rather than some other (hunger strikes, silent vigils), acquired significance as the college campus manner of expressing opposition. With each escalation of fighting in Vietnam, college towns came to expect further disruption and violence instead of a different expression of protest. In summary, our ability to forecast the rate of an activity such as rioting, which can derive from diverse underlying conditions, is hampered by this very fact and by the continual emergence of altogether new conditions for which the activity is functional.

Fads and Social Contagion

There are events of considerable importance for which a capability to forecast rates of occurrence[8] is unlikely ever to be developed because of their extreme sensitivity to suggestion, fad, and contagion. This remark is especially pertinent to activities that can be carried out by a solitary individual or that involve many persons but do not require coordination, a division of labor, or prior planning. Examples include plane hijackings, bomb threats, assassination attempts, self-immolations, and instances of "spontaneous" rioting (such as frequently occurred in black neighborhoods in the 1960s), in contrast to disorders which are outgrowths from demonstrations or planned confrontations.

The evidence for contagion among events of these kinds is substantial, based on the way they cluster in time and on the fact that novel features, particularly

---

[8] Note that we are not discussing the more difficult problem of forecasting individual events.

when paired with success and public attention, are quickly imitated. At the time of this writing a recent electric example is provided by the "cult of D. B. Cooper"—the parachute skyjacking in the Northwest which, in subsequent weeks, was followed by more than a dozen similar attempts.[9] A more ominous illustration is presented in Berkowitz and Macaulay (1971). Based on a statistical analysis of aggressive crimes in the temporal vicinity of John F. Kennedy's assassination and the Speck murders in Chicago, they report statistically significant increases in the national crime rates in the months after each of the spectacular murders. Judging from descriptions of several perpetrators of plane hijackings in this country, actions of these sorts appeal to alienated and disaffected individuals who apparently see in them an opportunity for momentary potency, glamour, and escape from a meaningless existence (Hubbard, 1973; pp. 177-195).

The large numbers of disorders in ghettos and on college campuses also reflect contagion processes. An outbreak of rioting in one city, on a school campus, or in a prison provides a behavioral model for persons in other locales who perceive themselves to be in a similar circumstance and are groping to devise some action appropriate to their situation; in short, to individuals who can identify with the rioters. Following the Attica rebellion, disturbances were reported in numerous other American prisons and even as far away as France. Indeed, in a New York Times (1971) article on the prison disorder in Clairvaux, France, it was reported that "two young guards resigned on the ground that they 'didn't want to die for 1,100 francs ($200) a month.' They complained among other things that recent reforms, permitting the prisoners to receive newspapers and to listen to the radio, had spread the news of the Attica, N. Y. mutiny among them."

Prison environments permit few alternative forms of protest. However, the range of activities available to deranged and socially marginal individuals who are not institutionalized is considerably broader; there often are several expressions which are substitutable in the sense that each is capable of articulating, or temporarily relieving, the underlying condition—"functional alternatives," in the disciplinary jargon. In terms of the perspective of this section, the particular

---

[9] Viewed from this perspective the history of skyjacking is quite interesting. The first attempt occurred in Peru in 1930. FAA records then show a 17-year interval without an incident. Between 1947 and 1950, there were 14 skyjacking attempts, of which 13 occurred on flights originating in Eastern Europe. All but one of these involved groups of persons, usually trying to escape to the West. The first skyjacking of a flight originating in the United States took place in 1961. Between that date and the end of 1967 skyjacking attempts on American flights averaged 2 per year. In 1968, 22 attempts occurred, and from 1968 to 1972 skyjackings of United States flights averaged 28 per year. In contrast with the early incidents in Eastern Europe, the American attempts have been carried out largely by solitary individuals and constitute the most contagious form of skyjacking. Data are from FAA records reported in Hubbard (1973, pp. 310-317).

activity that is undertaken may be largely fortuitous and would depend on which expression happened to occur at an auspicious time, proved newsworthy and received extensive media coverage, and "caught on." In contrast to the histories of social movements, the succession of expressions adopted by disorganized individuals lacks a developmental character; there is no learning, no organizational elaboration, no continuity, and therefore no coherence to the progression of activities. We have little reason to expect epidemics of skyjackings, shootings of random pedestrians, or phone calls announcing the placing of bombs in buildings, to follow one another in any meaningful sequence.

It is this substitutability among expressions which makes forecasting the next fad an impossible task. Yet, we can say that the most destructive expressions will usually have short lifetimes. Some incidents (e.g., bomb threats) are not so spectacular as to continually receive prominent media coverage, and decline in number from lack of propagation. Other types of events provoke governmental adjustments to reduce the vulnerability of the target. The parachute skyjackings referred to earlier were ended by altering the rear exit in passenger airliners so that the door could not be opened in flight. Skyjacking incidents of all types have now been sharply curtailed through the implementation of stringent search procedures at American airports.[10] Thus, although we may be unable to forecast the character of a new expression, merely knowing that adjustments will be made to an exposed institution, and that newsworthiness decays rapidly (and publicity given to violent and potentially contagious events may be limited intentionally), permits us to suggest that destructive expressions will be quickly extinguished.

The notion of substitutability among a collection of activities warrants additional comment. It was introduced above in the context of indicating the considerable difficulty in forecasting the next expression to be adopted by disorganized persons. Nonetheless, this concept can provide administrators with a powerful apparatus for predicting the consequences of particular policy changes. For certain categories of individuals a "hydraulic" model may appropriately characterize their rates of performing activities from a collection, in the sense that by removing the possibility of carrying out some, we raise the rates for others. As an illustration, narcotics addicts in New York City may be able to support the high price of their habits only by engaging in crime. If this presumption is correct, then the removal of one kind of potential victim would result in displacing criminal activity onto other targets, rather than in reducing the aggregate amount of crime. Some evidence for this possibility can be found

---

[10]It is not difficult to imagine innovations in skyjacking technique which would circumvent current search procedures. For instance, small plastic bombs could be placed in cigarette packs and would pass undetected by magnetic sensors. The danger comes not so much from innovation, however, as from communication of the techniques, and this raises the treacherous issue of media guidelines and freedom of the press.

in newspaper accounts which reported an increase in robberies of taxi drivers in New York City following the termination of selling transit tokens on city buses. It is also possible that the subsequent reduction in the victimization of cab drivers (accomplished by installing bullet proof partitions between the driver and the passenger compartment) was achieved at a cost of shifting criminal activity onto muggings of pedestrians. This is not the place to pursue these questions in detail; I simply wish to indicate that the complementary notions of substitutability and displacement are intriguing ones, and may be employed to advantage in forecasting the consequences of removing certain options from a class of alternatives.[11] In the preceding example, incidentally, if our concern is to reduce *violent* crime, one might conclude that the decision to remove bus drivers from the list of potential victims was an unfortunate one.

NUMBER OF OBSERVATIONS AND RESEARCH STRATEGY: SOME CONCLUDING REMARKS

Empirical research in sociology has become characterized increasingly by cross-sectional studies. This trend has occurred despite the fact that many influential early writers (e.g., Marx, Weber, Sorokin, Ogburn) showed a marked predilection for topics relating to social change and societal transformation, for which temporal data are relevant. There are a number of reasons for the ascendancy of cross-sectional investigation and its emergence as the dominant data analytic style. Perhaps most important is the consideration that the information gathering instrument can be designed so as to be fully appropriate to the research question at hand, and the required data can be quickly collected. In cross-sectional studies the data commonly pertain to current properties of the observational units (individuals, formal organizations, communities) or to past properties which nonetheless can be ascertained by interrogating and measuring the existing units.[12] By contrast, with studies involving time series data, if we wish the flexibility of designing the information base so it corresponds closely to the substantive issue we must conduct a panel study and possibly have to wait several years for the data, literally, to come into existence. Alternatively, we could resort to archival files or use materials collected by others, but this entails

---

[11] Evaluating the effects of saturating a city precinct with police, Press (1971) reports that, accompanying a general decrease in crime within the target area, the crime rates in neighboring precincts *increased*. Furthermore, there was a small increase in some categories of less visible, inside crime in the target area.

[12] It is common to collect retrospective information in surveys. Models of the status attainment process, for instance, incorporate variables which refer to different points in the life cycle: father's SES, respondent's education, prestige of respondent's current occupation. Nevertheless, the analytic perspective here is cross-sectional since these models do not involve repeated measurements on the same variables.

a cost of working with data prepared for different purposes and operating within the confines of that information base. In neither case does temporal analysis permit a researcher the possibility of responding to preliminary findings, or to the recent work of other investigators, by quickly returning to the field with an expanded or more directed schedule. This latter flexibility is a vital one for the rapid elaboration of empirically supported theory.

A second reason why cross-sectional analysis is attractive is because the powerful multivariate methodologies which can be brought to bear are simpler than the corresponding procedures for exploring time series data. In particular, the researcher using regression methods with data at one point in time need not concern himself with problems such as autocorrelation, time lags, transient responses, stability of the equilibria, or with other esoteric topics in systems analysis. It is not that these considerations are unimportant for elaborating and testing social theory, only that they would introduce unnecessary complications into many studies which do not require these concerns and which can be pursued more simply with cross-sectional data.

To capitalize on the advantages of cross-sectional analysis, it is necessary for both the target population and the sample to be large. The importance of a large population is that the sampling operation can be carried out in a manner which is appropriate for the specific research question. Social groups that represent small proportions in the population can be oversampled, variables that have little variation in the population can have their variation inflated in the sample (permitting more reliable estimates of effects), and multicollinearity can be reduced by the sampling framework. It is advisable to draw a large sample when many factors need to be controlled, when the form of response to key determinants may be non-linear (hence requiring several terms for representation), when there is interest in interaction effects, and when accurate estimation of the regression coefficients is important. In many respects the introduction of multivariate methods into sociology has been responsible for creating a need for large numbers of observations. Despite the saving in degrees of freedom that regression provides over tabular analysis, its greater flexibility has stimulated an interest in posing questions which require the preceding procedures; in particular, controls for many confounding factors.

In light of this discussion it is not surprising that the substantive areas which have developed most rapidly through application of cross-sectional methods have utilized either the individual as the observational unit (e.g., status attainment models), or some small structure such as the formal organization or the community. Before the advent of multivariate techniques it made little difference whether one studied individuals or nation-states because our technical ability to control simultaneously on several variables was non-existent. With the development of such a capability the drawback to the nation-state as an observational unit has become apparent: too few exist to tolerate the many control variables necessary to adjust for contextual differences among them[13] (e.g., level of economic development, availability of natural resources, ethnic and class cleavages, religious traditions) in order to estimate the relationship between a dependent variable (e.g., presence of a competitive party structure) and the specific determinants of interest. Thus, questions about nation-states do not lend themselves to powerful explanations by cross-sectional methods. Recent attempts to explain national differences in rates of violent acts (Gurr, 1969; Feierabend, Feierabend, and Nesvold, 1969) suffer in an especially serious way from this limitation.

It is to the credit of sociologists who study nation-state processes that most have resisted the trend to cross-sectional formulations. When the number of observations is small the principal recourse in empirical analysis is to time series data,[14] and the proper activity in theory construction is to pose questions which can be answered by examining temporal variations. The strategy in constructing *testable* theories about nation-state features must therefore assume a historical perspective and use the tools of that discipline, even though the emphasis in history is more on description and accounting for unique events than on generalization. Methodologically sophisticated analysis in macro-sociology must employ dynamic models, that is, system models of temporal change, and utilize long time series on features of the nation-states. With sufficient time points we could estimate the parameters of a model (theory of relationships) from a single observational unit. More likely, we would pool temporal and cross-sectional information from several units to increase the degrees of freedom. Verification would be accomplished by examining the fit of the model, by comparing its predictions with observed values from future time points, and by forecasting the variables of interest in other nation-states that are presumed to be characterized by the same process. Theoretical elaboration would proceed by showing that while a particular model applies to some states, other system models, representing different causal relationships, describe behavior in the remaining units. Comparative historical analysis has used this strategy to advantage,

---

[13] Studies which utilize the city as an observational unit are less handicapped by this difficulty. First, there are many more cities than nations so a greater number of control variables can be introduced and more extensive explanations tested. Second, many factors which must be controlled in cross-sectional analysis are approximately constant across U.S. cities and can be ignored.

[14] There is one alternative strategy, that of recasting the problem so it can be examined in a setting having a greater number of observational units. For instance, Lipset, Trow, and Coleman (1956), in an investigation of factors which contribute to the maintenance of democratic procedures in trade unions, based several of their findings concerning the importance of various structural features on the functions of these structures in *locals* of a single union. To increase the number of units they shifted the level of observation. See pages 425-427 of their report for an explicit discussion on this tactic.

although without formal quantitative models; for instance, Moore's (1966) case studies on the origins of dictatorships and democracies.

I do not wish to minimize the very serious difficulties that attend the analysis of temporal data. For many crucial issues the relevant time series will change too slowly for a model of the process to be estimated and verified. The notion of "sunk costs" again provides a pertinent illustration: once established, many arrangements are perpetuated because the cost of replacing them by more efficient operations would be exceedingly high. In technical language the problem is one of severe autocorrelation in that the continuation of an arrangement (such as the Electoral College procedure for selecting a president) is attributable only to a minor extent to the action of causal factors besides the prior existence of the institution. For this reason successive observations in a time series may contain little additional *new* information about temporal behavior, and the presence of observations at many time points may be deceptive with respect to the total amount of information contained in the data. An important point is that this difficulty is a consequence of how the time series has evolved and cannot be overcome by better analytic procedure.

Unfortunately, many issues of great significance in macro-sociology (e.g., the relative importance of various structural features for societal stability) are plagued by severe data inadequacies of this sort, and time series information will not salvage theory testing in regard to these topics. Our embarrassment here is that we are overly creative and able to construct several plausible explanations, each consistent with the small amount of data bearing on the issue. Our theories, in this circumstance, tend really to be perspectives for viewing a phenomenon (e.g., conflict versus consensus "theories" of societal stability) rather than sets of testable propositions. It is hardly peculiar, then, that ideological controversy is commonplace in macro-sociology, but not in fields which use the individual or the small organizational structure as an observational unit. The latter setting is not conducive to protracted controversy because, with cross-sectional data and many observations, it usually is possible to specify and rapidly collect the data that will distinguish between competing explanations.[15]

Yet, there are time series in nation-state features which show considerable year-to-year variation and would permit the estimation and testing of dynamic models. Examples are changes in partisan preference (in multi-party countries) especially during the months preceding an election, public opinion polls on a variety of topics, and rates for different kinds of crimes. The present interest in

---

[15] This is the typical manner in which theory is elaborated in science, so it is not surprising that, in the past decade alone, we have learned an enormous amount about the status attainment process from the work of Duncan, Sewall, and their colleagues. No comparable rapid cumulation of empirically supported theory can be cited for topics which use the nation-state as an observational unit.

social indicator construction and social forecasting is relevant to this concern as the system models likely to be developed for analyzing relationships among indicator variables and forecasting their trends should prove applicable more generally to the study of social phenomena where few observational units are available but considerable temporal variation is present. Quite possibly, then, one spin-off from methodological activity in this research area will be a new perspective on quantitative approaches to macro-sociological and historical issues.

REFERENCES

Bell, Daniel.
1964   "Twelve modes of prediction: A preliminary sorting of approaches in the social sciences." Daedalus (Summer): 845-880.
Berkowitz, Leonard, and Jacqueline Macaulay.
1971   "The contagion of criminal violence." Sociometry 34 (June): 238-260.
Brinton, Crane.
1952   The Anatomy of Revolution. New York: Random House.
Bronfenbrenner, Urie.
1958   "Socilization and social class through space and time." In Eleanor E. Maccoby, T. M. Newcomb and E. L. Hartley (eds.), Readings in Social Psychology (3rd. ed.). New York: Holt.
Cain, Glen, and Harold Watts.
1970   "Problems in making inferences from the Coleman Report." American Sociological Review 35 (April): 228-242.
Cambell, Angus, Philip E. Converse, Warren E. Miller, and Donald E. Stokes.
1960   The American Voter. New York: Wiley.
Coleman, James S.
1957   Community Conflict. New York: Free Press.
de Jouvenel, Bertrand.
1967   The Art of Conjecture. New York: Basic Books.
Duncan, Otis D.
1969   "Social forecasting: The state of the art." The Public Interest 17: 88-118.
Feierabend, Ivor, Rosalind L. Feierabend, and Betty A. Nesvold.
1969   "Social change and political violence: Cross-national patterns." In Hugh D. Graham and Ted Gurr (eds.), Violence in America. Washington: U.S. Gov't Printing Office.
Gurr, Ted.
1969   "A comparative study of civil strife." In Hugh D. Graham and Ted Gurr (eds.), Violence in America. Washington: U.S. Gov't Printing Office.
Hart, Hornell.
1945   "Logistic social trends." American Journal of Sociology 50 (March): 337-352.

Henry, Andrew, and James F. Short.
  1954   Suicide and Homicide: Some Economic, Sociological and Psychological Aspects of Aggression. New York: Free Press.
Hopper, Rex D.
  1950   "The revolutionary process: A frame of reference for the study of revolutionary movements." Social Forces 28 (March): 270-279.
Hubbard, David G.
  1973   The Skyjacker. New York: Macmillan.
Kmenta, Jan.
  1971   Elements of Econometrics. New York: Macmillan.
Kornhauser, William.
  1959   The Politics of Mass Society. New York: Free Press.
Lipset, Seymour M., Martin Trow, and James S. Coleman.
  1956   Union Democracy. New York: Free Press.
Lockwood, David.
  1958   The Black Coated Worker. London: Allen and Unwin.
Moore, Wilbert E.
  1964   "Predicting discontinuities in social change." American Sociological Review 29 (June): 331-338.
Moore, Jr., Barrington.
  1966   Social Origins of Dictatorship and Democracy. Boston: Beacon Press.
New York Times.
  1971   "Jail deaths in France lead Pompidou to question reform moves." (Sept. 24).
Press, S. James.
  1971   Some Effects of an Increase in Police Manpower in the 20th Precinct of New York. New York: Rand Institute Publication R-704-NYC.
Rossi, Peter H.
  1971   "Urban revolts and the future of American cities." In David Boesel and Peter H. Rossi (eds.) Cities Under Siege. New York: Basic Books.
Rule, James, and Charles Tilly.
  1972   "1830 and the unnatural history of revolution." Journal of Social Issues 28: 49-76.
Schuessler, Karl.
  1971   "Continuities in social prediction." In Herbert L. Costner (ed.), Sociological Methodology 1971. San Francisco: Jossey-Bass.
Spilerman, Seymour.
  1971   "Raising academic motivation in lower class adolescents: A convergence of two research traditions." Sociology of Education 44 (Winter): 103-118.
  1972   "The analysis of mobility processes by the introduction of independent variables into a Markov chain." American Sociological Review 37 (June): 277-294.
Spilerman, Seymour, and David Elesh.
  1971   "Alternative conceptions of proverty and their implications for income maintenance." Social Problems 18 (Winter): 358-373.

Sorokin, Pitirim.
1957   Social and Cultural Dynamics. Boston: Porter Sargent.
Walters, A. A.
1970   An Introduction to Econometrics. New York: W. W. Norton.

INDEX